THERAPEUTIC RECREATION PROGRAM DESIGN

second edition

THERAPEUTIC RECREATION PROGRAM DESIGN

principles and procedures

Carol Ann Peterson, Ed.D.
University of Illinois

Scout Lee Gunn, Ed.D.

PRENTICE HALL, Englewood Cliffs, New Jersey 07632

Library of Congress Cataloging in Publication Data

Peterson, Carol Ann, 1941–
   Therapeutic recreation program design.

   Rev. ed. of: Therapeutic recreation program design /
Scout Lee Gunn, Carol Ann Peterson. c1978.
   Includes bibliographies and index.
   1. Recreational therapy.   I. Gunn, Scout Lee,
1944– .   II. Gunn, Scout Lee, 1944– .   Therapeutic
recreation program design.   III. Title.
RM736.7.P48   1984   615'.8513   83-24695

ISBN 0-13-914839-6

90000

9 780139 148392

Cover design: 20/20 Services, Inc., Mark Berghash
Manufacturing buyer: Harry Baisley

  © 1984 by Prentice-Hall, Inc.
A Paramount Communications Company
Englewood Cliffs, New Jersey 07632

Printed in the United States of America

20 19 18 17 16 15 14 13

Prentice-Hall International (UK) Limited, *London*
Prentice-Hall of Australia Pty. Limited, *Sydney*
Prentice-Hall Canada Inc., *Toronto*
Prentice-Hall Hispanoamericana, S.A., *Mexico*
Prentice-Hall of India Private Limited, *New Delhi*
Prentice-Hall of Japan, Inc., *Tokyo*
Simon & Schuster Asia Pte. Ltd., *Singapore*
Editora Prentice-Hall do Brasil, Ltda., *Rio de Janeiro*

Contents

APPENDIXES

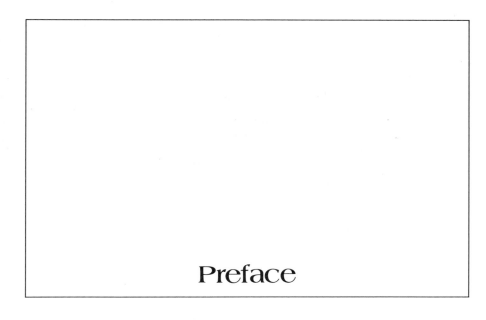

Preface

Therapeutic Recreation Program Design: Principles and Procedures is a text that appears to have widespread utilization and application in the growing field of therapeutic recreation. In order to improve and update its content, this second edition was requested. Numerous suggestions for revisions and changes have come from students, practitioners, and educators. The author also felt that much of the material needed revision and that sections of the book required reorganization. Recent changes in the field were also considered to be important and thus are included in this edition. The adoption of a philosophical position statement by the National Therapeutic Recreation Society (NTRS) in 1981 has major significance for the profession. This philosophy should influence the direction of the field and the content of therapeutic recreation programs. Thus, a major part of this edition has been focused on therapeutic recreation philosophy and program implications and applications. In addition, new information has been added related to assessment, documentation, and evaluation. Although the information related to the systems approach to therapeutic recreation program development remains somewhat the same, some revisions and expansion have been included.

A major revision is almost like writing a new book. Numerous people become directly and indirectly involved in the process. Their contributions are diverse and often difficult to acknowledge. I would like first to recognize those countless individuals who, through their comments and encouragement, have made this revision possible. Some people offered special support and assistance that deserve recognition. Dr. Joseph Bannon, Head, Department of Leisure Studies, University of Illinois, believes that creativity and productivity by faculty demand time and resources. He has freely given of both to support this effort. Nancy Rudins and Nellie Nason, departmental secretaries, contributed above and beyond the call of duty in the typing of the manuscript. Friend and colleague Dr. Barbara Sirvis reviewed the manuscript, made many helpful suggestions, and assisted the whole project through word processing. The work of numerous students is utilized throughout the book. These individuals are acknowledged where their contributions appear. This edition is strengthened by the addition of new material on several topics. Dr. Nancy Navar, Dr. Peg Connolly, Julie Dunn, and Carolyn Lemsky have written chapters of this book. Their participation is gratefully acknowledged and appreciated.

C. A. P.

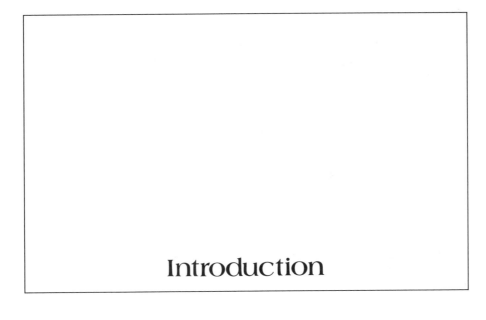

Introduction

This book is written for students in preparation for the delivery of therapeutic recreation services and for practitioners who are already in the profession. The profession of therapeutic recreation has many concerns, all of which directly or indirectly relate to the delivery of services to clients. This text focuses specifically on the design and development of therapeutic recreation programs. It is not an introductory text to the field. It assumes prior knowledge of illnesses and disabling conditions, the various settings where therapeutic recreation takes place, general therapeutic recreation history and theory, as well as specific activity content and basic intervention techniques. It also assumes general knowledge of leisure and recreation philosophy. It is not a text that addresses the various professionalization and professional issues and concerns such as credentialing, accreditation, professional preparation, standards, legislation, or advocacy. Some of these issues, however, are dealt with in the context of program development and if their content influences and impacts the planning of programs. The book does not attempt to present administrative concerns and techniques, although there are many direct implications for management within the material presented.

This is a book on therapeutic recreation programming. The topic is substantial enough to warrant exclusive coverage. The knowledge and skills required for program planning are numerous. They include knowledge of therapeutic recreation philosophy and theory, the leisure-related needs of various populations, areas of program focus, specific content for programs, as well as selection of appropriate intervention and facilitation techniques. Likewise, the process of program planning is important. This text presents one method of program development in depth. A systems approach is utilized. This approach, which is widely used in other professions, provides a logical and highly accountable method for the design, implementation, and evaluation of therapeutic recreation services. Thus, a thorough approach to program planning is attempted in this book. Content for programs is addressed, and a process for program development is described.

Programming is also presented on two levels. Overall or comprehensive program development for an agency or unit is presented. Developing and planning specific programs is also delineated.

The information presented is client-centered. Only those programs that directly involve clients are described. Many agencies are providing indirect services to clients such as community advocacy, education and awareness, accessibility activities, legislative action, information dissemination, professional preparation (practicum, field placement, and so on), and research. Although these activities can be considered programs, they are not addressed within this book. Many of the techniques and procedures described in this book could, however, be used for the planning, implementation, and evaluation of these indirect services.

The programming material provided in this text is intended for both clinical and community settings. The content for programs, derived from the NTRS philosophy, is appropriate for all settings where therapeutic recreation services are delivered. A given setting may, however, focus more on certain service components. The suggested procedure for developing these programs through specifying their objectives, performance measures, content, and process is the same. The book may appear at times to be somewhat biased toward clinical settings. When this is the case, it is because programming in clinical settings often requires more attention to specific information and procedures due to internal and external accountability demands.

The information presented focuses on group programming. While one-to-one services are provided in many settings, the greatest number of programs in therapeutic recreation are group-oriented. Thus, clustered leisure-related needs of clients appears to be a logical way to present programming information. This approach does not negate individualized planning or assessment. On the contrary, the total approach presented is based on selecting and developing group programs that address common identified leisure-related needs of clients. Individual assessment and/or referral is then conducted to determine which specific programs a given client may require or need.

One last introductory comment. Program planning is not viewed in this book as a singular or segmented procedure. Program planning is a comprehensive term which includes assessment, program development, implementation, monitoring, and evaluation. These topics are related and seen as components of the program planning process. In addition, documentation is a vital part of programming and is, therefore, included within this total approach. All of these areas are addressed within the text.

FORMAT AND ORGANIZATION

Three sections provide the organizational structure of this edition. Section 1 presents the conceptual background. Chapter 1 gives an overview of the philosophical approach utilized within the total text. Chapter 2 develops and expands the basic philosophy by providing a thorough explanation of the Leisure Ability philosophy utilizing a therapeutic recreation service model. Programmatic implications and applications are explored. This section provides the basic information related to the selection of content for therapeutic recreation programs.

Section 2 is devoted to the explanation of a systems approach to program development. Chapter 3 provides a rationale for, and basic overview of, the systems approach utilized. Chapter 4 presents information and procedures related to comprehensive planning of total unit or agency therapeutic recreation programs. Determining and writing statements of purpose and goals are highlighted as important aspects of developing general program direction. Chapters 5 and 6 provide detailed information on the design of specific programs. Chapter 7 describes evaluation procedures to be utilized with systems-designed programs.

Section 3 deals with concerns and procedures that are interrelated with the programming process. Chapter 8 focuses on activity analysis as a procedure to assist in the selection of appropriate activities for program inclusion. Chapter 9 is devoted to the essential topic of documentation. Various record keeping and documentation procedures are described and illustrated. The significance and relationship of documentation to the programming process is presented. Chapter 10 presents an overview of assessment procedures and addresses the relationship of assessment to program development and implementation.

The purpose of this book is to provide comprehensive and progressive program development information for the field of therapeutic recreation. Its focus is both content for programs and the acquisition of skills in the program development process.

THERAPEUTIC RECREATION PROGRAM DESIGN

A Philosophical Overview

PURPOSE: This chapter provides a basic definition of therapeutic recreation and an elaboration of the various aspects of the definition. The evolution, development, and acceptance of this definition as the endorsed philosophy of the therapeutic recreation profession is presented.

INTRODUCTION

Programming in therapeutic recreation requires understanding of two significant areas. One is the technical process of developing the program itself. Much of this text focuses on the techniques of a systems approach to program planning. Equally important is the second area of programming expertise: that is, understanding what content should be presented. Obviously, the two areas are interrelated and interdependent. Knowledge of one area and not the other will result in programs that are either inappropriate to clients' leisure-related needs or not adequate in terms of implementation, management, or accountability. This text attempts to address both issues, utilizing a comprehensive and integrated approach. The first two chapters will focus on a therapeutic recreation philosophy and the implications for program content. The second part of the book presents a procedure for program planning utilizing a systems approach. Together, these two parts enable an understanding of both the content and the process of programming.

All programs in therapeutic recreation service should be based on client needs. The problem, however, is determining the essence and meaning of the term *client need*. Whether clients are served in treatment, residential, or community settings, they have multiple and complex needs. The therapeutic recreation profession, like all other professions, must address this issue and determine what client needs they can and should address. Once this critical task of professional responsibility and authority is established, the question of program content is much easier to approach.

Therapeutic recreation has existed in the past with multiple definitions and philosophies. Since its beginnings as a professional area of service, it has functioned with diverse theories and loosely translated programmatic applications. In the past, most professionals operated with either a *recreation orientation* or a *therapy orientation*. This dichotomy existed in both clinical and community settings. Within both approaches, a concept of client need was implied. Unfortunately, within the therapy approach, the focus of therapy was never well defined.

In 1969, a statement of definition was formulated by leading professionals in the field. For a decade, it was the definition most often used by the profession. Therapeutic recreation service was defined as

> a process which utilizes recreation services for purposive intervention in some physical, emotional, and/or social behavior to bring about a desired change in that behavior and to promote the growth and development of the individual.[1]

This definition also implies or assumes client need. The definition, however, is broad and somewhat vague in its focus on *desired change in behavior* and general *growth and development of the individual*. Most human and health services would also fit this definition, the only difference being the use of recreation services as the medium or process of intervention. The resulting impact of this definition was the continued programming for clients based on the individual practitioner's or agency's interpretation of the definition. Client need could be viewed as almost anything that the therapeutic recreation specialist wished to address. During the decade of the seventies, many creative, innovative programs emerged for special populations in a variety of settings. Some of these programs brought new insight to possible alternatives for the field. The absence, however, of a clear definition of therapeutic recreation proved to be problematic in an era of rapid expansion.

The field grew in terms of the number of practitioners with professional preparation and training. Hundreds of agencies added therapeutic recreation to their services. The field also grew in its professionalization efforts and sophistication. The National Therapeutic Recreation Society and state therapeutic recreation societies, sections, and associations evolved as significant factors in the emergence of the field. Issues such as credentialing, professional preparation, accreditation of professional preparation programs, professional standards, continuing professional development, legislation, advocacy, and philosophy became important to the development and further establishment of the field.

---

[1]Statement formulated at Ninth Southern Region Institute of Therapeutic Recreation, University of North Carolina, 1969, in Richard Kraus, *Therapeutic Recreation Service: Principles and Practices* (Philadelphia: W. B. Saunders Company, 1978), p. 3.

Philosophy became a critical issue. The profession recognized that a clear and concise definition was essential to its immediate existence and future expansion. Direction for the delivery of service was at the core of this identified need. In addition, progress in all the professionalization issues required this input as guidance for further development.

Several newer conceptualizations of therapeutic recreation had emerged by the late seventies. The Therapeutic Recreation Service Continuum Model (Leisure Ability approach) had been developed by Peterson and Gunn. Witt and Compton[2] had developed a similar conceptual model. Meyer[3] had completed a thorough analysis of past and current therapeutic recreation philosophies and theories for the Philosophical Issue Committee of the National Therapeutic Recreation Society. His investigation not only described and contrasted the major components of the three major philosophical schools of thought, but also laid the groundwork for understanding the professionalization implications of each.

After many years of study and with input from the membership, the National Therapeutic Recreation Society adopted the Leisure Ability philosophy and model as its official therapeutic recreation position. That action, taken in the fall of 1981, gave the field a philosophical basis with well-defined direction for the conceptualization and delivery of therapeutic recreation services. (A copy of the endorsed NTRS Philosophical Position Statement appears in Appendix A.) The remainder of this chapter describes and expands this position. The focus of this explanation is the implications and applications of the philosophy for program development.

THERAPEUTIC RECREATION—A CONCEPTUAL DEFINITION

Within the Leisure Ability approach, therapeutic recreation can be briefly defined utilizing four descriptive areas. Figure 1-1 presents this information. The sections that follow elaborate on each of the identified components.

Purpose: to facilitate the development, maintenance, and expression of an appropriate leisure lifestyle

Play, recreation, and leisure experiences are an important aspect of human existence. The significance of these behaviors can be interpreted and understood from psychological and sociological perspectives. Within our technological postindustrial society, leisure appears to play an even greater role than in previous periods of history. Currently, the concept of

---

[2]Peter Witt and David Compton, "A Philosophical Statement for the National Therapeutic Recreation Society, a Branch of the National Recreation and Park Association" (Mimeographed paper, 1979).

[3]Lee Meyer, "Three Philosophical Positions of Therapeutic Recreation and Their Implication for Professionalization and NTRS/NRPA," *Therapeutic Recreation Journal,* 15, no. 2 (1981), pp. 7–16.

FIGURE 1–1 Therapeutic Recreation

PURPOSE:	To facilitate the development, maintenance, and expression of an appropriate leisure lifestyle
POPULATION:	Individuals with physical, mental, social or emotional limitations
PROCESS:	Selection, development, implementation, and evaluation of goal-oriented services Treatment Leisure education Recreation participation Based on individual assessment and program referral procedures
SETTINGS:	Treatment, residential and community-based health and human-service centers and recreation agencies.

quality of life is intimately associated with leisure experience and opportunities for self-development and self-expression.

Individuals with disabling conditions are entitled to a meaningful existence that includes satisfying recreation and leisure experiences. Unfortunately, the limitations associated with an illness or disability, as well as the attitudinal and architectural barriers imposed by our society, often inhibit or prohibit the leisure expression and involvement of these individuals.

Facilitating the development, maintenance, and expression of an appropriate leisure lifestyle for individuals with disabling conditions can be established as an area of human need and thus an area for professional service. Therapeutic recreation as a professional field of service has designated this purpose to direct its service interventions with clients and as its contribution to society.

Central to this statement of purpose is the concept of leisure lifestyle. Within the philosophy of therapeutic recreation, leisure lifestyle has a specific definition that provides understanding of the total approach as well as direction for program planning. Peterson has defined the term as follows:

> Leisure lifestyle . . . the day-to-day behavioral expression of one's leisure-related attitudes, awareness, and activities revealed within the context and composite of the total life experience.[4]

Within this definition, leisure lifestyle implies a philosophy of leisure that includes the significance of activities but also draws on the concepts of attitudes and awareness as equally influential in the expression and nature

[4]Carol Ann Peterson, "Leisure Lifestyle and Disabled Individuals" (Paper presented at Horizons West Therapeutic Recreation Symposium, San Francisco State University, San Francisco, September 26, 1981).

of the experience. Perhaps the most essential aspect of the definition is the focus on day-to-day behavioral expression. This implies that leisure lifestyle is a routine engaged in as a part of the individual's daily existence. The quality and nature of one's leisure lifestyle may vary, but the fact remains that each person has one. Traditional and nontraditional leisure activities and expressions are an ongoing aspect of living. Daily actions can thus be used to describe and characterize the essence of an individual's unique leisure lifestyle. Additionally, the leisure lifestyle of a person cannot be viewed independently of all other actions. Other aspects of the person's existence (work, school, religion, family, friends) interface with the individual's leisure lifestyle. Likewise, the individual's leisure lifestyle is influenced by collective and accumulated life experiences.

Thus, when the purpose of therapeutic recreation is stated as facilitating "the development, maintenance, and expression of an appropriate leisure lifestyle," it is implying a significant contribution. The improvement of the quality of an individual's life through a focus on the leisure component is much more complex than the provision of enjoyable activity or the delivery of some segmented therapy utilizing activity as the medium. Therapeutic recreation calls for a thorough understanding of the leisure lifestyle concept and the design of appropriate and comprehensive services that can be used to intervene in the lives of people in an influential and positive way.

Population: individuals with physical, mental, social, or emotional limitations

Any individual with a physical, mental, social, or emotional condition that limits leisure functioning is eligible and could potentially benefit from therapeutic recreation services. However, leisure functioning or dysfunction is not recognized within our society as a condition requiring remediation, treatment, or development. Consequently, individuals or populations are designated as service-eligible because of specific illnesses, disabilities, or conditions that are acknowledged by the health, human, or social classification schemes.

Traditionally, specific medical or psychiatric diagnostic terms are also used to designate the populations who receive therapeutic recreation services. Mental retardation, mental and emotional disturbance, physical and sensory impairments, acute and chronic illness, and substance abuse are the commonly identified conditions that place individuals into human and health-care systems where therapeutic recreation services are delivered. In addition, legal offenders in various detention and rehabilitation centers have been the recipients of therapeutic recreation services. This category of clients does not generally fall within the medical or psychiatric classification scheme. In this situation, deviance in normative or social behavior becomes the criterion for incarceration and, thus, specialized services.

Illness and disability are most often referred to by given medical or physical diagnostic terms. These terms frequently result in stereotypic interpretations of abilities and limitations. In order to avoid inappropriate stereotyping, it appears beneficial to look at specific conditions relative to the actual limitation that that condition imposes on the individual in terms of physical, mental, social, and emotional functioning. These actual limitations then need to be analyzed for their impact on leisure functioning. It is this analysis and assessment that provides the rationale as well as the content for therapeutic recreation service.

At the current time, individuals with medical and psychiatric conditions are the primary clients involved in therapeutic recreation. However, there appear to be substantial and logical reasons for expansion of populations in the future. As leisure becomes more significant to the society and claims a more central role in the lives of people, then leisure dysfunction may well appear as a major condition of importance. When and if that occurs, then any individual with problems or conditions that negatively impact on leisure functioning may seek and receive specialized therapeutic recreation services. These services would most likely be delivered through existing recreation and leisure service agencies, community mental health centers, and various public and private counseling practices.

Process: the selection, development, implementation, and evaluation of treatment, leisure education, and recreation participation services based on individual assessment and program referral procedures

Facilitating the development, maintenance, and expression of an appropriate leisure lifestyle requires careful planning of specific program interventions. Clients vary considerably in their understanding of leisure and their leisure functioning ability and potential. Three program service categories have been conceptualized that identify client need relative to leisure functioning.

Treatment services have as their focus the improvement of some functional or behavioral area of the client. Individuals with a disability or illness are assessed to determine their physical, mental, social, and emotional assets and deficiencies. Specific functional deficiencies that would limit or interfere with leisure involvement become areas for possible program intervention. Programs are then designed that have goals related to the identified functional improvement. Recreation and leisure activities are selected that contribute to the attainment of the improved behavioral areas. Staff interventions are carefully selected to facilitate the treatment and functional improvement. Within most illness and disability categories, certain functional problems are common. The likelihood of encountering similar problems among clients enables the development of group-oriented programs that can address these deficiency areas efficiently. Therapeutic recreation treatment-oriented services occur most frequently in clinical settings.

Leisure education services focus on the development and acquisition of skills, attitudes, and knowledge related to leisure participation and leisure lifestyle development. The ability to engage in meaningful leisure experiences appears to be dependent on an understanding of leisure as well as having a repertoire of leisure-related skills. Most clients can benefit from services that focus on these areas. Assessment plays a major role in determining areas of leisure ability and leisure dysfunction. Programs are designed with specific goals related to the development of leisure skills, knowledge, and attitudes. Leisure education services are a major client need area in both clinical and community-based settings.

Recreation participation services provide the opportunity for clients to engage in structured group recreation experiences for enjoyment or self-expression. In both clinical and community settings, these programs provide an important participation role. The acquisition of leisure-related skills appears somewhat inconsequential without the opportunity to utilize those skills. Although organized group-participation programs comprise only one aspect of comprehensive leisure involvement, such group-activity programs are significant in the social structure of our society. Individuals with disabilities in the community may need segregated programs that provide special assistance, different sequencing and pacing, modified equipment or activities, and/or special management or leadership techniques. Individuals in clinical settings also need recreation participation experiences. The situation of being in treatment does not eliminate the need for, or interest in, self-expression or enjoyment through recreation participation. Assessment in the usual sense is not an aspect of programming within the recreation participation component. Staff members are responsible for the selection and delivery of diversified program offerings that are compatible with the abilities and interests of the clients.

Within this conceptualization of three specific types of services (treatment, leisure education, and recreation participation), it is acknowledged that a given client or participant may require or need services in one, two, or all three areas. Although a continuum may be implied, in that improved functional ability may precede the acquisition of leisure-related skills, knowledge, and awareness, in many cases, these two service areas may be addressed simultaneously. In other cases, the functional problem may be identified, but not acknowledged as an area where improvement can be accomplished. Such an individual may thus benefit from leisure education services that "work around" the functional problem and focus on the acquisition of leisure skills and knowledge within the constraints of the illness or disability. Regardless of the functional problems requiring treatment as a service area, or lack of knowledge or skills that would warrant the provision of leisure education services, it is most likely that all clients would benefit from, or enjoy, recreation participation services. Comprehensive programming necessitates a willingness on the part of the therapeutic recreation specialist to look at all areas of clients' leisure-related needs simultaneously and then appropriately prioritize service delivery based on client need and the availability of resources. Likewise, a given client may only need therapeutic recreation services in one area and should not be submitted to a full range of programs if they are not warranted.

The three service areas (treatment, leisure education, and recreation participation) provide a conceptual scheme to assist in the identification of client needs relative to leisure. Specific programs can then be selected, developed, and implemented in all three areas. Regardless of the type of program, each should be developed to address specific goals that can be operationalized and thus evaluated. Assessments or referrals are an integral aspect of the overall process of matching clients with specific needs to the appropriate program offerings.

Settings: treatment, residential, and community-based health and human-service centers and recreation agencies

Any agency or center that serves individuals with limitations can be considered an appropriate setting for the inclusion of therapeutic recreation services. In clinical and residential human-service and health-care centers, therapeutic recreation is just one component of a comprehensive service package. Traditional examples of such settings would include community mental health centers; public and private psychiatric facilities or units; developmental disability centers; public and private mental retardation facilities; physical rehabilitation centers or units; general hospitals; extended-care and long-term health-care facilities; special residential schools and centers serving such groups as visually impaired, hearing impaired, emotional and behavioral disorders, severely multiply handicapped; correctional centers and facilities; community-based special education facilities; and year-round residential camps for emotionally disturbed. (Note: Residential or day camping could be a program of many agencies listed in this section. Camping is viewed in this context as a program, not a setting. It is listed here to denote a specific long-term treatment approach that is occasionally used with behaviorally disordered youth.)

Therapeutic recreation services are also included within many community-based human service agencies that do not necessarily have a clinical focus. Examples of these settings would include public park and recreation departments and voluntary agencies such as Easter Seal Societies, Associations for Retarded Citizens, Young Men's and Women's Christian Associations, Boy and Girl Scouts, Campfire, Inc. In these settings, therapeutic recreation is again only one aspect of a larger service offering.

There are some settings in which therapeutic recreation is the only service offered. Examples of these single-service agencies would be: Cheff Center for the Handicapped (focus on horseback riding—Augusta, Michigan), Recreation Center for the Handicapped (San Francisco), Stepping Stones (Cincinnati), Special Olympics, and BOLD (Blind Outdoor Leisure Development). These agencies are generally voluntary, nonprofit, or private in sponsorship. The focus of these organizations is either a specific activity or type of activity, or a specific disability or cluster of disabilities. Most often the orientation of the programs is leisure education or recreation participation.

It is indeed difficult to clearly identify the settings where therapeutic recreation takes place. One acknowledged problem is the differentiation of the terms—setting, agency, and sponsorship. The purpose of this section is merely to identify the variety and diversity of settings that provide therapeutic recreation services.

LEISURE ABILITY AS A HOLISTIC APPROACH

The Leisure Ability philosophy is appropriate for use in any setting where therapeutic recreation services are delivered. The three components (treatment, leisure education, and recreation participation) indicate areas of client need related to leisure. The nature of the setting and its mandate for service will determine which areas of program services are appropriate and justified for their clients. Although some settings, such as public recreation, may view their mandate for service as being leisure education and recreation participation, they can easily endorse the total philosophy, recognizing that treatment is a service component that is addressed in other settings. Likewise, some short-term clinical settings, because of time and length of stay, may only choose to deliver treatment and/or leisure education services while still recognizing and endorsing the total Leisure Ability philosophy.

The Leisure Ability philosophy also provides a solid and logical foundation for the movement of clients between various settings. Discharge of a client from a clinical setting to a community living situation is facilitated when both clinical and community agencies hold a common philosophical position regarding the nature of therapeutic recreation services. A continuity of therapeutic recreation service focus can thus be maintained regardless of the agency delivering services to the client at any given moment.

The profession of therapeutic recreation is on the verge of acceptance and recognition by other health and human-service professions and by the general public. A commonly held philosophy related to the nature of client needs and the role of program services can have a significant impact on the contribution of the profession.

SUMMARY

This brief conceptual overview provides the background for the program content portrayed throughout the remainder of the book. The Leisure Ability approach to therapeutic recreation gives specific focus to the delivery of service as well as direction for further development of the profession. The next chapter will further explore and expand the implications of this philosophy and approach for program development and delivery.

=========== **Suggested References** ===========

AVEDON, E. M., "A Critical Analysis of the National Therapeutic Recreation Society Position Statement" (Paper presented at a special seminar, Indiana State University, Terre Haute, Indiana, May 21, 1970).

——, *Therapeutic Recreation Service: An Applied Behavioral Approach.* Englewood Cliffs, N.J.: Prentice-Hall, Inc., 1974.

BALL, E. L., "The Meaning of Therapeutic Recreation," *Therapeutic Recreation Journal,* 4, no. 1 (1970), 17–18.

ELLIS, M. J., *Why People Play.* Englewood Cliffs, N.J.: Prentice-Hall, Inc., 1973.

FRYE, V., and M. PETERS, *Therapeutic Recreation: Its Theory, Philosophy, and Practice.* Harrisburg, Pa.: Stackpole Books, 1972.

KELLY, JOHN R., *Leisure.* Englewood Cliffs, N.J.: Prentice-Hall, Inc., 1982.

KRAUS, RICHARD, *Therapeutic Recreation Service: Principles and Practices* (2nd ed.). Philadelphia: W. B. Saunders Company, 1978.

LIEBERMAN, J. NINA. *Playfulness: Its Relationship to Imagination and Creativity.* New York: Academic Press, 1977.

MARTIN, F. W., "Therapeutic Recreation Service: A Philosophic Overview," *Leisurability,* 1, no. 1 (1974), 22.

MEYER, LEE, "Three Philosophical Positions of Therapeutic Recreation and Their Implication for Professionalization and NTRS/NRPA," *Therapeutic Recreation Journal,* 15, no. 2 (1981), 7–16.

NEULINGER, JOHN, *To Leisure: An Introduction.* Boston: Allyn and Bacon, Inc., 1981.

O'MORROW, G. S., *Therapeutic Recreation: A Helping Profession* (2nd ed.). Reston, Va.: Reston Publishing mpany, Inc., 1980.

PEARCE, JOSEPH CHILTON, *Magical Child.* New York: E. P. Dutton, 1977.

RUSALEM, H., "An Alternative to the Therapeutic Model in Therapeutic Recreation," *Therapeutic Recreation Journal,* 7, no. 1 (1973), 8–15.

2

Therapeutic Recreation
Service Model

PURPOSE: To present a model that conceptualizes and defines therapeutic recreation services, ranging from treatment to independent leisure functioning. The model includes the various expected roles and functions of the therapeutic recreator as they relate to the functional level of the client. The various categories of therapeutic recreation services are presented, with implications for the development and delivery of programs.

The Leisure Ability approach to therapeutic recreation defines and gives direction to the development and delivery of service. The philosophy requires expansion and interpretation to enable operationalization. The Therapeutic Recreation Service Model developed by Peterson and Gunn provides the opportunity for a more comprehensive understanding of the underlying concepts involved in the Leisure Ability approach.

The model (Figure 2–1) is a graphic representation of the various therapeutic recreation services. Service purposes, roles of the therapeutic recreation specialist, and the concept of degrees of freedom for clients are portrayed. The model also attempts to illustrate the concept of a continuum, implying movement through the various service components. The ultimate goal of independent leisure involvement and lifestyle is beyond the parameters of the model. The model itself only represents those services that would be designed and implemented under the auspices of various agencies involved in the delivery of therapeutic recreation.

Both advantages and difficulties are inherent in presenting a schematic representation of a multifaceted phenomenon. Very often a picture of a phenomenon or concept will make comprehension easier and more meaningful than the utilization of lengthy narrative descriptions. Relationships may be more clearly understood, and movement throughout a process

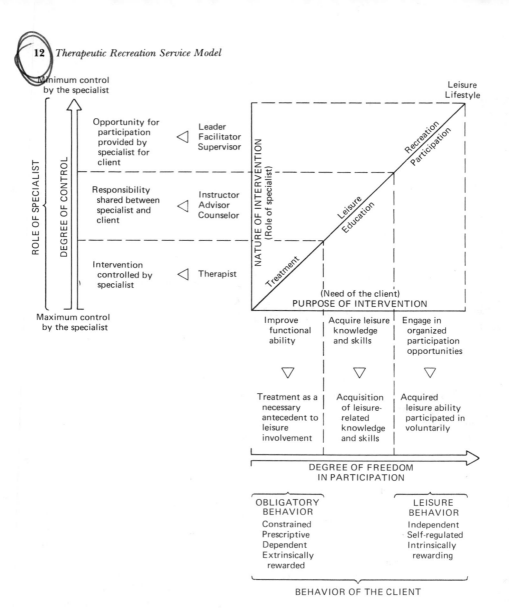

FIGURE 2–1 Therapeutic Recreation Service Model

may make more sense. However, the difficulties of a schematic model need to be mentioned so that the reader does not limit it to the two-dimensional characteristics of a page in a book.

The words chosen for schematic models are crucial in that space does not allow for extended explanations. It is also difficult to perceive movement or exact degrees of relationships on a static drawing. Additionally, models may be presumed to encapsulate a total concept, when in reality models can, at best, offer a visual clue to the basics of a concept or phenomenon. We acknowledge the limitations of schematics and ask that our readers be aware that the various domains of therapeutic recreation services are very often not distinctly separate units of service but, in fact, overlap or are conducted simultaneously.

Aspects of the model will be defined and described on the following pages. In addition, the reader may find that the model stimulates thought, discussion, and interpretation beyond the graphic illustration or the descriptions presented here.

A CLIENT-ORIENTED APPROACH

The Therapeutic Recreation Service Model is based on the concept of identified client needs related to leisure involvement. Each of the three categories of service (treatment, leisure education, and recreation participation) addresses a specific and different need that clients with disabling conditions may have. Programs are developed based on the analysis of clients served by a specific agency. The nature of the agency and its mandate for service is also a consideration. It is assumed that a given agency will provide services in more than one category. For example, most public recreation departments will provide leisure education and recreation participation programs for special populations. Those who work on an inpatient psychiatric unit or in long-term health-care facility will most likely find that their clients have leisure-related needs in all three categories of service. The issue remains: the need of the client determines the nature of programs provided. The nature of programs directs the content selected and the role of the therapeutic recreation specialist in that program.

A general analysis of clients served by a specific agency identifies the predominant areas of leisure-related client needs. This information provides the overall direction for the development of programs to be delivered. This basic program-delivery structure is then developed and operationalized. Individual client assessment techniques are then developed (and/or selected) and implemented. Individual clients can then be placed in, or referred to, the specific programs that focus on their individual areas of need. This overall approach utilizes the concept that within a given agency, client needs usually cluster. Thus, programs can be developed related to these common areas. However, clients are individually assessed and appropriately placed within those programs that relate to their unique problems, areas for development, or needs for participation. This scheme represents the current state of the art, where therapeutic recreation services are most often delivered through group-oriented programs. Consequently, the ability to address client needs must be conceptualized within the constraints of high-client/low-staff ratios and group structures. It is, however, possible to identify common leisure-related areas of need, program to meet these needs, and individualize within this situation. Even agencies with high-staff/low-client ratios find that group programs are an appropriate and highly beneficial way to address certain areas of behavioral change and leisure development. Most recreation participation programs by intent are group-oriented.

This approach addresses the need for individualized programming, which is a requirement within many agencies. The development of Individual Treatment Plans, Resident Care Plans, Individual Education Plans (or whatever individualized procedure is called for within a given agency) can be complied with by utilizing this approach. The initial conceptualization of client needs and the design of the basic service structure is the critical phase of the program development and delivery system.

PROGRAM FOCUS ON A SINGLE AREA OF PURPOSE

It is important to note that in using this approach, each program developed focuses on just one of the three major categories of service, or on an aspect of need within a major category. For example, if a program is designed for leisure awareness, it would focus only on that topic. Specific behavioral outcomes (performance measures) as well as the content (activities) and process (intervention techniques) are all developed with this singular emphasis. The program would not have elements of treatment or recreation participation within it by design or default. Similarly, a recreation participation program would be designed to facilitate leisure expression and enjoyment. It would not be used for treatment or leisure education purposes. This approach enables programs to be designed, implemented, and evaluated with a high degree of accountability. In the past, some agencies have used a more eclectic approach, where a given program was set up and client needs were individually addressed within the structure. An example of this would be the development of a general ceramics program in a long-term psychiatric facility. One client may be referred to the program to increase attention span; another client may be placed in the same program to develop social interaction skills. Another client is in the program to acquire ceramic skills, while other clients are voluntarily involved in the program because they enjoy crafts and specifically are interested in ceramics. This approach appears to be problematic on many levels. First, the program is limited by the activity selected as its focus. Second, the leader in charge must continuously interact with the various clients according to their specific reason for being in the program while simultaneously trying to keep the action for the whole group going. Third, specific outcomes are often narrowly conceived in order to be addressed within the context of the predetermined activity.

The systems approach utilized within this text focuses on the development of specific programs that address categories of client needs. This approach appears to be a more effective, feasible, and appropriate method of achieving positive client outcomes. It is acknowledged that initially this approach requires more planning and paper work, but the resulting program structure and content enable ongoing program operation and management that are both client-oriented and highly accountable.

TREATMENT AS A COMPONENT OF THERAPEUTIC RECREATION SERVICE

Within most clinical settings, therapeutic recreation services are established in order to contribute to the treatment and rehabilitation mission of the agency. Within these settings, therapeutic recreation services must be compatible with the central focus of treatment as well as make a unique contribution related to the leisure needs of clients. Since therapeutic recreation as a professional field of service is not well understood by most other disciplines, there has existed a great deal of confusion regarding its role in clinical settings. Part of the problem has been the absence of a clear position and definition by therapeutic recreators themselves. The result has been diverse interpretations of therapeutic recreation, often dictated by hospital administrators and medical personnel. The "diversion" concept, as well as the supportive-services designation, appears to be a by-product of this lack of clear professional definition, interpretation, and dissemination.

The Therapeutic Recreation Service Model provides an overall purpose for therapeutic recreation as well as specific definitions for the various categories of service. This information transferred to operational programs provides a strong rationale for, and understanding of, therapeutic recreation in any of the diverse clinical or community settings. Although the need for programs and the nature of content and intervention may vary depending on the specific population served, the overall purpose of facilitating the development, maintenance, and expression of an appropriate leisure lifestyle appears appropriate for all populations served. An understanding of the role and purpose of the treatment category of therapeutic recreation service within clinical settings is vital to overall comprehensive program development and implementation.

Several terms are used interchangeably within treatment. Treatment is perhaps the generic term, implying some specifically planned process to bring about desired positive change in behavior or pathology. *Rehabilitation, habilitation,* or *therapy* are terms that are often used to designate the same process within specific settings. When therapeutic recreators use the term *treatment,* they should be using it in the same way as all other health and medical personnel. Inherent in this term is a process. This process involves an assessment of need, a statement of the problem, formulation of treatment goal(s), design of a treatment plan, implementation, monitoring and progress reporting, and designation of criteria for decision-making regarding termination, continuation, or change. This procedure (or an agency-specific modification) is a necessary aspect of the planning and conducting of therapeutic recreation treatment-oriented services as well. Far too often in the past, therapeutic recreators have used the term "therapy" or "treatment" in a vague and general way to characterize their diverse and loosely defined programs.

Treatment not only implies a process; it also carries a connotation of focus or content based on the discipline or profession providing the specific service. Thus, psychotherapy, physical therapy, drug therapy, or any of the multitude of therapies denote an area of content that is applied through the designated and associated process. The treatment component of therapeutic recreation services also requires an area of focus if it is to be considered a legitimate therapeutic intervention. This important area of designation has been vague in the past, or at best, has been left up to the individual therapeutic recreation specialist within the given setting. For the most part, there has not even been a similarity of therapeutic recreation treatment purpose within settings serving the same population. Given this situation, it is no surprise that therapeutic recreation is not understood or recognized, let alone appreciated or acknowledged by other medical or health-related fields.

The Leisure Ability philosophy provides a foundation from which treatment-oriented therapeutic recreation services can derive a logical and appropriate purpose. Simply stated, if independent leisure functioning is the overall purpose of therapeutic recreation services, then the treatment component can and should address functional behavioral areas that are prerequisite to, or a necessary part of, leisure involvement and lifestyle. Behavioral areas can be identified by using the commonly acknowledged domains of physical, mental, emotional, and social functioning. Each of these areas has obvious significance for leisure involvement. In addition, they cut across all illnesses and disability classifications and thus are useful to a profession such as therapeutic recreation, which works with diverse populations in a variety of settings.

The designation of these four behavioral domains as the target area of concern in the treatment component of therapeutic recreation serves another important role. Assessing given clients using these four areas of functional ability gives a clearer and more objective picture of individuals and their capabilities and limitations. A given illness or disability affects different people in different ways. The diagnosis of a specific condition should not result in a stereotyped picture of the resulting functional or behavioral abilities. The utilization of an assessment approach that is not diagnosis-specific is therefore useful in determining clients' actual functional abilities and limitations.

In the medical model, the major concern is with the presenting pathology. Despite the frequent references to concern for the total person, more often than not, the major treatment is focused on the illness or disability itself, and not on how the condition affects the total person and the day-to-day living situation. There is little value in being overly critical of the medical or psychiatric professions. Perhaps the role of the allied health professions and ancillary services is to keep a focus on the total person. Therapeutic recreation is one of those professions that by definition is concerned with individuals and how they cope with, adjust to, or compensate for an illness or disability. Facilitating the development and expression of an appropriate leisure lifestyle is a purpose that goes beyond the disabling condition itself and seeks to assist the individual in establishing a meaningful and satisfying existence. Thus, in the provision of treatment-oriented therapeutic recreation services, the assessment of, and focus on, the actual behavioral and functional limitations imposed on the individual by the condition becomes a critical factor. In most cases, therapeutic recreation is treating, not the pathology itself, but the functional deficiency or limitation imposed by the pathology. The selection of the four areas of physical, mental, emotional, and social functioning enables an understanding of the actual results of an illness or disability and how these limitations may affect the living situation of the client. The therapeutic recreation specialist is particularly concerned with how these limitations relate to and influence leisure functioning.

An understanding of the physical, mental, emotional, and social-behavioral areas as they relate to leisure involvement and lifestyle gives the therapeutic recreation specialist a rationale and purpose for the development and implementation of treatment-oriented services. Clients are assessed for their functional abilities in these four areas as part of a comprehensive assessment related to all areas of leisure ability. If the analysis of assessment data indicates problems in the behavioral-functioning areas, then these problematic areas could be targeted for program intervention through treatment. This determination is made after careful consideration of the client's needs in all leisure-related areas. It is important to prioritize the client's needs. Functional problems may not be the client's major area of service need. A given client may have a greater need in the area of developing an awareness of leisure and acquiring some appropriate leisure skills. Some functional problems cannot be improved or changed. In these cases, a continued focus on the behavioral area would be shortsighted and not in the best interest of the client's eventual leisure lifestyle.

Many clients in clinical settings do have functional problems that relate to leisure involvement. Most of these problems can be addressed through treatment-oriented therapeutic recreation programs. Examples of this are found in Figure 2–2.

FIGURE 2–2 Functional Problems

CLIENTS WITH	POSSIBLE AREAS OF FUNCTIONAL IMPROVEMENT
Emotional disturbance	Staying in touch with reality Appropriate expression of emotions Appropriate social interactions
Mental retardation	Motor development Social development Increasing attention span
Physical disabilities	Increased strength Increased endurance Improved coordination

This list is not meant to be comprehensive. Each of the foregoing is merely an example of possible limitations that a *given individual* may display. Each of the limitations identified is a result of or directly related to the disability itself. Often a primary disability imposes other limitations on the individual. These are frequently referred to as *secondary disabilities*. An example of this might be an individual with a stroke who becomes withdrawn and begins to display symptoms of depression. Isolation and regressive social behavior are also common with many illnesses and disabilities. It is important to note that a secondary disability or disabilities are highly individual. They reflect a given client's response or reaction to the presenting primary disabling condition. The whole area of secondary disabilities is very significant to the therapeutic recreation specialist. Often it is these functional limitations that may require treatment. Indeed, they are as important to leisure functioning as the primary disability. Because the secondary disabilities are often in the social and emotional areas, they are very amenable to therapeutic recreation treatment-oriented services.

It is important to note that in the examples found in Figure 2–2 as well as in the examples related to secondary disabilities, there is a direct relationship of each of the problem areas to leisure functioning. Within the Leisure Ability approach to therapeutic recreation, this is the significant criterion as to whether the problem should be focused on through a treatment-oriented program.

When developing the treatment-oriented therapeutic recreation program, a group of related problem areas is usually clustered. An example would be a program that focuses on socialization or interaction skills. Another program may deal with physical or fitness-related areas. Programs can then be further developed, with objectives, performance measures, appropriate activities, and staff interventions. Each program, by addressing similar areas of functional ability and limitations, enables the referral and placement of clients by actual need. These needs can then be treated through a more thorough and focused group approach. In such programs, the activities are selected for their ability to contribute to the treatment goals and program objectives. Activity analysis (presented in Chapter 8) is a process that assists the therapeutic recreation specialist in the selection and modification of activities for treatment purposes. Activities selected and utilized this way can be a viable and dynamic treatment modality. The process, however, is a well-planned intervention to bring about specific behavioral change or improvement. Activities are used, not for their recreational or leisure potential, but rather for their specific inherent contribution to behavioral change.

Role of the Therapeutic Recreation Specialist

Figure 2–3, which displays only the treatment component of the total Therapeutic Recreation Service Model, indicates two other important concepts related to treatment services. These are the role of the therapeutic recreation specialist and the degree of freedom or choice on the part of the client. These concepts, along with the main issue of purpose of this

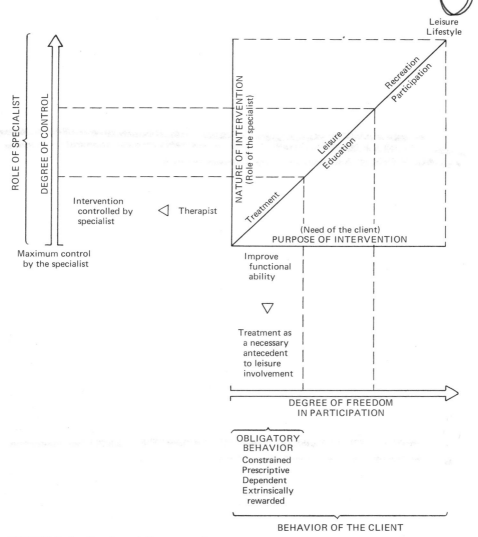

FIGURE 2–3 Treatment Component

service category, are vital to the understanding of the development and delivery of these services.

The primary role of the therapeutic recreation specialist while engaged in the design and delivery of treatment-oriented services is that of therapist. This term is not used merely to designate a role; rather, it implies the acquisition and appropriate utilization of a variety of therapeutic intervention techniques and strategies. The techniques needed depend on the population being served and also on the tradition or approach of the agency. For example, when working as a therapist with individuals with developmental disabilities, the therapeutic recreation specialist may be expected to utilize physical or environmental manipulation, verbal cueing, backward chaining, or behavior modification. In a psychiatric setting, therapeutic techniques, such as Reality Therapy, Reflective Listening, Transactional Analysis, or a vast number of other verbal and psychotherapy approaches, may be employed by the treatment team and thus are expected to be utilized by the therapeutic recreation specialist as well.

The role of therapist implies a carefully selected and appropriately implemented intervention technique that is used to bring about some specific behavioral change or improvement in clients. When a treatment-oriented therapeutic recreation program is being designed, obvious consideration is given to the development of the specific objectives that delineate the desired behavioral improvement. Careful consideration is also given to the selection of appropriate activities as the content that contributes to the attainment of the objectives. Equally important, however, is the selection and specification of the therapeutic-intervention technique to be used by the staff. The intervention technique used must be appropriate for the clients within the program, it must be compatible with the program objectives, and it must be feasible given the program content (activities). In addition, the staff member must be competent in the use of the technique, which must be within the designated authority of the therapeutic recreation staff member.

The selection of an appropriate therapeutic intervention technique should be based on the nature of clients and the purpose of the program. This implies that a good therapeutic recreation specialist needs a variety of intervention skills and techniques. It is inappropriate to assume that one technique will be appropriate for all clients or in all treatment-oriented programs. Similarly, the adoption of one therapeutic intervention approach based solely on the staff members' preference may be naive or self-serving.

Thus, in treatment-oriented therapeutic recreation services, the role of the specialist is that of therapist. The interactions and interventions within these programs are carefully designed to bring about predetermined client behavioral improvement or change. The role of therapist has inherent responsibilities and requires the acquisition of various therapeutic techniques and approaches. Different therapeutic strategies are used with different populations. Designing programs for a given population requires specific knowledge of appropriate, feasible, and effective therapeutic techniques.

Degrees of Freedom and Control

Engaging in an independent and meaningful leisure lifestyle implies freedom of choice on the part of the individual. Many of the definitions of leisure use the concept of freedom as a primary descriptor of the experience and phenomenon. The concept of freedom is part of the ultimate goal within the Leisure Ability approach to therapeutic recreation as well. However, within the treatment component, the freedom-of-choice issue is premature. Because of functional limitations, most treatment services utilize a program-referral or prescriptive approach. This implies that programs are developed and implemented to improve some functional skill or necessary behavioral area that is a prerequisite for leisure functioning and involvement. These assessments and judgments are most often considered to be the domain of professional decision-making and treatment planning. Thus, the client experiences little, if any, degree of freedom or choice while in treatment-oriented therapeutic recreation services. Control is in the hands of the therapeutic recreation specialist. Decisions regarding what functional problems and limitations will be addressed, as well as decisions regarding the nature and content of the programs, are made by the staff. This component parallels the medical model, where control of the treatment is the responsibility of the professional. As functional abilities improve, and as clients move into other areas of therapeutic recreation programming, the degree of freedom and control shifts from the therapeutic recreation specialist to the client. This shift will be further addressed in the following sections of this chapter.

Interdisciplinary Treatment

The information presented on the previous pages addresses specific treatment services as they relate to functional limitations as prerequisites to, or as a necessary aspect of, leisure involvement. Indeed, this is the unique contribution of treatment-oriented therapeutic recreation services. Many clinical settings, however, utilize an interdisciplinary-treatment approach. In an interdisciplinary approach, treatment goals are arrived at by the entire professional staff. Some goals are then addressed in treatment by a specific discipline. Other goals are focused on by all members of the team. When therapeutic recreation is part of an interdisciplinary-team approach, its focus of service would have a dual responsibility. One aspect of programming would be the implementation of programs and interactions addressing the general treatment goals determined by the team. The second area is more complex and difficult. It involves integrating the significance of leisure into the total rehabilitation concept and approach, so that specific treatment goals related to leisure functioning can be a part of the total treatment plan. Thus, when client cases are presented and discussed, the team will have a basis for setting up treatment goals that take this area of client need into consideration. The therapeutic recreation specialist must take the responsibility for interpreting and educating the entire team regarding the leisure area of rehabilitation and treatment. Much of the information on the previous pages and in the sections that follow can be used to present explanations and rationales for the inclusion of therapeutic recreation as a significant area of client need and treatment focus. In an interdisciplinary-team approach, it is essential that client-treatment goals related to leisure functioning be a part of the overall assessment and treatment plan. The absence of involvement at the critical client-assessment and treatment-planning stage would reduce the therapeutic recreation to a role of insignificance, with little or no impact. Once treatment goals related to leisure functioning are understood and accepted by the team, specific programs can be delineated and implemented to address those specific goals. Therapeutic recreation then becomes a legitimate part of the interdisciplinary-team and treatment approach, both contributing to general treatment goals and addressing specific leisure-related goals as well.

LEISURE EDUCATION AS A COMPONENT OF THERAPEUTIC RECREATION SERVICE

Leisure education is a broad category of services that focuses on the development and acquisition of various leisure-related skills, attitudes, and knowledge. The establishment and expression of an appropriate leisure lifestyle appears to be dependent on the acquisition of diverse knowledge and skills. A repertoire of activity skills is not the only requirement. A cognitive understanding of leisure, a positive attitude toward leisure experiences, various participatory and decision-making skills, as well as a knowledge of, and the ability to utilize, resources appear to be significant aspects of satisfying leisure involvement. These leisure education content areas can be operationalized into programs that have as their purpose the acquisition of appropriate leisure-related skills, knowledge, and attitudes. Figure 2–4 displays a model that breaks down and organizes this conceptualization of leisure education content. The various components will be elaborated on later in this section.

Play can be considered a basic behavior. This implies that play behavior is inherent, or a natural part of human existence and expression. The role and form of play behavior, however, are directed by societal influence and sanction. The play behavior of very young infants is similar

FIGURE 2–4 Components of the Leisure Education Content Model

LEISURE EDUCATION	
LEISURE AWARENESS 1.0	SOCIAL INTERACTION SKILLS 2.0
LEISURE RESOURCES 4.0	LEISURE ACTIVITY SKILLS 3.0

throughout the world and throughout history. The role, content, and structure of play for children, youth, and adults varies considerably based on the given culture. In postindustrial America, play has a significant role for individuals of all ages. The term *play* is not commonly used past the infant and childhood stages. Replacing "play" most often are the terms *recreation* and *leisure*. "Recreation" connotes to most people a vast variety of structured activities commonly sanctioned by the society and most frequently engaged in through some organized delivery system. "Leisure activities" seem to have a broader meaning and generally are accepted as activities and behaviors that are voluntarily engaged in by the individual for intrinsic and self-rewarding outcomes. It is not the intent of this text to explicitly define, defend, or differentiate between the various terms used within the leisure arena. The terms are introduced here only to assist in an understanding of the leisure education and Leisure Ability concept.

Play is most often understood as a behavior. It is a behavior that is identifiable, observable, and different from other forms of human behavior. It is content-free, implying that the behavior is displayed in many contexts. An individual can "play" within a structured, traditional recreation activity such as tennis or Backgammon, or can "play" within the unstructured form of daydreaming or watching TV. An individual can also display play behavior within other human contexts. Many social interactions are adult forms of play behavior. Likewise, one can have playful moments within the work situation. Play, then, is viewed as a behavior rather than a specific activity. The term *leisure behavior* is more commonly used within our contemporary society to identify this human behavior. This term will be used within this text to designate the wide range of human expressions that are engaged in voluntarily, possess the element of freedom of choice, are intrinsically motivated, and display the characteristics of being enjoyable and meaningful to the individual.

Although play and leisure behavior are considered basic behaviors and are viewed as a right and need of individuals, many people require some assistance in developing an appropriate and satisfying leisure lifestyle. There are many attitudinal blocks to leisure expression. The Protestant work ethic and its resulting impact related to idleness, self-enjoyment, and nonproductive activity still exert a strong influence on the lives of many people. In many ways, individuals with conditions of illness or disability are most often victimized by this influence. The disabling condition often removes individuals from productive activities (work) and leaves them without identifiable contributory roles. Unfortunately, a lingering view of leisure involvement is that leisure is earned as a reward for work, and, thus, the individual is not entitled to leisure benefits or enjoyment if they are not contributing to society in some recognized manner. Within our contemporary society and with the influence of more humanistic theories, this previous attitude has been largely rejected. The individual is seen as valuable and significant because he or she exists. The individual has rights and responsibilities like anyone else. Our human-service-system structure and legislative mandates support and reinforce this philosophy. The fact remains that many individuals with illnesses and disabilities are negatively impacted by previous attitudes and values of the society.

Because leisure is a significant component of contemporary life, it must also be viewed as an important and necessary aspect of existence for individuals with conditions of illness and disability. The concept of quality of life is very much related to the opportunities available for leisure involvement and expression. Individuals with disabling conditions, however, may need assistance in the development and expression of an appropriate leisure lifestyle. The leisure education component of therapeutic recreation services addresses this need in a direct and comprehensive manner.

The leisure lifestyle of most people in our society evolves and develops throughout the life span of the individual. Early childhood and family experiences and social interactions in the neighborhood and schools shape the foundation of attitudes and values related to leisure. The teen and young-adult years provide the opportunity for breaking away from family traditions and expectations and allow the individual to experiment with, and engage in, more self-initiated and self-directed forms of leisure. It is during the young-adult stage of life that leisure routines and lifestyle appear to become more stable and established for most people. Likewise, if conscious awareness of leisure and a valuing of the phenomenon occurs, it most likely takes place at this stage of human development.

Individuals with congenital illnesses and disabilities (or ones that occur very early in life) often are inhibited in normal play and socialization opportunities. Thus, the formulation of play and leisure attitudes and behaviors are frequently developmentally or experientially limited. Individuals who acquire a disabling condition later in life frequently have difficulties in the expression of previous leisure involvements and interest. Their condition itself may appear to inhibit or prohibit leisure involvement through imposed real or perceived limitations. In other cases, the individual may just dismiss leisure as a significant or possible component of living, since the focus of others and themselves shifts to the care and treatment of the disabling condition itself. Individuals with congenital as well as acquired conditions of illness and disability appear to have difficulty with leisure involvement and expression.

Since the development and expression of an appropriate leisure lifestyle is an important aspect of the human condition, there appears to be substantial reason for therapeutic recreation specialists to intervene. Even if the individual is not concerned about leisure, and even in the absence of widespread concern by other medical and health professionals, the profession of therapeutic recreation has a role to play in the preparation or rehabilitation of the client relative to leisure. The unique contribution of therapeutic recreation is significant to the total living experience of the individual, independent of its recognition by others.

Nature of Leisure Education Services

Leisure education services utilize an educational model, as opposed to the medical model. The educational model operates on the assumption that behavior can change and improve as the individual acquires new knowledge, skills, attitudes, and abilities. These changes occur through a learning process. The client is an active participant in the process, sharing responsibility for the change or growth that is targeted. Although illness or disability must be considered both in the content to be learned and the process through which learning takes place, the illness or disability is not the primary concern. Behavioral growth and change are sought independent of the condition. In leisure education, the focus of learning (or desired area of behavior change) is leisure ability.

It is difficult to determine the relationship between conditions of illness and disability, and leisure involvement and participation. The exact impact of any given condition on a specific individual is probably impossible to identify. Likewise, it is not of any significant value to attempt to categorize the impact or influence of the various kinds of illnesses or disabling conditions. A more realistic and useful approach appears to be the analysis of factors involved in successful leisure participation and utilization. The information gained through such investigation can then be conceptualized and organized in areas related to general program content. This program content can then be modified and operationalized for an individual or a group of individuals who have common characteristics or needs. The specific program design at that point takes into consideration the specific illness or disability. Content changes can be made based on the condition, and instructional strategies are selected that are appropriate for individuals of a given disability.

It is this approach that was utilized in the conceptualization and development of the leisure education model presented in this text. The model is based on a normalization concept. Nondisabled individuals were studied to determine components of successful leisure involvement. Observations and interviews were used as the primary methods of study. The information gained was analyzed and discussed with various professionals in the field. Four general categories of leisure-related skills emerged. Each of these was further conceptualized and developed. Figure 2–5 presents this expanded Leisure Education Content Model.

All models have conceptual weaknesses. This is particularly true of a model that attempts to describe a phenomenon as complex as leisure and an area in which so little agreement related to definition exists. The Leisure Education Content Model is thus subject to inherent and acknowledged limitations. Nonetheless, its conceptualization and the resulting components and content have proven to be useful in the design of leisure education programs for diverse populations in a variety of settings. The model provides both students and practitioners with identified areas of possible client need related to the development of various leisure-related skills, knowledge, attitudes, and abilities. Other models and approaches to leisure education have been developed and are currently being utilized. The Mundy and Odum model is one that the reader may find to be equally comprehensive and useful.[1] Most practitioners utilize some existing conceptualization of leisure education as the foundation for their programming. Noth-

[1]Jean Mundy and Linda Odum, *Leisure Education: Theory and Practice* (New York: John Wiley and Sons, 1979), pp. 44–116.

FIGURE 2–5 Leisure Education Content Model

LEISURE AWARENESS 1.1 Knowledge of leisure 1.2 Self-awareness 1.3 Leisure and play attitudes 1.4 Related participatory and decision-making skills <div align="right">1.0</div>	**SOCIAL INTERACTION SKILLS** 2.1 Dual 2.2 Small group 2.3 Large group <div align="right">2.0</div>
LEISURE RESOURCES 4.1 Activity opportunities 4.2 Personal resources 4.3 Family and home resources 4.4 Community resources 4.5 State and national resources <div align="right">4.0</div>	**LEISURE ACTIVITY SKILLS** 3.1 Traditional 3.2 Nontraditional <div align="right">3.0</div>

ing prohibits the individual therapeutic recreation specialist from conceptualizing one's own approach. It is, however, an awesome task to conceptualize and develop programs that are both appropriate and comprehensive in nature.

The Leisure Education Content Model presented in this text is generic in nature. It is not designed for one specific illness or disability. It crosses disability lines to identify aspects of leisure involvement and lifestyle development. Likewise, it is not specific for any given agency. Its content areas appear to be just as useful in community settings as in clinical settings. It has been used to design programs for nondisabled populations as well as special-need populations. Selection of content and the design of specific intervention techniques obviously will vary depending on the population and setting.

The various components of the model will be described further in the sections that follow. General program applications will be presented. Program-development applications for specific populations and settings will be left to the reader. Again, it is the intent of the authors to stimulate thought, further development, and promote applications that may extend beyond the limits of the model itself.

FIGURE 2–6 Leisure Awareness Component of the Leisure Education Model

---

LEISURE AWARENESS

1.1 Knowledge of leisure
1.2 Self-awareness
1.3 Leisure and play attitudes
1.4 Related participatory and decision-making skills

1.0

Content of Leisure Education Services

Four components have been conceptualized to identify the major aspects of leisure education content. Each of these four components will be described separately on the following pages. Figure 2–6 displays the first component of the total leisure education model previously presented.

Leisure Awareness. An important aspect of leisure lifestyle and involvement appears to be a cognitive awareness of leisure and its benefits, a valuing of the leisure phenomenon, and a conscious decision-making process to activate involvement. These cognitive aspects seem to be what was missing in so much of past recreation and therapeutic recreation programming. The historical assumption seemed to be that individuals only needed to acquire recreation activity skills, and from there, they would apply those skills in some meaningful pattern of leisure involvement. That approach did not seem to influence positively the leisure involvement of most clients beyond the actual participation in the segmented agency-sponsored programs. The more current approach, which focuses on some understanding of leisure, appears to have a better chance of facilitating the development and expression of an appropriate leisure lifestyle. Regardless of whether or not the individual immediately responds to the content of leisure education programs, they are still exposed to knowledge and information that may be useful to them at some later point.

Within the component of *leisure awareness,* at least four content areas can be identified that appear essential in facilitating the development and expression of an appropriate leisure lifestyle. The first of these is *knowledge of leisure.* This content area can address a variety of topics. The following topics are ones that have been found to be useful with many populations. Many other topics could be added.

What is leisure?
The difference between leisure behaviors and other behaviors
Benefits and possible outcomes of leisure involvement
Forms of leisure involvement
The concept of leisure lifestyle
The concept of personal responsibility for leisure lifestyle

A second content area is that of *self-awareness*. This area focuses on a more personal understanding of leisure and the individual. The following are possible topic areas for inclusion in this content area:

Actual and perceived abilities and limitations related to leisure involvement as a result of disabling condition
Past leisure and play patterns and activities
Current leisure involvement and satisfaction
Areas for future discovery and involvement
Personal resources for leisure involvement

This list could easily be extended to include many other related topics.

Because attitudes and values are so important to the acceptance, development, and expression of a leisure lifestyle, this content area is separated from the previous two. *Leisure and play attitudes* is the third content area of the first leisure education component. Within this area, existing attitudes about play and leisure can be explored. This topic can move from past, current, and future societal attitudes to the more personal exploration of one's own attitudes, their origin and impact. Often, values-clarification exercises are used in the presentation of this latter topic. The relationship between attitudes and behavior is another significant aspect of this content area. The therapeutic recreation specialist is not only interested in helping individuals to identify their own leisure attitudes, but also to assist clients in analyzing these attitudes to determine their appropriateness, level of satisfaction, and impact in terms of current and future leisure lifestyles. This is often a critical point in terms of redirecting, or moving toward a change in, leisure lifestyle development.

The fourth content area of the first component is entitled *related leisure participatory and decision-making skills*. Again, a variety of topics and processes can be identified for content inclusion in this area. Commonly identified areas include

Decision-making skills
Leisure planning
Problem-solving techniques

All of these three areas are processes that may require substantial time for learning. However, these skills appear essential if meaningful changes are to take place in the individual's leisure lifestyle and involvement.

This fourth area also includes topics that may vary considerably, depending on the specific population being served by the program. Examples of this may be such topics as the following:

Rehabilitation Center for Individuals with Spinal-Cord Injuries
Dealing with the accessibility issue at leisure-related facilities (restaurants, theaters, recreation centers, and so on)
Asking for assistance

How to locate information about accessibility

Interactions with nondisabled people in leisure participation (friends, staff, strangers)

Psychiatric Inpatient Unit

How to interact in recreation programs with nondisabled participants

How to locate information about appropriate leisure opportunities

Behavioral and emotional control in new situations

Group Home for Individuals with Mental Retardation

Appropriate behavior, mannerisms, and dress in programs with nondisabled participants

How to use public or special transportation

Related skills, such as money management, use of telephone, how to ask for directions or assistance

This limited list is for illustration only. Obviously, none of the lists of possible related participatory skills or topics is complete. In addition, many other populations and settings were not included at all. The reader, however, can develop such topic areas as needed.

This section has identified *content* related to the first component of the presented leisure education model. The identified content areas need to be conceptualized and developed into appropriate program structures prior to implementation. A few comments about program development will conclude this section.

The four content areas of the first component are rarely separated into different programs. Aspects of all four areas are generally combined into one leisure education program structure. The selection of topics is based on the specific population and their leisure-related information needs. In most cases, however, the information and skills found in the first component are not part of previously acquired knowledge. Thus, the conceptualization of the actual content for programs related to this component is at the discretion of the therapeutic recreation specialist designing the program.

The content or topic areas of this first component of leisure education are usually developed into programs that use a variety of cognitive and affective intervention techniques. Group discussion, paper-pencil leisure and self-awareness activities, individual and group verbal exercises, leisure information discovery or investigation games, mini-lectures, presentations, and use of various audiovisual aids are all common techniques utilized to facilitate an understanding and acquisition of the content. In the development of any therapeutic recreation program, it is important to select appropriate intervention or facilitation techniques. Again, the techniques utilized should be compatible with the content of the program and appropriate for the clients being served. Since the content of this first component of leisure education is primarily cognitive and affective, the interventions most often utilized are *instructional strategies or counseling techniques.*

Because of the use of counseling techniques, programs in this first component have frequently been called Leisure Counseling Programs. These authors object to the use of this title. It seems inappropriate to title a program by the intervention or facilitation technique used. The content of the programs most often focuses on leisure and self-awareness, leisure attitudes and values, participatory problems, and decision making. Thus, it would be more consistent to label the program by its content; for instance, Leisure Awareness or even Leisure Education. A variety of intervention techniques are indeed used, and aspects of various counseling techniques are very useful and appropriate. However, the use of a given counseling technique is not sufficient reason to include leisure counseling in the title.

There is a legitimate service area that can be called leisure counseling. It is, however, quite different and distinct from the leisure education programs presented here. *Leisure education* has a specific and *predetermined content,* which is operationalized into programs. This section of this chapter has delineated leisure education content and will continue to do so. Leisure counseling, as well as other forms of counseling, do not start with predetermined content. Rather, the problem or focus of counseling originates from the individual client. This major distinction between counseling and education is an important one. It is, however, common for counselors to use educational techniques within the counseling process. Likewise, educators often use counseling techniques within the educational process. Leisure counseling also has some significant differences when it comes to the issue of qualifications and credentials. In general, it is reasonable to assume that most therapeutic recreation specialists are qualified to use some basic counseling techniques. It is not appropriate to assume that they have sufficient training to utilize the title "counselor."

When developing and implementing programs related to the first component of the leisure education model, it is important to take into consideration the other leisure education needs that will be presented in the following sections. Likewise, client needs related to the *treatment* and *recreation participation* aspects of service must also be analyzed. This consideration, it is hoped, will enable the development of programs that will be complementary and, in some cases, will need to be sequential. This very issue is a good reason to engage in comprehensive program planning at the onset. Master planning enables appropriate identification of client needs and selection of program components from all levels of the Therapeutic Recreation Service Model to meet the identified needs. Client needs can be addressed within a comprehensive program structure. Specific programs are then developed with prior knowledge of resource (time, budget, staff, equipment, facility) availability. Such planning eliminates the all-too-often segmented approach found in the past.

Social Interaction Skills.

The leisure education model presented in this book has three other components. The second component focuses on social interaction skills. Figure 2–7 presents this segment of the larger model.

Social interaction is a major aspect of leisure lifestyle. This is particularly true of adult leisure involvement. In many situations, the social

FIGURE 2–7 Social Interaction Component of the Leisure Education Model

SOCIAL INTERACTION SKILLS

2.1 Dyads   ⎫
2.2 Small goups   ⎬   Cooperation
2.3 Large groups   ⎭   and
                                       Competition

2.0

interaction is more significant and important to the participants than the activity itself. The activity may be the reason to be together, but it is the social interaction that has real meaning for the people involved. Social dancing (ballroom, disco, rock, and so forth) is an example of this point. In other situations, the activity has significant meaning to the participants, but interaction abilities are essential for successful involvement. Playing bridge, which requires interaction between partners as well as bidding against others, illustrates this point. Most team sports also require interaction between and among team members for successful participation. A third situation involving social interaction skills can be identified. Some group-oriented leisure activities require little social interaction, but the participation and enjoyment seem to be heightened by social interaction. Square dancing or bowling are examples of this point. Within the comprehensive concept of leisure lifestyle, there are many leisure participation situations that do not involve traditional activities at all. In such a conceptualization, a social encounter that is exclusively a verbal interaction could be considered a leisure experience depending on the motivation, content, and outcomes. When we realize how often this type of social interaction takes place for most nondisabled individuals, it becomes a very important consideration. Simply stated, social interaction among adults may be the most frequent form of leisure participation. In all four of the foregoing situations, adequate and appropriate social interaction skills are necessary for satisfactory participation.

Many individuals with conditions of illness or disability have less-than-adequate social interaction abilities. This may be the result of the primary pathology itself or a reaction to the major problems, which then becomes a secondary disability. With handicapped children, parents often protect or shelter the child, which frequently results in few early and normal socialization opportunities. With adults, social isolation often is a defense or form of self-protection. In some cases, there are simply limited opportunities for social interaction. Regardless of the cause, the resulting inadequate social interaction skills interfere with, or create barriers to, leisure participation.

Since social interaction appears to be such a significant aspect of leisure participation and lifestyle, it is included as a component of leisure education. The skills and abilities involved in social interaction can be learned. They can be conceptualized into program structures. What is more important, they can be learned through involvement in various recreation and leisure activities and thus take on a more dynamic, action-oriented dimension. Acquiring social interaction skills in the context of activities allows for more realistic learning and application. Generally, learning interaction skills through activity involvement is enjoyable for the client as well. Fortunately, traditional recreation activities have within their structures all the various and basic interaction skills normally required within our society. Careful assessment of the client's existing social interaction skill level and the analysis of additional interaction skills needed can be conducted. Activities can then be selected that have the appropriate inherent interactional requirements to facilitate the acquisition of the designated social interaction skills. Activity analysis (presented in Chapter 8) provides valuable information related to the process of activity selection for the development of social interaction skills.

The acquisition of social interaction skills, like any other skill acquisition, requires the planning of specific programs designed to facilitate the learning of the designated behavior. If social interaction skills are identified as a major area of client need, then specific programs addressing these skills need to be developed. Depending on the population and setting, social interaction skill development may be a significant aspect of the comprehensive leisure education and therapeutic recreation mission. An example of this point may provide some clarification. Individuals with moderate mental retardation may need specific programs to develop appropriate social interaction skills. Individuals in a substance-abuse program or in a short-term psychiatric facility may only need to have appropriate social interaction skills reinforced through other types of therapeutic recreation programming.

When developing and implementing programs that focus on the acquisition of interaction skills, the therapeutic recreation specialist functions in the role of *educator*. The interventions and facilitation techniques are selected from various *instructional strategies*. Although a therapeutic recreator can counsel a client regarding the need for interaction skills, the actual acquisition of those skills involves a learning process. Thus, instructional techniques are the most frequently used interventions with social interaction skill-development programs.

There are many ways to conceptualize social interaction skills. Models have been developed to characterize the various aspects and areas of interaction. Social-development schemes have been provided by various disciplines. Applications of these have been made for some categories of disability, such as the developmentally disabled. It is not the intent of this section to focus on social interaction in depth or comprehensively. A brief conceptual scheme is presented as part of the social interaction skill component. This scheme is general and is intended to cut across all disability categories. It is very limited, however, when applied to a specific disability group or to a given individual. The scheme is described here to provide just one brief view of some considerations within the social interaction area.

Interaction skills can be conceptualized by number of people involved and by nature of the interaction. A simple three-by-two matrix emerges as shown in Figure 2–8.

FIGURE 2–8 Social Interaction Matrix

	DUAL	SMALL GROUP	LARGE GROUP
Cooperative			
Competitive			

This conceptualization is meant to identify very basic interactions required within leisure activities. These same interactions are basic to other human-communication and social situations. Thus, there is obvious generalization of the skills even though they may be addressed and developed within an activity context.

Dual. *Dual* implies an interaction between two people. This is probably the most common and frequent interaction between people. It can be further characterized as having two dimensions—*cooperative* and *competitive*. "Cooperative" designates verbal and nonverbal interactions that are mutual and positive in intent and content. A casual social conversation between two friends or two people engaged in sailing a boat together are examples of this behavior. Although frequently taken for granted, there are many abilities and skills required in such interactions.

"Competitive" in this context does not necessarily mean competing to win or beat the other person. Rather, it implies a variety of interactions of unequal outcomes or conflict. Arguing, disagreeing, asserting, and criticizing are all aspects of this dimension, as well as the traditional concept of competing. Thus, engaging in a game of Backgammon or being involved in a fair and appropriate argument with a peer would be considered competitive dual interactions. Again, a variety of skills and abilities is needed to be competitive in the various dual-interaction situations. A given client may need interaction skills in the dual category. Cooperative and competitive abilities should be assessed and possibly included within the intervention program. Because of the frequency of these interactions and their potential for leisure enjoyment, this category of interaction is probably the most important.

Small Group. A *small group* has from three to approximately ten participants. It is best defined as a group where all members are expected or able to interact with each other. Thus, the upper limit is more dependent on the nature of the activity than an absolute number. The skills involved in small-group interactions are quite different from the dual interaction. The number of participants places different demands on the individual. Two primary skills can be identified. One is the ability to compromise and cooperate with the other members. The second is appropriate self-initiation and self-assertion. These characteristics need to be employed in two ways. In small-group activities, there are interactions that are required and necessary within the activity itself. In addition, there are interactions that enhance and expand the social experience within the group and activity.

It is this latter set of social interaction skills that are more difficult to acquire and utilize appropriately.

The small-group interactions also include the dimensions of cooperation and competition as defined in the dual category. Examples of cooperative small-group interactions would be a square-dance set or small social gathering of friends. An example of competitive small-group interaction would be a poker game. It is obvious that in many situations, there are times when both cooperative and competitive transactions occur simultaneously. The small-group interaction is again a vital area of social interaction ability. The skills are important not only to leisure involvement, but also to other human communication and living situations. Families, work, and many adult social situations require small-group interaction skills.

There are many specific skills involved in small-group interactions. These skills need to be identified and conceptualized for various client populations. Appropriate assessment techniques can then be designed. The development of program structures to address the skills follows assessment.

Large Group. A *large group* is usually considered to be ten or more people. Each group member is not expected to interact with all other group members. They are considered a group by the fact they are all geographically in proximity to one another. The interactions are most likely to be among and between individuals within the context of the larger group setting. Again, the skills of self-assertion and self-initiation are needed to be a successful participant. This is even more true in the large group than in the small group, since the activity itself is not usually demanding of the individual. Some of the skills from the dual category are also required. Within the large group, the responsibility of "making things happen" really falls on the individual. Without the ability to take this responsibility, the individual can easily get lost in the crowd.

The cooperative and competitive dimensions also exist in the large group. These dimensions are most often displayed among or between a few individuals rather than with the group as a whole. Examples are large-group activities and situations that could include the following: a large-group picnic, roller-skating, attending a rock concert.

In many ways, large-group social interaction skills are not as important or needed as frequently as dual or small-group interaction skills. They are mentioned, however, because the skills involved are quite different from those required in the other two categories.

Social interaction ability is an essential aspect of successful leisure involvement and lifestyle. Since the behaviors and skills involved can be learned and are, for the most part, independent of the illness or disability itself, it is included as a component of leisure education. If the development of interaction skills is a need of clients, then appropriate programs need to be conceptualized and implemented that focus on this area. The absence of adequate interaction ability can be as much a barrier to leisure involvement as the absence of activity skills or knowledge of leisure and its significance.

This section does not intend to discount or ignore those leisure activities and experiences that the individual engages in and enjoys while alone. Indeed, there is a great need to assist individuals in developing a repertoire of activities and interests that can be done alone. Likewise, helping them to understand the need for, and develop a positive attitude toward, solitary leisure involvement appears to be a significant aspect of an overall leisure lifestyle. This section, however, focuses on interaction skills that are not utilized within solitary leisure experiences.

Leisure Skills Development. Expressing a satisfying leisure lifestyle implies that the individual has a sense of freedom and choice in leisure involvement. Choice involves having options and alternatives. Consequently, it appears logical that a repertoire of leisure activities and related interests is necessary for meaningful experiences. The issue is not simply one of acquiring as many leisure skills as possible. It seems more important to assist the individual in selecting and developing adequate skills in a number of activities that will potentially be a source of enjoyment and personal satisfaction for the individual.

The concept of developing an appropriate leisure lifestyle implies a shifting of responsibility to the individual and to one's ongoing leisure expressions. Once leisure skills are acquired, it is expected that they will become a meaningful aspect of the individual's leisure lifestyle. Some of the activities may be participated in through an organized delivery program, such as a bowling league, ceramics program, or photography club, but many of the skills will be utilized independent of any agency. These skills will be engaged in through commercial leisure opportunities, at home (or in a facility) alone, or with others in a social situation.

The role of the therapeutic recreation specialist is thus twofold relative to the leisure skill-development component. One role is that of educator. Teaching a specific skill, or group of skills, requires the use of various instructional strategies and techniques. The major criterion is the appropriateness of the selected instructional technique to the skill being taught and to the learning style of the client. This obviously requires that the effective therapeutic recreators have at their command a repertoire of instructional strategies appropriate for use with the types of clients being served. The second role related to leisure skill development is more difficult to characterize. It involves assisting the client in the selection of appropriate leisure skills to be acquired. In that sense, the role requires that the therapeutic recreation specialist has a knowledge of, and the ability to use, some counseling techniques and skills of the therapeutic recreation specialist. It also requires a thorough understanding of the concept of leisure lifestyle and its various dimensions, which are significantly different from traditional activity skill programming. This point, it is hoped, will become clearer through the remainder of this section as specific leisure skills are addressed in more depth.

In the past, most activity skill development programs have focused on traditional recreation activities. These activities are ones commonly identified as recreational and sanctioned by the society. They have been promoted and programmed by the leisure and recreation profession. Countless classification and categorical systems have been developed to identify them. The following list is an example of the types of activities frequently referred to within the traditional recreation category.

Traditional—Categories of Commonly Identified Forms of Recreation

sports	dance
aquatics and water-related activities	drama
	other expressive arts
outdoor	mental games and activities
music	hobbies
arts and crafts	

There is nothing inherently wrong or inappropriate with activites that fall under the label of traditional recreation. Indeed, individuals with disabling conditions may need and want activity skills from the traditional categories. The problem, however, is the assumption that these activities, and only these activities, are important or appropriate. When we accept the concept of a leisure lifestyle, we recognize that there is a multitude of leisure experiences and interests that extend far beyond traditional recreation activities. Observing what adults actually do with their leisure results in a very different list of activities and events. The following list attempts to identify by category the types of adult leisure pursuits and involvements that are common in our culture. These are in addition to the traditional activities previously identified.

Nontraditional—Categories of Adult Leisure Involvement

social interaction	living-things maintenance—pets and plants
spectating and appreciating	
leadership and community service	self-development
fitness	education
relaxation and meditation	self-care
cognitive and mental	travel
eating	fantasy and daydreaming
food preparation	intimacy and sexually related activity
shopping	
home improvement	substance use—alcohol, drugs, tobacco
home maintenance	nothing

Involvement in these leisure activities more adequately represents the content and nature of adult leisure lifestyles. Many of the actions are engaged in alone or with significant others as opposed to organized activity-centered groups. Many of the activities are less structured with fewer exact procedures or rules. Most often the environment for participation is the home or some general environment as opposed to a specific recreation activity or facility. The dimension of time is also different for many of the activities. Nontraditional activities are less likely to require a specific amount of time or time scheduled by someone else. An immediately obvious difference between these activities and traditional recreation activities is the absence of a program structure sponsored by a leisure service delivery agency.

It is important to note that the leisure involvements and activities identified as nontraditional do require various skills, knowledge, and participatory abilities. Many people evolve into, and engage in, these leisure pursuits without specific programmed instruction. However, it is possible to analyze these activities and develop programs that would systematically address the acquisition of the various skills. Individuals with disabling conditions may need this specific form of leisure skill development. If leisure lifestyle development and expression are the concern of therapeutic recreation service, then the understanding, selection, and programming of skills related to these leisure pursuits may take precedence over the traditional forms of recreation activities.

Assisting the client in the development of appropriate leisure skills takes on new dimensions when using this leisure lifestyle approach. The concern shifts from focus on the skills of a specific traditional activity to broader participatory abilities that include knowledge of leisure possibilities, selecting and learning appropriate leisure activities, and integrating leisure involvement within the total life situation. This does not mean that specific leisure activity skills are not part of the total programming focus. It merely means the specific activity skills must be viewed and selected within a broader context. Far more attention must be given to the individual and the development of leisure skills and related participatory abilities for a unique lifestyle and situation.

In clinical and community settings, there is a need for leisure skills development programs for individuals with disabling conditions. Indeed, many of our clients lack specific and general leisure activity skills appropriate for a meaningful ongoing leisure lifestyle. The task of the therapeutic recreation specialist is the selection of appropriate content for these leisure skill development programs. The concept of leisure lifestyle and the previously identified lists of activity categories may be useful in the selection process.

Several other factors must be considered when conceptualizing and selecting content for leisure skill development programs. The identified leisure activity skills must be within the ability range of the individual in terms of functional behaviors. The activities should be feasible within the resources (money, equipment, access to facilities) of the individual. Likewise, the skills should be compatible with the overall life situation of the individual and, in many cases, compatible with leisure interests of those with whom the individual may live. Activity skills ought to be age-appropriate and also provide opportunity for continued development and involvement at later life stages. Other considerations such as socioeconomic status, educational level, ethnicity, and religion may have direct implications for activity selection and development. Of primary concern, however, is the involvement of the individual in the selection process. If individuals are to value the activity and find some meaning and satisfaction through participation, then it is imperative that they be a part of the selection procedure. All of these considerations place an emphasis on the individual and one's continuing leisure involvement rather than on an immediate clinical or community program structure. That indeed is the intent. Assisting the client in the development of leisure skills must be futuristic in orientation. The focus is continuously on transferring responsibility for leisure involvement to clients and helping them define and prepare for a leisure lifestyle independent of the current agency program structure.

It is obviously difficult to determine how many and what kinds of leisure activity skills an individual needs. There are no absolutes or established standards that can be applied. Indeed, the absence of such criteria should be respected. The concept of an individualized and unique leisure lifestyle and activity repertoire deserves to be protected. Professional knowledge and judgment of the therapeutic recreator, with input from the client, becomes the basis for decision making related to the development of a leisure skill repertoire of a given client.

Some agencies have established guidelines to assist in the assessment and decision-making process related to leisure skill development. The STILAP is an assessment-programming procedure developed for use in the Leisure Services Program at the State Technical Institute and Rehabilitation Center (Plainwell, Michigan).[2] This procedure utilizes fourteen categories of adult leisure involvement as the basis for analyzing a client's current leisure skills, judging their appropriateness, and determining areas for additional skill development. Flexibility is built into the procedure, in that many traditional and nontraditional activities fit the requirements of each of the fourteen categories. Thus, when a given client is being assessed and program referrals are being made, maximum individualization can occur. Clients are advised and counseled regarding the need for, and benefits of, leisure involvement as well as given guidance in the selection of specific skills to be acquired.

A procedure such as STILAP is agency-specific. That is, it is only appropriate when designed for a given agency serving a specific population. Other assessment-programming procedures have been, and need to be, developed that take into consideration the general characteristics of a given population and give direction to leisure skill development needs. It is important to state, however, that the basis and theoretical foundation for such procedures should be conceptualized carefully to prevent overly simplistic or otherwise inappropriate decision-making or programming approaches.

---

[2]STILAP. State Technical Institute Leisure Assessment Process is described in greater detail in the following publications:

Nancy Navar, "A Rationale for Leisure Skill Assessment with Handicapped Adults," *Therapeutic Recreation Journal*, 14, no. 4 (1980), pp. 21–28.

Nancy Navar, "Leisure Education Techniques," *Expanding Horizons in Therapeutic Recreation VIII*, ed. Gerald L. Hitzhusen (University of Missouri, Technical Education Services, Columbia, Missouri, 1981), pp. 116–233.

Nancy Navar and Therese Clancy, "Leisure Skill Assessment Process in Leisure Counseling," in *Expanding Horizons in Therapeutic Recreation VI*, eds. David J. Szymanski and Gerald L. Hitzhusen (University of Missouri, Technical Educational Services, Columbia, Missouri, 1979), pp. 68–81.

A well-developed comprehensive scheme or model of leisure lifestyle that includes leisure skills can be very useful in the assessment and programming efforts related to this component of leisure education.

Within community and clinical settings, the conceptualization, selection, development, and implementation of actual leisure skill development programs will be dependent on the nature of clients served. Their specific limitations and abilities, status within their life span development, and predominant place of residence will give direction to determining appropriate leisure skill needs and thus give direction to programs which develop these skillls. The nature and mandate of the agency delivering the services is also a significant factor in program direction and content. In general, however, it is quite clear that leisure skill development is a primary need of most clients and well within the mandate of the majority of agencies offering therapeutic recreation services. The amount of programming conducted in the leisure skill development component, however, must be carefully balanced with other client program needs identified within the Therapeutic Recreation Service Model.

The designing of leisure skill development programs, like all other programs in therapeutic recreation, requires the specification of objectives and performance measures, and the delineation of task-analyzed activity content to assist in the learning of the material. The predominant intervention style is instructional. This requires that the program designer and program implementers have a good command of a variety of instructional techniques, so that interventions can be selected that are compatible with the activity being learned and appropriate for the individual clients in the program. The learning of any activity skill can be greatly facilitated by good instructional techniques. Most therapeutic recreators could increase their impact substantially by acquiring greater expertise in the understanding, selection, and use of instructional strategies.

In some ways, the design of good leisure skill development programs is easier than other kinds of therapeutic recreation programs. The desired outcomes are specific leisure skills. These skill behaviors are concrete, they are observable, and, in most situations, they can be adequately described and thus accurately measured. A high degree of accountability is achievable in such programs.

Leisure skill development programs are usually designed to be implemented independent of other leisure education programs. This means that the focus of the program is the specific leisure skill or cluster of related leisure skills. It is possible, however, to include objectives and content related to leisure resources, social interaction skills, and other content from the leisure awareness component. When these additions are included, they need to be related to the specific leisure skill being presented. A program of this nature can help clients to integrate the concepts, knowledge, and skills.

Leisure Resources. The Leisure Resources component adds another important dimension to the leisure education category of program content. Knowledge of leisure resources and the ability to utilize these resources appears to be a significantly important factor in the establishment and expression of a leisure lifestyle. All too often, it is assumed that clients have a basic knowledge of information acquisition and utilization. In other cases, therapeutic recreators have just not processed the importance of identifying resources and assisting the client in acquiring the ability to be independent through the use of such resources. The concept of an independent leisure lifestyle requires that the client be able to seek out information and use it appropriately.

Leisure is not a well-understood phenomenon in our society. Thus, it is not unusual that many people, nondisabled as well as disabled, are at a loss when it comes to an awareness of leisure resources and how to use them. Individuals with some disabling conditions may be at an even greater disadvantage, in that they may have been protected or isolated from resource-information utilitization in general. A well-planned, comprehensive leisure education program must include information and utilization skill development related to the topic of leisure resources. Such programming gives to clients the tools for their own exploration, expansion, and participation in leisure involvement. Independent leisure involvement is probably not possible without such knowledge and ability.

There are many ways in which the content of Leisure Resources can be identified and categorized. The possible areas of content related to the topic are enormous. Likewise, a given client's leisure-resource needs will vary considerably. There is an obvious advantage in starting with a basic conceptualization of leisure resources prior to selecting specific content for programs. Figure 2–9 presents a conceptual scheme related to leisure resources. It is presented as one example of a resource conceptual model. Other conceptualizations could be developed that would be equally useful. The present scheme is general and not developed with a specific population in mind. The unique characteristics of a given population would obviously give direction to the conceptualization of a model that could more appropriately meet the resource needs of that particular group of individuals.

This model focuses on two areas related to Leisure Resources. The first is the delineation of *types of information* the client may need. Each of these is expanded below.

FIGURE 2–9 A Leisure Resources Conceptual Model

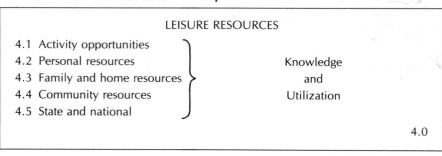

LEISURE RESOURCES

4.1 Activity opportunities
4.2 Personal resources
4.3 Family and home resources
4.4 Community resources
4.5 State and national

Knowledge
and
Utilization

4.0

Activity Opportunities. Many clients may need information regarding the vast number of different leisure activities available. Thus, just identifying possible leisure activities could be a valuable area of program content. The intent here is both to expand the clients' awareness of leisure opportunities as well as to assist them in identifying preferences for possible inclusion in their personal repertoire.

Personal Resources. Because leisure is not well understood, many individuals may have limited awareness of possible leisure involvements that are already within their ability and experience. Identifying these resources can expand individuals' leisure repertoire considerably by merely bringing attention to the opportunity. Examples of this would include the following: verbal and interaction ability can be used for leisure enjoyment. For the person who is ambulatory, walking and jogging are possible leisure activities. This category can also be expanded to identify functional abilities and limitations that influence leisure. Other characteristics, such as finances, educational level, and past leisure experiences, can be explored for possible current and future leisure involvement.

Family and Home Resources. The people with whom one lives (family members or individuals in the facility) can be considered leisure resources. Thus, the identification of leisure interests of others can expand the repertoire of leisure possibilities for a given client. The "home," whether it is the client's own house or a facility in which he or she lives, is another source of potential leisure involvement. Since most people spend a considerable amount of time in the place of residence, the home becomes an important leisure resource. Assistance is frequently needed to help the client identify various aspects of the home that are possible leisure resources. Obvious ones, such as the TV, books, magazines, and games, are easily identified. However, general objects and places are often more abstract. Newspapers, the kitchen, a garage, plants, and pets are often overlooked as leisure resources. When engaged in such discussion, identifying "what is" can be supplemented with "what could be." How objects or places could be used for leisure involvement is an interesting and expanding experience, especially for those individuals for whom the home may be the primary environment for leisure involvement.

Community Resources. Most communities have a variety of agencies, commercial enterprises, places, and facilities that are leisure resources. It cannot be assumed that a given client is aware of these opportunities. Thus, some aspect of programming needs to focus on the identification of these leisure resources, as well as on a consideration of the participatory requirements. Most commonly recognized recreation resources would include the public recreation programs, services, and facilities, such as a city's recreation department or park district; programs offered through the school district, often listed as adult education or community education; and the voluntary, nonprofit-agency programs and facilities, such as the YMCA, YWCA, scouting, Campfire, Boys' and Girls' clubs. Within the leisure lifestyle philosophy, many other leisure resources would be identified. Commercial recreation plays a major role in the leisure involvement of most people; therefore, these resources also need to be identified and understood. Bowling alleys, movie theaters, pool halls, dance studios, golf courses, game arcades, and roller- or ice-skating rinks are a few examples of commercial recreation-activity establishments. Swim clubs, racket clubs, health spas, and fitness centers are examples of another type of commercial leisure agency. Restaurants and bars provide a frequent form of commercial leisure involvement. The commercial category can be extended to a wide variety of other establishments. For example, arts and crafts, fabric and yarn, and photography stores often sponsor classes and other group-participatory opportunities. Within most communities, a large number of nonagency-sponsored clubs exist. Examples would be a square-dance, bridge, or model-airplane club. Youth and adult social and service organizations and clubs are also considered part of the leisure resource network. Thus, groups like Altrusa, Lions, and Rotary International need to be identified as possible leisure resources. In addition, the multiple opportunities for volunteer work or service can be viewed as a leisure opportunity. Obviously, a complete list of possible leisure resources in a community cannot be identified here. The issue remains: a broad conceptualization of community resources is needed, and an appropriate method of introducing this information to clients is important.

State and National. In addition to the personal, immediate home environment and community resources, there are leisure opportunities on a state and national level that may be appropriate to introduce to clients. This area can be conceptualized in many ways, since there are multiple public and commercial resources and opportunities. By definition, information about travel is imperative within this category.

The *knowledge and awareness* of leisure resources is only one aspect of this component of leisure education. Equally important is the area of *utilization skills* related to the resources. Of primary significance is assisting clients in being able to identify and locate leisure resources on their own. This information, along with a knowledge of various participatory and utilization aspects, is vital in the process of facilitating an independent leisure lifestyle.

The nature and amount of leisure resource content to be programmed is dependent on two factors. First is the type of clients being served, their resource information needs, and processing skills. There is wide variability in the populations being served by therapeutic recreation. Since the leisure resource category is very cognitive in nature, programming approaches and processes need to reflect the abilities and limitations of the specific individuals or groups. For example, an individual with mild to moderate mental retardation may have difficulty processing information about resources and their utilization. Thus, programming may need to be substantial to assist in the acquisition of the information. An individual with a college degree who has recently acquired a spinal-cord injury may be able to acquire information quickly about leisure resources and apply this information immediately to the community after rehabilitation. An individual residing in a long-term health-care facility on a permanent basis has a different kind of leisure-information need. In this case, the information will be centered on resources of the facility and the individual's own personal resources. Programming needs to reflect these differences in the clientele being served.

The second factor influencing the nature and content of leisure resource information programming is the other areas of client need that must also be addressed through the various therapeutic recreation programs. Total available programming time must be balanced among the diverse areas of client need. Leisure resource knowledge and utilization skills are important, but must be analyzed and selected within the context of total programming concerns. Leisure resource content can be programmed in many different ways. Specific and separate programs can be structured to focus exclusively on this content. Most often, however, the content is presented in combination with other areas of the leisure education model. The content is very compatible with information and content from the leisure awareness category. Or the content can be combined with leisure skill development programs. In this case, resources are generally selected that relate directly to the leisure skill being taught.

As in all other components of leisure education and therapeutic recreation programming, objectives must be specified and content and process descriptions delineated to facilitate the acquisition of the leisure resource information. An understanding of clients' informational needs and a sound conceptual scheme related to leisure resources is fundamental to this type of program development.

Leisure resource content is most often structured and delivered through instructional methods. Although some counseling techniques related to the transfer of information may be used, instructional strategies are the primary intervention mode. Thus, the therapeutic recreation specialist is functioning in the role of educator within this component of leisure education programming. This educator role implies a sharing of responsibility with the client for the teaching-learning process.

Leisure Education: A Priority Program Focus

Four areas of leisure education program content have been described in this section. Rationales and implications for program development have been presented. It is our hope that this information enables a greater comprehension of, and appreciation for, the leisure education service component and its contribution to the overall therapeutic recreation mission.

Figure 2–10 displays the leisure education component within the context of the total Therapeutic Recreation Service Model. The major points of leisure education are highlighted in terms of need of the client, purpose of the intervention, relationship of the services to independent leisure behavior, role of the specialist, and the degree of control and freedom in participation. In many ways, the leisure education component appears to

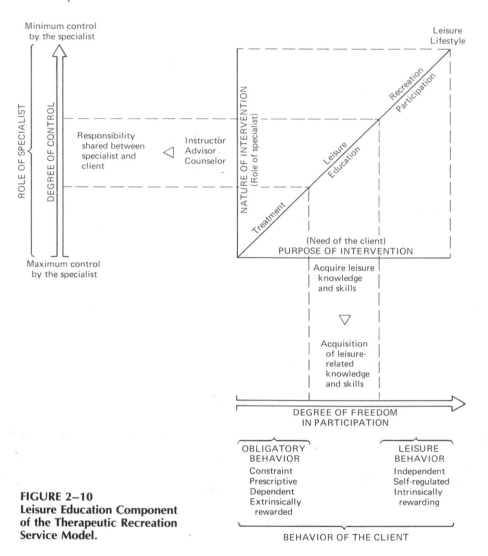

FIGURE 2–10
Leisure Education Component
of the Therapeutic Recreation
Service Model.

be the most important program service area within therapeutic recreation for most clients. This component contains the essential knowledge and skills necessary to develop an appropriate and meaningful leisure lifestyle. Regardless of the disabling condition and the limitations or barriers it presents, the individual has the right to experience leisure involvement and satisfaction. This opportunity, however, is dependent upon sufficient leisure-related knowledge and skills. Programs emerging from the leisure education concept and models provide for an understanding of leisure and the acquisition of participatory abilities and skills.

RECREATION PARTICIPATION AS A COMPONENT OF THERAPEUTIC RECREATION SERVICE

The third major component of the Therapeutic Recreation Service Model is entitled *recreation participation*. It encompasses a specific type of programming that is distinctly different from the previous two components. Its contribution to the overall goal of Leisure Ability is, however, equally significant. Treatment and leisure education programs can be viewed as prerequisite or developmental in relation to the leisure lifestyle concept. Recreation participation programs, on the other hand, are part of the expression of leisure lifestyle.

Recreation participation delineates a type of structured and delivered program. The purpose of such a program is to provide opportunities for fun, enjoyment, and self-expression within an organized delivery system. Like recreation participation programs provided for nondisabled individuals, the motivation to participate and the outcomes of involvement are determined primarily by the individual. The agency basically provides the opportunity for participation by organizing diverse programs and participation experiences that are of interest to the clients.

Recreation participation programs are an essential part of the total Therapeutic Recreation Service Model and the Leisure Ability philosophy. One aspect of independent leisure involvement is the opportunity to select and engage in organized activities and leisure opportunities with others through a structured delivery system. Although these programs represent a small percentage of leisure involvement for most people, they do contribute a unique opportunity to participate. These programs can be described by the following activity or participatory characteristics:

1. Activities that require many participants and an administrative structure. Leagues and tournaments are examples of these types of activities.
2. Activities that are enjoyed in groups and are facilitated by an administrative structure. Activities such as dramatics, arts and crafts, and music are often provided through a group or club program.
3. Activities that require a specific facility or type of equipment not usually owned by the individual. Fitness and exercise programs, ceramics, and square dancing are illustrations of such recreation participation programs.
4. The provision of a specific facility, place, or equipment to be used by the participant for self-initiated and self-directed involvement. A park, playground, swimming pool, and drop-in center or program illustrate this point.

All four of these characteristics have one common dimension. The program or service is provided with the assumption that the participant has the activity skills and participatory ability necessary for satisfying or enjoyable involvement. The agency has the responsibility for providing the opportunity; the participant holds the responsibility for the individual experience and outcome. Unlike the treatment component, which has a specific predetermined outcome—improved functional ability—or the leisure education component, which has predetermined outcomes in terms of the acquisition of various leisure-related knowledge, skills, and abilities, the recreation participation component states broad, general outcomes of enjoyment and self-expression. Specific outcomes are not predetermined by the agency or program designer.

Programs in the recreation participation component do need to be designed carefully, just like programs in any other component of the Therapeutic Recreation Service Model. Specific activities are described. The nature of the intervention and the facilitation techniques to be used are specified. Other aspects of implementation and program operation are delineated. These aspects of design are necessary in order for the program to be evaluated appropriately and thus be accountable. The only aspect of the full systems design approach that is absent in these programs is the specific objectives and corresponding performance measures.

Although the nature and content of recreation participation programs are extremely diverse, there are three aspects that are constant. First is the issue of control by the individual. Individuals voluntarily choose to participate. They select the activity or program to engage in. They also control the nature and intensity of their involvement. Thus, there is a high degree of freedom and participant control in these programs.

The second aspect focuses on the role of the therapeutic recreation specialist or staff member. In recreation participation programs, the staff member facilitates the involvement of the individuals. The role can be that of *leader* or *supervisor*, depending on the type of program. In the *leadership role*, the staff member directly interacts with the individuals or group to heighten, encourage, support, reinforce, or expand their participation. A variety of leadership techniques and strategies can be used. The specific technique employed should be appropriate for the individuals involved and compatible with the activity or nature of the program. Leadership is thus seen, not as one type of intervention, but as a variety of strategies to be acquired and utilized in a suitable way. The *role of supervisor* is quite different from the role of leader. The supervisor interacts with the participants only in a regulatory way, for safety of the individuals or protection of the facility or equipment. A staff member lifeguarding in a swimming program illustrates this point in the purest sense. Verbal or nonverbal interactions are strictly for safety or protection. A staff member may supervise a crafts area or a gym or a multipurpose area. In each of these situations, their presence is needed for legal as well as regulatory purposes. They are, however, facilitating involvement through this important role. Indeed, participation in the chosen activity or experience would not be possible without the supervisory function. In many programs, the roles of supervisor and leader are combined. The staff member is supervising in a regulatory sense but may also enhance participation through verbal and nonverbal leadership interactions.

In recreation participation programs and services, the roles of leadership and supervision can greatly enhance the quality of the experience for the individuals involved. Thus, the acquisition and appropriate utili-

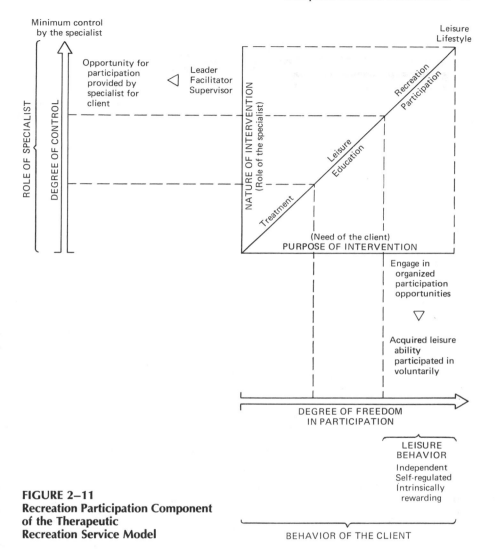

FIGURE 2–11
Recreation Participation Component
of the Therapeutic
Recreation Service Model

zation of good leadership and supervisory techniques are a vital part of the therapeutic recreation specialist's total repertoire of facilitation skills.

Figure 2–11 displays the recreation participation component within the context of the total Therapeutic Recreation Service Model. The major points presented in this first section are summarized within the dimensions of the model.

Recreation participation programs need to be further elaborated on within the context of community and clinical settings. The rationale for their provision, as well as the nature of content, varies considerably because of the uniqueness of these two very different settings.

Community-based Settings and Recreation Participation Programs

In community-based settings, recreation participation programs serve a variety of functions that may be perceived as slightly different from the function of these services in clinical settings. Although the purpose of these special programs remains the same—that is, the opportunity to engage in self-selected organized activity with others—this function must be understood within the context of some broader philosophical issues.

At the onset is the issue of mainstreaming and integration. It is the absolute belief of these authors that individuals with disabling conditions should be integrated into ongoing recreation programs provided for the general population. This integration, however, is dependent on several factors. First, the individual with a disabling condition must have the activity skills, as well as the interaction skills, required to function within that program. Second, the service providers of general recreation programs in the public, voluntary, and private sector must view the involvement of all individuals, including those with limitations, as part of their basic service responsibility. Our society is slowly moving toward this broader understanding and acceptance of the rights and abilities of disabled individuals. Until this attitude is common and widespread, the issue of integration remains a difficult one. Currently, the burden of integration lies on disabled individuals themselves. Consequently, it is quite understandable that many disabled individuals choose not to engage in ongoing leisure and recreation programs provided for the general public. If the intent of these experiences is enjoyment, fun, and/or self-expression, the disabled individual may find that the attitudinal and architectural barriers block any possible opportunity to have these experiences within the existing service structure. Nonetheless, this ultimate goal of integration is worthy of pursuit.

Likewise, there are responsibilities inherent in the adoption of a totally integrated approach for the disabled individual as well. Individuals with a disability need to view the existing service structure as legitimately their domain. Clients' acceptance of personal responsibility for their own leisure lifestyle, the acquisition of leisure skills and interests, and the ability to function in an integrated setting are all parts of the integration issue. Obviously, some of the responsibility for this approach lies with professionals within the human-service fields of special education, early childhood development, rehabilitation, social work, and therapeutic recreation, as well as the medical and health fields.

As we move toward the ideal of a totally integrated society, there are still issues to be addressed in the current situation of recreation participation programs. Therapeutic recreation specialists working in the community setting have at least four major roles. They need to be involved actively with recreation service providers in *advocacy, consultation,* and *training* roles. The purpose of this involvement is to open up opportunities for individuals with disabilities to engage in recreation participation programs within the community. The sharing of information regarding the rights and abilities of disabled individuals and an understanding of limitations, assistive techniques, and activity and leadership modifications is a major contribution of the therapeutic recreation specialist. Likewise, the provision of information on the removal of architectural barriers and barrier-free facility design is equally important. Throughout these interactions, attitudinal and general integrative information can be transmitted. Although this function of the therapeutic recreation specialist is an indirect service function, it is vital to the immediate and eventual integration of disabled individuals in ongoing recreation programs in the community.

The fourth major role of the therapeutic recreation specialist is the *provision of appropriate recreation participation programs* for designated special populations. Given that the right to engage in structured group recreation activities is established, the following situations appear to justify the separate delivery structure for certain special-need populations.

1. The severity of the limitations imposed by the disability requires special sequencing for participation, unusual amounts of assistance by leader, or an unusual degree of activity modification. An example of this would be a crafts program for severely physically disabled children (for instance, quadriplegic athetoid cerebral palsy, Duchenne muscular dystrophy, severe osteogenesis imperfecta).

2. The absence of previous and appropriate socialization experiences that would enable the individual to participate in a general recreation program provided by a community recreation agency. An example of this would be an active-games program for moderately retarded individuals.

3. The absence of appropriate activity skill level that would enable the individual to participate in a general recreation program provided by a community recreation agency. An example of this would be a general recreation program for autistic children.

4. The condition of the individual(s) requires special behavior management or unusual supervision demands to ensure safety and/or appropriate participation. An example would be a creative movement program for emotionally disturbed children.

5. The expressed preference of an individual or group for special segregated programming. An example would be a recreational volleyball program for adult individuals with hearing impairments or a social club for physically disabled adults or young-adults. Note that in these illustrations, we are dealing with individuals who are accepting responsibility for their own leisure choices and have expressed a desire for services, assistance, or facilities based on their personal preferences for separate programming.

6. The absence of general organized recreation participation opportunities in the immediate community. In some places, usually smaller cities, towns, and rural areas, there are few, if any, organized community recreation programs for children, youth, or adults. Nondisabled individuals may not be as victimized by the absence of organized recreation, since other forms of play and leisure involvement are more readily accessible to them. In such situations, special recreation programs for individuals with disabilities may be viewed as an important recreation service and given priority.

Although the six criteria just presented may appear a bit restrictive, it seems necessary to establish some guidelines to justify segregated programming. In far too many communities, special segregated programming is being promoted without examination of the reasons or need. In many cases, the specialized programming merely perpetuates the isolation of the individual with a disabling condition and removes integrated programming responsibility from the public recreation service provider.

Assuming that segregated special recreation participation programs are justified, the therapeutic recreation specialist in the community has the responsibility of developing and implementing appropriate recreation participation programs. The content of these programs should parallel the content of similar programs for nondisabled individuals. Most often this implies offering programs for specific age groupings. Once the program is in operation, leaders should interact with the participants in such a way as to encourage age-appropriate behaviors and normalized involvement within the activities presented.

Clinical Settings and Recreation Participation Programs

It has been previously stated that being in treatment does not remove the individual from the need for, or right to, leisure involvement. However, the individual in treatment may require assistance with leisure involvement, since the daily hospital routine is different from the home environment and since many familiar resources have been removed from use. In most situations, the individual leisure lifestyle of the client will be severely interrupted by the hospitalization. The nature of the illness or disability may make involvement in previous leisure patterns impossible. In other cases, hospitalization and treatment may render the previous leisure lifestyle unimportant. The clients themselves may or may not view leisure involvement as necessary or of any concern. Nonetheless, clients still have a need for leisure involvement, even if its nature and intent have changed. Distraction, alleviation of boredom, release of emotions, and an opportunity to engage in action other than conversation and watching TV are often cited by clients as reason for desiring recreation participation programs while in treatment. These reasons in and of themselves can easily justify the establishment and operation of recreation participation programs.

The therapeutic recreation specialist sees other reasons for the necessity of recreation participation programs within the clinical setting. Ongoing leisure participation enables some normalization within the atypical environment of constant treatment focus. Recreation programs provide an opportunity for "well" aspects of the client to be utilized and maintained. They provide socialization opportunities. They may facilitate adjustment to illness or disability by providing an opportunity for clients to maintain a perspective on what they can do. Emotional equilibrium is also frequently cited as a benefit or outcome of participation.

Countless reasons exist for providing recreation participation programs in the clinical setting. A more important issue may be the identification of types of programs and identifying appropriate content. A major difference can be noted between long-term and short-term treatment situations. In the short-term setting (up to three months), treatment is usually intense. The daily schedule is often full, and there is little time for recreation participation programs. What is offered is often delivered in the evenings and on weekends. In this situation, it is very difficult to provide programming based on expressed patient interest. Generally, the therapeutic recreation specialist will attempt to design programs that will have a high appeal to a large number of patients (and often their families or friends). Constraints of equipment, supplies, facilities, staff, and time direct the activity selections. Given these constraints, many creative, enjoyable programs can still be offered. The difficulties and problems of these recreation participation programs should not result in their elimination or low prioritization.

Recreation participation programs in long-term settings (more than three months) take on a different dimension. In these settings, the provision of opportunity for self-directed leisure and recreation participation assumes a greater significance, owing to the length of time involved in treatment or care. In these situations, the recreation participation programs must reflect the concept of leisure lifestyle. For the patient or resident, these programs provide the opportunity for ongoing leisure participation and expression within the hospital or care setting. The therapeutic recreation specialist must carefully plan a full range of program and service offerings that adequately address the specific interests, preferences, and skills of the clients. Unfortunately, traditional activities such as Bingo, bowling, movies, and birthday parties dominate in many existing facilities. These authors strongly object to this type of stereotyping. It would appear that in the long-term setting, recreation participation programs should provide a great deal more variety. Ideally, the nature and content of programs should be much more individualized and normalized, to reflect appropriate adult and youth programs conducted for the same age groups living within the community.

In those long-term and permanent-care settings where the therapeutic recreation program utilizes a comprehensive approach incorporating treatment, leisure education, and recreation participation, the recreation participation program can and should include another aspect of program focus. As new leisure skills are learned, logically there needs to be an opportunity for engaging in those skills for enjoyment and self-expression. Thus, ongoing programs must parallel and provide the opportunity for personal choice within the leisure lifestyle that is being developed by the individual.

Many of the settings where therapeutic recreation is offered are those in which the clients will live their entire lives. Leisure lifestyle for these individuals must be viewed within the limitations of the disability and the long-term setting. Nonetheless, personal responsibility for one's own leisure lifestyle can be developed. The total program focuses on this concept in all components of therapeutic recreation and culminates in the individual's choice and expression within many of the recreation participation programs.

SUMMARY

The Therapeutic Recreation Service Model was developed to provide a descriptive and conceptual scheme for understanding the Leisure Ability philosophy. Each component (treatment, leisure education, and recreation participation) has been presented in depth within this chapter. The purpose, nature, and content of each of the three components has been explored in order to provide a rationale for programming as well as to give direction for program selection and development. The next section of this book will present a systematic and thorough approach to the design of programs.

========================= **Suggested References** =========================

BURDETT, C., and M. E. MILLER, "Mainstreaming in a Municipal Recreation Department Utilizing a Continuum Model," *Therapeutic Recreation Journal*, 13, no. 4 (1979), 41–47.

CARRIE, D., and S. SYGALL, "A Consumer Needs Based Approach for Recreationists," *Leisurability*, 8, no. 3 (1981), 14–15.

DIXON, J., "Expanding Individual Control in Leisure Participation While Enlarging the Concept of Normalcy," *Therapeutic Recreation Journal*, 13, no. 3 (1978), 20–24.

HOWE-MURPHY, R., "A Conceptual Basis for Mainstreaming Recreation and Leisure Services: Focus on Humanism," *Therapeutic Recreation Journal*, 13, no. 4 (1979), 11–18.

HUTCHINSON, P. and J. LORD, *Recreation Integration*. Ottawa, Ont., Canada: Leisurability Publications, Inc., 1979.

JOSWIAK, K., "Recreation Therapy Assessment with Developmentally Disabled Persons," *Therapeutic Recreation Journal*, 14, no. 4 (1980), 29–38.

KINNEY, W. B., "Clinical Assessment in Mental Health Settings," *Therapeutic Recreation Journal*, 14, no. 4 (1980), 39–45.

MUNDY, J., and L. ODUM, *Leisure Education: Theory and Practice*. New York: John Wiley and Sons, 1979.

NAVAR, N., "A Rationale for Leisure Skill Assessment with Handicapped Adults," *Therapeutic Recreation Journal*, 14, no. 4 (1980), 21–28.

REYNOLDS, R. P., "The Changing Role of Leisure Services in Residential Facilities: Implications and Challenges," *Leisurability*, 5, no. 3 (1978), 34–37.

RIOS, D., "Leisure Education and Counseling with Severely Emotionally Disturbed Children," *Therapeutic Recreation Journal*, 12, no. 2 (1978), 30–34.

SCHUM, R. L., M. SULLIVAN-LUPETIN, and A. MESSMER, "A Residential Program for Children with Communication Disorders," *Therapeutic Recreation Journal*, 15, no. 1 (1981), 18–23.

VIRTUE, J., "The Role of Recreation/Leisure and the Recreationist within Institutions," *Leisurability*, 5, no. 3 (1978), 39–41.

WEST, R., "Therapeutic Recreation Services as a Component of Optimal Health Care in a General Hospital Setting," *Therapeutic Recreation Journal*, 13, no. 3 (1979), 7–11.

3

A Systems Approach
To Program Planning

PURPOSE: To present an introduction to, and overview of, the systems approach to program planning. Basic concepts are explained and a rationale for the approach is given. A description of the procedure utilized in this book is delineated.

Programming is the main focus of therapeutic recreation. The design and delivery of services is the reason for the profession's existence. However, despite the fact that the delivery of services is the central concern of the field, little definitive information has been developed related to program planning techniques and procedures. The absence in the professional literature of defined procedures for program planning leaves administrators and therapeutic recreation specialists with the hit-or-miss method or, worse yet, the we've-always-done-it-this-way method. In other situations, concerned professionals have developed their own planning methods. This has resulted in unique programming approaches that often cannot be generalized to other populations or settings.

As a profession, therapeutic recreation needs to develop and accept some defined procedures for the planning and delivery of services. This mark of a profession—standardized procedures—has been frequently absent in the therapeutic recreation field.

It would be naive to assume that one method of program planning can be determined and implemented across the board. However, program planning guidelines or models can be developed that would be appropriate for all types of settings and populations and for different levels of program involvement. The interdisciplinary tool of systems planning approaches gives us such models.

SYSTEMS PLANNING APPROACHES

The general theory of systems is based on two concepts. The first is the concept of "wholeness." This implies that any entity can be viewed as a system and can be studied for its dynamics as a complete entity. Although the parts can be identified, broken down, analyzed, and studied, the total entity has characteristics and dimensions that are greater than the sum of the parts. Thus, viewing just the parts or components does not give a realistic picture of the total entity.

The second concept of general systems theory is that of "interrelatedness." This concept attempts to explain that parts or components of a system interrelate with one another. These interrelationships between parts are as important as the individual parts. Systems theory, including the concepts of "wholeness" and "interrelatedness," has brought a new perspective to the study of many entitites—natural phenomena, man-made entities, organizations, and human-service delivery systems. The systems concept has facilitated the understanding of complex human, social, and natural entities.

Systems theory, however, is more than a method of analysis and description. It has been translated into many practical applications. One of the most common applications is to the process of program planning.

Systems planning models provide developed steps or procedures for program *design, implementation,* and *evaluation.* The models are not designed for one discipline, but rather are procedures that can be used in any field of service.

The flexibility of the systems approach enables diverse program content and structure to exist. The planning, implementation, and evaluation procedures guide the planner systematically through program development without dictating actual content or implementation strategies. However, the method facilitates logical design in interrelated stages, providing continuity and accountability to the program plan.

Simply stated, a systems approach to program planning focuses on three basic concerns:

1. determining what the program is to accomplish (where you're going)
2. designing a set of procedures to get to those goals (how you're going to get there)
3. developing criteria to determine if the program did what it was designed to do (how you know if you got there?)

Many systems planning models have been developed and implemented for various planning needs. Some are very complex and rely on computer technology; others are quite simple and basically outline the major stages of program development. Regardless of the level of sophistication, seven basic components are built into any systems planning model:

1. determining the purpose, goals, and objectives
2. designing a specific set of procedures and content to accomplish the purpose, goals, and objectives

3. specifying implementation of delivery strategies
4. designating an evaluation procedure
5. implementing the program
6. evaluating the program
7. revising the program based on evaluation data

These steps are presented as a model in Figure 3–1. The solid arrows indicate the sequence of steps to be followed. The dotted line is a feedback loop and shows that information acquired during evaluation can be used to improve the program, and that revision may occur at any stage of the planning operation.

Planning is more than just one step. Systems planning approaches are dynamic and cyclical. Planning is always followed by implementation, evaluation, and revision. Each cycle should improve the program's ability to come closer to its intended purpose. The term *dynamic* indicates that programs are always in a state of change. Constant program evaluation and resulting improvements are expected.

RATIONALE FOR USING A SYSTEMS APPROACH TO PROGRAM PLANNING

The systems approach provides a framework from which programs can be logically planned, conducted, and evaluated. The resulting programs are completely client-centered. They are based on an initial analysis of clients' leisure-related needs. Goals and purpose statements are then developed that address these identified needs. The specific programs are designed to

FIGURE 3–1
Program Planning Model

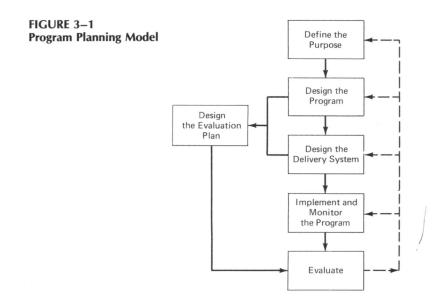

accomplish the specified purpose and goals. This procedure provides a structure for evaluating how well programs are operating and allows a type of accountability not feasible in traditional program planning approaches. In other words, therapeutic recreators who use systems approaches can determine how well their programs facilitate behavioral improvement. This ability to account to clients, administrators, sponsoring agencies, and tax-payers is particularly important now that all types of human services are being questioned for their value and effectiveness.

Systems approaches to program planning also provide the staff with a clear view of program direction. In a systems approach, all aspects of the program are thoroughly designed, including the evaluation plan, prior to its implementation. This technique implies that the staff has thought through all facets of client needs, agency philosophy, and program potential and problems before moving into the actual delivery of the service.

A specific plan of action resulting from a systems-designed program is beneficial in setting up and operating a program. Staff members who have implemented systems-designed programs find that they feel better about themselves because they know what is expected of them. Instead of dealing with the vague notions of the purposes of traditional programs, the specificity of systems designs allows members of the staff to understand their roles and functions, as well as assisting them in determining and evaluating the outcomes of their efforts.

Most important is how systems-designed programs benefit clients. When client needs and problems are identified and stated as program objectives and then procedures are designed to facilitate the accomplishment of those objectives, clients can realistically see justifiable reasons for their participation in the program. In the past, this concept of explaining purpose to clients has been ignored in therapeutic recreation programs. Clients were often the last to know why their involvement in programs was desired or prescribed. The staff often only gave general reasons for client involvement. Therefore, the benefits of involvement were also nebulous. Clients wondered what improvement was supposed to look like or feel like. The specificity of the systems approach to program planning enables both staff and clients to know the intended outcomes of involvement. Each program has definitely stated purposes and objectives, as well as criteria for determining the clients' progress in the program. Usually, this information can be shared with the client, although it is not always feasible or desirable to share program objectives and outcomes with clients who have certain disabilities or illnesses, such as profound retardation.

Systems-designed programs have other distinct advantages. A specific design enables staffing requirements to be determined, including the nature and extent of in-service training (paid and volunteer). The necessary facilities, equipment, and supplies can also be determined more accurately. Budgeting becomes somewhat less confusing, since each program can be budgeted separately. Cost effectiveness can also be determined by comparing the results of the program to the resources (staff, equipment, facilities) used. The advantages of this type of budgeting are numerous;

among them, decisions can be made about how best to distribute resources based on priority needs and program effectiveness.

A SYSTEMS PROGRAM PLANNING PROCEDURE FOR THERAPEUTIC RECREATION

A variety of systems program planning models exists. Most of these are general and delineate various stages in program design and employ diverse levels of sophistication and complexity. In order for any of these models to be useful to a given profession, they need to be refined and described, utilizing the characteristics and specific dimensions of the given field of specialization. The following four chapters of this book take a basic systems planning approach and convert it into a detailed planning procedure for use in therapeutic recreation. An inclusive model is presented. It incorporates program planning from the comprehensive level of an agency, unit, or department, through the planning of specific programs. It also includes the important stage of developing the assessment (referral or selection) procedures that will be used to place individuals appropriately into program components. The remainder of this chapter defines and describes the various levels, stages, and terms incorporated within the total planning model.

Defining the Term *Program*

The word *program* is somewhat confusing, since it is used in so many ways and for so many different levels of services. Often, it is used to indicate a broad range of services offered by an agency or unit. In this context, we would be referring to the therapeutic recreation program of an agency or of a unit. The same word "program" is used to delineate a specific program, such as a swimming program, that is a part of the broader therapeutic recreation program. Our first task is to give some definition to the term "program" so that we use it in a consistent manner and avoid misinterpretation.

For the purpose of this book, the term "program" will be used in two different ways. We will use the term *comprehensive program* and the term *specific program.* "Comprehensive program" will be the broader term; it implies the total range of specific programs designed and delivered to clients by an agency or unit. The term "specific program" is defined as

> a designated set of activities and interventions designed to meet predetermined objectives for a specific group of clients. Each specific program is planned, implemented, and evaluated independently of all other specific programs.

The systems approach to planning presented in this book provides procedures for the development of both the comprehensive program and specific programs.

Where to Initiate Comprehensive Program Planning

The next area of concern is determining where comprehensive program planning begins. Throughout this book, there is frequent use of the phrase "agency, department, or unit." This phrase is employed to indicate the level of comprehensive program development. In different settings, comprehensive planning occurs at different levels. We will be using the term *comprehensive program planning* to indicate the level where decisions are made for a designated population. For example, a community mental health center is an agency comprised of several different units. An example might be the adult inpatient unit, the partial-hospitalization unit, the substance-abuse unit, and the children's psychiatric unit. In this case, comprehensive program planning would begin at the *unit* level, since that is the level where decisions are made for a specific population. One would expect that the therapeutic recreation comprehensive program for each of the four units would be conceptualized, developed, and implemented quite differently. Likewise, in a municipal recreation department or agency, there

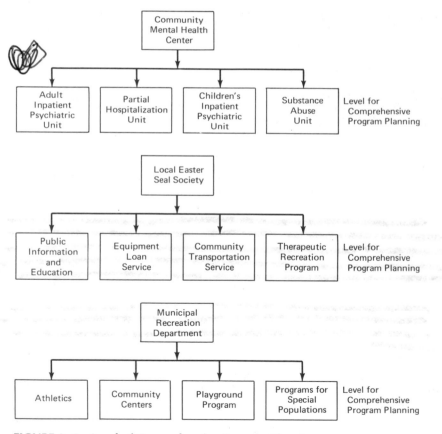

FIGURE 3–2 **Level of Comprehensive Program Planning**

is breakdown of units or divisions. Comprehensive program planning would most likely take place, not at the agency level, but at the unit or division level. Similarly, an Easter Seal Society is an agency. Comprehensive therapeutic recreation program planning would not take place at the agency level, but rather at the department, unit, or division level. Figure 3–2 illustrates this concept of the level at which therapeutic recreation comprehensive program planning takes place.

Although general policy and philosophy may originate at the agency level in most settings where therapeutic recreation services are delivered, the actual responsibility for program planning and delivery takes place at the next level of the administrative or organizational hierarchy. For our purposes, it will be this secondary level or organization where comprehensive program planning is initiated. If the reader is working in an agency where the organizational structure is different, it is still possible to study the agency and determine where comprehensive planning is most appropriate and apply the planning model, with additional stages of breakdown as needed.

The Program Planning Model

The complete program planning model and specific procedures are described in depth in the following four chapters. A brief overview of the model is presented in Figure 3–3 to give the reader a holistic picture of the various stages and content. Equally important is the concept of the sequence and interrelationship of the various stages. The accompanying narrative is intentionally brief, since detail is addressed in later chapters.

Comprehensive Program Planning. This major level of planning focuses on determining program direction for the therapeutic recreation services of a given agency, unit, or department. Four stages are included:

1. *Analyzation.* In this significant first stage, the targeted clientele is studied and major factors that influence program direction are identified and analyzed. Understanding the clients, their characteristics, and their leisure-related needs is a priority task. This is followed by studying the nature of the agency, identifying available and potential resources, understanding the community, and investigating various aspects of the therapeutic recreation profession. All of this information is used as the basis for conceptualizing the comprehensive program.

2. *Conceptualization.* At this stage, the important task of deriving and writing the statement of purpose and developing goals for the comprehensive program takes place. These statements take information gathered in the analyzation stage and convert it to directional statements, which will guide all further development.

3. *Investigation.* In this stage, potential ways of converting goals into operational program components are investigated. Alternative program components are acquired through brainstorming and creative thinking. The resulting potential program components are then studied for their feasibility and practicality within the constraints of the agency and available resources. They are also reviewed for their ability to appropriately address the content of the goals.

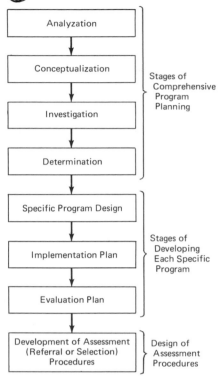

FIGURE 3–3
Therapeutic Recreation Program Planning Model

4. *Determination.* At this next stage, the program designers actually select the program components that will be used to operationalize the intent of the statement of purpose and goals.

Comprehensive program planning involves interrelated stages that originate with an understanding of clients' leisure-related needs and progress through sequential stages to arrive at operationalizable program components. The result is logically derived, feasible, and appropriate specific programs that directly address stated goals. In combination, these separate specific progams provide a comprehensive approach to meeting identified client needs.

Developing the Specific Programs. The comprehensive program is made up of a number of different program components or specific programs. Each of these specific programs requires development and written specifications. The model indicates three stages of development for each specific program.

1. *Specific Program Design.* At this stage, several sequential design tasks are undertaken. A statement of purpose is written; terminal program objectives,

enabling objectives, and performance measures are developed. Program content and process are designed to address the intent of the objectives.

2. *Implementation Plan.* This plan details how the specific program will be implemented. The sequencing of material within each session, as well as the sequencing of the sessions, are specified. Additional general implementation information related to clients, staff, and resources is delineated.

3. *Evaluation Plan.* In this method of systems program planning, each specific program is developed, implemented, and evaluated independently of all other specific programs. Thus, an evaluation plan is needed for each specific program. The procedures and content of the evaluation plan are developed to acquire information about the specific program's outcomes, processes, implementation, and resource utilization. The evaluation plan is implemented simultaneously with the program. The resulting information is used to improve and revise the specific program and to make judgments about the value and effectiveness of the specific program.

Procedures involved in the design of specific programs enable systematic development and specification of therapeutic recreation services. The resulting specific programs are highly accountable because of their measurable objectives and specified process and content descriptions. Written implementation strategies and evaluation procedures add to the credibility of the approach.

Design of Assessment Procedures. The comprehensive program planning process starts with an analysis of clients and their leisure-related needs. This general analysis results in goals, which then dictate overall program direction. These goals are then operationalized into specific programs. Each specific program addresses an intent of a given goal or combination of goals. Thus, the various specific programs have different purposes and content, which relate back to the generalized client leisure needs identified in the initial, analyzation stage. When all this interrelated comprehensive and specific program development is completed, there remains the task of designing the method of placing individual clients into appropriate specific programs. Thus, the final stage of program planning is the development of the assessment procedures to be used in conjunction with the overall program. In most clinical settings, the terminology *assessment procedures* is common and appropriate. In community settings, an exact parallel process does not exist, nor is it a necessity. However, there should be some method of assisting the individual (or family) in making an appropriate selection of specific programs. Thus, a *selection* or *referral* procedure should be developed for use in community programs. Within this program model, the general term "assessment procedure" is used to imply the process of individual assessment in clinical settings or the process of individual referral or selection in community settings.

SUMMARY

This chapter presented an overview of a systems planning model for use in the development of therapeutic recreation programs. This approach provides a logical, feasible, and accountable method of planning, which starts with an analysis of clients' leisure-related needs and systematically evolves through various developmental stages to produce specific programs. These specific programs include implementation strategies and evaluation mechanisms. The development of assessment procedures completes the total planning process.

=============================== **Suggested References** ===============================

BANATHY, B. H., *Instructional Systems*. Palo Alto, Ca.: Fearon Publishers, 1968.

BUCKLEY, W., *Sociology and Modern Systems Theory*. Englewood Cliffs, N.J.: Prentice-Hall, Inc., 1967.

CHURCHMAN, C. W., *The Systems Approach*. New York: Dell Publishing Co., Inc., 1968.

CLELAND, D. I., and W. R. KING. *Management: A Systems Approach*. New York: McGraw-Hill Book Company, 1972.

HARTLEY, H. J., *Educational Planning, Programming, Budgeting: A Systems Approach*. Englewood Cliffs, N.J.: Prentice-Hall, Inc., 1968.

SUTHERLAND, J. W., *A General Systems Philosophy for the Social and Behavioral Sciences*. New York: George Braziller, Inc., 1973.

VON BERTALANFFY, L., *General Systems Theory*. New York: George Braziller, Inc., 1968.

WEINBERG, G. M., *An Introduction to General Systems Thinking*. New York: John Wiley and Sons, 1975.

4

Comprehensive
Program Planning

PURPOSE: To provide information related to comprehensive program planning. Analysis of the various factors that must be considered in program conceptualization are presented. The process of deriving and specifying an agency, departmental, or unit level's statement of purpose and goals will be described. Selecting program components from goals is also covered. Sample program-conceptualization models for a variety of agencies are included.

One of the most important tasks for the program designer[1] is initially to conceptualize the overall or comprehensive program for a unit, agency, or department. (Hereafter, the term *agency* will be used to imply any one of these three units.) This task is extremely vital. Without a systematic method of determining client needs and converting these into a comprehensive program scheme, the staff often finds itself with segmented programs that reflect tradition, individual staff interests, or other nonjustifiable program offerings. The systems approach provides a sequential method of conceptualizing and developing the comprehensive program. This approach derives its direction from appropriate analysis of clients and other factors which are a significant influence in program design and operation. Figure 4–1 provides a model of the procedural steps for the development of the comprehensive program. Each of these steps will be described within this chapter.

---

[1]As a general rule, it is advisable to have more than one person involved in the comprehensive program planning process. The entire therapeutic recreation staff is often included in the process. Clients, or representatives from client populations, are considered valuable to good planning. In some settings, staff members from other disciplines are also included. In this chapter, to avoid problems with plurals, the term *designer* will be used. It should be read to include whomever could be a part of the planning function, as opposed to one individual.

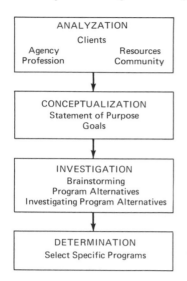

FIGURE 4–1
Comprehensive Program Planning Agency, Unit, or Department Level

ANALYZATION

A well-planned comprehensive program, which can be appropriately operationalized to address clients' leisure-related needs, must have a clear picture of its reason to exist. A statement of purpose and a set of goals provide this direction and definition. Prior to developing the statement of purpose and goals, a stage of analysis is required. The purpose of this analysis is to investigate thoroughly the clients and their leisure-related needs. In addition, it is necessary to study the various factors that influence the selection of the program direction and, eventually, the operation of the total program. Five areas of analysis have been identified. These are the clients, the agency, resources, the community, and the therapeutic recreation (TR) profession. Within these five areas, there may be an overlap of some concerns and issues. However, if each of the five is addressed seriously and carefully, the program planner should have sufficient information for solid decision-making in the program development stages that come later.

Clients

The comprehensive program will be developed to address the leisure-related needs of the clients. Thus, at this first step of analysis of the total planning process, as much information as possible must be gathered about the clients to be served. This is a general analysis of the client population, not an assessment of specific individuals (development of the individual assessment occurs at a later stage). It is assumed that the agency, unit, or department serves an identifiable clientele and that the individuals served will have many of the representative characteristics of the overall target population. Thus, a thorough analysis of the general clientele can and should produce information that will allow an appropriate statement of purpose and goals to be derived. Specific programs can then be selected and developed to address the goals. Individual clients will be assessed and referred to specific programs that are already identified and developed. Given the procedure, it is easy to see the importance of a thorough initial analysis of clients.

Analysis of the clients is undertaken with the knowledge that the eventual outcome will be the determination of leisure-related needs. This concept is important so that demographic, illness, and disability information is gathered and viewed from the onset with a specific purpose in mind. At each phase of the analysis, the programmer asks, "What does this tell me about clients' leisure-related needs and, thus, eventually, program considerations?" The following questions provide direction for the client analysis:

Who are the clients to be served?

How many clients are to be served?

What are their ages and age characteristics?

What disability or disabilities do they have?
   Disability is being used here in a general way to include illnesses, physical or mental disabilities, or any condition that is the reason for receiving services of an agency.

What is the level(s) of severity of the disabilities?

What are the secondary disabilities?
   Secondary disabilities refer to the resulting problems or limitations that often accompany or result from a given primary disability. Many of these are social or emotional in nature.

What is the usual percentage breakdown of males and females?

What are the socioeconomic, occupational, and educational characteristics?

Are there predominant religious and/or ethnic groups served?

Is the target population in transition?
   Some agencies find that their target population is shifting. An example might be from clients with acute conditions to those with more chronic or continuing problems.

Where will the clients be living after discharge, and to what type of agencies will they be referred?

Where do the clients currently live, and will those residential situations change?

After the initial demographic, disability, and general characteristics information has been gathered, the designer analyzes the target population relative to its leisure-related needs. A series of questions such as the following can help in this type of analysis:

1. What functional problems do the clients have that would inhibit or prohibit leisure involvement?

2. Can these functional problems be addressed and improved through treatment-oriented therapeutic recreation services?

3. What secondary disabilities do the clients have that would inhibit or prohibit leisure involvement?

4. Can these secondary disability problems be addressed and improved through treatment-oriented therapeutic recreation services?
5. Do the clients have an awareness of leisure, an understanding of their responsibility for leisure, and an understanding of their potential in leisure?
6. Do the clients have adequate leisure activity skills?
7. Do the clients have knowledge of leisure resources and their utilization?
8. Do clients have adequate social interaction skills for leisure involvement?
9. Do clients have the ability to plan for and make decisions relative to leisure?
10. What additional barriers to leisure exist for these clients (architectural barriers, stigma, fiscal resources, and so on)?
11. What strengths and abilities do these clients have relative to leisure involvement?
12. What would an appropriate leisure lifestyle look like for these clients?

Other questions about the clientele can be raised and investigated in addition to those mentioned here. The purpose of all questions is to uncover as much information as possible about the targeted population. It is important to note that the nature of, and answers to, these questions will vary, depending on the type and size of the agency. For example, a public recreation department may have the entire disabled population of a given community as its potential target clientele, whereas an inpatient children's psychiatric unit has a relatively small and easily identifiable target group. The fact remains that the program designer must start the entire comprehensive program planning process with a clear understanding of the clients to be served, their characteristics, and their leisure needs.

Agency

The nature and type of the agency directly affect the content of the statement of purpose. One would expect a psychiatric facility to be involved in treatment or rehabilitation programming. Similarly, one would expect a municipal recreation department to be engaged in instructional and recreation participation programs. Each agency has a mandate for the kind of services it provides, based on the type of agency and, in some cases, legislation and regulation. Most agencies will stay within their mandates, although they often can extend their services and do more than their primary function would indicate. Analysis and thorough understanding of the agency's mission is vital to comprehensive TR program planning.

Although an agency's history is important, the program planner should not be biased by tradition in determining appropriate program direction. Contemporary ideas and new directions in therapeutic recreation services should be reflected in the statement of purpose. Reviewing the history and background of a given agency does provide useful information to the program designer. Often, this information helps in understanding traditions that may appear illogical or inappropriate. In addition, the background knowledge may give clues to resistance to progress or change and, thus, be helpful in determining strategies for overcoming problems.

A major factor that must be analyzed related to clinical agencies is the presence and type of regulatory bodies that accredit that facility. Most health-related facilities must comply with a set of standards established by a recognized accrediting group. The most common regulatory bodies are the Joint Commission on Accreditation of Hospitals (JCAH) and the Commission on Accreditation of Rehabilitation Facilities (CARF). Each of these accreditation bodies has standards that have direct implications for therapeutic recreation services. Knowledge of the appropriate standards and the agency's use of them will have an immediate impact on the type of comprehensive TR programming that is required or needed in a given agency. To date, similar external accreditation procedures do not exist for community-based recreation departments serving special populations.

Some agencies may be directly impacted by various forms of federal, state, or local legislation. Legislation may have implications for programming requirements. The astute program designer becomes aware of such existing legalities prior to formulating the comprehensive program direction.

Analysis of the organizational and administrative structure of the sponsoring agency is also important. Although this analysis may not give immediate direction to the content of the program, it is vital to the design of a program that can be implemented within the given structure.

An additional area of agency analysis is the consideration of the various functions of the agency that may have little to do with the therapeutic recreation service. The overall agency may have diverse roles and functions. A conscientious therapeutic recreation designer will recognize the value in understanding the total agency prior to narrowing one's concerns to the specifics of the therapeutic recreation program.

Resources

Before developing a statement of purpose and goals and prior to conceptualizing operational programs, the designer needs a good grasp of available and potential resources. Understanding resources at this level enables the designer to make program choices at a later time with these constraints in mind. Likewise, he or she makes initial conceptual decisions based on this important knowledge. At the analyzation stage, the designer attempts to identify all available resources. In addition, one tries to identify potential resources so that the conceptualization and development of the program are not too narrowly defined. The following questions relate to various resources that may be of concern to the program designer:

Staff
How many TR staff are there?

What are their skills and abilities?

What is the likelihood of increasing the TR staff?

What is the nature of the non-TR staff? Can they be used indirectly in programs? Can they be used in a supportive way?

Are volunteers used within the program? Can they be used?

Are families involved in the program? Can they be included?

Are student interns used? Can the internship program be expanded? Should it be?

Facilities and Equipment

What facilities within the agency are available for use in the TR program?

Can other areas be used or converted for use?

What community facilities might be available for use?

What equipment and supplies are available?

Budget

What is the nature and amount of the current budget?

What is the process for increasing the budget? How feasible is an increase?

What are the resources for external funding (grants, foundation support, contributions)?

Is fund raising permissible?

What is the potential for third-party reimbursement?

Services

What kinds of services can be obtained from outside (service and community) groups?

Are contractual services possible or desirable?

What services can be acquired from other health agencies or public, voluntary leisure agencies?

Many other questions can be generated to discover the nature and availability of resources. The more that is known about existing and potential resources, the better. Comprehensive program planning without an understanding of the resource base could result in well-conceived programs in terms of client needs but be totally inappropriate in terms of feasibility in operations.

Community

Knowledge of the surrounding community is also useful prior to deriving the statement of purpose and goals. The designer should investigate other agencies and the services that they deliver. Unnecessary or inappropriate repetition can be avoided in this way; gaps in service can also be discovered.

Identifying available program resources is another benefit of community investigation. Far too often, programs tend to reflect an "in-house" orientation. Programs are designed and provided all within the facility itself. This approach is narrow in terms of preparing the client for use of community-based services. Likewise, it is very expensive. Even in clinical and residential programs, the services and facilities of other agencies can be used.

Most contemporary clinical therapeutic recreation programs have a futuristic focus, which implies programming for where the client will be after discharge or termination. If the client is returning to the community, a thorough understanding of that community is needed. If the client currently lives in the community, there is still the need to study that community, so that the therapeutic recreation program can facilitate the effective or increased utilization of other services within it. Thus, an understanding of the predominant leisure lifestyles within a specific community is important. Programs that emerge out of the statement of purpose and goals need to reflect common community interests. Clients should be able to move comfortably into leisure interests within the community after being involved in therapeutic recreation programs. It is acknowledged that there is no one community leisure lifestyle. There are, however, identifiable leisure lifestyle subgroups based on the geographic and seasonal variables, age groups, ethnic and religious orientations, and availability of various resources and services.

The Therapeutic Recreation Profession

The professional therapeutic recreation specialist will want to investigate aspects of the profession in the development of a comprehensive program. Several areas of the profession have direct bearing on program decisions.

Philosophy of the Profession. As stated in Chapter 1, the National Therapeutic Recreation Society has recently adopted a philosophical position (see Appendix A). A conscientious TR professional would most likely want to consider the essence of that philosophy when making the initial decisions related to program direction. Obviously, there are variations in the interpretation of the existing philosophy, as well as multiple ways to conceptualize and operationalize the philosophy within a given setting. Nonetheless, the NTRS philosophy appears to be a central consideration in the analyzation stage prior to formulating the comprehensive program's statement of purpose and goals.

Standards. Most professions develop and endorse standards for the delivery of their services and for the various desired professional behaviors of their practitioners delivering service. The National Therapeutic Recreation Society has followed this professionalization route. Three specific documents identified various standards and guidelines that should be investigated by the TR professional who wishes to develop and deliver high-quality therapeutic recreation services.[2]

1. *NTRS Standards of Practice for Therapeutic Recreation Service.* This officially endorsed set of professional standards sets forth directions for the entire profession. A copy appears in Appendix B.

---

[2]The three standards documents are available for purchase from The National Recreation and Park Association, 3101 Park Center Drive, Alexandria, Va. 22302.

2. *NTRS Guidelines for the Administration of Therapeutic Recreation Service in Clinical and Residential Facilities.* This document offers additional direction for program development and operation within clinical settings.
3. *Guidelines for Community-Based Recreation Programs for Special Populations.* This document offers useful information for program development in public recreation agencies.

Professional standards are developed and supported by practitioners in an attempt to be appropriately self-regulating as a profession. Although there is no external enforcement of these standards, the conscientious professional voluntarily attempts to comply with their intent and content. Thus, familiarity with these standards becomes important to the therapeutic recreation administrator at the analyzation and developmental phase of comprehensive program planning.

Credentialing. The qualifications and abilities of the staff implementing programs appears to influence significantly the quality of therapeutic recreation services. The credentialing program provided by the National Council for Therapeutic Recreation Certification (NCTRC) offers a recognized procedure for identifying qualified therapeutic recreation personnel at the professional and associate level.[3] This credentialing program does interface with the standards of various health-agency accrediting bodies. In the cases where the standards of accrediting bodies specify the requirements for "qualified personnel," the NCTRC credentials meet the personnel requirement in the area of activity and therapeutic recreation services.

Professional Preparation in Therapeutic Recreation. Current information about TR curricula and the preparation of TR students is a consideration in comprehensive program planning, especially in those agencies that plan to sponsor interns. Information about professional preparation programs, curriculum standards, and fieldwork standards are available from the National Therapeutic Recreation Society.

Continuing Professional Development. NTRS and the various state therapeutic recreation sections offer a variety of professional development opportunities. Conferences, workshops, and institutes provide training and educational experiences that may be needed by the staff of various agencies. This is a consideration in the analysis stage, since the program developer may want to make conceptual programming decisions that may be beyond the staff's current level of knowledge or ability. The question, "Can the members of my staff receive the training they need to implement various aspects of this program?" is often answered positively if the designer knows in advance about various continuing professional development opportunities.

---

[3]The National Council for Therapeutic Recreation Certification, 3101 Park Center Drive, Alexandria, Va. 22302. Applications for certification, as well as information regarding the current standards and requirements, can be obtained from the Council at this address.

Publications and Professional Documents. A variety of printed materials is available through the National Therapeutic Recreation Society that may be useful in program development, as well as in implementation. Awareness of this professional service may be significant in terms of timely and useful information.

Examples of these follow:[4]

> *Issues and Guidelines for Establishing Third-Party Reimbursement for Therapeutic Recreation.* Ingber, Fran K. And West, Ray E.
>
> *Quality Assurance: Concerns for Therapeutic Recreation.* Navar, Nancy and Dunn, Julie (Eds.)
>
> "NTRS Field Placement Guidelines"
>
> *Therapeutic Recreation Journal*

Membership in NTRS and State Therapeutic Recreation Societies. Although membership in a professional society per se has little to do with comprehensive program development, there are several benefits that may enhance the quality of planning and delivery of service as well. Association with other professionals increases the network of resources, knowledge, and expertise available to the program planner. This linkage with other TR colleagues can be used to enhance programming ability and problem solving through the sharing of information and experience. The identification and opportunity for interaction is most often possible through membership in a professional organization.

Trends and New Directions. The professional organization of any field emerges as the focal point for gathering and disseminating information to the people who work in that profession. Thus, an investigation of current professional and program trends can be very useful to the program designer. Specific trends in programming for various populations and agencies can be identified through professional contacts and professional organization information networks.

A significant amount of information about the profession has been identified in this section. Although this information may appear to have a somewhat indirect relationship to the act of comprehensive program planning, it is included because of the authors' belief in the importance of professional affiliation and the potentially beneficial influence of the profession on the design and delivery of therapeutic recreation services.

CONCEPTUALIZATION

The first major task of the conceptualization stage is to develop and write the statement of purpose. The statement of purpose is generally a one-sentence statement that concisely indicates the purpose of the comprehen-

---

[4]The publications and documents identified can be obtained or purchased by writing to the NTRS Liaison at the address given in footnote 2.

sive therapeutic recreation program. Once written, this statement becomes the core from which the entire comprehensive program evolves.

Content for the Statement of Purpose

Once the essential factors related to the clients, agency, resources, community, and the TR profession have been identified and studied, the designer is ready to develop the statement of purpose. Chapter 2 presented a comprehensive Therapeutic Recreation Service Model. An abbreviated version appears in Figure 4–2. Briefly summarized, this model indicates that program direction can be categorized by looking at three areas of therapeutic recreation service. These areas are

1. *Rehabilitation or treatment.* Programs with this intent focus on the improvement of a client's physical, social, mental, and/or emotional behaviors.
2. *Leisure education.* Programs of this nature focus on assisting the client in learning new leisure skills, acquiring social skills, establishing an awareness of self and leisure, and acquiring knowledge related to leisure-resource utilization.
3. *Recreation participation.* Programs in this category provide the individual with the opportunity to engage in leisure activities and programs of one's choice.

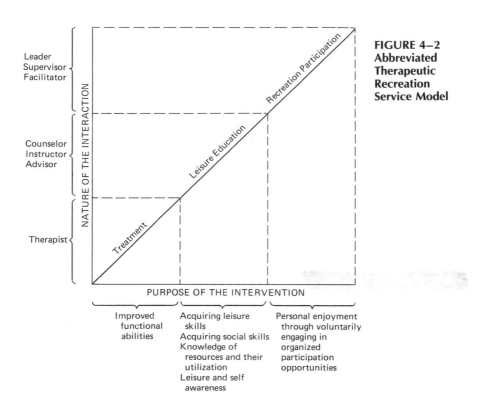

FIGURE 4–2 Abbreviated Therapeutic Recreation Service Model

The model can thus be used for conceptualizing the basic content for the statement of purpose. Program direction can focus directly on any of the three areas or can reflect components or combinations of all three. It is common for a statement of purpose to focus on one or two of these areas.

Selecting the exact content for a statement of purpose for a given agency, unit, or department is dependent on the nature of the agency, the type of clients served, and the nature of their leisure needs. The information acquired in the previous, analyzation stage gives the designer the necessary background to make the appropriate decisions regarding the clients' leisure needs within the context of the agency's mandate.

Writing the Statement of Purpose

The statement of purpose should be comprehensive yet brief. It should explain the reason for the program's existence without going into detail. The words selected should give a concise and clear message. Several examples are provided next.

Example 1. Therapeutic recreation program in a vocational rehabilitation center

Statement of purpose. To provide a wide range of recreation and leisure services to enable the acquisition and application of skills, knowledge, and attitudes necessary for successful participation in community leisure life.

Example 2. Therapeutic recreation program for a local Easter Seal Society

Statement of purpose. To provide opportunities for physically disabled residents of the community to develop recreational skills appropriate to age and limitation, and to acquire knowledge of available and accessible community recreational facilities and resources. *leisure ed*

Example 3. Therapeutic recreation program for a children's inpatient psychiatric unit

Statement of purpose. To facilitate the acquisition and/or improvement of social, emotional, cognitive, and physical functional abilities as they relate to play and recreation participation and to overall development and adjustment. *tx.*

Example 4. Therapeutic recreation program for a long-term health-care facility[5]

Statement of purpose. To provide comprehensive leisure services which are designed to improve functional abilities related to leisure; promote the acquisition and application of leisure-related skills, knowledge, and attitudes; and to provide opportunities for voluntary involvement in leisure interests and activities both within the facility and the community. *leisure ed, tx, rec. participation.*

Statements of purpose will vary somewhat in their content, format, and wording. Usually, they are one sentence long. They do not indicate how the service will be delivered. They focus on purpose or intent of the

[5]Used with permission of the designer, Cynthia Carruthers DeFord.

comprehensive program. Statements of purpose are the backbone of the planning process. Each successive stage of program development will reflect the direction of the statement. Therefore, careful consideration should be given to the content of the statement.

Goals

Once a statement of purpose has been derived for a unit or agency, the next step is to develop goals. Goals describe aspects of the statement of purpose in greater detail. They develop the comprehensive program's purpose. Usually, goals are idealistic; yet, they are capable of being put into operation through program components. Goals are not directly measurable; they are statements of intent. Various examples of goal statements are provided. They correspond with the programs used in the sample statements of purpose.

Example 1. Vocational Rehabilitation Center

Goals
1. To provide services and resources to enable students to acquire new leisure skills appropriate to their limitations and future lifestyles
2. To provide the opportunity and structure to facilitate the students' regular participation in previously obtained and newly acquired activity skills and interests
3. To provide counseling and educational services to assist students in understanding the significance of the leisure phenomenon and in the acceptance of their personal responsibility for leisure utilization
4. To provide information related to leisure resources and experiences involving the utilization of resources
5. To provide information and activity experiences to promote and enable the understanding and acceptance of ongoing health and physical fitness practices
6. To provide opportunities to improve or increase social interaction abilities that will expand or facilitate the enjoyment of leisure activity participation

Example 2. Easter Seal Society

Goals
1. To facilitate the acquisition and dissemination of information regarding opportunities for recreational participation of physically handicapped community residents
2. To provide an opportunity for physically handicapped community residents to gain new and well-balanced interests in leisure skills appropriate to age and limitation
3. To provide the opportunity to participate in recreative activities in order to maintain and expand existing skills and interests
4. To counsel physically handicapped persons about personal responsibility for meeting their own leisure needs
5. To provide knowledge and experience to enable the utilization of community recreation resources
6. To encourage the integration of the physically handicapped into ongoing community recreation programs

Example 3. Children's Inpatient Psychiatric Unit[6]

Goals

1. To develop and/or improve social interaction skills
2. To develop gross and fine motor skills
3. To facilitate more appropriate means of emotional expression
4. To improve cognitive functioning
5. To improve perceptual-motor skills
6. To develop basic concepts of leisure
7. To provide opportunities for learning new leisure skills
8. To provide opportunities for experiencing enjoyment and contentment
9. To provide opportunities for recreation participation
10. To develop and/or improve play skills
11. To provide opportunities for creative expression
12. To provide information about community leisure resources

Example 4. Long-Term Health Care[7]

Goals

1. To improve and maintain the cognitive functional level of the residents in order that they may interact more effectively with their environment
2. To improve or increase social interaction skills
3. To foster the development of a personal awareness of leisure and its significance
4. To assist residents in the investigation and evaluation of their current leisure values and attitudes
5. To acquire or increase leisure decision-making and planning skills that will promote and encourage the assumption of personal responsibility for leisure utilization, and facilitate the independent leisure functioning of the residents
6. To provide knowledge and experiences which enable the utilization of facility and community recreation resources
7. To promote the integration of the resident into the community
8. To enable residents to utilize previously acquired leisure skills or acquire new leisure skills appropriate to their limitations and future lifestyle
9. To increase community and agency awareness of, and involvement with, disabled populations and therapeutic recreation services
10. To contribute to the professional development of persons in therapeutic recreation

Writing Goals

Because goals play the major role in determining program content and direction, they should be developed carefully and with much attention to alternatives, resources, and desired interpretation of the statement of purpose. Content is of vital significance. Equally important are the format and wording of the statement. The following steps should be useful in deriving and stating goals:

---

[6]Used with permission of the designer, Kathy Murphy.
[7]Used with permission of the designer, Cynthia Carruthers DeFord.

Process for Deriving and Stating Goals

1. Review the statement of purpose.
2. Review the characteristics and needs of the population.
3. Review the nature and purpose of the agency, resources, and constraints.
4. Brainstorm possible goal areas.
5. Determine the appropriateness of goal areas for the specific population.
6. Develop goal statements.
7. Analyze goal statements. A criteria list follows that may be used for this final check of goal appropriateness and technical quality.
8. Refine and rewrite goal statements.

Criteria for Judging Goal Statements

1. The statement clearly delineates the goal area:
   a. The statement focuses directly on the key concept words.
   b. The surrounding wording does not change possible interpretation of the goal statement.
2. The statement has appropriate level of generality and specificity:
   a. The statement excludes material that describes actual implementation concerns and strategies.
   b. The statement avoids levels of generality that are too broad to direct reader to specific intent.
3. Statements are parallel in style and general level of content:
   a. Statements are consistent in wording and format.
   b. Statements are consistent in nature of content presented.
4. Statements are both appropriate and feasible for population and agency:
   a. Goals can be substantiated through professional knowledge as appropriate for development or performance expectations.
   b. Goals reflect the philosophy and nature of the agency and are feasible within time, budget, and staffing constraints.
5. Statements reflect the nature and intent of the statement of purpose.

Each agency or unit should develop its own goal statements, reflecting the unique needs of its population, the nature of its setting, and the philosophy of its staff. Generally, however, the content for goal statements reflects the three functions of therapeutic recreation service: treatment, leisure education, or recreation participation. From these three areas, numerous specific goals can be formulated. The following suggestions for goal content are offered merely as a stimulus to the program developer. The areas are generic and not related to specific illnesses, disabilities, or settings. Each is presented as a content area and is not a fully developed goal statement.

Rehabilitation or Treatment Goals

1. To improve physical fitness
2. To increase physical functioning
3. To stimulate physical development
4. To maintain current levels of physical functioning

5. To increase cognitive (mental) functioning
6. To stimulate cognitive development
7. To maintain current levels of cognitive functioning
8. To improve social and interactional skills
9. To increase verbalization and self-expression
10. To stimulate affective responses
11. To facilitate appropriate expressions of emotion
12. To assist in the adjustment to a condition of illness or disability
13. To decrease atypical behaviors or mannerisms
14. To increase avoidance behaviors
15. To increase independence and the ability to make decisions
16. To increase awareness of personal feelings

Leisure Education Goals
1. To develop awareness of leisure and its significance
2. To develop self-awareness related to play and leisure
3. To explore personal leisure attitudes and values
4. To develop leisure problem-solving abilities
5. To acquire knowledge of leisure resources and their uses
6. To facilitate integration into community recreation programs
7. To expand knowledge of leisure opportunities
8. To stimulate self-directed leisure behavior
9. To assist in the development of a personal leisure philosophy
10. To develop social and interactional skills
11. To acquire new leisure skills
12. To increase personal repertoire of leisure skills
13. To provide exposure to new leisure skill areas
14. To develop advanced levels of leisure skill areas

Recreation Participation Goals
1. To facilitate participation in previously acquired leisure skills
2. To facilitate self-expression in leisure
3. To provide opportunities for social interaction
4. To encourage ongoing conditions of health and fitness
5. To provide an environment for the integration of diverse physical, mental, social, and emotional skills
6. To provide opportunities for the reinforcement and support of other treatment programs
7. To provide opportunities for creative and self-directed leisure involvement
8. To provide opportunities for experiencing enjoyment and contentment

These suggested goal areas can be made more precise and appropriate once a specific population and setting are identified. For example, if a population is composed of severely mentally retarded children, a general physical goal might become more definitive; for example, "to develop physical coordination and basic body movements." The program planner is urged to make those refinements when selecting and developing goal statements. A vast number of goal areas related to therapeutic recreation programs are not mentioned here because of their uniqueness to a given setting, population, or approach. For example, a goal area for a long-term health-care facility might deal with the reduction of disoriented behaviors. The planner can be concerned with the uniqueness of a particular population and, at the same time, refer to general lists such as the ones provided.

Note, in the various examples on the preceding pages, the wording and format of goal statements. Goals clearly delineate an area of behavioral improvement, acquisition, or expression. They do not indicate how this will be accomplished. The next stage of comprehensive program development will address that issue. Goals identify major areas for intended program focus. They are brief, concise statements written to define and further clarify the intent of the statement of purpose. Generally, there will be from five to ten goals for a comprehensive therapeutic recreation program.

INVESTIGATION

After the statement of purpose and the goals are written, the next stage in comprehensive program planning is to select program components. *Program components are the operational units for implementation of the program.* Each program component carries out some aspect of the statement of purpose and goals. The number of components depends on the resources available to the therapeutic recreation staff, as well as on the scope of the goals. Regardless of the number and type of components, it is essential that they flow from the goals that have been determined. Each component selected will later be refined and designed in detail. The term "specific program" is used to identify program components when they have been selected and are in the development process. The general term *program component* is used at the conceptualization, investigation, and determination stage to identify the programmatic idea that will be used to translate goals into operational units. The terms can be used interchangeably, if desired.

Basically, a program component or specific program is a set of activities and an interactional procedure that are designed for a defined group of clients for some predetermined purpose. Each component can be distinguished by its intended purpose, area of content, and interaction process. Each component is implemented and evaluated separately from the other components.

The process of converting goals into program components is a difficult and challenging one. It calls for experience, expertise, and creativity. A wide range of possibilities exist for transforming goals into program components. The planner is free to choose from existing program models or to create new delivery concepts. Familiarity with a large number of other programs and their implementation strategies is obviously useful to the planner, but more essential is the ability to conceptualize the components logically.

Several important concerns need to be kept in mind when investigating and selecting program components. First, *the intent of every goal must be translated into some aspect of operationalized program components.* The very essence of all program components evolves from the goals. This direct relationship of programs to goals is what has often been missing in the past. Many agencies have written goals and filed them in a drawer. Programs are created and implemented at the whim of the staff. In a systems-designed comprehensive planning approach, this is not the case. Each program component is selected for its ability to address the intent of one or more of the goals. Thus, there is a direct relationship between the operationalized programs and the agency's TR statement of purpose and goals.

The second concern is that *the goals state the intent of the comprehensive program.* Operationalizing that intent can be complex. Six goals do not translate into six program components. That is an oversimplifcation. A given goal may require several program components to address it appropriately. Likewise, the intent of two or more goals may be combined into one program component. If a large and diverse population is served by the agency, one goal may need a different program component for each identified population subgroup or functional level. In other cases, one goal may be written to address the needs of one subgroup, and, thus, one program component for that one goal may be sufficient. The issue remains: selection of program components to address adequately the intent of the goals is complex and difficult.

A third concern to consider is that of *resources.* Analyzing goal statements and selecting program components must be undertaken with a constant awareness of the available resources (staff, facilities, time, and budget). Without this reality in mind, it would be easy to select far more program components than could be feasibly implemented. Thus, the constraint of resources becomes a critical factor in the conceptualization and eventual selection of program components. It is important to keep in mind that, in the future, other program components can be added or existing ones expanded if, and when, additional resources become available or can be justified. These additional program components will also emerge from the existing goals, maintaining the integrity and interrelatedness of the systems approach. The statement of purpose and goals are written initially from an analysis of clients' leisure-related needs. Thus, these goals are sound, whether or not they can be operationally addressed as thoroughly as the designer would want at the beginning of the total program implementation.

The fourth concern related to transforming goals into program components focuses on *knowledge of possible program structures.* Program structure implies the nature of the format or organization of the program component. Avedon,[8] and Farrell and Lundegren,[9] have provided classifications

---

[8]E. M. Avedon, *Therapeutic Recreation Service: An Applied Behavioral Approach* (Englewood Cliffs, N.J.: Prentice-Hall, Inc., 1974), pp. 161–164.

[9]P. Farrell and H. M. Lundegren, *Recreation Programming: Theory and Technique,* 2nd ed. (New York: John Wiley and Sons, Inc., 1983), pp. 82–98.

of program structures or formats. Their material is integrated to provide the following list of possible program structures:

1. one to one
2. group—treatment, club, activity focused
3. instructional classes
4. competition—leagues, tournaments, contests
5. special events
6. mass activity—entertainment, large-group participation
7. open facility—drop-in or scheduled open use of activity areas

A given program component uses *one* of these common leisure service structures. Each of these structures has identifiable dimensions and characteristics. The appropriate structure needs to be selected to facilitate the desired outcomes of a given program component. For example, a treatment-oriented program component might use the group or one-to-one structure; a league or open-facility structure would not likely be compatible with the desired behavioral change. Likewise, a leisure education program component would most likely use an instructional class or group structure. Various structures are by definition more compatible with various categories of the TR Service Model. The initial conceptualization and investigation of possible program components uses this concept of structure to help give it definition and direction. However, the selection of structure must be followed by further explanation, specification, and description in order to be operational (see Chapter 5). At the current level of planning, it is helpful to explore and identify program components by indicating the basic structure that could be used.

The fifth concern in translating goals into program components is the issue of *priority of goals.* Although eight or so goals may have been identified and stated for a comprehensive TR program, quite often some goals are conceptualized and viewed as being more important than others. When this is the case, it is logical to assume that those priority goals will most likely be operationalized through more program components or through more substantial or intensive program components. Identifying priority goals should be undertaken prior to investigating alternative program components.

The concept of *multiple ways to operationalize a given goal* is the sixth area of concern. The intent of any goal can be accomplished programmatically in many ways. The astute designer will brainstorm and investigate many possible program components before arriving at a decision. Experience is important in this task, but creativity is of equal value. Brainstorming helps in clearing the mind of traditional or assumed ways of doing things. Often, creative, workable ideas emerge when a group of planners feels the freedom to really explore alternative ways of addressing the intent of a given goal. Ideas that result from this process are often more efficient and may still be effective. When many goals are a part of a comprehensive

TR program, multiple methods must be identified and considered prior to making the final program component selection.

The last concern when converting goals into program components is the issue of *equal consideration for all goals.* When the designers initially derived and stated goals, they were, in essence, saying that all goals are important and represent significant aspects of clients' leisure-related needs. An important responsibility of the designer at the investigation stage is to address each goal thoroughly. This is best done by brainstorming and investigating program components for all goals before making any decisions. By using this holistic approach, the goals at the end of the list will have a chance of receiving equal attention and consideration.

Procedural Steps in the Investigation Stage

The following specific procedural steps are presented to assist the reader in understanding the investigation stage:

1. Review all goals for the purpose of understanding their intent.
2. Identify priority goals if desirable.
3. Brainstorm each goal for possible program components (including identification of possible program structure).
4. Review the goals for possible areas of combination.
5. Brainstorm combination program components.
6. Investigate each brainstormed idea for feasibility, practicality, and usefulness.
7. Discard ideas that are determined to be of no value.

DETERMINATION

The next stage in the comprehensive program planning process is the actual selection of program components that will operationalize the intent of the statement of purpose and goals. Many ideas and alternative program components were generated in the investigation stage. This information becomes the source for the determination process. The process starts by reviewing the possible program components and ascertaining their relationship to the established goals. Each alternative program component is studied for its strengths and weaknesses, its demands on resources, and its compatibility with other goals and program components. Eventually, after careful consideration, the designer selects the most appropriate and desirable program components. A final check is made to be sure all goals are adequately addressed through the selected program components. The designer then moves on to the actual development and specification of each program component. Chapter 5 describes the process of development for the program components.

Obviously, the determination stage uses the human decision-making process. If each of the previous stages has been carefully completed, the decisions required in the determination stage will be made utilizing good information and will allow the designer to be as objective and logical as possible. The program components that are selected will be directly related to the statement of purpose and the goals. These goals and purpose statements should adequately represent the leisure-related needs of clients. The end result is a systematically derived comprehensive program plan that is both internally consistent and externally justifiable.

AN EXAMPLE OF THE INVESTIGATION AND DETERMINATION PROCEDURE

To further illustrate the process of converting goals to program components, the following descriptive narrative is presented. Although it is brief, it does give the reader some additional understanding of the thought process and decision making that accompanies the conceptual and developmental steps presented in this chapter.

Vocational Rehabilitation Center, Plainwell, Michigan

Population.   Four hundred students, ages seventeen to sixty, male and female, mild to moderate physical disabilities (including visual and hearing impairments), emotional disabilities, substance abusers, legal offenders, and chronic physical conditions (cardiac and respiratory illnesses)

Setting.   Residential trade school offering vocational training in many areas. Average program length is one to two years

Staff.   Nine full-time therapeutic recreation staff members: one with master's degree, six with bachelor's degrees, two technicians

Recreation Facilities.   Indoor facilities—swimming pool, bowling alleys, gym, multipurpose rooms, craft rooms, and fitness rooms. Outdoor facilities—tennis and volleyball courts, softball diamond, lake, and wooded area

Purpose Statement.   To provide a wide range of recreation and leisure services to enable the acquisition and application of skills and knowledge necessary for successful participation in community socio-leisure life

> *Goals*
> 1. To provide services and resources to enable students to acquire new leisure skills appropriate to their limitations and future lifestyles
> 2. To provide the opportunity and structure to facilitate students' regular participation in previously obtained and newly acquired activity skills and interests
> 3. To provide counseling and educational services to assist students in understanding the significance of the leisure phenomenon and in the acceptance of their personal responsibility for leisure utilization
> 4. To provide information related to leisure resources and experiences involving the use of resources
> 5. To provide information and activity experiences to promote and enable the understanding and acceptance of ongoing health and physical fitness practices
> 6. To provide opportunities to improve or increase social interaction abilities that will expand or facilitate the enjoyment of leisure activity participation

Narrative Description of a Comprehensive Therapeutic Recreation Program Using the Systems Approach

The purpose statement for the trade school indicates that the focus is on acquiring and applying leisure skills and knowledge for continued leisure participation, once the student has completed vocational training. The goals refine this purpose by indicating the need for students to acquire new skills that are appropriate to physical, mental, emotional, and social functional levels and that will provide lifelong leisure participation opportunities. In fact, many of the vocational students had developed leisure skills, but they were appropriate to the younger years and included a heavy emphasis on team sports. The goals also addressed the need to learn about available leisure resources and how to use them. These goals tie in with the school's concern that many former students, well trained vocationally, were not maintaining jobs, and that a partial explanation was inadequate leisure lifestyles. Inadequate social skills also seemed significant. Ongoing health and fitness appeared important regardless of types of disability. Since the school is residential and located far away from a large community, the designer felt responsible for providing ongoing opportunities for recreational participation.

The result of the analysis of the goals, students, and resources was a decision to plan a comprehensive program with the following categories[10] and program components.

Assessment and Prescription. In this program component, each student is first interviewed, with the use of an instrument designed for the program, to determine the current level of leisure skills and frequency of participation. As part of this component, students are introduced to the total program's purpose, content, and process. Included in these counseling sessions is information related to leisure, its implications, and potential. A prescriptive program is then worked out for the student that takes into account the areas of leisure skill weakness, social interaction needs, and recreational participation opportunities. Thus, this component is directly concerned with Goal 3, although the component indirectly relates to all the goals. This program component is implemented on an individual basis, as new students arrive at the school.

Skill Development Category. The purpose and goals emphasize leisure skill development. The skill development category addresses this issue. Thirty-five program components were developed, using a class structure. These programs focused on eight areas of common, adult leisure activities: (1) individual and dual sports, (2) aquatics, (3) fitness, (4) expressive arts, (5) home and family, (6) community service, (7) mental activities, and (8) outdoor activities. Each specific program was developed with behavioral

---

[10]The use of the concept *program category* is an adaptation to the described process. It is basically a middle-level breakdown before specific program components are identified.

performance objectives. These objectives not only deal with the actual activity skill involved, but also with the social behaviors necessary for participation and with learning about the resources involved with the activity. The skill development category thus deals directly with goals 1, 4, 5, and 6. Students are enrolled in courses according to information gained in the assessment process relative to areas of weakness, interest, and leisure lifestyle development.

Recreation Participation Category. The third category deals most directly with Goal 2, although it has implications for goals 3, 4, 5, and 6. This category intends to provide a comprehensive set of leisure opportunities in which students can engage voluntarily. These leisure opportunities are designed to simulate experiences available in communities. The category is subdivided into four subcategories: (1) intramural or athletic competitions, (2) drop-in use of the facilities, (3) clubs and special-interest groups, and (4) special and social events, including entertainment groups, dances, picnics, trips, and sports car rallies. Students are urged to establish an ongoing pattern of leisure involvement through these opportunities. Although they are usually voluntary activities in nature, occasionally some aspect of this category is prescribed so that a student may obtain additional development in social interaction or exposure to other leisure activities not offered in the skill development category.

Before arriving at these three categories, the planner discussed and analyzed countless other alternatives. The designer felt that the resulting conceptualization was the best and most feasible program for this population and setting.

OTHER COMPREHENSIVE THERAPEUTIC RECREATION PROGRAM EXAMPLES

Long-Term Health-Care Facility[11]

Statement of Purpose. To provide comprehensive leisure services that are designed to improve functional abilities related to leisure; to promote the acquisition and application of leisure-related skills, knowledge, and attitudes; and to provide opportunities for voluntary involvement in recreational interests and activities within both the facility and the community

Goal Statements
1. To improve and maintain the cognitive functional level of the residents in order that they may interact more effectively with their environment
2. To improve or increase social interaction skills
3. To foster the development of a personal awareness of leisure and its significance
4. To assist residents in the investigation and evaluation of their current leisure values and attitudes

[11]Materials used with permission of the designer, Cynthia Carruthers DeFord.

5. To acquire or increase leisure decision-making and planning skills that will promote and encourage the assumption of personal responsibility for leisure utilization, and facilitate the independent leisure functioning of the residents
6. To provide knowledge and experiences to enable the utilization of facility and community recreation resources
7. To promote the integration of the resident into the community
8. To enable residents to utilize previously acquired leisure skills or acquire new leisure skills appropriate to their limitations and future lifestyle
9. To increase community and agency awareness of and involvement with disabled populations, and therapeutic recreation services
10. To contribute to the professional development of persons in therapeutic recreation

Program Component Titles

Treatment

Sensory Stimulation	Remotivation
Reality Orientation—Basic	Individual Contacts
Reality Orientation—Advanced	Attending

Leisure Education

Communication Skills
Leisure, Self-Awareness, and Decision Making
Leisure Resources
Leisure and Alcoholism
Leisure Skills—Physical
Leisure Skills—Mental
Leisure Skills—Expressive
Leisure Skills—Lifestyle
Leisure Skills—Music and Dance
Self-Esteem

Recreation Participation

Community Involvement
Special Events
Resident Council
In-House Resident Volunteers
Newspaper
Creative Leisure
Religious Services and Study

Indirect Client Service

Public Awareness
Internship
Inservice and TR Awareness
Volunteer
Continuing Education

In-Patient Psychiatric Children's Unit[12]

Statement of Purpose. To facilitate the acquisition and/or improvement of social, emotional, cognitive, and physical functional abilities as they relate to play and recreation participation and to overall development and adjustment

Goal Statements
1. To develop and/or improve social interaction skills
2. To develop gross and fine motor skills
3. To facilitate more appropriate means of emotional expression
4. To improve cognitive functioning
5. To improve perceptual-motor skills
6. To develop basic concepts of leisure
7. To provide opportunities for learning new leisure skills
8. To provide opportunities for experiencing enjoyment and contentment
9. To provide opportunities for recreation participation
10. To develop and/or improve play skills
11. To provide opportunities for creative expression
12. To provide information about community leisure resources

Program Component Titles

Treatment
Therapeutic Recreation Group—ages 5–7
Therapeutic Recreation Group—ages 8–10
Task-Oriented Group
Perceptual-Motor Group
Movement Group
1-to-1 Treatment

Leisure Education
Play Group
Family Leisure Group

Recreation Participation
Recreation Group
Outings

SUMMARY

The systems approach provides a logical and useful way of conceptualizing clients' leisure-related needs and converting them into operational program components. This approach to comprehensive planning insures that each of the development stages is interrelated, resulting in programs that address specific client needs within the context, resources, and constraints of a given agency. The process starts with a thorough analysis of targeted clients, and the professional and agency factors that influence program development.

[12]Materials used with permission of the designer, Kathy Murphy.

This information is used to derive a statement of purpose and goals that will give direction to the comprehensive program. The goals are then investigated to generate possible program components. These potential program components are then analyzed for their practicality, feasibility, and appropriateness. Finally, the designer selects the actual components that will be used in the comprehensive program based on their ability to translate the intent of the goals into operational programs within the resources and constraints of the agency.

============ **Suggested References** ============

AUSTIN, D. R., *Therapeutic Recreation: Processes and Techniques.* New York: John Wiley and Sons, 1982.

AVEDON, E. M., *Therapeutic Recreation Service: An Applied Behavioral Approach.* Englewood Cliffs, N.J.: Prentice-Hall, Inc., 1974.

BANNON, J. J., *Leisure Resources. Its Comprehensive Planning.* Englewood Cliffs, N.J.: Prentice-Hall, Inc., 1976.

EDGINTON, R. E., D. M. COMPTON, and C. J. HANSON, *Recreation and Leisure Programming: A Guide for the Professional.* Philadelphia: W. B. Saunders, 1980.

FARRELL, P., and H. M. LUNDEGREN, *Recreation Programming: Theory and Technique,* 2nd ed. New York: John Wiley and Sons, 1983.

KRAUS, R., *Social Recreation: A Group Dynamics Approach.* St. Louis: The C. V. Mosby Company, 1979.

MAGER, R. F., *Goals Analysis.* Belmont, Ca.: Fearon Publishers, 1972.

O'MORROW, G. S., *Therapeutic Recreation: A Helping Profession,* 2nd ed. Reston, Va.: Reston Publishing, Inc., 1980.

Programming Trends in Therapeutic Recreation. Creative Leisure Services, 2225 E. McKinney, Denton, Tx. 76201. Six issues per year.

STROBELL, A., *Creative Recreation Programming Book.* Alexandria, Va.: National Recreation and Park Association, 1977.

5

Developing
Specific Programs

PURPOSE: To provide information and a detailed description of the systems procedures used in the development of specific programs. Included are sections on the
program's statement of purpose, terminal program objectives, enabling objectives, performance measures, and the design of the content and process related to each enabling
objective. Each developmental stage is described, and examples are given to assist in
the learning of these design procedures.

THE SPECIFIC PROGRAM

After a statement of purpose and goal statements are determined for a
unit or agency, the program designer is faced with the task of developing
specific programs. Specific programs are the operational units that put the
goals and purpose into action. As discussed in the previous chapter, agency
or unit goals must be translated and transformed into actual operational
programs. In a systems approach to planning, these specific programs need
to be developed and described in a very detailed manner, so that desired
outcomes are directly related to planned interventions and activities. This
chapter focuses on the techniques and procedures related to developing
specific programs.

A specific program can be defined as

> a set of activities and their corresponding interactions that are designed to
> achieve predetermined objectives selected for a given group of clients. The
> specific program is implemented and evaluated independently of all other
> specific programs.

Aspects of this definition require further exploration. Implied in the definition is the concept that each specific program identifies and addresses some major aspect of treatment, leisure education, or recreation participation. One specific program cannot focus on all of these areas of client need. Thus, specific programs are selected and developed that relate to different categories of client need. Some programs will address various treatment concerns; others will be developed to focus on the diverse aspects of leisure education; still others will center on recreation and leisure participation opportunities.

Once the general topic of a specific program is selected, objectives will be derived and stated. These objectives will be delineated for a given group of clients (usually a subgroup of the total population served by the agency). Activities will then be developed that relate directly to the identified objectives and are appropriate for the designated clients. "Activities" in this context does not mean just traditional recreation or leisure activities. It implies a broader category of actions or program content, which can include such areas as discussions, lectures, and written or cognitive exercises as well as traditional or nontraditional recreational activities. Thus, the term *activity* refers to the action, content, or media presented to the clients to address the objectives and, it is hoped, to achieve the desired outcomes.

Similarly, specific interactions will be designed to be used with those activities for that particular set of clients. The program is designed to be implemented independently of other programs. Its objectives, activities, and interventions have their own timelines, staff, resource allocations, and designated evaluation mechanism. A given client is placed or referred to one or more specific programs based on the client's need and the program's designed ability to address that need. This method of programming enables the individual leisure-related needs of clients to be met. It also allows for specific programs to be added, deleted, or changed as clients' needs dictate. Because each specific program has its own focus (purpose and objectives), it can be evaluated based on its contribution to the overall mission of the therapeutic recreation unit, agency, or department. Likewise, the progress of an individual client can be carefully monitored, based on achievement and participation within each assigned or designated program.

Specific programs need to be developed and described so that they can be implemented by the specialist in a consistent manner. This description also allows the program to be repeated by the same implementer, or implemented by someone else. The thorough written description is also of value for the purpose of evaluation. Additionally, it allows the agency to maintain a high level of accountability in that all programs are documented before, during, and after implementation.

The total development of the specific program requires three stages of design: developing the program plan, developing the implementation plan, and developing the evaluation plan. Each of these stages has sequential procedures and tasks. Figure 5–1 presents an overview of the entire process. This chapter presents the information necessary for the

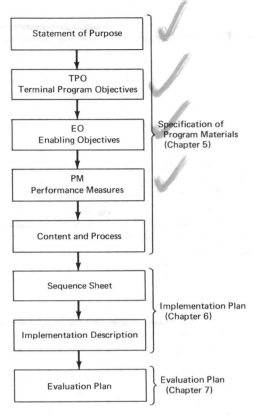

FIGURE 5–1
Development of the Specific Program

design of the first stage—developing the program plan. Included are sections on the following:

1. Statement of Purpose
2. Terminal Program Objectives
3. Enabling Objectives
4. Performance Measures
5. Content and Process Descriptions

Each of these steps builds on the previous material, so that the entire program is developed to accomplish its purpose through the use of systematic and interrelated parts.

STATEMENT OF PURPOSE

The design of every program starts with a clear understanding of the program's intended purpose. The most appropriate way to insure this understanding from the onset is to determine and write a brief statement of purpose for the specific program. Normally, this statement is a concise, one-sentence explanation of the program's focus. It delineates whether the program is treatment-oriented, leisure education-oriented, or recreation participation-oriented. The purpose, however, goes beyond the general category of service. It is as precise as possible in its description. Consider the following example purpose statements for various programs:

To provide the opportunity to improve physical fitness

To provide opportunities to acquire, improve, and utilize social interaction skills within a leisure context

To facilitate a personal understanding of leisure and its potential utilization

To provide the opportunity to gain knowledge of leisure, awareness of personal attitudes and values related to leisure, and to acquire knowledge of resources that would help facilitate leisure involvement

To provide opportunities to acquire basic water readiness and safety skills necessary for advancement into a beginner-level swimming program

To provide the opportunity to acquire wheelchair-maneuvering skills and basic basketball skills required for playing competitive wheelchair basketball

Each of these examples pinpoints the intent of the program in clear and concise language. The statement of purpose is just that—a statement of intent. It is written from the point of view of the sponsoring agency or unit. The language used states what the program is intended to provide. Note also that the statement of purpose does not state how the program will accomplish this. The remainder of the program system will delineate the "how." Nor does the statement of purpose need to describe for whom the program is designed. That information, although vital to the program specification, is presented in the implementation description.

In order to address the diverse goals delineated by the therapeutic recreation agency, unit, or department, a variety of specific programs is generally selected. Each of these specific programs will require a statement of purpose. These combined purpose statements provide the overall operational definition of the previously delineated agency's or unit's goals. Checking back this way is also an important monitoring step. At this point, the designer can verify that the more generalized intent of the goals has been reflected in actual programming efforts.

It is important to note that some agencies or units may not be using a comprehensive approach to therapeutic recreation program planning. Even if an agency does not use this method, it is still possible, and desirable, for an individual therapeutic recreation specialist to develop specific programs using the systems design procedures. If this is the case, the designer identifies a specific program concern and then starts the development process with a statement of purpose. One would then proceed on with the steps delineated in this chapter and in chapters 6 and 7.

Program Titles

Most programs are given a title, which is used in presenting the program to clients and other interested staff members, families, or outside groups. Often, the title given does not directly identify the purpose of the program—nor does it need to. The title is simply a code for communication and identification purposes. For example, a program may be entitled "Jogging." This title does not tell us if the program is teaching jogging, providing jogging for clients who want to jog for enjoyment or fitness, or whether it is a treatment-oriented program used in the rehabilitation of cardiac patients. Often, agencies use even more indirect program titles, such as "The Clang Gang," "Early Riser," or "Staying Alive." These examples illustrate that the title often gives little indication of the purpose or nature of a given program. Thus, the statement of purpose becomes even more important, at least to the designer, implementer, and administrator. Whenever possible, it appears appropriate to title a program so that it does imply the purpose. This simple act can do much to help clients and others understand the program, its purpose, and the reason for their involvement. Titles such as "Instructional Jogging," "Leisure Awareness," and "Conversational Skills" imply purpose and, thus, assist clients and the staff in understanding the role and nature of the various specific programs.

TERMINAL PROGRAM OBJECTIVES

After the specific program component has been identified and a statement of purpose has been written, the designer develops the Terminal Program Objectives (frequently referred to as TPOs). TPOs are best described as general outcome statements. They are written in language that specifies anticipated outcomes related to the client. Thus, the phrase "to demonstrate . . ." will always characterize the TPO.

Terminal Program Objectives are not complete behavioral objectives, since they do not identify conditions, specific behaviors, or criteria, which are all necessary parts of a measurable objective. This aspect of further development and specification will come later. Terminal Program Objectives identify more global behavioral outcomes. Their role is to break down the intent of the statement of purpose into separate identifiable and general outcome behaviors. Normally, each TPO can stand somewhat independently of the other TPOs. However, each TPO is needed to address adequately the overall concern or intent of the program. TPOs are the first-level behavioral outcome statements of the specific program. As such, they are not immediately measurable.

Several examples of TPOs are provided to illustrate their role, content, and language. Note the global nature of their content, the concept of independence between and among them, and yet the element of interrelatedness.

Instructional Cross-Country Skiing Programs

TPO 1.   To demonstrate the ability to cross-country ski

TPO 2.   To demonstrate knowledge and ability related to maintenance of equipment

TPO 3.   To demonstrate knowledge of resources related to cross-country skiing opportunities

TPO 4.   To demonstrate knowledge related to the purchase of equipment and clothing

Political Action Program for Senior Citizens[1]

TPO 1.   To demonstrate knowledge of the significance of one's participation in the election process

TPO 2.   To demonstrate knowledge of the relationship between political issues and the election process

TPO 3.   To demonstrate the ability to identify political issues of concern and how they relate to the election process

TPO 4.   To demonstrate knowledge related to the voting procedure

Leisure Awareness and Planning Group[2]

TPO 1.   To demonstrate an awareness of the concept of leisure and personal responsibility in leisure

TPO 2.   To demonstrate knowledge of leisure resources and their utilization

TPO 3.   To demonstrate the ability to plan for personal leisure participation

Social Interaction Skills[3]

TPO 1.   To demonstrate the ability to listen to others

TPO 2.   To demonstrate the ability to assert oneself

TPO 3.   To demonstrate the ability to cooperate with others

Activity Group Therapy[4]

TPO 1.   To demonstrate the ability to work with and relate positively to the group

TPO 2.   To demonstrate the ability to utilize the group in a therapeutic manner

In all of these illustrations, the Terminal Program Objectives state the terminal or outcome behaviors expected of the client in the program. The combination of the TPOs for a given program is a further explanation or definition of the program's purpose.

Deciding on an appropriate level for the TPOs is often a problem for

[1]Used with permission of the designer, Marty Golub.
[2]Used with permission of the designer, Sandra Wolf Klitzing.
[3]Used with permission of the designer, Laura J. Young.
[4]Used with permission of the designer, Kathy Van Houten.

the beginning systems designer. Obviously, there are many ways in which the TPO could be written.

Choosing the appropriate level for the TPOs is dependent on the population, its functional ability, and the nature of the program. For example, TPOs for a program developed for trainable, moderately mentally retarded individuals may delineate smaller units of outcome behavior, whereas total activities or groups of related behaviors may be appropriate for other populations. Generally, a specific program has a minimum of two TPOs. A program with more than five TPOs will become very lengthy and may need to be separated into two different programs—a beginners' level and an advanced level. Thus, a basic rule of thumb is to conceptualize the intent of the statement of purpose in two to five Terminal Program Objectives.

Each TPO requires further breakdown. A TPO as written is not specific enough, nor is it measurable. The designer must analyze each TPO to derive Enabling Objectives and Performance Measures. Terminal Program Objectives serve as the general outcome behavior statement, indicating a broad category of knowledge, skill, or ability that a client will be expected to acquire.

To assist in the description and organization of a systems-designed program, several forms have been developed. Figure 5–2 presents a blank Objectives and Performance Measures (OPM) sheet. This form provides a space for the Terminal Program Objective, and the next level of breakdown into Enabling Objectives and Performance Measures. It also identifies the name of the program and can be modified to include other additional information. One Objectives and Performance Measures sheet is used for each TPO. Figure 5–3 presents a sample OPM form filled in for one TPO from the Relaxation System (Appendix C) to illustrate the positioning and nature of the various items that are found on this useful form.

ENABLING OBJECTIVES

Analyzing the Terminal Program Objectives for Enabling Objective Content

Each TPO needs to be broken down into smaller behavioral units. These units, called Enabling Objectives (EOs), are the specific targeted behaviors around which the rest of the program system is designed. The selection of content and process is focused on these units. In addition, EOs are specific enough to be used for measurement purposes. In many ways, they are the most important and essential aspect of a systems-designed program.

EOs are conceptualized and selected through analysis of the TPO. The designer studies the intent of the TPO to arrive at necessary or desired units of behavior, skill, or knowledge that are appropriate for that topic and appropriate for the nature of the given population. During this process of analysis, the designer attempts not only to identify desired or necessary

FIGURE 5–2

Objectives and Performance Measures

PROGRAM: _____

TERMINAL PROGRAM OBJECTIVE: _____

ENABLING OBJECTIVE	PERFORMANCE MEASURE

FIGURE 5–3

[handwritten: at the start of the activity ... by power ... because ...]

Objectives and Performance Measures

PROGRAM: Relaxation

TERMINAL PROGRAM OBJECTIVE: 1. To demonstrate knowledge of the concept of relaxation

ENABLING OBJECTIVE	PERFORMANCE MEASURE

1. To demonstrate knowledge of the potential benefits of using relaxation techniques.	1. Upon request, the client will demonstrate knowledge of the potential benefits of using relaxation techniques by stating (either verbally or in writing) one of the following concepts related to the benefits of relaxation:
	   a. increase in a sense of control over behavior when tense,
	   b. decrease in physical tension, or alleviation of some symptom related to physical tension,
	   c. decrease in feelings of anxiety or some symptom of anxiety,
	as judged appropriate by the therapeutic recreation specialist.

2. To demonstrate an awareness of stress and its sources.	2. Upon request, the client will demonstrate an awareness of stress and its sources by stating one personal source and one symptom of stress that he or she has experienced, as judged appropriate by the therapeutic recreation specialist.

3. To demonstrate the ability to identify physical manifestations of stress.	3. Upon request, the client will demonstrate the ability to identify physical manifestations of stress by:
	   a. locating a symptom of tension using another client or leader as a model, and
	   b. verbally identifying muscle tension in his or her own body,
	as judged appropriate by the therapeutic recreation specialist.

behavioral units, but also to arrive at units that are somewhat parallel in their content and level.

Some TPOs break down easily into logical areas of behavior. These are *concrete TPOs,* and they usually result in very *concrete EO* behavioral units. Here is an example of a concrete TPO and its resulting concrete EO behaviors. Assume the TPO states, "to demonstrate the ability to play table tennis." An analysis of this TPO produces the following EO content units:

1. serving
2. forehand
3. backhand
4. drop shot
5. smash
6. lob
7. rules
8. scoring
9. etiquette
10. strategy

Although there could be some disagreement over the possible number and types of behaviors, skills, and knowledge that could be included in the program, most people would agree that these ten areas comprise the essential aspects of playing table tennis. What is important is to identify the actual areas necessary for the game. Because we are dealing with a specific game and with accepted procedures and rules, the areas of behavior are relatively concrete and direct. Many leisure activities and skills fall into this category of concrete TPOs and EOs. However, most treatment and leisure education (excluding activity skills) programs are more difficult to conceptualize, since they fall under the category of abstract TPOs and EOs.

When programs have *abstract or indirect TPOs and EOs,* the designer must conceptualize and define the meaning of the TPO, because the content is subject to multiple meanings or interpretations. Take, for example, the TPO "to demonstrate conversational skills with authority figures." In this case, the developer must determine the content areas that represent the intent of the TPO for the specific population. Analysis is still part of the process. It is used to arrive at the specific content areas that define the meaning or intent of the TPO. The following illustration is of an activity program that intends to establish conversational and verbal-interaction skills with five- to nine-year-old emotionally disturbed children.[5]

TPO 1.   To demonstrate conversational skills with authority figures

EO content areas arrived at through analysis:

1. Making a request
2. Initiating basic conversation

[5]Material included with permission of the designer, Linda Henrichs.

3. Receiving instructions
4. Receiving criticism or correction

When analyzing abstract TPOs, the designer must carefully conceptualize the EO content areas. The EO content areas should be logical and, when added together, represent an adequate definition of the intent of the TPO. The EOs should each be related to the topic of the TPO and provide an appropriate coverage of the TPO's meaning.

Whether the designer is dealing with an abstract TPO or a concrete TPO, the process of analysis is essential. The EO behavioral areas that result from analysis are the designer's interpretation of the meaning or intentions of the TPO. It is critical that the EOs be logical and appropriate for the population being served. For example, the number, nature, and level of EO content areas would be quite different for a social interaction program designed for trainable mentally retarded and one designed for individuals with cerebral palsy. The EO content areas operationally define the TPO for the group under consideration. Those who disagree with the breakdown still cannot refute the fact that the TPO has been operationally defined.

Stating the Enabling Objectives

As discussed, Enabling Objectives are units of behavior that are essential divisions of a Terminal Program Objective. An EO is a specific behavioral statement indicating a unit of knowledge or skill that the client is expected to accomplish. Doing an analysis of the TPO to derive EO content areas makes the job of writing the actual EOs much easier. Essentially, the designer takes the different EO content areas and converts them into behavioral terminology.

The EO is written as a client outcome and is stated behaviorally. It differs from a TPO only in that it deals with a smaller unit of behavior. Examples of EO content areas converted into Enabling Objectives are the following:

1. Ping Pong
   EO content area: Serving
   Enabling Objective: To demonstrate a legal service
2. Conversational skills for emotionally disturbed children
   EO content area: Making a request
   Enabling Objective: To demonstrate the ability to make a request

Each TPO for a specific program is analyzed to derive the EO content areas. The EO content areas are then stated as Enabling Objectives. The Objectives and Performance Measures sheet presented in Figure 5–2 provides a column for writing the EOs derived from, and related to, the particular TPO. Figure 5–3 presents a completed version of the sheet to illustrate the numbering and positioning of the EOs and their corresponding Performance Measures.

To assist the reader in understanding the concepts of TPOs and EOs within specific programs, the TPOs and EOs for several different programs are presented on the following pages. Note the levels, language, format, and content of these TPOs and EOs. In addition, the reader can refer to Appendix C to view these concepts within a fully developed systems program that utilizes the various operational and descriptive forms mentioned thus far in the chapter.

Leisure Awareness and Resources Program—Community Mental Health Center Clients[6]

TPO 1. To demonstrate an awareness of the concept of leisure and personal responsibilities in leisure

EO 1. To demonstrate knowledge of the meaning of leisure

EO 2. To demonstrate knowledge of when personal free time occurs

EO 3. To demonstrate knowledge of personal leisure activities

EO 4. To demonstrate knowledge of personal leisure opportunities

EO 5. To demonstrate knowledge of the beneficial effects of leisure

EO 6. To demonstrate knowledge of personal blocks to leisure

TPO 2. To demonstrate knowledge of leisure resources and their utilization

EO 1. To demonstrate knowledge of one's personal leisure resources

EO 2. To demonstrate knowledge of leisure resources owned by the facility

EO 3. To demonstrate knowledge of leisure resources within walking distance of the facility

EO 4. To demonstrate knowledge of leisure resources that are accessible primarily by car

EO 5. To demonstrate knowledge of information sources that can be used to identify or locate community leisure resources

TPO 3. To demonstrate the ability to plan for personal leisure participation

EO 1. To demonstrate the ability to identify and express leisure interests

EO 2. To demonstrate the ability to develop a plan for participation in expressed leisure interest

Social Interaction Skills—Emotionally Disturbed Children[7]

TPO 1. To demonstrate the ability to listen to others

EO 1. To demonstrate the ability to maintain eye contact with a speaker

EO 2. To demonstrate the ability to maintain appropriate body position and spatial relationship with the speaker

EO 3. To demonstrate the ability to allow others to finish speaking without interruption

EO 4. To demonstrate an understanding of the intent of the speaker

EO 5. To demonstrate the ability to make appropriate verbal responses

[6]Material used with permission of the designer, Sandra Wolf Klitzing.
[7]Materials used with permission of the designer, Laura J. Young.

TPO 2. To demonstrate the ability to be self-assertive
    EO 1. To demonstrate the ability to ask a question
    EO 2. To demonstrate the ability to make a request
    EO 3. To demonstrate the ability to offer suggestions and criticisms
    EO 4. To demonstrate the ability to initiate a discussion
    EO 5. To demonstrate the ability to share feelings
TPO 3. To demonstrate the ability to cooperate with others
    EO 1. To demonstrate the ability to share in decision making
    EO 2. To demonstrate the ability to follow club rules
    EO 3. To demonstrate the ability to comply with group decisions
    EO 4. To demonstrate the ability to accept constructive criticism
    EO 5. To demonstrate the ability to share

Basic Water-Readiness Program—Moderately Mentally Impaired Children[8]

TPO 1. To demonstrate the ability to perform basic water-readiness skills
    EO 1. To demonstrate the ability to enter the pool independently
    EO 2. To demonstrate the ability to exit from the pool independently
    EO 3. To demonstrate an ability to feel secure in the water
    EO 4. To demonstrate an ability to put face in the water
    EO 5. To demonstrate the ability to perform a front float
    EO 6. To demonstrate the ability to perform a back float
    EO 7. To demonstrate the ability to perform a front glide
    EO 8. To demonstrate the ability to perform a back glide
TPO 2. To demonstrate a knowledge of basic water-safety skills
    EO 1. To demonstrate a knowledge of safe areas to swim
    EO 2. To demonstrate a knowledge of pool rules
    EO 3. To demonstrate a knowledge of what to do if a water accident occurs
    EO 4. To demonstrate a knowledge of ways to avoid water accidents

A final word about developing and stating Enabling Objectives. The EOs represent the core of the systems-designed program. The content and process of the program are developed to bring into existence the behaviors that are identified in the EOs. The measurement of the clients' achievement is focused on the intent of the EO. Thus, when developing the EOs, the designer is determining and specifying what the program intends to achieve. Although the EOs should be comprehensive enough to cover the topic appropriately or address desired or necessary behaviors, it is advisable to keep the number of EOs to a minimum. Additional or supplemental information, skills, and activities can always be added to the content of the program. This does not mean that additional EOs must, or should, be added. Rather, the EOs should address only those essential aspects of the program. EOs indicate the behavioral areas for which the program will be held accountable. Each EO specified and stated will be measured in terms of client gains and outcomes. Specific interactions and activities will be

[8]Material used with permission of the designer, Elaine Dempsey.

designed to achieve the intent of the EO. Thus, careful consideration must be given to the selection and specification of each EO. Once an EO is included in a program, the designer makes a commitment to the importance of that EO and to facilitating the clients' accomplishment of that behavior.

EOs should be logical, appropriate for the intended client population, and compatible with the context of the overall program. They should be written in clear and concise language. Each EO statement starts with the phrase, "To demonstrate." It continues with an exact behavioral phrase, which is as brief as possible. This conciseness should enable absolute understanding of the targeted behavior, skill, or knowledge.

The EOs for a given TPO define and specify the meaning of the TPO. When a client has achieved all EOs for a given TPO, the implication is that the TPO has been mastered. When all EOs of all TPOs have been achieved, then it can be inferred that the client has accomplished the intent of the program's Statement of Purpose. In a systems-designed program, this concept of levels or hierarchy is central. A program starts with a statement of purpose. This statement of purpose is broken down into Terminal Program Objectives. TPOs, in turn, are broken down into Enabling Objectives. The EO level is of major significance, because it is at this level that exact specification and measurement take place. Behaviors, skills, or knowledge at the EO stage are at an appropriate and feasible level for accurate observation and evaluation. In addition, they are at a level that allows for the comprehensive identification and selection of program content (activities) and process (interactions).

PERFORMANCE MEASURES

Enabling Objectives identify the selected and desired outcome behaviors of the program. These behaviors are the skills, knowledge, or abilities that the program specifies as the targeted areas for behavioral change, improvement, or acquisition. After the EOs have been selected, all remaining developments and specifications of the program focus on them.

The first task after the determination of the EOs is the development of the Performance Measures (PMs). *The Performance Measure is a statement of the exact behavior that will be taken as evidence that the intent of the EO has been achieved or accomplished.* Whereas the EO delineates an area of behavioral concern, such as a specific skill or category of knowledge or unit of behavioral improvement, the Performance Measure identifies an exact definition of a behavior that is observable and measurable and can be taken as appropriate representation of the EO.

A Performance Measure is a complete behavioral objective, which includes three specific parts—the desired behavior, the conditions under which the desired behavior will occur, and the criteria or standards for judging the behavior. As a behavioral objective, its role is different from that of the Enabling Objective. The Performance Measure indicates and specifies the nature and type of measurement for the purpose of evaluation. There are several reasons for separating the EOs from the Performance

Measures. First, the EOs identify the targeted behavioral areas of concern for the program. All EOs are conceptualized and written prior to developing the Performance Measures. Thus, the identification and specification of EOs is a conceptual stage. When the EOs are written, they can be reviewed, and revised if necessary, to insure that all of the essential or desired EOs are included. Then the designer moves on to the next stage, developing the Performance Measures. The second reason is simply an issue of clarity in reading. Often, a Performance Measure becomes very lengthy, especially when many criteria are used as part of the measure. Interested readers can easily identify the focus of a program by scanning the Enabling Objectives. They can then go on to read the Performance Measures if they are interested in the measurement aspect of the program. In short, the technical nature of the format and language of a Performance Measure makes it difficult to identify easily the behavioral component, which is frequently the area in which an administrator or staff member is most interested. The third reason is probably the most important. The EO is the vital element of concern in the program. The actual activities and interventions of the program are selected to address the full intent of the EO. EOs are quite broad in their concern for a given skill, knowledge, or ability. The Performance Measure, by definition, can only select and define *a representative task, behavior, or action* for observation and measurement. Rarely can the full intent of an EO be incorporated into a PM. The Performance Measure in essence cannot, and should not, expect to be as comprehensive as the intent of the EO.

Each Enabling Objective will have a corresponding Performance Measure. Since EOs identify the desired target behavior for improvement or acquisition, it is only logical that each of these behavioral areas be evaluated. Thus, a Performance Measure must be developed for each EO.

The form in Figure 5–2 has been developed as a tool for organizing and displaying the Terminal Program Objectives, the Enabling Objectives, and their corresponding Performance Measures. Figure 5–3 displays a developed Objectives and Performance Measures Sheet. Additional examples are found in Appendix C. Note the positioning of the Performance Measures relative to their corresponding Enabling Objectives.

Earlier, it was stated that Enabling Objectives provide the operational definition of the Terminal Program Objective. That concept can be further refined with the addition of Performance Measures. Each Enabling Objective has a corresponding Performance Measure that delineates the standards of behavior that are reasonable representations of the desired outcome. Thus, when a client has achieved or obtained all of the EOs, as evidenced by his or her ability to demonstrate the actions or behaviors specified in the Performance Measures, the client has in essence achieved the Terminal Program Objective. A simple way of stating this is, "The sum of the EOs and their Performance Measures equals the Terminal Program Objective." Following this line of thought, a client who achieves each of the separate EOs for a given program, as designated by the Performance Measures, has also demonstrated the intent of the TPOs. This is a useful concept, but it also means that the Enabling Objectives and corresponding Performance Measures must be complete and logically derived and specified.

Writing Performance Measures

The therapeutic recreation specialist works primarily with clients to bring about desired and meaningful behavioral changes and improved skills for leisure expression. The program designer needs to be especially sensitive to these concerns while writing Performance Measures. Performance Measures that require too much time to evaluate or are too demanding in terms of the level or amount of behavior to be observed, measured, and recorded will quickly be neglected or totally rejected by the program implementer. Thus, the designer must develop appropriate and reasonable Performance Measures. *A basic rule of thumb is to look for, and select, the least amount of behavior that is still representative of the intent of the Enabling Objective.* For example, if the EO states, "To demonstrate dyad skills," then the designer will attempt to write a Performance Measure that selects a good representation of dyad interaction, but with the least amount of behavioral display possible. Likewise, if the program is teaching specific computer games and the EO states, "To demonstrate the ability to play Pac Man," then the designer selects the least amount of game time that is representative of the ability to play the game and still be appropriate. Thus, the criteria might state one game, as opposed to three or more games.

Another principle is *to observe and measure the behavior in the most natural environment or situation possible.* Evaluation of the Performance Measures should be as unobtrusive as possible. Thus, good Performance Measures attempt to evaluate the behavior in the context of an activity itself, rather than in an obvious testing situation. In therapeutic recreation, this calls for the creative design of Performance Measures that provide for necessary measurement while allowing the action and nature of the program to continue.

These two principles (least amount of behavior and the most natural measurement situation possible) are critical to good program design and evaluation as well as vital to the acceptance of systems programs by implementers.

Three Aspects of a Performance Measure

A Performance Measure is a complete behavioral objective, and, as such, has three distinct parts: the conditions, the behavior, and the criteria.

Conditions. A condition is the situation under which the desired behavior will occur. Phrases that indicate common conditions include

On request . . .
When given the necessary equipment . . .

When given a choice of three activities . . .
With an opponent of equal ability . . .
On a written exam . . .

Sometimes conditions are unique to a situation, setting, population, or program. An example follows:

While involved in a trip in the community with the therapeutic recreation specialist and after completing the program of assertive training, the client will . . .

Conditions of a behavioral objective primarily set the stage, by identifying necessary equipment, activities, time lines, or other events that are essential to the performance of the desired behavior. Normally, the condition is the first phrase of the Performance Measure. It starts with a preposition and is set off from the rest of the PM by a comma. Occasionally, the conditions are scattered throughout the Performance Measure. Conditions occur throughout the following PM and are italicized for identification:

On request, the client will play a game of checkers *with an opponent of equal ability,* maintaining contact with reality throughout the activity as evidenced by continuous attention to the game and completion of the game within a reasonable amount of time,
as judged by the therapeutic recreation specialist.

In this example, some conditions are not mentioned but implied. The checker game itself is not specified. Often, when a condition is very obvious, it can be eliminated to reduce the length of the complete Performance Measure.

Behavior. The behavior identified in the Performance Measure is the central focus of a behavioral objective. It is the phrase that identifies what the client will be doing to demonstrate the desired knowledge, skill, or ability. The behavior must be observable and measurable in order to meet this requirement. Although measurement of the specific action is most often dealt with in the criteria section of the PM, the behavior focuses the attention of the reader on the general area of concern. Some examples of the behavioral part of a PM are:

. . . the client will demonstrate knowledge of leisure resources in the home . . .
. . . the client will demonstrate increased endurance . . .
. . . the client will demonstrate an understanding of the difference between work and leisure . . .
. . . the client will demonstrate knowledge of a leisure-planning process . . .
. . . the client will demonstrate a forehand shot . . .
. . . the client will demonstrate the ability to initiate dyad interaction . . .

The behavior section of the PM is, in most cases, an exact replication of the behavior stated in the Enabling Objective. The wording always includes the phrase "the client will," followed by an action verb. The criteria section defines more specifically the exact act or representation of the behavior stated, along with standards of form, frequency, or other behavioral descriptions.

Selecting Representative Behaviors. Selecting the representative behavior from the Enabling Objective to be included in the Performance Measure is a major task in writing Performance Measures. In a *concrete* Enabling Objective, the task is somewhat easier. For example, if the EO is a specific skill from a leisure activity, such as "To demonstrate a legal service" (Ping-Pong), the representative behavior would logically be executing legal serves. The client would be asked to show the program implementer that he or she can execute a serve, either upon request or while playing a game. It would be ridiculous to ask the client for a written description of serve in this case. The designer must describe in the criteria how many serves must be executed accurately. In other words, the behavior selected for inclusion in the Performance Measure for a concrete Enabling Objective is the stated behavior itself: a simple direct translation from EO to PM, with just the criteria and conditions requiring development.

On the other hand, when dealing with an *abstract or indirect* Enabling Objective, the designer has a more difficult task in selecting a representative behavior. For example, assume the EO from a leisure education program states, "To demonstrate knowledge of leisure resources in the home." This is an abstract EO, since there are so many things that could be involved and included in the EO. In this situation, the task of identifying a good representative behavior becomes more difficult. The challenge is to select an observable and measurable action that captures the essence of the EO content. An example might be:

> Upon request, the client will demonstrate knowledge of leisure resources in the home by verbally identifying five resources and giving a description of each resource, which includes how it has been used in the past and how it can be used differently in the future,
> as judged appropriate by the therapeutic recreation specialist.

Note that in this PM, the behavior of the EO is repeated in the PM: ". . . the client will demonstrate knowledge of leisure resources in the home." The PM continues with the representative behavior ". . . by verbally identifying five resources and giving a description of each. . . ." This representative behavior is taken to be adequate evidence that the client understands the broader concept of leisure resources in the home. There is probably no way to test the entire concept of leisure resources, nor would it be desirable to do so. The issue is that of identifying a representative slice of the knowledge for the purpose of the PM. One must also note that there is some overlap between the behavior description and the criteria in a PM of this nature. Stating "five resources" is a criterion measurement, but it is interrelated with the behavior being identified as well. This overlap between behavior and criteria is common.

Selecting appropriate representative behavior for abstract Enabling Objectives is a difficult task, and one that requires experience, trial and error, and patience. As the designer's skills improve and observation abilities increase, one becomes somewhat more comfortable with the task and even finds it challenging.

Criteria. The criteria in the Performance Measure delineate the exact amounts and nature of the behavior that can be taken as evidence that the objective has been met. A criterion is a precise statement or standard that allows individuals to make judgments based on observable, measurable behavior. Good criteria statements are so clear that two or more different evaluators have no problem making the same decision about whether or not the desired behavior occurred.

Writing criteria statements requires that we select representative behaviors and then describe the amounts and nature of those behaviors. Criteria can be written in many ways. Selecting the right, or most appropriate kind of, criteria is directly related to the nature of the knowledge or skill identified in the EO. The following sections identify and describe the commonly used types of criteria.

1. Number of Trials. Some behaviors occur by chance, and thus the criteria need to be written in the standard format, "*x* out of *y* attempts." For example, hitting a target with darts or catching a ball or executing a Ping-Pong serve can occur by chance if just one trial or attempt is called for. In situations such as these, the designer is wise to use a numbers of trials as criterion. An example of this follows:

> On request, the client will demonstrate the ability to execute a legal Ping-Pong serve three out of five times,
> as judged by the instructor.

It is unlikely that the client can serve the ball three out of five times by chance. Note also that the word "legal" designates a criterion. There is a standard definition of legal serve, and thus the criterion does not need to be further defined.

2. Level of Accuracy. Certain behaviors require a criterion of accuracy to be useful. Ability to throw a baseball, putt in golf, or bowl is usually judged by a degree of accuracy in order to be credible. An example of level of accuracy reads:

> Given a putting green with a circle one yard in radius drawn around the hole, and upon request, the client will putt six out of ten golf balls into the circle from a distance of ten yards,
> as judged by the instructor.

Note that this Performance Measure combines accuracy and number of trials.

3. Amount of Time.   Some behaviors are best judged by utilizing time as a criterion. Here is an example of this type of criterion:

> On request, the client can run the hundred-yard dash within twenty seconds, as judged by the instructor.

Note that this behavior may not need a number of trials. The client either can or cannot run that fast. The same can be said for such activities as bike riding or swimming. A client either can or can't do the activity. In other words, it would be unlikely that the behavior could occur by chance alone. Thus, increasing the trials only increases the amount of evaluation time required.

4. Percentage or Fractions.   Certain behaviors are valid only if they are maintained over time. The problem is that all activities are not consistent in terms of the amount of time required for action or number of opportunities available. A percentage criterion allows for such variation. A Performance Measure of this nature might read:

> While engaged in a basketball game, the client will demonstrate the ability to make baskets by hitting one-quarter of the attempted field shots, as judged by the instructor.

5. Form.   Some Performance Measures require the specification of form in order to be appropriate. This is often the case when dealing with activity skills that include an aspect of physical performance, such as sports and dance. For example, form is important in executing a forehand shot in tennis, a specific stroke in swimming, or a golf swing. Likewise, form is vital to ballet, gymnastics, and many other motor skill activities or, in these cases, is highly related to success or accuracy within the activity. There are several ways in which this can be described:

1. Relate the Performance Measure to an existing, known standard that is generally respected and accepted. For example:
   > On request, the client can swim twenty-five yards using the side stroke as described in the Red Cross WSI Manual, as judged by the instructor.

2. Judgment of an expert. A good golf instructor knows and can judge form with reliable and valid consistency. In this case, the Performance Measure might read:
   > On request, the client can drive a golf ball a minimum of 100 yards with acceptable form, as judged by the instructor.

   Note that this PM combines form and distance for a thorough criterion.

By now you might have noticed that all PMs contain the phrase "as judged by . . . ." Regardless of the type of behavior and criteria used, all PMs must be viewed and judged by someone. Although it may appear tedious to place this phrase in all PMs, it is a necessary aspect of the PM. In most of the examples given so far, the criteria are very explicit, and almost anyone could view the behavior and make the judgment based on the criteria. However, there are many PMs where this is not true, where the judgment by an expert is an essential part of the criteria itself. The previous PM example on driving a golf ball illustrates this point of professional judgment by an expert. Many of the programs in therapeutic recreation that deal with improved functional behavior and leisure awareness will require this judgment by an expert to make the PM credible. The system in Appendix C demonstrates the inclusion of this professional judgment requirement throughout the system. However, the program designer must be warned that professional judgment alone, without other stated criteria, defeats the purpose of Performance Measures. Observable and measurable behavioral descriptions are by definition a necessary part of the Performance Measure. Several examples of *poor PMs* may help to illustrate how vague the PM is without criteria for the desired behavior. They also show how nebulous the PM is when only the judgment of the TRS is stipulated.

> Upon request, the client will demonstrate increased endurance,
> as judged by the therapeutic recreation specialist.

> Upon request, the client will demonstrate awareness of leisure preference and patterns,
> as judged by the therapeutic recreation specialist.

The absence of representative behaviors and criteria for judgment in each of the foregoing examples makes these PMs useless.

    6. *Procedures and Characteristics.* Many PMs for therapeutic recreation programs deal with content and behavior that are not adequately specified by criterion statements using form, number of trials, percentages, or accuracy. Countless situations exist where the best criteria would be statements that are developed to describe the specific procedure or characteristics of the representative behavior itself. These characteristic statements are appropriate, valid, and reliable. They can be observed and measured. In most cases, they enhance the quality of the PM because of their specificity and direct application to the behavior being addressed in the particular PM. PMs using the procedures and characteristics criteria use the phrase "as characterized by" right after the identified behavior and then go on to list in narrative form the selected statements. The following PM illustrates this type of criteria use. Note that other types of criteria are often used in combination with this approach.

> During an evening meal, the client will demonstrate dyad conversational ability by conducting a minimum of two conversations during the meal as characterized by the following:

1. initiates a conversation with another resident
2. listens to the other resident's response
3. continues conversation on an appropriate topic
4. speaks in acceptable tone and at an appropriate volume
5. maintains appropriate eye contact and body positioning throughout
6. concludes the conversation in an appropriate manner,
   as judged by the therapeutic recreation specialist.

Most often, when these types of criteria are used, they also require the use of the phrase "as judged by" as a necessary aspect of the criteria. The phrase indicates that some knowledge and expertise are held by the person making the judgment. In the preceding Performance Measure, there is a variety of "appropriate" topics, tones, volumes, and completions of the conversation that may fulfill the specified criteria. The specialist is expected to make those judgments based on experience, previously discussed acceptable behaviors, and common sense. The criteria in the example are a bit vague, but they still serve as adequate guidelines for judging whether the client has acquired the desired behaviors.

Here are two other examples of PMs that use the procedure and characteristics criteria:

PM from a Beginning Jogging Instructional Program

Upon request, the client will demonstrate the ability to take own pulse rate as characterized by the following:
1. placing second and third fingers on neck
2. finding pulse and maintaining finger position
3. counting number of beats for thirty seconds
4. doubling that number to get heart rate,
   as judged by the therapeutic recreation specialist.

PM from a Leisure Awareness Program for EMR Adults

Upon request, the client will demonstrate knowledge of personal leisure activities as characterized by the following:
1. completing "My Leisure Coat of Arms" form
2. verbally describing a specific participation experience for each activity depicted on the form,
   as judged appropriate by the therapeutic recreation specialist.

The use of the procedures and characteristics criteria is very common in the writing of PMs for therapeutic recreation programs. The value of this type of criterion cannot be overemphasized. This approach allows the program designer, implementer, and evaluator to focus on behavioral descriptions that capture the essence of the desired representative behavior in the most precise and meaningful way possible.

Multiple Performance Measures

Sometimes the area of concern identified in the Enabling Objective is too complex to be evaluated adequately by one Performance Measure. In other cases, the EO may require measurement of some knowledge, as well as the ability to perform some task. Often, the behavior is very abstract, and two or more different testing situations are needed to verify that the behavior in the EO has really been acquired or internalized. In these situations, it is appropriate to use multiple Performance Measures. This basically means writing two or more PMs for one EO.

For illustration, we will take an EO from a tennis instructional program. Assume that one of the EOs states: "To demonstrate knowledge of the rules and scoring." The program designer decides that he or she wants evidence that the client knows the rules and can utilize them in the regulation and scoring of tennis. Two Performance Measures are thus used to address these two concerns:

PM 1. While playing a set of tennis, the client will demonstrate knowledge of the rules and scoring by determining the winner of each point and calling out the correct score before each point and each game,
as judged by the opponent, who has previously demonstrated knowledge of the rules and scoring procedures.

PM 2. On a written test, the client will demonstrate knowledge of the rules and scoring by achieving a score of 80 percent or higher,
as judged by the instructor.

In this case, the second Performance Measure is used, since it is unlikely that all of the issues or situations related to the rules and scoring would arise during a game. By giving a written exam in addition to the actual playing, the instructor can include situations that are unique or problematic related to the rules and scoring. Thus, the instructor can more effectively test the student's knowledge of the rules and ability to keep score and utilize the rules in the actual playing situation.

Although multiple Performance Measures are discussed here, it is not meant to imply that they are always needed and should be used. Quite the opposite is true. One good PM for each EO would be most desirable.

Additional Comments About Performance Measures

Performance Measures are written for individuals. Although the kinds of programs described in this text are designed primarily to take place in a group context, the PM always focuses on one individual. The phrase "the client will . . . ," "the patient will . . . ," or "the student will . . ." implies this focus on the individual. Also implied is that each person within the group program will be individually evaluated by the stated Performance Measure.

The purpose of the Performance Measure is to provide specific observable and measurable evidence that the intent of the EO has been achieved or accomplished by the client. Thus, the issue of when the PM is used within the implementation of the program becomes important to the development of the PM and how it is written. Most EOs address a behavior that is to be improved or increased, or a skill or knowledge that is to be acquired. These kinds of behavioral changes do not occur easily or quickly. They take time to evolve. Once the program is implemented, it is expected that each Enabling Objective will be addressed on a regular basis—meaning in more than one session. This allows the desired behaviors to be addressed, practiced, and, it is hoped, internalized. Stated another way, the intent of the program is to produce a permanent behavioral change that will remain after the program is completed. However, the PM is utilized within the program itself. The evaluation of the clients' progress or gains is part of the program process.

The PM is written to be used within the program *after* the EO has been addressed in a sufficient number of sessions. This does not mean that the last session of every program should be devoted to the evaluation of clients utilizing the PMs, nor does it mean that the PM can or should be used on the same day that a particular EO is introduced. The PM should be used when there has been adequate time to acquire and practice the given behavior. It is, therefore, a "test" situation to see if the client has achieved the intent of the EO.

There are basically two ways to set up the evaluation of the PMs within a program. One is to designate time within certain sessions of the program to evaluate selected PMs. For example, if EO3 of some program is introduced in session 2, and reviewed and practiced in sessions 3, 4, and 5, then on the Sequence Sheet for session 6, there may appear a comment in the Description column that states, "Evaluate EO3." (A complete description of the role and nature of the Sequence Sheet is presented in the next chapter. The reader may also want to review the system in Appendix C for an illustration of how the PMs are incorporated into the Sequence Sheet.) In other programs, there is no singular designated session for the evaluation of the Performance Measures. The evaluation is described as being *ongoing*. This implies that the program implementer is continuously observing the designated behaviors as specified in the PM, and documents the achievement of the PM when it occurs. This approach does imply, however, that the various behaviors of the EOs are being addressed and practiced throughout various sessions, so that the implementer has many opportunities to observe the behavior as it is being demonstrated. The latter approach does have the advantage of allowing for more variance in the individual's ability to acquire or improve some behavior within the time lines of the program.

The purpose of the Performance Measure is to specify the exact behavior that will provide evidence that the intent of the objective has been met. As such, the conditions under which the behavior is expected to be performed, the representative behavior, and the criteria for judging whether the behavior has occurred are all extremely important. Regardless of whether or not our criteria are as specific and precise as we desire, we are still accomplishing more than before in terms of accountability and improved services by even attempting behavioral descriptions. The following behavioral objective checklist is provided to assist in the development of technically correct Performance Measures. In order for a Performance Measure to be technically acceptable, you must be able to answer each of the questions positively as it relates to the Performance Measure:

1. Can you readily identify the behavior that is to be demonstrated by the client to show that he or she has acquired the objective?
2. Can you readily identify the conditions under which the behavior will be demonstrated?
3. Can you readily identify the standard to which the client's behavior must conform?
4. If two staff members looked at this Performance Measure and a client's performance, could they agree whether or not the standards and limits had been achieved?

Writing and reading Performance Measures are enhanced by using a standard format. It is highly recommended that the sequence of the parts be the same for all PMs. The format most frequently used arranges the parts in the following sequence: conditions, behavior, and criteria. The phrase "as judged by . . ." appears as the last line. This format allows designers, implementers, and other readers to identify the various parts easily and quickly.

A final word about Performance Measures is warranted. Performance Measures are a vital aspect of the systems-designed program. They are, however, no more important than the other parts of the system. For many beginning program designers, the Performance Measures are initially the most difficult part of the system to develop, in terms of both content and technical correctness. Like any other programming skill, the development of good Performance Measures takes time to acquire. The initial inability to derive great Performance Measures does not imply that the whole systems approach is not valuable. Effective programs can still be developed using this approach, since the steps that come before the PMs and the steps that come afterward are of equal importance. Over time, most programmers find that their skills in writing PMs improve substantially. Often, development of the rest of the program system and the implementation and evaluation processes help the designer to see ways to improve the PMs as well as other aspects of the program.

DESIGNING CONTENT AND PROCESS

After Terminal Program Objectives, Enabling Objectives, and Performance Measures have been derived and stated, the program designer moves on to the development of the content and process of the program. Within a systems-designed program, there is a very defined way of developing and stating the content and process. Each Enabling Objective is analyzed for its unique contribution to the program. Content and process descriptions are then developed to address each Enabling Objective as a separate unit. By developing a program this way, the designer, and later the implementer, know that each important aspect (EO) of the program will be focused on through designated activities and interventions.

Content

To begin this stage of systems development, the EO and its corresponding PM are analyzed to determine what needs to be done to accomplish or establish the designated behavior. This step starts with task analysis. The EO is broken down into concrete tasks, behaviors, and activities that the designer feels are necessary to accomplish the intent of the EO. This breakdown produces the content for that EO. *Content can be summarized by stating that it is what is to be done in the program to achieve the intent of the EO.*

Several factors must be considered in the development and specification of content. The designer must continuously be aware of the type of clients for whom the program is intended. For example, designing content for individuals with moderate mental retardation may require more attention to the detailed breakdown and specification of a given skill or knowledge. Age characteristics, the size of the intended group, the availability of resources (supplies, equipment, facilities), and the length of the program will all play an important role in determining the level and amount of content that is appropriate for a given EO.

Task analysis of the EO itself is a primary concern. The designer needs to study carefully the intent of the EO and select the content that appropriately covers all necessary or desired aspects of the specified behavior. This procedure varies with the type of EO under consideration. A *concrete* EO, such as "to demonstrate a legal serve (Ping-Pong)" is relatively easy, since the parts of serving will be basically the same—grip, stance, hitting action, and definition of legal serve in terms of where it lands in the opponent's court. The designer can decide to add elements to this basic content, such as serving strategy and types of serves. However, the basic elements are pretty much determined and apparent in a concrete EO. An *indirect* EO requires that the designer literally determines what is meant or intended by the EO. In other words, the design of content for an indirect EO requires the specification of the operational definition of the EO. Once the operational definition is determined, then that information becomes the information to be task-analyzed. For example, an EO from the sample system in Appendix C states, "To demonstrate knowledge of the potential benefits of using relaxation techniques." This is an indirect EO, since there are potentially many ways to interpret its meaning. The designer first operationally defines what is meant or intended for the EO to cover. Once this is accomplished, the information can be task-analyzed to determine what activities, discussion topics, and the like must be presented to cover the topic adequately. True, two different designers may interpret the EO differently, but as long as both come up with adequate information or definitions that logically relate to the stated EO and appropriately specify that content, there is no error in design. Indirect EOs will always be subject to disagreement in terms of analysis and definition. The issue in systems is not one of absolute rightness or consensus. Rather, the issue is the fact that the *designer's interpretation* is specified. We know what the designer intended and thus can use the system and evaluate it on its ability to produce what it operationally defines.

Indirect EOs do give direction to the designer. Note the implied general content of the following EOs from different systems:

> to demonstrate knowledge of leisure resources in the community
>
> to demonstrate the ability to use a leisure planning technique
>
> to demonstrate dyad conversational skills

For any of these three EOs, it is possible to define their meaning operationally for a given population, setting, and leisure context. Once they have been thus defined, that definition or understanding can be task-analyzed to determine the actual content that needs to be developed for the EO within the program.

In program systems in which the EO calls for the selection of traditional or nontraditional leisure activities, a procedure called "activity analysis" can be very useful. Chapter 8, in the last section of this book, presents a comprehensive explanation of activity analysis. The material presented in that chapter enables the thorough examination of activities. Information gained through activity analysis can then be used to determine if the selected activities will be helpful in accomplishing the intent of the EO. Activity analysis is a valuable tool for use in the selection of content for treatment and leisure skill development programs where leisure activities are a major aspect of the program content.

Designing content for a given EO, whether it is a concrete or an indirect one, is a technical as well as a creative procedure. Determining and selecting the actual activities, skills, knowledge, or topics that must be covered to relate logically to the EO is the more technical aspect of design. However, most EOs can be addressed in several ways, and, thus, the creative aspect of design comes into existence. A good programmer thinks about the target population, the EO, and the many possible ways that that content could be designed. Then one selects and specifies the content one wants to incorporate into that program. The amount of creativity and variety found in any given system is the product of the designer's ability. Systems can be designed to be very simple, basic, or even rigid, or they can be exciting, fun, unique, or complex, depending on the designer's ability, experience, and originality. It is the content selection and description that is the critical aspect of design in systems-developed programs. Although the TPOs and EOs determine the intent and outcome behaviors of a program, it is the content that delineates how the program will actually be presented.

Many beginning systems program designers ask the question, "How much content should be included in the specification of a program?" An obvious answer would be, "The more content and detail related to content, the better." Comprehensive specification enables more thorough evaluation of the total program process. However, most program designers have limited time for the writing of programs; thus, efficiency is a factor. One rule of thumb to follow is to determine a level of content information and be consistent with that level for all EOs throughout the system. The program system in Appendix C displays this concept of consistency of amount and level of detail for all of the EOs. The level chosen appears to be adequate to give the implementer sufficient information about program content for each EO. An illustration of a much more detailed system can be found in Joswiak's published materials on leisure counseling for the mentally impaired.[9] Regardless of the level of detail selected, the system is enhanced by consistency throughout, as opposed to having some EOs with high levels of content specified and other EOs with little detail presented.

Throughout this chapter, it has been mentioned that the EOs provide the real focus of the system. The PMs are merely the selected representative behaviors that can be used as evidence that the intent of the EO has been demonstrated in an observable, measurable form. Consequently, when task-analyzing to determine and select the content for the program, the focus should be on the EO, not the PM. The EO by definition will always encompass a broader concern than the PM can measure. This concept is vital in the development of the content section of the system. By focusing on the EO, the designer is likely to develop a more complete and appropriate program. A thorough analysis of the EO enables a more comprehensive approach to the intent of the EO. The content sections of the system will thus frequently deal with information, skills, or behaviors that are beyond the scope of the one representative slice of behavior found in the PM. A well-developed system will always expand the content section to deal with the full intent of the EO. Additional, ancillary, or supportive information is also appropriate to include in the content section. Thus, another procedural guideline in systems development is *to focus the content description on the full intent of the EO, not merely the PM.*

Specifying the content for an EO is organizationally made easier by the use of a form. Figure 5–4 displays a blank Content and Process Description (CPD) sheet. Note that this form identifies the TPO number, the EO number, and the complete statement of the EO. The left-hand section is designed for the description of the content, which has been task-analyzed and selected for specification. Figure 5–5 displays a completed Content and Process Description sheet that shows the positioning of content relative to its corresponding process information on the CPD sheet. Also, review Appendix C for other illustrations of this use of the CPD sheet.

---

[9]Ken Joswiak, *Leisure Counseling Program Materials for the Mentally Impaired* (Washington, D.C.: Hawkins and Associates, 1976). Note the detail in the leisure-counseling activity sheet. A system of this type enables a recreator to implement the program fully, independently of the designer.

FIGURE 5–4

Content and Process Description

TPO No.: _____

EO No: _____

EQUIPMENT: _____

CONTENT	PROCESS	

FIGURE 5–5

Content and Process Description

TPO No.: 2

EO No.: 2   To demonstrate basic physical warm-ups and relaxation activities

EQUIPMENT: Mats or blankets

CONTENT	PROCESS

1. The purpose of warming up
 	
  a. The warm-up serves as a transition into a session of relaxation activities.
 	
  b. The warm-up functions as a physical preparation by helping to prevent injuries by easing muscles into physical activity, helping to identify points of physical tension and initiating the process of releasing it, encouraging body awareness.
 	
  c. The warm-up aids in mental preparation for a session of relaxation by providing an activity that is relatively easy to concentrate on and is therefore useful in clearing the mind of daily stress.
 	
2. The processes of warm-up activities
 	
Total Body Stretch—Warm-up Activity A
 	
  a. Make your body as long as possible, stretching your hands over your head.
 	
  b. Stretch the right side, making it as long as possible, leaving the left side relaxed.
 	
  c. Repeat above for left side, leaving right side relaxed.
 	
  d. Make your body as wide as possible, stretching your arms out to the side, and standing in a straddle.
	Have participants stand in a circle at arms length from one another.
	
	Introduce the warm-ups by reviewing the purposes of warming up. Tell participants that the beginning of each session will be spent doing warm-ups and that you will be starting with some simple movements or stretches.
	
	Explain that most of the warm-ups include breathing with the movements. Tell them it is important in getting full benefit from the warm-up to pay careful attention to the breathing instructions.
	
	Introduce the total body stretch by asking the participants to stretch as if they had just awakened from a night's sleep. The leader may want to demonstrate if the group is slow in getting started.
	
	Discuss: Ask, "Why do you think we want to stretch in the morning?" (Focus: it helps to get blood back into muscles that haven't been working all night. That is how we get started in the morning, so it is a logical place to begin with warming-up.)
	
	Take participants through steps verbally and with demonstrations. Repeat 2–3 times.

Process

After the content has been specified for an EO, the designer develops the process for that content. *Process refers to the way the content is presented to the clients.* The process information, which appears on the right-hand side of the Content and Process Description sheet, is a detailed breakdown of what the therapeutic recreation specialist will do with the content of that particular EO. The content is broken down, expanded, and explained in the content column. Paralleling each part of the content will be statements delineating how that content is to be handled by the specialist.

Chapter 2 presented the concept of the utilization of different intervention styles by the therapeutic recreation specialist, depending on the nature of the program (treatment, leisure education, or recreation participation). By the time a program has been developed to the current stage, it has already been determined whether it is a treatment-oriented, leisure education-oriented, or recreation participation-oriented program. Thus, the general intervention style is also known. The program will be utilizing therapeutic techniques (treatment), instructional and/or counseling techniques (leisure education), or leadership and/or supervisory techniques (recreation participation). However, each of these categories of intervention styles is broad and encompasses many different types of specific intervention strategies. Within the systems-designed program, very specific information is needed regarding the particular intervention strategy or strategies that are to be used. It is the Process section of the Content and Process Description sheet that allows for this type of written description of the intervention strategies that are selected for use.

In addition, specific parts of the content may require different intervention techniques; thus, delineating the specific process or intervention strategy for each part of the EO's content breakdown is essential. For example, assume the content of one EO relates to teaching a specific aspect of a leisure skill. The information in the content column breaks down the skill to its component parts. In the process column, a detailed description of how that skill will be taught appears. Several different instructional strategies may be incorporated. For some aspect of the skill, group instruction may be designated. For another aspect of the skill, one-to-one instruction may be desirable. Practice time requires a different form of intervention. Perhaps a game situation is used to practice the skill further. The game situation may require additional forms of intervention, including leadership and supervision. All of the information is described in the process section of the CPD sheet related to a given EO and its content.

The Process section enables the designer to describe fully the overall intervention strategy to be used, as well as the specific processes as they relate to the different aspects of the EO. Breaking down process statements so that they parallel the content enables the designer and the implementer to have a much better explanation of "how" the program is intended to be presented. Figure 5–5 illustrates this concept of processs paralleling content. Appendix C can also be reviewed to see the expanded use of this approach.

The concept of diverse intervention techniques and the need to specify them is important to the systems-developed program. Knowing what to do and how to do it is vital to the implementation of the program. The more detail that is specified related to content and process, the greater the likelihood that the program can and will be implemented appropriately. When a program is implemented as designed, more accurate information can be acquired through the evaluation process. This evaluation information can then be used to indicate areas for improvement. Specifically, content and process can be thoroughly reviewed for their contributions to the program. Changes can be made to improve the content or process or both. However, if detailed information is not included at the time of design, the implementer may not be able to follow exact content or process procedures, and thus the evaluation process becomes vague as well.

Several other issues can be discussed relative to the design of the process section. The first is the issue of choice and decision making related to process. For any content specified for a given EO, there are many alternative ways in which that content could be presented. Diverse therapeutic techniques exist, and there are countless instructional strategies and many counseling techniques; likewise, there are many styles of leadership. Deciding what techniques to use within each of these categories can be confusing. A few basic principles may be helpful to the beginning designer.

Program time is a scarce commodity in most agencies. Thus, several factors need to be kept in mind when programming. One of these is *efficiency*. Efficiency refers to producing results with the least amount of energy, time, and/or resources. A designer, when selecting the intervention techniques to be used in a given program, should consider this issue. What technique or techniques will produce the desired outcomes with the least expenditure of time, energy, or resources? An example of this might be using a standard "demonstrate, explain, practice" group instructional technique as opposed to one-to-one instruction with the use of video-tape equipment for feedback. Many would agree that the latter technique may be more effective; however, the number of clients, number of staff, and available time and resources may make the group instructional situation the most efficient.

The second principle is that of *effectiveness*. Effectiveness refers to results and the ability to achieve the desired outcomes. Although there are usually multiple intervention techniques that can be used with any given content, some techniques may be more effective with certain kinds of content. Selection of an appropriate intervention technique should therefore consider this issue of effectiveness. One of the major pitfalls to avoid in therapeutic recreation programming is becoming overly committed to a given intervention technique without seriously looking at its ability to contribute to the desired outcomes. In the past, this problem has occurred most frequently in the area of counseling strategies. Some programmers appear to be more concerned with the utilization of a given intervention technique than they are with achieving the desired outcomes of the program.

A third principle to follow in the selection of intervention techniques is that of *careful consideration of the targeted client population*. Specific intervention techniques have been developed for use with certain populations. These techniques may not be effective or efficient with other populations. For example, backward chaining is often used to teach skills to individuals with mental retardation. This same technique would be unnecessary and even boring to individuals of normal intelligence. Likewise, basic techniques used with nondisabled individuals may be totally inappropriate for a given special population. For example, a very cognitively-oriented counseling technique may be beyond the mental functioning of a confused elderly person. Thus, knowledge of diverse intervention strategies as they relate to different populations is vital for the appropriate selection of any technique. In addition to information related to a given disability, the designer must consider the *age* of the individuals involved and the *number* of individuals to be included in the program. Intervention techniques appropriate for young children could be totally inappropriate for use with adults. Likewise, a technique that is effective for a group of three or four will most likely be useless with a group of twenty.

The last principle to consider in the selection of intervention techniques is the *program context.* The intervention strategies and processes selected must be appropriate for the clients; they must also match the content of the program. Ease of use and the skills of the implementer are considerations. The strategies eventually included are selected for their ability to contribute to the attainment of the program's desired outcomes. They should, therefore, "fit" or match with all of the previously mentioned concerns. Common sense, logic, and experience all contribute to this selection process.

Many beginning program designers run into some debate over what is content and what is process when developing a systems program. This confusion is understandable when we look at common use of the two words, content and process. Many programs are a teaching process: the process of decision making, the process of leisure planning, the process of relaxation, the process of making or constructing something. Redefining the terms *content* and *process* for use in systems design may help. *Content is the breakdown of the skills, knowledge, or behavior related to the program* and the client. The content description includes the activities and essence of the program focus. Therefore, if the program content is addressing a process or procedure such as a relaxation technique, the description of that relaxation technique would be found in the content section of the CPD Sheet. *Process,* on the other hand, *is what the therapeutic recreation specialist will do with the content* to present it to the clients. Thus, process statements will always focus on the intervention of the specialist. In the case of the relaxation technique, the technique itself is content; how the therapeutic recreation specialist is to teach the technique will appear in the process section. Reviewing Appendix C with careful note of the division of content and process should help in understanding the role of these two sections and what material appears in each. The rule of thumb remains: the description and breakdown of information about the EO's intent is content. The description of what the specialist does with that content is process.

When the concept of content and process is understood, the designer proceeds to develop the written content and process descriptions for each EO in the program. In other words, each EO and its corresponding PM will have at least one Content and Process Description sheet (depending on the level of detail that is selected for use in the program). The Content and Process Description sheet describes in detail what is to be done and how it will be presented to the clients. If the program is designed well, the activities or actions should produce the desired results. If not, through the evaluation process, the designer has a more reasonable and systematic way of determining what worked and what didn't. This information can then be used to revise and improve the system.

SAMPLE PROGRAM SYSTEM

Throughout this chapter, reference has been made to the sample program system "Relaxation," found in Appendix C. These references were made to help illustrate a specific stage or aspect of the systems design procedure. At this point, the reader may wish to review again the sample system in order to see the various parts as they interrelate with one another. The holistic reading of the system should help in the understanding of the separate parts in context. The "Relaxation" system is used primarily to illustrate systems technology. It is acknowledged that the program content area is only appropriate for specific populations in certain situations.

RECREATION PARTICIPATION PROGRAMS

The development of specific programs as presented in this chapter is appropriate for treatment-oriented and leisure education-oriented programs. These types of programs are designed to bring about some kind of predetermined behavioral change (improvement, establishment, or acquisition). Thus, specific objectives and performance measures are necessary to identify desired areas of behavioral change and to evaluate progress in the acquisition of the targeted behaviors. Recreation participation programs are designed to facilitate individuals' expression of leisure interests. It would be inappropriate to predetermine specific outcomes in such programs. This does not mean that recreation participation programs should not be well developed and specified. It does mean that specific behavioral objectives and performance measures would be inappropriate. Many other aspects of systems design can be used to develop the recreation participation programs. A modified form of session content and process descriptions, sequence sheets, and implementation plans are all valuable ways to specify and describe the recreation participation program.

Other modifications of the systems approach can be used in the delineation of the recreation participation programs. A common method is the use of a Management-by-Objectives approach, which basically indicates objectives related both to what the leadership will be doing as well as to management of resources and participation factors.[10] Such a method still can be evaluated, the difference being that specific behavioral outcomes for the participant are absent. They are replaced by management objectives focused on leadership and delivery concepts.

SUMMARY

Determining and writing Terminal Program Objectives, Enabling Objectives, and Performance Measures start the design procedure for a specific program. This stage is followed by developing and delineating the content and process for each EO. When all of these stages are completed, the designer has a well-developed and logical program description that should be appropriate for the designated population; feasible, given the agency's constraints and resources; and compatible with other agency programs and services. However, the program design is not complete at this stage. Two additional aspects need to be developed: the implementation plan and the evaluation plan. These two parts of the total program plan are presented in chapters 6 and 7.

=========== **Suggested References** ===========

ARMSTRONG, R. J., T. D. CORNELL, R. E. KRANER, and E. ROBERTSON, *The Development and Evaluation of Behavioral Objectives.* Worthington, Oh.: Charles A. Jones Publishing Company, 1970.

AUSTIN, D. R., *Therapeutic Recreation: Processes and Techniques.* New York: John Wiley and Sons, 1982.

BRAMMER, L. M., *The Helping Relationship: Process and Skills.* Englewood Cliffs, N.J.: Prentice-Hall, Inc., 1973.

GRONLUND, N. E., *Stating Behavioral Objectives for Classroom Instruction.* London: The Macmillan Company, 1970.

HACKNEY, H., and L. S. CORMIER, *Counseling Strategies and Objectives* (2nd ed.). Englewood Cliffs, N.J.: Prentice-Hall, Inc., 1979.

HOWARD, D. R., and J. L. CROMPTON, *Financing, Managing, and Marketing Recreation and Park Resources.* Dubuque, Ia.: William C. Brown Company Publishers, 1980.

KRATHWOHL, D. R., "Stating Objectives Appropriately for Program, for Curriculum, and for Instructional Materials Developed," *Journal of Teacher Education,* 16 (1965), 83–92.

————, *Taxonomy of Educational Objectives, Handbook II: Affective Domain.* New York: David McKay, 1964.

MAGER, R. F., *Preparing Instructional Objectives.* Palo Alto, Ca.: Fearon Publishers, 1962.

MUNDY, J., and L. ODUM, *Leisure Education: Theory and Practice.* New York: John Wiley and Sons, 1979.

PETERSON, C. A., *A Systems Approach to Therapeutic Recreation Programming.* Champaign, Il.: Stipes Publishing Company, 1976.

[10]A good, thorough explanation of Management-by-Objectives can be found in D. R. Howard and J. L. Crompton, *Financing, Managing, and Marketing Recreation and Park Resources,* Chapter 13, "Managing by Objectives in Recreation and Parks." (Dubuque, Ia.: William C. Brown Publishers, 1980), pp. 250–274.

6

Specifying
the Implementation Plan

PURPOSE: To present information pertinent to the implementation plan for systems-designed programs. Included is material related to the length and number of sessions; sequencing; input requirements, such as staff, facilities and equipment; as well as description of the targeted client population.

A systems-designed program specifies Terminal Program Objectives (program goals), which are then broken down into Enabling Objectives (EOs), with corresponding Performance Measures (PMs). Each EO and PM is then task-analyzed to produce the content and process necessary for bringing the desired behaviors into existence. Although the program planners design a program with general implementation considerations in mind, up to this point the implementation strategy has not yet been delineated. This step, however, is vital and must be specified in detail as part of the overall program plan.

In a systems approach, the designer is saying that a particular program, implemented in a particular manner, should produce the desired results. If the desired results are not achieved, then a variety of factors can be analyzed and changed, if necessary, to improve the likelihood of success in the future. The program, its implementation plan, and the evaluation plan are closely interrelated. Many times programs do not work, not because of their content, process, or objectives, but because the implementation strategy was deficient. Obviously, it is easier to revise the implementation plan than it is to rewrite the program.

The implementation plan is comprised of two separate parts. Both are vital to the entire systems-designed program. One part is the *Sequence Sheet.* This is a form that specifies what is to be included in each session.

The second part is the *Implementation Description.* This is a written description of the general implementation strategy for the overall program.

THE SEQUENCE SHEET

In previous chapters, a description of the development of Enabling Objectives (EOs), Performance Measures (PMs), and Content and Process Descriptions (CPDs) was presented. From that material, we learned that *each* EO and its corresponding PM contains a thorough description of activities (content) and procedures (process), which are designed to facilitate the accomplishment of the objective. This description, the Content and Process Description, presents information about the implementation of that particular objective; it does not indicate how that objective is interrelated with the rest of the program. This is the role and function of the Sequence Sheet.

The Sequence Sheet is a session-by-session description of how the total program is designed to be implemented. It includes what Enabling Objectives will be addressed in each session, what aspects of the Content and Process Description are to be implemented, along with time estimates for each of these activities. The Content and Process Description sheet *does not* indicate the time allowed for any given objective or activity. It merely delineates the process designed to address that objective. The Sequence Sheet is the only place in the system where time allocations are specified. Figure 6–1 presents a blank Sequence Sheet. A completed Sequence Sheet for a system is found in Appendix C.

Programs that are designed utilizing a systems approach can be of two different types: *The set-number-of-sessions program,* or the *continuous-session program.* The program with a set number of sessions implies that it is developed and will be implemented with a predetermined number of sessions. Many community-based recreation programs for special populations are of this type. The program is usually set up on a seasonal schedule of eight, ten, or twelve weeks. Some programs in treatment or residential settings also use this approach. With this type of program, the designer knows from the beginning how many sessions will be held and the length of each session. The design of the content sequence of the program must take into account the number of sessions available. A later section of this chapter deals with the continuous session program. The following pages focus on the set-number-of-sessions type of program.

The Sequence Sheet does several other things that are not indicated on the Content and Process Description sheets. It indicates practice time and review opportunities. Many objectives are complicated and cannot be acquired in a given session. The Sequence Sheet allows the program designer to specify the various sessions in which a given objective is to be reviewed or practiced. Most specific leisure skills require this type of reinforcement through practice if they are to be mastered. Likewise, in a treatment-oriented program, a given targeted behavior for improvement would need time allocated over several sessions if permanent change in that behavior is to be expected. The Sequence Sheet carefully lays out this

FIGURE 6–1

Sequence Sheet*

TPO	EO	DESCRIPTION	SESSION NO.	TIME (MIN)

*Evaluation should take place on an ongoing basis. Performance Measures should be reviewed prior to each session, and clients' progress should be recorded during or directly after groups.

kind of information so that the program staff can address objectives in a systematic manner over the various sessions. An example of the specification of objectives to be addressed and the concept of review and practice is found in Figure 6–2.

The Sequence Sheet serves another important function. It indicates when and how the observation and recording of the achievement of objectives is to be carried out. Time is actually scheduled on the Sequence Sheet for this evaluation of the clients' progress toward accomplishing the objectives. This kind of observation time may be indicated on the Sequence

FIGURE 6–2 Section of a Sequence Sheet for a Racquetball Skill Program
Sequence Sheet*

TPO	EO	DESCRIPTION	SESSION NO.	TIME (MIN)
		Warm up	2	5
1	2	Introduce backhand shot grip, position, swing, follow through	2	10
		Practice exercise		15
1	1	Review forehand	2	10
		Practice		10
1	5	Rules and scoring	2	15

*Evaluation should take place on an ongoing basis. Performance Measures should be reviewed prior to each session, and clients' progress should be recorded during or directly after groups.

Sheet. A tournament near the end of a leisure-skill program may be the specified evaluation time for checking various skills. The Sequence Sheet would include this information for the given session. An example is given in Figure 6–3.

The Performance Measure indicates how a given objective is evaluated. When scheduling time on the Sequence Sheet, it is important to note how the PM is written, so that the appropriate activity, time, or structure is set up for the evaluation process. Equally important is the manner in which the evaluation of objectives takes place. In therapeutic recreation, it would appear desirable to have the evaluation of objectives be as unobtrusive as possible. Thus, the utilization of free play, tournaments, practice sessions, or some program activity itself as the context for the evaluation of objectives keeps the focus on program participation and not on testing.

In some programs, the evaluation of the accomplishment of the objective is continuous, throughout the program. As the program staff members observe the achievement of objectives, they record the information on the *Performance Sheet*. In these kinds of programs, the explanation of how objectives are to be evaluated should appear somewhere in the program materials. This information can be in the introductory Implementation Description or appear as a note on the Sequence Sheet.

FIGURE 6–3 Section of a Sequence Sheet for a Racquetball Skill Program

TPO	EO	DESCRIPTION	SESSION NO.	TIME (MIN)
1	1,2,3,4,5	Singles tournament (staff evaluates designated EOs)	6	50
2	1	Racquet-ball facilities in the community	6	10

A Performance Sheet is a simple form used to record the attainment of objectives. Clients' names are placed in the numbered, left-hand column. All of the Enabling Objectives of the program are placed across the top of the form, on the diagonal lines. This is usually done by indicating the TPO number, the EO number, and an abbreviation of the EO content. A blank Performance Sheet appears in Figure 6–4. A completed Performance Sheet can be found in Appendix C.

The attainment of objectives can be recorded in various ways. A simple √ can be used to indicate achievement. Some programmers have devised other recording methods, such as a date, which is placed in the appropriate box when the objective has been achieved. If pretesting is used, a code can be created to indicate if the client had the skills or knowledge of the objectives at the beginning of the program. Another variation of coding is some numerical system indicating degree of attainment; for instance, 3 = can do with difficulty, 2 = can do with occasional difficulty, 1 = can do consistently and correctly. The Performance Sheet enables the programmer to keep an easy record of the accomplishment of objectives. Later, in the evaluation stage, this form provides quick access to information about individual achievement as well as information about problematic objectives.

The Sequence Sheet is the tool that is used to assist the designer in achieving a well-balanced and interesting program. At each session, the nature of the clients, their age, their abilities and limitations, and their number should be taken into account. Attention span, learning style, and participation concerns are also important. Rarely would the staff address just one objective in a given session. Variety and balance are an issue when putting together a program. The Sequence Sheet is the place in a systems-designed program where these considerations are addressed. Each session should be designed with attention not only to covering the important aspects of the objectives, but also to the design of an interesting and balanced session as well.

The Sequence Sheet has one additional function and feature. The EOs and PMs of a program indicate the minimal material to be covered in the program. They indicate the basic areas of a program that the staff members have delineated for accountability purposes. The total program can address other areas in addition to the specified EOs and PMs. This additional material will be indicated on the Sequence Sheet. For example, in the racquetball skill program illustrated in Figures 6–2 and 6–3, the designer may wish to include a brief history of racquet ball, information about doubles play, and perhaps some advanced shots. However, the designer decides that this is not essential material and thus does not have Enabling Objectives, Performance Measures, or Content and Process Descriptions related to these three areas. In other words, the clients are not being evaluated on this material, nor is the instructor being held accountable for the learning of the material. The material will be presented, however. Thus, it will appear on the Sequence Sheet in some appropriate session or sessions. Essential material, or the basic material for which the program plans to be accountable, will always be included as Enabling Objectives. EOs are always evaluated, and thus the PM is written for each EO. Additional or supplemental material appears only on the Sequence Sheet. This

FIGURE 6–4

Performance Sheet

PROGRAM: _____ Relaxation _____

STAFF: _____

DATE: _____

ENABLING OBJECTIVES

NAMES

1.
2.
3.
4.
5.
6.
7.
8.
9.
10.
11.
12.
13.
14.
15.

indicates its inclusion in the program, although acquisition of the knowledge or skill is not essential and thus is not evaluated by a Performance Measure.

This concept of the inclusion of additional information or material on the Sequence Sheet also enables the design of more creative and balanced sessions and of the total program as well. Introductory material can be added to the first session; warm-ups or get-acquainted activities can be added to any session. A party or presentation to parents could be scheduled for a concluding session. The issue remains: all of this information appears on the Sequence Sheet. This important form maps out in advance the entire program as it is designed to be implemented.

The Sequence Sheet is a guideline or map to the implementation of a program. Since it is developed in the design stage of program planning, its content and time estimates are coming from the program designer's experience and best professional judgment. Obviously, errors in judgment may exist regarding the length of time that it takes to learn a given skill or acquire certain behaviors. Likewise, the sequence of activities in a given session or throughout the total program could be less than desirable. This information, however, will be discovered and documented as the program is implemented and evaluation information is recorded after each session (or at designated times). The existence of the Sequence Sheet, however, gives the program staff direction for implementation. The documentation and recording of information about the program's adequacy and usefulness give concrete information for program revision. The reader is encouraged to review the Sequence Sheet that appears in Appendix C for a more thorough understanding of the content and design of this important aspect of program development.

Sequence Sheet and Session Format Description for a Continuous Session Program

The Sequence Sheet as described in the previous pages has obvious advantages for programs that have a *set number of sessions*. Many public recreation programs for special populations fit this model of programming; for example, a ten-week program with one-and-a-half-hour sessions once a week. Some clinical or treatment facilities utilize this type of program structure as well. Many programs, however, especially in the clinical setting, are continuous. Clients are admitted and discharged from the facility at various times. Thus, the systems-designed therapeutic recreation programs must operate with a different structure than the carefully designed sequence plan for a program with a set number of sessions.

One method of scheduling the continuous program is to again set up a definite number of sessions for the program. The number of sessions (and number of weeks) would be less than the average stay of clients. The EOs, PMs, and Content and Process Descriptions would remain as before. The Sequence Sheet, however, would be designed so that there is no real beginning or end to the program, although each session would be designed to be as complete as possible in addressing a given objective. Clients are then referred to the program at any point in the sequence. They would stay in the program until they had participated in all of the sessions through one complete cycle. At that point, they would be referred to another program, remain in the targeted program for another cycle, or be terminated from the program. The Sequence Sheet is still used in such a program, primarily as a guide for the implementation of each session. Evaluation of objectives, as well as the evaluation of the entire program, is still very appropriate with this variation of the program structure.

This method of scheduling the continuous program has worked very well with many treatment programs as well as with leisure education programs. The program staff needs only to be aware of the need to orient new clients individually as they enter a given program and to introduce newcomers to the rest of the group. In programs of this type, some review and practice time can be built in for the objectives of previous sessions. Such practice or review time, however, should be individualized for the members of the program, based on how long they have been in the program and how many objectives they have been presented with previously.

Another method of scheduling the continuous program is to do away with the Sequence Sheet altogether and replace it with a *Session Format Description*. In this alternative method of sequencing, the program still has EOs, PMs, and CPDs. The program staff looks at the clients in the program and selects EOs, PMs, and CPDs for each session on a day-to-day basis. The staff selects the objectives to be addressed based on the composition of the group currently in attendance and according to common needs within the content of the program. This method of scheduling also allows for objectives to be selected and implemented based on the progress of individuals within the group. New objectives are only selected when the group is ready to move on.

When a continuous program uses this method of scheduling, the Sequence Sheet is not needed or appropriate. It is desirable to replace it with a Session Format Description. The Session Format Description describes the content of a basic session. It indicates the length and structure of the session but leaves the specific content open to selection by the staff. An example of an implementation plan using the Session Format Description is presented below. Additional information about the system is included to assist in the understanding of the total program.

Aspects of an Implementation Plan for a Program That Is Ongoing
Peer-Interaction Program for Developmentally Disabled and Emotionally Disturbed Children[1]

Agency and Population Description.   This program is designed for short-term residential treatment for emotionally disturbed and developmentally disabled children ages five to fifteen.

Program Purpose.   To help emotionally disturbed and developmentally disabled children to interact socially in play.

System.   The peer-interaction program is an *ongoing program* that meets in the gym four times each week for one hour each time. The program helps the participants

[1]Materials presented with permission of the designer, Mary Patricia McCreary

learn cooperative play. At any one time, there may be six to fifteen children involved; children move in and out of the group as they are admitted and discharged from the facility.

Program Referral and Basic Structure. When children are admitted to the facility, their social skills are assessed and, if need is indicated, they are assigned to the peer-interaction group. Games are introduced to the children over a period of several months. As the children grasp the rules of one or two games, another game is taught. Once half of the children can play half of the games when given external cues, new games are introduced. The session begins with a familiar game, and then a new game is taught. Sessions continue to include familiar games to help the continuity of the activity and to give the children continued success.

Terminal Program and Enabling Objectives

TPO 1.   To interact in a structured activity with assistance
   EO 1.   To play games according to the rules, with assistance
   EO 2.   To interact using verbal or nonverbal communication, with external cues
   EO 3.   To choose to play games with other children, with assistance

TPO 2.   To interact in a structured activity without external cues
   EO 1.   To play games according to the rules, without external cues
   EO 2.   To interact, using verbal or nonverbal communication, without external cues
   EO 3.   To choose to play games with other children, without assistance

TPO 3.   To interact with peers in a free-time activity with external cues
   EO 1.   To initiate a game, with external cues
   EO 2.   To complete a game, with external cues
   EO 3.   To interact, using verbal or nonverbal communication, with external cues
   EO 4.   To choose to play games with other children, with assistance

TPO 4.   To interact with peers in a free-time activity without external cues
   EO 1.   To initiate a game, without external cues
   EO 2.   To complete a game, without external cues
   EO 3.   To interact, using verbal or nonverbal communication, without external cues
   EO 4.   To choose to play games with other children, without assistance

Sample Session Format

1. Fifty minutes of teaching and playing games
   Duck, Duck Goose
   Stone
   Fox and Squirrel
   Flying Dutchman
2. Five minutes of quiet rest
3. Five minutes of clapping time
   Children who did a "super job" (meaning that they played the games with external cues and attended to the activity throughout to the extent that they did not disrupt the ongoing activity) that day will get clapped for. Children's names are called individually, and if they did a good job, they are clapped for. This gives the children reinforcement for a job well done!

Program Materials. The leader selects appropriate Enabling Objectives and corresponding Content and Process Description sheets from the program materials, based on the assessed level of the group. A full description of techniques for working on that EO is found in the process column of the CPD. Twenty-six games are provided in the appendix of the system. They are rated by level of difficulty in terms of interaction requirements.

Whether a program has a set number of sessions or is ongoing, a description of its implementation by session is needed. The Sequence Sheet or the Session Format Description provides this information. This information not only allows the program to be implemented correctly, but later allows for the utilization of evaluation information regarding the appropriateness of the sequencing and time allocations for various activities in relation to the achievement of objectives.

THE IMPLEMENTATION DESCRIPTION

In addition to the Sequence Sheet or the Session Format Description, a systems-designed program requires a specified *Implementation Description*. This description is general in nature and refers to the overall strategy for implementing the entire program. In systems-designed programs, the given objectives and their corresponding Content and Process Descriptions are to be implemented in a specific way for a designated population and with other specific identifiable inputs. When the program is implemented as planned, it should achieve the Performance Measures and thus accomplish the program's purpose. Although no system is perfect by design, this procedure does enable the collection of evaluation information, which can be used to make objective decisions regarding program revision. Thus, general implementation information is vital to the operation of the system. In a package of systems-designed program materials, the Implementation Description appears in the introductory section. The general Implementation Description contains information on the following areas: description of the clients for whom the program is designed, description of the staffing requirements, description of the required equipment and facilities, and a description of the number, length, and frequency of the program sessions. Additional or explanatory information can be added to the implementation plan as needed.

Description of the Population

A systems-designed program is developed for a specific population. The characteristics of that population are taken into account as Enabling Objectives and Performance Measures are written. Likewise, the Content and Process Descriptions are developed based on the characteristics of the selected population. The Sequence Sheet or Session Format Description takes into consideration the nature of the targeted population. Given this information, one would not expect the system to work with another population. Consequently, at the beginning, it is necessary to specify the intended population and the characteristics that are important relative to the specific program. Merely delineating that clients are mentally retarded or emotionally impaired is not sufficient. The designer describes actual limitations or abilities that are important. In some cases, prerequisite skills may also be described if they are important to the given program. An example of this would be basic swimming skills as a prerequisite for a canoeing class. Part of the population description is the identification of the age range and number of clients for whom the program is designed.

All of this information is important for the appropriate selection of clients for actual program involvement. Equally significant is the use of this information in the evaluation process. If a given client had difficulty with the achievement of objectives, the staff would first check to see if that client had the characteristics indicated for that program. Obviously, the program staff members would not revise a total program because of one client who was not within the intended target group; rather, they could individualize for that client within the program or refer the client to a more appropriate program.

An example of a *Description of Population* is found in the sample program system in Appendix C.

Number, Length, and Frequency of Sessions

At the beginning of the Implementation Description, some basic aspects of the program's structure are identified. The *number* of sessions, the *length* of session (for instance, one hour, forty-five minutes, one-and-a-half hours) and the frequency of sessions (number of sessions per week) are delineated. Although the number of sessions and length of sessions appear as part of the Sequence Sheet, it is useful to have this general information appear at the beginning of the program materials as well.

The determination of the number, length, and frequency of sessions is also an important aspect of decision making in program development. Client characteristics as well as program content are important factors to consider when making these decisions. For example, shorter sessions several times a week may be better for severely retarded individuals. Often, constraints of the agency or unit must be considered in making these decisions. The ideal implementation for a given program might be every day; however, consideration of other therapies may make this type of schedule impossible. The program must be compatible in its environment as well as appropriate for its objectives and clients. In other settings, such as community-based recreation programs for special populations, transportation may be an important issue. Thus, we often find these programs meeting once a week. Number, length, and frequency of sessions are determined after considering the population, the program content, and the constraints of the agency or unit. A description of *Number, Length, and Frequency of Sessions* is found in Appendix C.

When a designer decides to run a program for ten weeks for an hour and a half each week, the designer is indicating that the objectives and performance measures should be possible to achieve within that time. In evaluating such a program, the amount of time spent on each EO is compared to the results achieved. Discrepancies or program failures can then be realistically analyzed relative to the amount of time needed to accomplish the program content. Revisions based on data can then be made. For example, a program may require more sessions or longer sessions to produce the desired outcomes. In other cases, the content of the program may need to be reduced to allow for the achievement of the objectives within the time available.

Description of Staff

Systems-designed programs are planned with certain constraints and resources in mind. The *Implementation Plan* needs to identify these factors. Staffing requirements are central to the effective implementation and outcomes of the designed program. The Implementation Description identifies the number of staff members needed as well as the qualifications required. Here is an example of such a description for a bowling-instruction program for physically handicapped individuals.

Staff. One therapeutic recreation specialist with knowledge of physical disabilities, bowling, methods of adapting and modifying bowling equipment and procedures, and ability to use appropriate teaching techniques and physical-assistive techniques. One adult volunteer or staff assistant for each alley used.

The failure or less-than-satisfactory results of a program can often be attributed to the absence of the appropriately trained staff or numbers of staff as described in the Implementation Description. We would not revise the program materials in this case, but rather implement the program again with the designated trained staff, in order to determine the value or adequacy of the program.

There is one additional consideration in the category of staff description. Staff descriptions should be based on what the program really requires for implementation. To designate a position title—such as "therapeutic recreation specialist"—is not sufficient. The exact skills and knowledge needed by the staff to implement the program is the issue.

Facilities, Equipment, and Supplies

Systems-designed programs may require specific facilities, equipment and/or supplies. Part of the Implementation Description delineates the necessary facilities and objects. Although equipment and supplies for a given EO are identified on each corresponding Content and Process Description sheet, it is of value to have a master list of all needed items at the beginning of the program materials. Examples of *Facility, Equipment, and Supply Descriptions* are found in Appendix C.

SUMMARY

An implementation plan is vital to a systems-designed program. The program itself designates objectives and performance measures and details the activities and procedures needed to bring about the desired outcomes. However, the program materials do not identify many factors and conditions necessary for the program's operation. Thus, an implementation plan is needed. This plan has two parts: the general Implementation Description and the Sequence Sheet. The information presented in these two parts of a systems-designed program indicates the necessary implementation and operational components of the program.

7

Program Evaluation
Peg Connolly [1]

PURPOSE: To provide a rationale for, and information about, an evaluation process that can be used with systems-designed programs. The methodology presented makes possible data-based decisions for program revisions and improvements, and provides a foundation for making statements about program effectiveness.

Evaluation! The term frightens the practitioner and student. Some envision incomprehensible statistics. Others imagine computers and piles of print-outs. Yet others think about some insensitive outside team briefly surveying their programs and then pronouncing harsh judgments about the program or the staff's inadequacies. Many resent the concept of evaluation because they see it as interfering with vital direct client-service time. To others, it implies additional amounts of paper work. Although most practitioners and students agree that evaluation is needed to determine the outcomes of programs and to justify therapeutic recreation service, there still remains a fear of the evaluation process. Much of that fear is probably based on a lack of knowledge and skill related to evaluation techniques and procedures.

This chapter will provide some basic information about one program evaluation process. The method selected is interrelated with program design and implementation. It is meant to be conducted by the program's staff. Its purpose is the improvement of programs through adequate documentation of the program's operations and outcomes.

[1]The major portion of this chapter was written by Dr. Connolly and used with her permission. The authors acknowledge her expertise in the area of evaluation and express appreciation for her willingness to contribute this material.

DESCRIPTION OF EVALUATION

The word *evaluation* is used in many different ways, within many diverse contexts, and often on a variety of levels. As a result, it is hardly strange that confusion and misinterpretation surround its existence. However, common to all usage is the concept of judging the merit of some phenomenon. Program evaluation, aided by new techniques in evaluation research, is attempting to make the judging process more accurate and objective. This is accomplished by determining in advance the criteria by which to judge outcomes.[2] Systems-designed programs fall neatly into the category of entities that can be evaluated by certain predetermined criteria, since specific behavioral objectives and performance measures, which serve as standards for judgment, are inherent in program design. Evaluating a program that has been designed with a systems methodology is a much easier process than evaluating programs that have no predetermined or specifically stated outcome behaviors or procedures for achieving those outcomes.

The process is still not all that simple or automatic. Information (data) needs to be collected systematically and consistently, which allows the program staff to analyze findings later to make solid revision decisions. Collecting good information is dependent on asking appropriate questions and developing good instruments for the collection of information.

Evaluation in this chapter is viewed as a method of documenting program operations and outcomes to determine the strengths and weaknesses of the program. As previously stated, all evaluation approaches involve the judgment of the merit of some phenomenon. Two important aspects are inherent in this characterization of evaluation. One is that we can ascribe value or merit to programs that meet some standard of quality. The other is that all evaluation involves judgment. The collection of evaluation data aids both in clarifying the program's level of merit and in making factual judgments.

The evaluation procedure presented in this chapter employs the concepts and procedures of evaluation research. It is based specifically on two broad-based evaluation approaches, congruence models[3] and the utilization-focused model.[4] The congruence models of evaluation include the discrepancy evaluation model (DEM)[5] and Stake's countenance model.[6] Both of these models rely on the assumption that evaluation is an integral part of program planning and operations and that meaningful evaluation requires the specification of standards or behavioral objectives in the program design stage. Evaluation with congruence models is accomplished by

[2]Carol H. Weiss, *Evaluation Research: Methods of Assessing Program Effectiveness* (Englewood Cliffs, N.J.: Prentice-Hall, Inc., 1972), p. 1.

[3]Don E. Gardner, "Five Evaluation Frameworks: Implications for Decision Making in Higher Education," *Journal of Higher Education*, 48 (1977), pp. 571–593.

[4]Michael Quinn Patton, *Utilization-Focused Evaluation* (Beverly Hills: Sage Publications, 1978).

[5]Diane Kyker Yavorsky, *Discrepancy Evaluation: A Practitioner's Guide* (Charlottesville, Va.: University of Virginia, Evaluation Research Center, 1976).

[6]Robert E. Stake, "The Countenance of Educational Evaluation," *Teachers College Record*, 68, no. 7 (1967), pp. 523–540.

analyzing program outcomes and processes that occur during actual implementation in comparison to the intended standards and objectives in the program design.

The utilization-focused evaluation model focuses on broader concerns than meeting standards of design. This model is designed to evaluate intended as well as unintended program operations and outcomes in order to collect information that is useful to program designers and administrators. While being able to judge how adequately the design standards function in yielding planned outcomes, the utilization-focused model directs us to question the initial design. Here we look for areas that may be added or deleted from the design, based on evaluation information. More importantly, we evaluate because we intend to "utilize" the findings. We do not stop at our judgment of program merit, but we go to the point of using evaluation data to direct program revision toward improving the program design.

A plethora of evaluation procedures, models, and approaches is available. The evaluation procedure presented here is based on the foregoing two evaluation approaches in view of the program evaluation needs in therapeutic recreation service. This procedure was developed primarily with systems-designed programs in mind, along with its feasible use as an internal evaluation process within therapeutic recreation services. Prior to examination of this specific procedure, an explanation of evaluation concerns and premises will be presented.

THE PURPOSES AND FUNCTIONS OF EVALUATION

What does judging the worth or merit mean in terms of a program? *First, evaluation, systematically conducted, leads to information related to program improvement.* Most of us want to know where and how to improve what we do. Observing our programs for the purpose of improving services is a reasonable and justifiable expenditure of time and effort. Evaluation of a systems-designed program produces explicit information about what revisions need to be made for program improvement.

The second major purpose of evaluation is related to judging the effectiveness of programs. Programs designed with a systems methodology have clearly stated objectives, along with specific procedures for achieving them. These procedures, accompanied by systematic evaluation, allow professionals to state accurately the effects or outcomes of their programs. Evaluation of this type does not rely merely on intuitive feelings or on random success stories, but rather on accurate, data-based statements of achievement. For example, stating that "80 percent of the clients reached the designated objectives" is a definitive and supportable report of the program's operation. Although a program may not prove to be totally effective, at least criteria can be established and decisions made based on actual performance compared with predetermined standards. Objective judgment and accurate reporting related to program outcomes and procedures are necessary responsibilities of professionals in the human-services fields. Evaluation allows for this level of documentation and accountability.

Whether evaluation is conducted for program revision and improvement or for judging program effectiveness, the systems approach to program planning used with evaluation serves the vital function of facilitating decision making. Information is systematically gathered on major aspects of design and operation, which enables objective decisions to be made. Programs can be expanded, maintained, revised, or terminated. Such decisions, which in the past have often been made without adequate evidence, can now be based on actual program performance.

RATIONALE FOR EVALUATING PROGRAMS

Evaluation takes time. It requires paper work. It adds additional responsibilities to program implementers and administrators. "So why bother?" some professionals might ask. The answer comes back loud and clear—accountability! All kinds of human services are having to justify their existence. Accountability and justification go hand in hand. People want to know the reason for programs and their effects.

Most concerns about evaluation have arisen in relation to accountability demands placed on human-service delivery systems over the past twenty years. Accountability has become a more dominant issue as fiscal restraints have placed limits on service delivery. As budgets have become tighter, there has been a greater demand to justify that the services we deliver are accomplishing their purposes in the most effective and efficient manner. In fact, accountability is a relative term that indicates the professional service deliverer can justify that program services and activities are effective and efficient in relation to outcomes achieved and service dollars expended. The accountability issue permeates our practice on every level. We can see its effect in the delineation of standards by the profession and standards from outside bodies to the profession. Issues such as quality assurance are certainly representative of the accountability concerns.

Often, evaluation is perceived as one method of demonstrating accountability. If an administrator tells the practitioner to justify why a specific program is being delivered, the major tool available to accomplish this request is usually an evaluation of some sort. Certainly, the administrator is going to respond more favorably to some facts and figures that substantiate the practitioner's justification of accountable program services than to a philosophical argument about why the program is good for the clients. When accountability is the issue, hard data seem to be the most powerful response, and evaluation activities are tools for gathering these hard data.

Four groups of people are usually interested in accountability. Although their interests differ, they each have a concern and a right to hold therapeutic recreation services accountable.

Clients

The individuals who receive therapeutic recreation services are the primary group to whom we need to be accountable. All too often they are the last ones to understand why they are scheduled for certain programs or what outcomes should result from their participation. Systems-designed and evaluated programs can resolve these issues. Clearly stated objectives and performance measures enable clients to know what is expected of them and how well they are doing. Program evaluation can be used to review and revise programs continuously, so we can be reasonably sure that clients are receiving the best services possible.

The Funding Source

Funding of therapeutic recreation services comes from a variety of sources: taxpayers, insurance companies, direct fees and charges, grants through foundations and agencies, as well as from voluntary contributions. The funds are controlled, managed, and distributed by the sponsoring agency. Administrators at different levels are accountable for the allocation and expenditure of the funds. Tighter controls, seemingly fewer resources, and more demands for services describe the contemporary agency. Justification for services and accountability are demanded in such a situation. Administrators want to know why programs are needed, what exact objectives and procedures will be employed, and how program effectiveness will be determined. Again, systems-designed and evaluated programs meet the requirements for this level of justification and accountability. Program results are easily determined and can be objectively recorded and reported.

The Therapeutic Recreation Profession

One of the characteristics of a profession is that there exist established procedures related to its area of service. In the past, therapeutic recreators have had a difficult time delineating such procedures. Systems-designed and evaluated programs contribute greatly to this goal. Over time, information can be gathered and distributed that can standardize procedures. Therapeutic recreation specialists can say, "This program, with these objectives, implemented in this way, produces these results." Program evaluation is obviously needed to substantiate and support such statements. The profession stands to gain credibility and respect through such efforts. We are accountable to ourselves for the development and utilization of professional procedures. Program planning and evaluation methods are among the procedures that need standardization.

The profession of therapeutic recreation has made great strides in terms of standardization and accountability. We now have two documents that guide internal accountability demands and procedures. *Standards of Practice for Therapeutic Recreation Service*[7] and *Guidelines for the Administration of Therapeutic Recreation Services in Clinical and Residential Facilities*[8] specify accountability expectations in practice. The overall goal of meeting these professional standards is to demonstrate quality care to clients. Demonstration of accountability and quality care may best be accomplished through evaluation and documentation.

[7]National Therapeutic Recreation Society, *Standards of Practice for Therapeutic Recreation Service*. (Alexandria, Va.: National Recreation and Park Association, 1980).

[8]National Therapeutic Recreation Society, *Guidelines for the Administration of Therapeutic Recreation Services in Clinical and Residential Facilities* (Alexandria, Va.: National Recreation and Park Association, 1980).

As we look closely at these professional service standards, we see that the primary mandate is to document that the intent or purpose of each standard is occurring in practice. From the traditional sense of standards, we can see that service practices are not bound by rigorous or ridiculous criteria of the extent to which the standard is to be met. The standards set forth are minimal and open to a variety of evaluative approaches. There is the freedom to address each standard based on agency criteria or norms for client services within minimal time line demands. Therefore, the major responsibility is to develop evaluative approaches and document evidence that each standard is met in service delivery.

External Accrediting Groups

The accountability demands faced by human-service deliverers are best exemplified in the standards of external accrediting bodies, such as the Joint Commission for the Accreditation of Hospitals (JCAH), the Commission for the Accreditation of Rehabilitation Facilities (CARF), and other similar groups. Today, our accountability demands extend far beyond our profession, our clients, and funding sources to interdisciplinary quality assurance concerns in relation to specific service settings and facilities.

As you review the standards of any one of these external accrediting groups, you can quickly determine that the demand is often for evaluation to justify adherence to standards. Demonstrating quality assurance is the overriding purpose of using service delivery standards. While quality assurance and evaluation are not definitively synonymous, program and service delivery evaluation comprise a large portion of demonstrating quality assurance. Accurate and effective evaluation approaches and procedures, including specific program evaluation, are essential to the development of a comprehensive quality assurance plan. While no one evaluation effort will address the overall quality assurance concern, no comprehensive quality-assurance plan is possible without adequate evaluation efforts. Evaluation and quality assurance go hand in hand and have become a primary concern in the delivery of therapeutic recreation services.

TYPES OF EVALUATION

Two types of evaluation are related to program planning and decision making. Although they serve different functions, each contributes to the total process.

Formative Evaluation

Formative evaluation refers to evaluation efforts and processes that are conducted while a program is being planned or during its implementation. *The purpose of formative evaluation is to improve the program's effectiveness.*[9] Data are collected to help decision makers revise and improve the

---

[9]Michael Scriven, "The Methodology of Evaluation," in *Perspectives of Curriculum Evaluation,* ed. Ralph Tyler, Robert M. Gagne, and Michael Scriven (Chicago: Rand McNally and Company, AERA Monograph Series on Curriculum Evaluation, no. 1, 1967), pp. 39–83.

program. The revisions can be made at any time: before the program is actually put into operation, during the implementation, or after a program is concluded. Sophisticated formative evaluation plans might call for the collection of data and revisions at all three stages. Regardless of the depth of the evaluation, the concern is the same: gathering information to further develop and improve the program's effectiveness. Much of the evaluation discussed in this chapter is formative in nature.

Summative Evaluation

Summative evaluation is conducted on a program in operation to determine its value. *Its purpose is to judge the program's overall effectiveness.*[10] Normally, summative evaluation requires experimental or quasi-experimental designs with control group or comparative studies between programs with similar goals but with different procedures, in order to make judgments about the best or most efficient way of conducting a program. In therapeutic recreation, we rarely have the time or resources for such in-depth comparative studies. It is important to note, however, that statements about a program's effectiveness can be made from data collected during formative evaluation. The same evaluation questions, asked for the purpose of improving and revising systems-designed programs, can also yield information necessary for making basic judgments about a program's effectiveness.

PRACTICAL CONCERNS ABOUT EVALUATION

Practicality must be an issue in program evaluation. Four concerns emerge as useful in this regard. First, the evaluation needs to be *efficient.* In other words, the evaluation should take as little time as possible. Evaluation, after all, is not the primary focus of therapeutic recreators; service to clients is. Consequently, any evaluation effort should be possible within appropriate time considerations.

Second, program evaluation should be *feasible.* The staff members who conduct the evaluation must have the necessary skills. To be meaningful, evaluation efforts require the support of the staff and administrators. Actions that are subverted or resisted destroy the intent and value of program evaluation. Part of feasibility includes the willingness of administrators to allow the time for evaluation efforts as well as to provide other necessary resources, such as secretarial help and financial assistance.

Third, meaningful program evaluation must be *appropriate within the context of the setting.* Agency attitudes and philosophies must be considered, as well as operational priorities. No one is going to get excited about program evaluation if it disrupts the entire agency schedule and operation on a day-to-day basis. This does not mean evaluation is not important; it does mean that it needs to be tempered with good judgment and some public relations efforts.

Fourth, evaluation should be *useful.* When evaluation is done because of professional standards, external standards, or agency requirements, and

[10]Ibid.

is not directed toward improving services, it can become a moot activity. Evaluation of service delivery cannot be viewed as an end in itself. It is a means to an end: a procedure to collect useful information to be used to improve services and programs. It can become easy to collect a great deal of evaluation data that have little or no functional use for the practitioner. However, this is a frivolous waste of valuable time and resources. On the other hand, some do not want to know what is weak or less than effective in programs and services, for that may practically mean more work in the revision of programs. Nevertheless, we can neither afford to collect evaluation information that is not useful to our services nor to ignore the use of evaluative findings that disconcert our professional egos or require remediative actions to correct.

CHARACTERISTICS OF PROGRAM EVALUATION

Basic program evaluation, as presented in this chapter, has a variety of characteristics that are important to identify and that refine our understanding of the term.

Program evaluation is part of *program planning*. Sequentially, the steps are to—

1. conceptualize the specific program;
2. design the program, including terminal program objectives, enabling objectives, performance measures, and the content and process for each EO;
3. develop the implementation plan; and
4. design the evaluation plan.

Determining at the outset what information, procedures, and levels of evaluation are needed or desired simplifies the total process and makes it more relevant. Effective program evaluation cannot be conducted after a program is terminated. Data need to be collected throughout the program, and that means that the plans for its collection must be determined and developed prior to implementation.

Program evaluation is also an ongoing process during *program operation*. The basic evaluation questions normally asked in program evaluation are ones that require continuous attention. The most useful data are collected after each session. No staff member should be expected to remember details about some activity or session that occurred ten weeks before. Useful and accurate information is best obtained as the program is implemented on a regular basis.

Program evaluation is part of the *implementation strategy*. Time needs to be built into the implementation schedule for the required evaluation tasks. For some programs, evaluation of progress toward achievement of objectives is a regular part of each session. For other programs, progress toward objectives is scheduled intermittently or at the end of the entire program. Thus, one aspect of evaluation, documentation of the achievement of objectives, takes place during actual program implementation.

In addition to monitoring the achievement of objectives, actual program time is also spent observing other aspects of the program's operation. Watching various activities for their appropriateness in contributing to attainment of the objectives and monitoring time spent on various activities are illustrations of such evaluation concerns. This time should be considered as part of implementation and operation of the program.

The evaluation procedure described here is designed to be conducted by the person who implements the program. This is referred to as *internal evaluation*. There is some controversy over the issue of internal versus external evaluation. External evaluation involves the use of an expert who is not involved in the program or, in many cases, is from outside the agency. However, few agencies have the resources to hire outside evaluators. Most agencies do not have an evaluation expert on their staff either. Thus, if evaluation of programs is to be conducted regularly, internal evaluation procedures must be used. The procedure presented in this chapter is designed for use by program staff members and is, therefore, considered within the responsibilities of the professional therapeutic recreation specialist. Some additional knowledge and skills may need to be acquired by the therapeutic recreation specialist in order to conduct appropriate internal program evaluation.

Program evaluation has many forms, levels of sophistication, and methodologies. The procedure suggested in this chapter is selected for its implementation feasibility by therapeutic recreation specialists, its compatibility with systems-designed programs, and the usefulness of its results for revision decisions and preliminary statements of program effectiveness. The references suggested at the end of this chapter supply the reader with resources for other evaluation procedures and information.

EVALUATION MODELS

Discrepancy Evaluation

One of the methods of program evaluation we favor is called *discrepancy evaluation*.[11] In simplest terms, discrepancy evaluation compares actual outcomes with desired or planned outcomes. The area of difference, or discrepancy, between the real and intended outcomes isolates the area for investigation. It leads to the identification of factors that can be changed to improve the program. Answers to questions relevant to the components of the program's design and operation help to explain the discrepancies. Discrepancy evaluation is concerned with three areas: inputs, process, and outcomes (see Figure 7–1).

Input. Input refers to necessary people and objects involved in the program. Normally, the input of a therapeutic recreation program is comprised of (1) staff, (2) clients, (3) supplies, (4) facilities, and (5) funding.

---

[11]Information presented on discrepancy evaluation is adapted from two evaluation models and approaches, primarily taken from Stake, "Countenance of Evaluation," pp. 523–540, and Yavorskv, *Discrepancy Evaluation*, pp. 47–84.

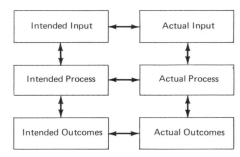

FIGURE 7–1
Discrepancy Evaluation Model

The program and implementation plans, as presented in previous chapters, describe the need to specify the characteristics of input in the design stage. Later, during evaluation, the question will be asked, "Was the program implemented as designed?" The actual input will be compared to the intended input. If there is a discrepancy between the two, it may well explain why desired outcomes were not achieved. For example, suppose that the program staff did not have the required training and that certain staff skills were necessary to enable clients to achieve the program objectives. This discrepancy could explain deficient program results and point to an area of program improvement; for instance, provide the necessary staff training or select staff members who have the training. If this were the true cause of the problem and if staff changes were made or training provided, one would expect the program to come closer to its desired performance the next time it was implemented.

The clients are considered to be input. Programs are designed for a specific group of individuals. When there is a discrepancy between the actual clients involved in a program and the description of clients for whom the program was intended, program revisions or a different screening procedure may be in order.

Designated supplies, facilities, and funding are also considered input. Discrepancy between actual and intended outcomes can often be explained by investigating differences in these areas.

Process. Process refers to the actions and activities described in the program plan. A systems-designed program specifies the content and process that are to be used to achieve the program's objectives. In the evaluation, a careful investigation of the process is undertaken. There are two major areas of concern. First, were the designated content and process followed? Second, were the activities and processes that were implemented appropriate and useful in achieving the objectives? Here again is the concept of intended versus actual. If a program was not implemented as designed, one can understand its failure to achieve objectives. Sometimes implementation problems have nothing to do with the program per se. Other priorities at a treatment facility, for example, could prevent sessions from taking place or disrupt the operation of a given session. In this case, the evaluator can explain the failure of the program but may not need to make program revisions. In other cases, the program may not have been feasible to implement as designed because of problems in the program's design; for example, there was too much or too little content in a given session. Here the evaluator has specific information to work with in actual program revision.

Part of the process of evaluation is to investigate the activities and interactions designed for the program. The designer wants to know how well they worked and what improvements can be made. The program staff is, therefore, asked to keep an account of the session's process in order to provide information for revision. The best ideas of the designer can prove inadequate in the actual operation of a program. Much of the task of evaluation, consequently, is checking out and attempting to improve the content and process of the program, thus increasing the probability of achieving desired outcomes.

Outcomes. Intended outcomes are the Terminal Program Objectives and Enabling Objectives of a program. The designer selects them with great consideration and formulates the Performance Measures to assess the achievement of the desired outcomes. In the evaluation process, the implementer checks and records the progress toward the attainment of the objectives. Usually, the first evaluation question asked is, "Did the clients achieve the objectives?" Normally, some standard is predetermined for a program, such as, "We will consider this program effective if 80 percent of the clients reach 90 percent of the objectives." Checking intended outputs against program results provides the necessary information for judging program effectiveness.

The gap between actual and intended outcomes is equally important for revision decisions. The question, "Did we reach our desired level of attainment of objectives?" must be followed with the question, "What aspects of the program contributed to, or hindered, the achievement of the objectives?" The evaluator wants to know precisely what parts of the program were good or bad. Only this type of information will lead to solid revisions. It is always possible for clients to reach objectives by chance or even despite the program. The program designer is, consequently, interested in knowing if the designated activities and process of the program contributed to the achievement of the objectives. Questions about why the program did or did not work focus on inputs and process of the program.

The discrepancy evaluation model depends on well-constructed programs that show logical relationships between input, process, and outcomes. Thus, program results can be compared to the intended plan, and changes can be made about its design and operation.

Utilization-focused Evaluation

Because of the identification of concerns related to the lack of use and the inherent lack of usefulness of many evaluation approaches, a new area of feasible, service-delivery–oriented approaches to evaluation have evolved. One of these approaches is the Utilization-focused Evaluation approach (UFE). Rather than being focused on highly technical, rigorous research methods of evaluation, Utilization-focused Evaluation places a dominant emphasis on the usefulness of evaluation information collected. This is not to say that Utilization-focused Evaluation has no concern for appropriate methodology; rather, the main concern is for useful evaluation findings. A simplistic evaluation methodology is preferable to a rigorous research design if the information generated from the simplistic design is highly useful for program improvement.

The Utilization-focused Evaluation approach offers a more realistic guide to program evaluation and is especially adaptable for use by the internal evaluator. This evaluation approach differs from early evaluation models in several ways. First, it emphasizes formative rather than summative evaluation concerns. This is especially valuable to therapeutic recreation services. Merely knowing the overall effectiveness of a program in terms of outcomes does not give sufficient information on how the program might be revised and improved. The focus on formative evaluation efforts directed toward program improvement is of paramount importance, especially in the early stages of program development.

Second, Utilization-focused Evaluation focuses on the nature of evaluation information in relation to the informational needs of program decision-makers. In other words, what does the program designer want, or need, to know about the program? While an administrator may juggle numbers to allocate resources, the programmer needs descriptive data not only to identify program strengths and weaknesses but also to do something about correcting such weaknesses.

Third, utilization approaches focus on the applicability of methodology to both the nature of evaluation concerns and the nature of the applied program setting. In studying evaluative approaches and procedures, it is fairly easy either to develop a fear of methods or to become a methods snob. We have been advised to accept experimental design as the epitomy of quality evaluation. However, in reality, any one of a number of methods is appropriate, depending on the nature of evaluation and the real-world constraints of applied settings. Utilization-focused Evaluation provides "methods flexibility" as opposed to "methods blinders."

THE FORMATIVE PROGRAM EVALUATION PROCEDURE

The Formative Program Evaluation Procedure (FPEP) was designed specifically for therapeutic recreation service programs.[12] It was developed in view of the current philosophical position of the National Therapeutic Recreation Society and is to be used with programs in either the treatment (rehabilitation) or leisure education areas. While it can be used with any well-developed therapeutic recreation program, it is most suitable for use with systems-designed programs, as described in previous chapters. The following description and guidelines for using this procedure will be presented in relation to systems-designed therapeutic recreation programs.

The purpose of the FPEP is to collect evaluation information during the

[12]Margaret L. Connolly, "Analysis of a Formative Program Evaluation Procedure for Therapeutic Recreation Services" (unpublished doctoral dissertation, University of Illinois at Urbana-Champaign, 1981).

implementation of the program in order to identify program strengths and weaknesses to revise and improve the program. In order to accomplish this purpose, the FPEP provides an evaluation design with questions and concerns related directly to the adequacy of therapeutic recreation programs. Any good evaluation activity will include the selection of an appropriate design, development of an effective and efficient evaluation plan, the appropriate implementation of evaluation strategies and techniques, and will culminate in the use of evaluation findings for the revision and improvement of the program. All of these evaluation procedures have been incorporated into the development of the FPEP. Rather than starting from scratch, the practitioner need only operationalize or prepare the FPEP for use with one's specific program.

As soon as the program plan is developed but prior to implementation, the evaluation plan should be developed for using the FPEP on a specific therapeutic recreation program. There are two primary evaluation concerns to be addressed in the evaluation of a systems-designed therapeutic recreation program:

1. How well does the program function in actual implementation?
2. What outcomes do clients attain as a consequence of participating in the program?

These two evaluation concerns relate directly to the purpose of the FPEP evaluation procedure. Again, if the purpose is to identify program strengths and weaknesses in order to revise and improve the program, then information is needed about both how the program functions and whether or not clients attain the planned outcomes of the program.

With systems-designed programs, program objectives are developed to meet certain identified client needs. Program process and content are selected to provide clients with the opportunity to attain the developed objectives. The use of resources and the structuring and organization of program content and process also play a significant role in whether or not clients attain, or at least have the opportunity to attain, program objectives. In order to evaluate a systems-designed therapeutic recreation program, all of these issues must be taken into account.

Too often, we are most concerned with only one issue in evaluation; that is, whether or not program participants succeed in accomplishing program objectives. This is certainly very important in terms of justifying our services, but just knowing what objectives are accomplished does not give the program developer enough information to really improve and revise the program. Therefore, in order to collect useful evaluation information that will provide the therapeutic recreation practitioner with adequate direction to improve and revise the program, the evaluation design must take into account information regarding both the implementation of the program and the outcomes of the program. Analysis of information in both of these areas of evaluation concern will lead to revision of the program plan, including revision of program objectives, program content, processes, resources, structure, and organization.

The program evaluation plan, then, is developed after the program plan and implementation plan are completed. The purpose of the evaluation plan is to prepare a systematic and comprehensive strategy for evaluating the program. The FPEP is one such strategy or procedure, which is designed specifically for the internal evaluation of therapeutic recreation programs. A variety of instruments in the FPEP are designed to collect evaluation information about program operations and outcomes during implementation. In order to develop a specific program evaluation plan, the practitioner needs only to decide on how to appropriately apply the FPEP instruments and procedures to the specific situation. Details concerning possible applications and variations will be provided throughout the discussion of the FPEP.

A number of evaluation instruments or tools have been developed as part of the FPEP. Some of these instruments—the Post-session Report Form, Performance Progress Instrument, and the Client Performance Sheet—are used to collect evaluation information during program implementation. Other instruments—such as the Client Profile Form, Post-session Analysis Form, and the Modifications Analysis Form—are used to summarize and interpret evaluation data in order to revise and improve the program. First, each instrument will be described in terms of what it is designed to do. Then an explanation of how each instrument is used in the evaluation procedure will be presented.

Evaluating Program Operations

One instrument, the Post-session Report Form, is designed to examine the actual functioning of the program in day-to-day operations. The overall evaluation concern is: how well does the program function when it is actually implemented? The overall concern is broken down into specific evaluation questions about the program, including the following:

1. Was the session implemented as designed? If not, what changes or modifications were made?
2. How appropriate were the activities (content) used in relation to program objectives addressed in this session?
3. How appropriate were staff interaction or intervention strategies (process) in this session?
4. Did the sequence of activities appear to be logical and appropriate?
5. Was a sufficient amount of time available for the objectives and activities planned for this session?
6. Were required materials, supplies, equipment, and facilities available for this session?
7. Was an adequate number of staff members, appropriately trained, involved in this session as planned?
8. What was the nature of client and staff involvement in this session?
9. What unanticipated events or outcomes occurred in this session that were not planned in the original design?

It is important to understand both the rationale behind each of these questions and the aspects of the program that will be examined to answer each question throughout program implementation. As you can see from these questions, the major program aspects to be evaluated during day-to-day operations are implementation of program design, appropriateness of activities, appropriateness of staff interactions and interventions, sequencing of activities, sufficiency of time, availability of resources, staffing, nature of client and staff interactions, and the nature of unplanned or unanticipated program events. Just as these aspects are combined in a program design to create a viable and logical program-delivery approach, so too must they be examined during implementation to evaluate whether the combination of aspects is in effect efficient and appropriate to accomplish the program's purpose. Each of the foregoing evaluation questions will be examined individually in relation to related program aspects. This will present a better picture of what is actually involved in evaluating program functioning during implementation.

Information Examined on Program Operations. First, *implementation of the program design* relates to a concern about whether or not what was planned in the program design was actually implemented. As we design specific programs, we include our knowledge and judgments about what the needs of our service recipients are and the best way or approach to address those needs given the mission and resources of our particular environment or agency setting. In order to evaluate this program aspect during program implementation, we need to examine how the program design is put into action. Is it implemented as we planned? Did we make changes or modifications to the design during implementation? Within this area, the programmer is dealing with two basic issues: (1) whether or not the program is put into action as planned and (2) if it is not implemented as designed, what is the nature of, and rationale for, the implemented changes or modifications? This information will be essential in interpreting how well the program has functioned and in determining specifically how the program will be revised and improved.

Evaluating the *appropriateness of activities* (content) within the implemented session allows the programmer to look specifically at the nature and content of planned activities in terms of the objectives they are designed to address. It is hoped that during program design, consideration was given to the logical appropriateness of activities. During implementation, the programmer collects data on activity appropriateness in relation to objectives by observing how well activities operate, how well they are received by program participants, and how logical they appear to be in actual operations.

Staff interventions and interactions (process) are selected for the program design based on their appropriateness to the nature of planned activities, the needs of program participants, and their relevance to the achievement of program objectives. During program implementation, we want to examine how well the planned interventions and interactions actually work. Are they appropriate during implementation? Are there other, more appropriate interventions that are being, or that could be, used in relation to specific program session activities? Are they the most appropriate in relation to the actual participants in this program, or are there more appropriate methods available for program participants? We want to examine closely what is done during implementation of intervention and interactions to refine this area.

Sequence of activities within the program session can be a significant determinant of whether or not the program functions adequately or, perhaps more importantly, of whether or not program participants attain objectives. If the program session is not running smoothly, we may wish to attempt a variation in activity sequencing. Another sequencing issue we may wish to examine is whether adequate segments of warm-up, transition, or wrap-up activities are included within the session sequence sheet. Evaluating this program aspect can yield data that provide direct implications for program revision and improvement. Collecting evaluation information on how logical and appropriate is the sequence of session activities will allow for improvements in this area.

Behavior change and subsequent learning through therapeutic recreation programs takes time. When a systems-designed program is planned, judgments are made as to a scheduled amount of time for each program session (see previous chapters for a description of the Sequence Sheet). Session activities are then sequenced and structured within this planned, and somewhat arbitrary, time pattern on the program's Sequence Sheet. It is during program implementation that we must evaluate the *sufficiency of time* planned for participant achievement of objectives addressed within each session. The assumption is not that participants should acquire all planned session objectives during initial exposure, but rather that, given the objectives and activities planned for each session, there was sufficient time allowed for such within the session. Some of the judgments about sufficiency of time planned will depend on the nature of participants involved, and some of the judgments will depend on the nature of activity content to be presented. Both areas should be examined in making judgments about the sufficiency of time allotments within sessions.

Often times, the majority of our program planning efforts are focused on the development of objectives and program content and process. *Availability of resources* is one program aspect that deserves systematic examination during implementation. The actual availability of materials, supplies, equipment, and facilities within the program session must be examined along with the appropriateness of these resources during implementation. Lack of planned resources can seriously hinder the achievements of program participants. Similarly, inclusion of inappropriate resources can be detrimental. Specific evaluation information on both of these resource issues is necessary to improve resource selection decisions for program success.

Staffing patterns or issues are another program aspect to be evaluated during implementation. It is important that an adequate number of appropriately trained staff members be involved in the program session as planned. Here both practical and ideal concerns may be examined during implementation. Often times, we make professional judgments as to the desirable ratio of staff members to program participants. Included in these judgments is a realization of staff availability. While a smaller participant-staff ratio may be desirable within a program, such ratios may not be feasible because of staff availability. On the other hand, some programs may not be safely implemented without an adequate number of staff members. Likewise, during actual program operations, we can get a better idea if the staff is adequately trained for a specific program, if additional or specialized training is necessary, or if staff members without highly specialized skills may adequately conduct the program. Evaluation data on staffing concerns will be collected during program implementation and provide useful information for future staffing decisions in regard to the program.

The previously discussed program aspects are very specific, and directed toward predetermined concerns about the efficiency and effectiveness of the systems-designed program. The two remaining program aspects are a bit more general in nature and may not be as apparent as a concern until the program is actually implemented. Again, the program designer assumes that the program plan has been carefully developed to insure positive results, but program functioning cannot be put to the true test until it is implemented. During actual implementation, some unanticipated events or outcomes may occur. Additionally, all of the best planning and structuring of the design will not yield an accurate description of the nature of actual staff and participant interactions within the program until such interactions occur. The Post-session Report Form includes evaluation questions on both these areas in order to collect data on spontaneous, unplanned interactions and events, both positive and negative, as the final areas of concern to be documented during program implementation.

The programmer documents descriptions of *the nature of participant and staff interactions* throughout program implementation. The initial evaluation question is not specific as to whether such interactions are positive or negative, appropriate or inappropriate, authoritarian or participatory, although these may be issues of concern to particular programmers. The general intent is to document descriptions of what is observed in participant and staff interactions within program operations. Some programmers have focused on the level of participatory involvement, while others have focused on resistiveness and/or cooperation. The general descriptions regarding this program aspect may be analyzed and interpreted based on issues that are discovered in interactions through implementation.

Similarly, one cannot plan to observe or evaluate *unplanned or unanticipated program events or outcomes* in a specific sense. However, concerted efforts should be made to document any unplanned or unanticipated events or outcomes at the conclusion of each program session. This idea of evaluating unplanned or unanticipated events relates to the parody of evaluation. Sometimes it is difficult to know what specific effects we are looking for until the event or action is completed. Saying, "That was good," or "That was bad," are past-tense analyses possible only after we have experienced the event. And yet, if we do not *plan* to collect some general data on *unplanned events* that may occur, our judgments of such will be based on memory, which is too easily distorted. The parody, then, is that if you do not plan to evaluate the unexpected, you will not be able to analyze accurately the results of unanticipated events or outcomes, which may justifiably be planned for in program revision and improvement.

A little more discussion of what is meant by unplanned or unanticipated events or outcomes seems worthy of attention here. What is an unanticipated event or outcome of a specific program? A case in point might be a skill-development program. The emphasis of program outcomes is on learning the skills of a sport or game—for example, softball skills for adult developmentally disabled individuals. An unanticipated or unplanned outcome may be discovered in that a strong peer culture develops in this specific program. While social and peer interaction skills were not indicated in program objectives, these outcomes may evolve during program implementation. If these unanticipated outcomes were considered important for this group of clients, they might be incorporated into the revised program design as specified program objectives. In another instance, staff members and participants may develop a sense of respect for one another in a leisure education group focused on the development of leisure attitudes and values. While not initially planned as an outcome, the program objectives may be revised to include an emphasis on mutual respect. The possibilities are unending if we tune our evaluative senses toward the actions and interactions that occur in program implementation. We must look for more than what is planned; in this case, to remain cognizant of the many possibilities, both positive and negative.

In summary, the Post-session Report Form is designed to collect evaluation information on how well the systems-designed program functions during actual implementation, including an examination of program aspects such as implementation of program design, appropriateness of activities, appropriateness of staff interventions and interactions, sequence of activities, sufficiency of time, availability of resources, staffing, nature of participant and staff interactions, and the nature of unplanned or unanticipated program events. The actual Post-session Report Form instrument is shown in Figure 7–2.

Using the Post-session Report Form. You will notice in Figure 7–2 that two types of evaluation data are required to complete the Post-session Report Form. The majority of questions require a simple quantitative or numerical response in the form of a "yes" or "no" or a rating of 1 to 5 on a Likert Scale. All questions require the documentation of qualitative or descriptive information in relation to the numerical response. This feature of collecting both qualitative and quantitative information was built into the form for two very specific reasons. First, *quantitative* or numerical information aids in the summary and analysis of evaluation data for all sessions of the program. Ratings for all program sessions can be summarized, and yield an average figure for a particular program aspect. For example, in question 3, regarding staff interactions and intervention strategies, at the end of ten program sessions, the programmer can add up all ratings, divide by ten, and come up with an average rating or value for this particular program aspect.

FIGURE 7–2 The Formative Program Evaluation Procedure

Post-session Report Form

DIRECTIONS: A POST-SESSION REPORT FORM is to be completed at the conclusion of each regularly scheduled program session. Please provide as much detailed information as possible for each question below.

PROGRAM TITLE: _____

SESSION No: _____ SESSION DATE: _____
NUMBER OF CLIENTS PRESENT: _____

NUMBER ABSENT: _____ NAMES OF ABSENT CLIENTS: _____

1a. Was the session implemented as designed? (circle one)

Yes (skip to question #2) ... 1

No 2

1b. If no, please describe the changes or modifications made during implementation and the reasons for making changes:

CHANGES OR MODIFICATIONS	REASONS OR RATIONALE

1c. How effective do you feel these changes or modifications were in comparison to the original session design plan? (circle one)

1	2	3	4	5

very effective   very ineffective

1d. Are there any additional changes or modifications in the session design that would further improve this session? (circle one)

Yes 1
No (skip to question #2) ... 2

If yes, please explain the additional changes or modifications: _____

_____

_____

FIGURE 7–2 (*Continued*)

2. How appropriate were the *activities* used for this session in relation to program objectives addressed in this session? (circle one)

1	2	3	4	5

    very appropriate   very inappropriate

    Please explain your answer: _____

    _____

    _____

3. How appropriate were *staff interaction or intervention strategies* used in this session in relation to session activities, nature of clients, and achievement of program objectives? (circle one)

1	2	3	4	5

    very appropriate   very inappropriate

    Please explain your answer: _____

    _____

    _____

4. Did the *sequence of activities* in this session appear to be logical and appropriate? (circle one)

    Yes (skip to question #5) ... 1

    No 2

    If no, please identify changes that may be made to improve the sequence:

    _____

    _____

5. Was the *amount of time* allowed for client achievement of program objectives in this session sufficient? (circle one)

1	2	3	4	5

    very sufficient   insufficient, more or less time needed

    Please explain your answer: _____

    _____

    _____

6. Were planned resources (i.e., materials, supplies, equipment, and facilities) available for this session? (circle one)

    Yes (skip to question #7) ... 1

    No 2

    If no, please explain: _____

    _____

FIGURE 7–2 (*Continued*)

7. Were *adequate numbers and appropriately trained staff* involved in this session as planned? (circle one)

Yes (skip to question #8) ... 1

No 2

If no, please explain: _____

_____

_____

8. What was the *nature of client and staff involvement* in this session?

_____

_____

_____

_____

9. What unanticipated events or outcomes occurred in this session that were not planned in the original session design?

POSITIVE UNANTICIPATED EVENTS OR OUTCOMES: _____

_____

_____

_____

NEGATIVE UNANTICIPATED EVENTS OR OUTCOMES: _____

_____

_____

_____

10. Additional comments on this session: _____

_____

_____

_____

_____

_____

When analyzing the evaluation results, the use of these average ratings for each program aspect will allow the programmer to pinpoint areas of concern. If the average of all ratings on staff interaction and intervention strategies is 1.3, the programmer may conclude that, overall, staff interventions and interactions functioned very appropriately during program implementation. On the other hand, if the average of all ratings on this program aspect was 4.5, the programmer may conclude that there are some problems in this area as they were usually rated as functioning very inappropriately. More information will be provided on specific analysis and interpretation procedures later in this chapter. This example merely explains why this concern is important.

While quantitative data are very helpful in the analysis of evaluation information, numbers alone do not give the programmer sufficient direction or information about why there were problems in a specific aspect of the program, or what might be done to revise and improve a particular area of the program. For this reason, *qualitative* or descriptive information is also collected on the Post-session Report Form. When qualitative and quantitative evaluation data are analyzed at the end of program implementation, the programmer can pinpoint areas of concern by examining average ratings. When concerns or problems are identified, descriptive evaluation data can be analyzed to decide what revisions or changes to make in order to minimize or eliminate identified problems.

Now that the type of evaluation data to be collected on the program have been presented, the following question is usually raised: "How do you collect these evaluation data?" In evaluating how well the program functions during actual implementation, evaluation information is collected through systematic observation and documentation of the program aspects examined with the Post-session Report Form. There are a few variations on how and who observes, but the basic method remains *observation in the naturalistic setting*. Let's examine this method a little more closely.

Why observation? In any evaluation procedure, you want to select the most accurate, efficient, and feasible method of collecting information. When evaluating program functioning during implementation, observation is the best method in therapeutic recreation programs. This choice is made based on an understanding of the phenomenon to be evaluated, which, in this case, is a program design. This design is conceptualized and developed by the programmer as a plan of action to address specific client needs through service delivery. The program design equals the best plan available based on the programmer's professional judgments of the needs of program participants, therapeutic recreation service delivery trends and approaches, as well as knowledge of program-development techniques. Based on some professional, theoretical, and conceptual beliefs about therapeutic recreation service delivery, we can make some evaluative judgments about the worth or value of the program by examining the program plan. However, the real test of program effectiveness comes when the program is implemented.

During implementation, program concepts and constructs are translated into actions by the staff and participants. The best way to collect evaluation information on this translation from concept to practice is to observe program operations systematically. By observing and documenting descriptions of how well the design is implemented, of what modifications are made and why, of the appropriateness of activities, of sufficiency of time allotted, and of other program aspects, we can gather data that allow for judgments of how well the program plan actually functions during implementation.

The next question that comes up is: "But how objective can the evaluation data be if they consist of judgments based on observations?" The answer here is that the data collected will be as objective as the observer wants them to be, given that a human being with personal values and biases is recording the observation. Perhaps this is the bottom line: there will be objectivity limitations resulting from human observation, just as there are implementation limitations in human-designed programs. Through some careful planning, specific evaluation questions, and observational safeguards, you try to minimize as much bias as possible in human observation. However, you cannot eliminate or disregard the most accurate, feasible, and efficient method because of inherent problems with its use.

At this point, the reader is encouraged to explore further study on the use of observational methods in the naturalistic or applied setting.[13,14] For the use of observation within the FPEP, here are a few guidelines. First, if you are the program designer and you also intend to evaluate your program during implementation, you need to keep a few things in mind. Of primary importance are your own beliefs about the program. If you want the program to be successful at all costs, you will tend to perceive it favorably during program implementation. Believe it is perfect and you will probably record evaluation data that support your belief! Now, it would be just as biased to take the stance that the opposite is true and, by self-fulfilling prophecy, have your program fail. But keep this simple principle in mind: *no program is perfect or without the potential for further improvement.* With this prescript in mind, you can collect evaluation data that question how well the program functions by documenting observed strengths and weaknesses of various aspects of the program.

The second principle is to refine your observational skills. Become an expert at differentiating between overt and covert behaviors and events, at what can be seen and what cannot be seen through human observation. Practice your observational skills and improve your accuracy in observational recording. One way to verify your accuracy in observation and documentation is to see what the level of inter-observer objectivity is. This is the third principle: *check your observational accuracy against that of another human observer.* In order to practice this, choose a situation in practice and predetermine what behaviors are to be observed. Having selected a specific behavior in a specific setting, two individuals take independent recordings. These observational recordings may then be compared to check the level of inter-observer reliability.

[13]Michael Quinn Patton, *Qualitative Evaluation Methods* (Beverly Hills: Sage Publications, 1980).

[14]John Lofland, *Analyzing Social Settings* (Belmont, Ca.: Wadsworth Publishing Company, 1971).

Of course, there are more sophisticated methods of analyzing situations or events in practice. One could video-tape program sessions and examine the filmed recordings to document evaluation data. Another approach would be to have one or more observers collect data during program sessions. These methods of observation may not be practical because of the amount of resources or staff time involved. Even if such resources and staff time are available, there will always be a human observer involved to some degree in the recording of evaluation data, even with sophisticated methods.

Whichever structure and mechanics are employed to collect evaluation information through observation, remember that there will always be the chance that error may occur in such recordings. The more one practices observational techniques, the more definitive one is in predetermining what is to be observed. The more concrete one is in observational documentation, the more confident one can be about the evaluation information collected.

When to Use the Post-session Report Form. So far, we have covered what the Post-session Report Form examines in terms of program aspects during implementation, what type of data are collected, and the method used to collect data. The next issue is when the Post-session Report Form is used. When implementing a program for the first time, or if a program has not undergone comprehensive evaluation, then evaluation information should be collected using the Post-session Report Form after each program session. This allows for comprehensive documentation of program operations and is very crucial in the early stages of program development and evaluation. There are certainly several ways to adapt the FPEP, but initially you will want as much evaluation information as possible to be able to analyze program functioning in order to revise and improve the program.

This discussion has covered how program functioning is evaluated in day-to-day implementation. The major instrument used is the Post-session Report Form. Evaluation data are collected at the conclusion of each program session through observational documentation with this instrument. The other major evaluation concern addressed with the use of the FPEP relates to client outcomes or performance in the program. This aspect of the FPEP will be discussed next.

Evaluating Client Performance

The purpose of the FPEP is to collect evaluation information during implementation in order to identify program strengths and weaknesses. The intent is that this evaluation information will help the programmer revise and improve the program plan. Documenting client performance as a result of program participation is a key element in program evaluation. After all, the bottom line of designing a program is to put together a strategy, intervention, or approach that will aid those who participate in the program to accomplish behavioral change in the form of improved functional abilities and/or the acquisition of new knowledge and skills. One measure of the effectiveness of a program, therefore, is documenting the outcomes clients attain as a consequence of participating in the program.

Two processes of data collection may be employed in the FPEP to document client outcomes or performance within the program. One concern relates to overall performance, and evaluation data for this area is collected on the Client Performance Sheet. The other concern is client progress throughout the program, and the Performance Progress Instrument is used to collect evaluation information for this area. Let's examine the purpose, structure, and use of the Performance Progress Instrument first.

An important concern in the delivery of therapeutic recreation services is how well individual clients are progressing within the service-delivery setting. While specific programs are designed with a set of objectives and performance measures delineating exact expected outcomes for clients, one may also be concerned about ongoing performance or progress of clients prior to outcomes attainment, especially in the early stages of program development. The Performance Progress Instrument depicted in Figure 7–3 is used for this purpose.

Using this instrument, ongoing ratings and observational recordings are documented on client participation in the program in relation to program objectives. There are two ways to use this form. First, one copy of the form may be used for each program participant. In this case, entries on individual client progress are recorded on the form after each program session. At the end of the program, you can analyze each individual client's performance throughout all program sessions. Another possible way to use the form is to copy one form for each program session and record individual entries about all program participants on the same form after each session. In this way, you have evaluation information on the progress or performance of all program participants for each particular program session. Either variation may be appropriate, depending on your specific evaluation concerns.

Suppose, for example, you are more concerned about how the group of program participants are responding to each program session. You want to get an idea of how well the session activities are being perceived, how well this grouping of participants works together within this program, what differences there are in terms of the progress of various participants in relation to the entire program group, or any other concern that relates to total participation in each program session. If this is the case, then it would be logically appropriate to collect evaluation data on performance progress of all program participants with the same instrument on a session-by-session basis. If, on the other hand, your major concern is to show the progress of individual clients across all program sessions, then your choice would be the use of the Performance Progress Instrument for each individual program participant.

The use of the Performance Progress Instrument is most important during the early stages of program development. Ultimately, the information collected on this form will be analyzed to help determine how the program may be revised and improved to enhance performance based on knowledge of how clients progress through the program. The method of data collection is, again, systematic observation and professional judgment.

FIGURE 7–3 The Formative Program Evaluation Procedure

Performance Progress Instrument

PROGRAM TITLE: _____

Circle One: Individual Client Progress for Total Program . . . 1   add session number and date _____
Session Progress Notes for All Clients 2

NAME OR DATE	PROGRAM PERFORMANCE PROGRESS NOTES

The real measure of program outcomes is collected with the Client Performance Sheet, which is shown in Figure 7–4.

Let's examine the measurement of client performance outcomes. Each systems-designed program is developed to allow clients to acquire a set of outcome behaviors, skills, and knowledge. When clients are assigned as participants in a specific program, two assumptions are made. First, it is assumed that the clients will benefit in some way from the acquisition of program objectives. The second assumption is that the client does not currently possess the outcome behaviors. These two assumptions are logical concerns for program development and assignment, but they become crucial concerns in program evaluation. After all, if a measure of the effectiveness of a program is that clients achieve the performance outcomes as a result of program involvement, then there must be some way of documenting that clients do not have the outcomes when they enter the program.

Documenting that clients will benefit by the acquisition of the program outcomes may, initially, be a logical professional judgment based on the overall purpose of agency services, assessment of client needs, and the matching of individual needs to the specific program purpose and objectives. This documentation of need prior to program involvement is relevant to broader evaluation concerns than program evaluation, such as follow-up evaluation post-discharge. But, documenting client performance in relation to program objectives must be done in two ways in relation to program involvement.

Upon, or prior to, entry into the specific program, some measure must be made of the baseline skills of clients in relation to program objectives. These baseline data may be generated through what is called a pre-test. This pre-test, regardless of method used, gives the programmer a rating of the clients' entry-level skills on program objectives, which will later be used in order to make judgments about performance outcomes.

Various methods may be employed to collect these baseline data, all depending on the nature, content, and intent of program objectives. In some instances, the programmer will be able to administer a structured test or instrument that measures baseline skills related to program objectives. In other cases, the clients may participate in a series of tasks or activities where performance measures may be applied prior to program delivery in order to collect baseline data. If neither of these methods seems appropriate for the client-participants or the nature of the program, then the practitioner must rely on professional judgment, related assessment data, or observational recordings of client behaviors and abilities in relation to program performance measures.

Regardless of the method employed, there must be documentation of baseline performance related to program objectives. Without such baseline data, it is very difficult to justify program outcomes as an indication of how effective the program is. If clients come into the program having already attained program objectives, or if program objectives are attained through some means other than program involvement, then we cannot give the credit to the program for such client accomplishments. In using

FIGURE 7–4 The Formative Program Evaluation Procedure

Client Performance Sheet

DIRECTIONS: Using the coding system below, record program outcomes when individual clients achieve program objectives.

CODING SYSTEM:

+   indicates *able to perform objective behavior after instruction*

x   indicates *unable to perform objective behavior after instruction*

*   indicates *able to perform objective behavior before instruction*

PROGRAM TITLE: _____

OBJECTIVES

CLIENT NAME

the FPEP, the programmer documents client abilities in relation to program objectives either prior to client involvement in, or at the beginning of, the program. The results of this pre-test information may be recorded on the Client Performance Sheet, dated, and marked, "Baseline Performance Data."

Once baseline data on performance are documented, clients participate in the program as planned. The programmer then decides when performance outcomes data will be collected, again depending on the nature of the specific program and in view of some basic concepts about learning and behavior change. For example, systems-designed programs are structured so that, for each session, there is a specific objective or a number of objectives to be addressed through related content and process. One would not expect clients to have fully attained the session objectives by participating in one session or by one exposure. While this immediate outcome attainment may be possible for some individuals, a more realistic assumption is that learning takes time and practice. Therefore, the programmer may wish to monitor progress on a session-by-session basis but not attempt measurement of performance outcomes until the clients have had time to be exposed to the objective activities and to practice the behaviors. In some programs, all performance outcome measures will be taken at the end of the program. In other programs, performance outcome measures may be spaced throughout the program, as long as adequate time has been allowed for client acquisition of performance outcomes. In either case, the Client Performance Sheet will be used to document client outcomes.

What method will be used to evaluate client performance outcomes? This is the real advantage of systems-designed programs, because evaluation criteria and conditions are built into all program performance measures. Performance measures may indicate the completion of a test or structured instrument, or they may indicate the completion of a task or display of a specific behavior to be judged by the programmer according to predetermined criterion statements or specifications. To evaluate outcomes of a systems-designed program, the therapeutic recreator need only follow conditions and criteria of the Performance Measures and record a judgment about whether or not the client has attained specific behaviors. These recordings of client outcomes are documented on the Client Performance Sheet and used through analysis and interpretation as an indication of program strengths and weaknesses.

Analysis of Program Evaluation Data

Program evaluation data collected during program implementation will be analyzed in two sections: (1) analysis of program functioning during implementation and (2) analysis of client performance. After evaluation data are summarized and organized in both of these areas, they will be ready for interpretation of both strengths and weaknesses in program functioning and client performance, as well as overall strengths and weaknesses of the program as a whole.

How is analysis of evaluation data conducted? Analysis involves summarizing all evaluation data from all program sessions in relation to specific program aspects and client outcomes. In other words, you will be compiling or aggregating data from each program session, organized according to specific evaluation issues as previously discussed, such as compiling or grouping all evaluation data on the appropriateness of activities or the appropriateness of staff interventions and interactions. You want to group or organize all of these data so you can get an overall picture of how adequate the program is in general and, in a specific sense, how appropriate individual program aspects were throughout implementation.

Several analytical procedures and instruments were developed to aid in the analysis and interpretation of program evaluation data collected through the use of the FPEP. An in-depth discussion of the analysis of evaluation data on program functioning during implementation and client performance outcomes should provide a clearer understanding of how this phase of evaluation is completed. The discussion of analysis of evaluation data will be presented separately, regarding program functioning during implementation and analysis of client performance outcomes.

Analyzing Evaluation Data on Program Functioning. Analysis of evaluation data collected on program functioning during implementation is done by summarizing the information that has been documented on the Post-session Report Forms after each program session. This includes a comprehensive summary of evaluation data on previously discussed program aspects: implementation of program design, appropriateness of activities, appropriateness of staff interactions and interventions, sequencing of activities, sufficiency of time, availability of resources, staff, nature of client and staff interactions, and the nature of unplanned or unanticipated program events.

Two specific instruments and the procedure of grouping qualitative descriptions in table form have been developed for the analysis of evaluation data from the Post-session Report Forms. Remember, you are going to organize and summarize the data so that they are ready for interpretation. Without this analysis to summarize and organize the data, such interpretation may be difficult, if not impossible.

The first stage of analyzing program functioning is to summarize all quantitative data from the Post-session Report Form. This summary is accomplished by organizing evaluation ratings on the Post-session Analysis Form, which is shown in Figure 7–5. Information on quantitative ratings from each Post-session Report Form is recorded on the Post-session Analysis Form under the appropriate session column. When all information is summarized on this analysis form, then the average of ratings for each program aspect is computed. Let's examine the use of the form in a little more detail in relation to the information required for each of the program aspects listed under the column heading "Evaluation Questions."

The first three entries—date, number present, and number absent—are somewhat self-explanatory. The date of each session is documented, along with the number of clients present and the number absent for each particular session. An average rating of session dates is not taken; however, averages are computed for both the number of clients present and those

FIGURE 7-5 Post-session Analysis Form

EVALUATION QUESTIONS	SESSIONS										AVERAGE OF RATINGS
	1	2	3	4	5	6	7	8	9	10	
Date											
No. present											
No. absent											
Implemented as designed											
Changes or modifications											
Effect of changes											
Other changes											
Activities appropriate											
Intervention appropriate											
Sequence of activities											
Amount of time											
Resources available											
Adequate no. of trained staff											
Client/staff interactions											
Unanticipated positive events/outcomes											
Unanticipated negative events/outcomes											
Additional comments											
Evaluator notes											

absent across all program sessions. The ratings on the remainder of aspects listed under evaluation questions are recorded based on the type of information documented on the Post-session Report Forms. In other words, if a Likert Scale rating was used for a program aspect on the Post-session Report Form, then the actual Likert Rating (that is, 1 through 5) is recorded for each program session. As you can see from the Post-session Report Form, in Figure 7–2, Likert Scale ratings were used for the following program aspects: effect of change or modification, appropriateness of activities, appropriateness of staff interventions and interactions, and sufficiency of time allotted. For program aspects requiring a yes or no rating (that is, implemented as designed, additional changes or modifications, sequence of activities, availability of resources, and adequate numbers of trained staff), a 1 is recorded if the answer to the evaluation questions was yes, and a 2 is recorded if the answer was no. For recorded changes or modifications during session implementation, client and staff interactions, and unplanned events or outcomes, a 1 is recorded if observational data were documented in relation to these particular aspects for a particular program session, and a 2 is recorded if there were no observational data recorded. The *average* of all ratings for all sessions is then recorded in the final column of the Post-session Analysis Form by simply adding all ratings in a row and dividing by the total number of program sessions.

The Post-session Analysis Form takes care of summarizing all quantitative data related to program functioning during implementation. Before proceeding to further analysis of program functioning, it is important at this time to analyze the nature of average ratings. If positive or favorable average ratings are found for all program aspects, further analysis of program-functioning evaluation data may not be necessary. In other words, if the program sessions were all implemented as designed, no modifications or changes were documented, no other modifications were indicated, all Likert Scale rating averages were at the level of 1 or 2, the sequence of activities was appropriate, resources and trained staff were available, and no recordings were documented on client/staff interactions or unanticipated events/outcomes, then you may presume your program has functioned well during implementation, and there is no need to further analyze post-session evaluation data. If, on the other hand, session modifications were made, Likert Scale ratings on any program aspect ranged between 3 and 5, any program aspect was rated as not available, or recordings were documented on client/staff interactions or unanticipated events/outcomes, then further analysis is required to summarize specific evaluation findings that may help pinpoint problems in these aspects.

A specific analysis instrument has been developed for in-depth examination of modifications to the program design made during implementation, and is shown in Figure 7–6. If more than two or three program sessions were modified during implementation, then it may be desirable to record these on the Summary of Session Modifications Analysis Form. Once all modifications for the program are compiled on this analysis form, along with a brief description of the rationale for each, data will be ready for interpretation of these modifications in relation to the program design.

FIGURE 7–6 Summary of Session Modifications Analysis Form FPEP

SESSION NUMBER	RECOMMENDED MODIFICATIONS	RATIONALE	COMMENTS/ CRITIQUE AND PRIORITY/ FEASIBILITY

ADDITIONAL COMMENTS AND CONCLUSION/INTERPRETATION:

FIGURE 7–7 Therapeutic Recreation Specialist's Observational Notes on the Sufficiency of Time

SESSION	THERAPEUTIC RECREATOR OBSERVATIONAL NOTES
1	Clients not tested, only introduced to objectives.
2	90 minutes is almost too much time. 60 minutes would be more appropriate.
3	90 minutes too much time. Clients' attention to the game decreased after 60 minutes or so.
4	90 minutes was very good because it allowed enough time for each client to take hitting practice and to play several different positions.
5	Too hot!
6	With water break, time allowed proved to be sufficient.
7	Less time was needed to accomplish the performance tests; however, the remaining time was used effectively.
8	For a practice game, 85 minutes is enough time to complete 3 innings.
9	We were able to complete 4 full innings in the practice game— over 90 minutes. Any more time might have lost interest of clients.
10	90 minutes is just about the right amount of time for a practice game.

Another analytical procedure that may be employed to compile qualitative data on all other program aspects where low average ratings were computed on the Post-session Analysis Form is to use tables to summarize observational recordings for a particular program aspect across all program sessions. For example, Figure 7–7 shows observational notes recorded in relation to evaluative ratings on the sufficiency of time for a systems-designed program on softball skills for developmentally disabled adults.[15] In the evaluation of this specific program during implementation, it was found that the average overall rating for the sufficiency of time for all program sessions was 3 on a 5-point Likert Scale. This average rating of 3 indicated that it would be desirable to see where revisions might be made to improve this program aspect, so the table was compiled to organize all observational data for more accurate and specific interpretation. Such tables may be compiled for any program aspect indicated as receiving a low-average rating on the Post-session Analysis Form.

That concludes the description of analytical instruments and procedures employed on evaluation data from program implementation. The first step is to analyze all quantitative ratings from program sessions on the Post-session Analysis Form. Depending on the level of average ratings obtained through this summary of evaluation data, further analysis may be necessary of qualitative recordings of session modifications or other program aspects where average overall ratings indicate potential program-function problems and areas for revision.

Analyzing Evaluation Data on Client Performance. Several analysis procedures and one instrument are employed to analyze evaluation data on client performance outcomes from the program. Evaluation data collected on client performance included: (1) baseline data on clients' entry-level skills in relation to program objectives, (2) outcome data on clients' attainment of program objectives, and (3) recorded data on client performance progress throughout the program. These data need to be organized and summarized for interpretation, and one additional instrument needs to be completed for analysis of client performance.

The Client Profile Form, shown in Figure 7–8, is designed to compile information regarding the characteristics of program participants. While specific programs are designed for a particular target group of clients, it is important to document the specific characteristics of actual client participants. This information on client profiles becomes an integral aspect in interpretation of client performance outcomes.

Outcome data collected on clients' attainment of program objectives are analyzed in two ways. First, all program objectives are listed in relation to both the total number of sessions designed to address each objective and the total number of clients attaining each of the program objectives. The diagram in Figure 7–9 shows how this information can be laid out for analysis.

[15]Connolly, *Analysis*, p. 183.

FIGURE 7-8 The Formative Program Evaluation Procedure

Client Profile Form

DIRECTIONS: The purpose of this form is to gather background information on clients who participate in the program.

PROGRAM TITLE: _____

CLIENT NAME OR IDENTIFICATION NUMBER	REASON FOR PARTICIPATING OR ASSIGNMENT IN THE PROGRAM	AGE	PRIMARY DISABILITY	SECONDARY DISABILITIES	SPECIAL NEEDS, RESTRICTIONS, OR PRECAUTIONS	OTHER REASONS FOR CLIENT INVOLVEMENT OR OTHER COMMENTS

FIGURE 7–9 Client Outcomes on Program Objectives

PROGRAM OBJECTIVES	1	2	3	4	5	6	7
NO. OF SESSIONS ADDRESSING	7	4	5	6	5	6	7
NO. OF CLIENTS ATTAINING	3 of 4	1 of 4	4 of 4	4 of 4	2 of 4	3 of 4	4 of 4
TOTAL PERCENT OF CLIENTS ATTAINING	75	25	100	100	50	75	100

It can be seen that a numbering system is used as a reference for each specific objective, which is described in detail in the program plan. In the first column, objective number 1 was addressed on some level in seven program sessions (i.e., introduction of the objective, direct instruction, or practice opportunity for the objective behaviors), and three of four clients attained this objective within the program by performing favorably on Performance Measures.

The second method of analyzing client-outcome data is to summarize individual client gains. These data may be organized as presented in Figure 7–10.

FIGURE 7–10 Individual Client Gains

CLIENT	SPECIFIC PROGRAM OBJECTIVES ATTAINED (BY NO.)	PERCENT OF TOTAL OF PROGRAM OBJECTIVES ATTAINED
A	3, 4, 7	43
B	1, 2, 3, 4, 5, 6, 7	100
C	1, 3, 4, 5, 6, 7	86
D	1, 3, 4, 6, 7	71

Again, a numbering system was used to refer to program objectives. Based on the analysis of client outcomes in terms of program objectives and individual client gains, outcome data are now ready for interpretation.

The final analytical task in relation to client performance is to compile documentation on client performance progress throughout the program. Since previous decisions were made about whether to record progress on an individual basis or on a session-by-session basis, these evaluation data are merely grouped with either outcome data regarding client performance on program objectives or individual client gains, depending on the type of performance progress data collected. These performance progress data are not analyzed any further, but are used during interpretation of client performance in relation to the specific program.

Based on the compilation and summary of evaluation data regarding both program functioning during implementation and client performance outcomes, the analysis phase of the FPEP is completed. All analyzed evaluation data are now ready for interpretation. Note that analysis has consisted primarily of summarizing and organizing the evaluation data so that program strengths and weaknesses can be identified. The next phase of the FPEP—interpretation—involves making judgments about the analyzed data in order to revise and improve the program.

Interpretation of Program Evaluation Data

Interpretation of evaluation data involves making judgments. While evaluation data become the dominant factual basis for these interpretive judgments, evaluation data will not provide you with a definitive answer on how to improve your program. The interpretation phase of the FPEP, or of any evaluation procedure, can be thought of as the "jigsaw puzzle" stage. You now have most of the pieces before you, but it will take some patience and a touch of professional creativity to put it all together. It may be difficult for some to conduct analysis of the data without adding their interpretations, but it is very important to keep analysis and interpretation activities separate. There are two reasons for keeping these stages separate. First, you want to make sure you analyze all data before making any interpretive decisions. We have dissected the program design into key aspects that would be evaluated during implementation. It is important to put all the pieces back together prior to interpretation, so that decisions made are based on the whole program, not just a few parts.

The second reason for keeping these two separate is to allow for more than one independent interpretation of the analyzed evaluation data. Patton strongly recommends keeping the two activities separate.[16] This way, if you want to check on your own interpretations, you might share the analyzed data with another therapeutic recreator or other staff member to see what interpretations he or she perceives. By keeping analysis and interpretation separate, you may ask these other professionals to indicate the strengths and weaknesses they identify in the program, without contaminating their professional judgments with your interpretations.

The primary purpose of the interpretation phase is to identify program strengths and weaknesses. This is done in relation to program functioning and client performance first, and then an overall summary of program strengths and weaknesses is made by combining results from both areas. Two sets of interpretive questions have been developed to direct this phase of evaluation. One set of questions is designed to assist in interpreting data on program functioning, and the other set is designed to assist in interpreting client performance outcomes.

Interpretation of Program Functioning.   The evaluation concern specifically related to the adequacy of the program is: how well does the program function in actual implementation? The FPEP calls for the collection of evaluation data on specific program aspects presumed to affect

[16]Patton, *Qualitative Evaluation*, p. 258.

this functioning. During interpretation, the programmer focuses on answering the following questions when examining analyzed evaluation data:

1. How extensive and how relevant were the content modifications made during implementation? How appropriate are these content modifications in relation to the intent of the specific program?
2. How well did the planned program activities, processes, and resources function during implementation? What strengths and weaknesses are identified in implementing program content, processes, and use of resources?
3. What was the nature of staff and client involvement in this program? What are the strengths and weaknesses, as well as general characteristics, of planned and unanticipated interactions, events, and outcomes?

Given the foregoing questions and the analyzed evaluation data, the programmer examines the summaries on the Post-session Analysis Form, Summary of Session Modifications Form, and any other tables of qualitative data in relation to identifying strengths and weaknesses of program functioning. You may wish to organize your interpretation so that you literally look at each program aspect separately and decide if analyzed data reveal any particular strengths or weaknesses. Were there a number of participants absent throughout the program? Were sessions implemented as designed, or were a number of changes and modifications made? Continue with this type of questioning, listing strengths and weaknesses within each program aspect. After this is done, make a list of all program aspects where no, or only minor, weaknesses were identified, and a list indicating program aspects where weaknesses are identified. Now construct a summary of program function, indicating overall program strengths and weaknesses or concerns. Through interpretation, indicate the implications you arrive at in regard to program weaknesses. Do you have any judgments regarding probable cause or an idea of how the weaknesses might be modified or changed to improve them?

At this point, you have summarized your interpretation of the functioning of the program during implementation. You should have an idea of program strengths and a list of program weaknesses. You have not only listed weaknesses, but you should have indicated some judgments as to what corrective actions might be pursued to revise these areas or what events may have occurred to lead to the weaknesses in program aspects.

Interpretation of Client Performance. The evaluation concern related specifically to client performance is: what outcomes do clients attain as a consequence of participating in this specific program? During interpretation, the programmer focuses on answering the following questions when examining analyzed data on client performance:

1. How many program objectives do clients achieve in this program? What is the distribution of client outcomes in relation to program objectives?
2. What are individual client outcomes for this program? What is the nature of client outcomes and progress within the program?

3. What are the strengths and weaknesses of program objectives? Given program outcomes and individual client outcomes, how relevant and appropriate do program objectives appear to be?

With the foregoing interpretive questions and the analyzed evaluation data on client performance, the programmer interprets strengths and weaknesses of client performance. In program outcomes, examine all gains on all program objectives. Are there some objectives where fewer or no clients show gains? Indicate which objectives reveal favorable gains and which show fewer favorable gains. The objectives with fewer favorable gains may be determined as a weak area of program objectives. Interpret what might be the cause and corrective action to be taken to improve these objectives. Were they adequately addressed in enough program sessions? What sources of information can you find that might indicate why low, or no, achievements were attained on these objectives?

Next, examine individual client gains. Do all clients do well in performance outcomes? If not, question why some clients do better than others. Were clients absent from sessions? Compare information on individual gain to information on client profile (refer to Figure 7–7). Do lower achievers have different characteristics in terms of age, primary disability, secondary disability, or special needs? If there are differences in client characteristics between high and low achievers in the program, this may be an indication of the need for more careful selection of appropriate clients for program participation. On the other hand, if greater selectivity is not possible, it may be an indication of program revision to accommodate a greater diversity of client characteristics. You may also decide to examine closely performance progress recordings to determine if any of these observations provides information to aid in interpreting individual gains.

The final area involves interpretation of client performance outcomes in relation to program objectives. At this point, you have data on how well individual clients achieved, as well as an idea of how all clients did on all program objectives. Now consider the planned objectives in relation to the outcomes. Are they still relevant and appropriate? Are there other objectives that should be added in view of program and client outcomes? You may wish to reexamine unanticipated events and outcomes that were recorded within post-session evaluation data. Some of this information may indicate how planned objectives may be revised.

Now, just as you did with program functioning, construct a summary of overall strengths and weaknesses of client performance outcomes. Pinpoint all strengths and weaknesses in program outcomes, individual client gains, and planned program objectives. The interpretation of client performance data, along with the interpretation of program functioning, is now suitable for preparing an overall interpretation of the specific program.

Interpretation of Overall Program Strengths and Weaknesses. It is now time to do an overall interpretation of the specific program. The summary of strengths and weaknesses regarding program functioning is combined with the summary of strengths and weaknesses concerning client performance outcomes. Interpretations are made as to the major strengths and weaknesses in both areas. Weaknesses are then prioritized in terms of how important each is in relation to the intent of the program. In other words, the most severe weakness may be the first priority for revision. If this weakness is not corrected, the program design may not function adequately during the next implementation, nor may planned objectives be obtained.

Once interpretation and priorities are set for the program, the programmer has a list of areas where revision is indicated. All important revisions will be directed toward a change or modification to the program plan. Figure 7–11 shows the top priorities for revising a softball skill development program for developmentally disabled adults. The major weaknesses interpreted in this program were: (1) the actual client population was lower-functioning than the target population, (2) program outcomes were low, (3) many clients had a high number of absences throughout the program, (4) heat problems presented a significant problem in this summer/ outdoor program, and (5) the sessions were too long for the clients involved. Based on these findings, the priorities in Figure 7–11 were established. As you can see, each priority relates to a specific program area in the program plan and is accompanied by a specific revision or concern for revision.

This concludes the aspect of interpreting evaluation data. Again, this phase of evaluation has included judgments about the meaning and implications of analyzed evaluation data. Do not be surprised if two different therapeutic recreators come up with different interpretations of the meaning and implications of the evaluation data. Since judgment is involved, there is room for differing interpretations. It is highly advisable for the programmer to seek other interpretations of the evaluative data for a specific program. However, the ultimate decisions about exactly where and how the evaluation findings are used to revise and improve the program remain with the program designer. If other interpretations differ, interpret all of these in relation to the program intent and the needs of the target client group.

Reporting Evaluation Results

After all evaluation phases are completed, a final evaluation report should be prepared on the specific program. This report should include a summary of all evaluation activities and findings. Keep the report as simple and straightforward as possible. You might start the report with a statement explaining why you conducted the program evaluation, along with a very brief history of the program, indicating its reason for, and state of, development. The next thing to include would be a brief description of the evaluation procedure used, which, in this case, would be the FPEP. It will also be helpful to include a general description of how the program was

FIGURE 7–11 Priorities for the Revision of the Program Based on Interpretations of the Evaluation Findings

PRIORITY	PROGRAM AREA	REVISION OR CONCERN
1	Objectives and client population characteristics	Examine objectives in relation to intended client population characteristics and either (a) Revise program objectives and performance measures for lower-functioning clients or (b) Enroll in the program only those clients whose skill levels and characteristics match those for whom the program was designed.
2	Content	If objectives are revised, revise program content appropriately, especially if program is revised for a lower-functioning group where major activity-format changes may be necessary due to lower skill levels
3	Client involvement	Explore methods of reducing client absences, which may be affecting performance and program outcomes
4	Process	If this is to continue as a summer program, revise structure to incorporate rest and water breaks
5	Process	Consider reducing program session time from 90 minutes to 60 minutes to accommodate ability and attention span of clients and/or consider adding more weekly program sessions

implemented, over what length of time (that is, number of days or weeks), the days of the week on which program sessions were held, and any other general information deemed important in regard to the implementation of the program.

The rest of the report should include information on the interpretation of evaluative data and priorities for program revision. Any other information, such as copies of FPEP instruments or actual evaluative data, should be attached as appendices. A copy of the implemented program design might also be included.

Why develop a report if you have all the information you need to revise and reimplement the program in the future? One reason is that if you do not document the evaluation findings and implications, they will be lost, thanks to the distortion of memory. Another reason is for documentation in relation to demonstrating quality assurance. A third issue is that such documented information could be very useful in staff training or orientation. A final concern is for program continuity. With a report on file, if staff turnover occurs, incoming staff members have documentation of the nature of program functioning and outcomes to start with, to insure continuity of program services for clients. All of these reasons make an evaluation report a valuable piece of documentation in service delivery.

Revising the Program

The final phase of the FPEP is to actually revise the specific program. If the evaluation activity stops at the final report and actual program revisions are not made, then the activity may be worthy but not very useful. And usefulness is what evaluation is all about! The program should be revised based on the evaluation findings and priorities, and a new program plan should be developed for future implementation of the program. This completes the cycle from the original program plan, implementation plan, and evaluation plan to actual implementation and evaluation of the program. The cycle is complete when the program plan is revised based on evaluation data.

SUMMARY

Program evaluation planning is the third and final aspect of the systems design for a specific program. The Formative Program Evaluation Procedure provides a detailed plan of action for the evaluation of specific programs. For newly developed programs, this comprehensive approach to program evaluation is very useful. Since the FPEP is designed specifically for therapeutic recreation, the programmer need only operationalize the procedure for the specific program, and the evaluation plan is ready for program implementation.

======================= **Suggested References** =======================

Annand, V. S., "A Review of Evaluation in Therapeutic Recreation," *Therapeutic Recreation Journal*, 11, no. 2 (1977), 42–46.
Attkisson, C. C., W. A. Hargreaves, M. J. Hozowitz, and J. E. Sorensen (Eds.), *Evaluation of Human Services Programs*. New York: Academic Press, 1978.

BRASKAMP, L. A., and R. D. BROWN (Eds.), *Utilization of Evaluative Information*. San Francisco: Jossey-Bass, Inc., Publishers, 1980.

BULLOCK, C. C., "Interactionist Evaluators Look for 'What is' not 'What Should Be,'" *Parks and Recreation*, 17, no. 2 (1982), 37–39.

CONNOLLY, M., "Analysis of a Formative Program Evaluation Procedure for Therapeutic Recreation Services." Unpublished doctoral dissertation, University of Illinois at Urbana-Champaign, 1981.

CONNOLLY, P., "Evaluation's Critical Role in Agency Accountability," *Parks and Recreation*, 17, no. 2 (1982), 34–36.

———, "The Formative Program Evaluation Procedure: An Internal Tool for Therapeutic Recreation Services," in *Extra Perspectives: Concepts in Therapeutic Recreation*, ed. L. L. Neal and C. R. Edginton, pp. 41–56. Eugene, Or.: Center of Leisure Studies, University of Oregon, 1982.

DATTA, L. E., "Interpreting Data: A Case Study from the Career Intern Evaluation," *Evaluation Review*, 4, no. 4 (1980), 481–506.

EDGINTON, C. R., and G. A. Hayes, "Using Performance Objectives in the Delivery of Therapeutic Recreation Service," *Leisurability*, 3, no. 4 (1976), 20–26.

FILSTEAD, W. J., "Using Qualitative Methods in Evaluation Research: An Illustrative Bibliography," *Evaluation Review*, 5, no. 2 (1981), 259–268.

GARDNER, D. E., "Five Evaluation Frameworks: Implications for Decision Making in Higher Education," *Journal of Higher Education*, 8, no. 5 (1977), 571–593.

GIROUX, H. A., "Overcoming Behavioral and Humanistic Objectives," *The Educational Forum*, 43, no. 4 (May 1979), 409–419.

GUBA, E. G., *Toward a Methodology of Naturalistic Inquiry in Educational Evaluation*. Los Angeles: Center for the Study of Evaluation, University of California, 1978.

HOLSTI, O. R., *Content Analysis for the Social Sciences and Humanities*. Reading, Ma.: Addison-Wesley Publishing Co., 1969.

HOUSE, E. R., "Assumptions Underlying Evaluation Models," *Educational Researcher*, 7 (1978), 4–12.

HUTCHINSON, P., and R. C. MANNELL, "Practical Approaches for Learning How to Evaluate," *Parks and Recreation*, 17, no. 9 (1982), 74–76.

ISAAC, S., and W. B. MICHAEL, *Handbook in Research and Evaluation*. San Diego: Edits Publishers, 1972.

KENNEDY, D. W., and H. M. LUNDEGREN, "Application of the Discrepancy Evaluation Model in Therapeutic Recreation," *Therapeutic Recreation Journal*, 15, no. 1 (1981), 24–34.

LOFLAND, J., *Analyzing Social Settings: A Guide to Qualitative Observation and Analysis*. Belmont, Ca.: Wadsworth Publishing Co., 1971.

MORGAN, M. K., and D. M. IRBY, *Evaluating Clinical Competence in the Health Professions*. St. Louis: C. V. Mosby Co., 1978.

NAVAR, N., and J. DUNN, *Quality Assurance: Concerns for Therapeutic Recreation*. Champaign, Il.: Department of Leisure Studies, University of Illinois, 1981.

PATTON, M. Q., *Creative Evaluation*. Beverly Hills: Sage Publications, 1981.

———, *Qualitative Evaluation Methods*. Beverly Hills: Sage Publications, 1980.

———, *Utilization-focused Evaluation*. Beverly Hills: Sage Publications, 1978.

ROSSI, P. H., H. E. FREEMAN, and S. R. WRIGHT, *Evaluation: A Systematic Approach*. Beverly Hills: Sage Publications, 1979.

ROSSMAN, J. R., "Evaluate Programs by Measuring Participant Satisfactions," *Parks and Recreation*, 17, no. 6 (1982), 33–35.

SADLER, D. R., "Conveying the Findings of Evaluative Inquiry," *Educational Evaluation and Policy Analysis*, 2, no. 2 (1980), 53–58.

SCRIVEN, M., "The Methodology of Evaluation," in *Perspectives of Curriculum Evaluation,* ed. R. W. Tyler, R. M. Gagne, and M. Scriven, pp. 39–83. AERA Monograph Series on Curriculum Evaluation, no. 1. Chicago: Rand McNally and Company, 1967.

STAKE, R. E., "The Countenance of Educational Evaluation," *Teachers College Record,* 68, no. 7 (1967), 523–540.

STEVENSON, J. F., and R. H. LONGABAUGH, "The Role of Evaluation in Mental Health," *Evaluation Review,* 4, no. 4 (1980), 401–438.

8

Activity Analysis

PURPOSE: To present a definition, rationale, and description of activity analysis. One detailed procedure of activity analysis is provided. Various applications of activity analysis are described.

Once program goals and objectives are specified, using the systems method, the designer has the task of selecting content (activities) for the program. This process is often taken for granted and traditional activities are selected blindly, based on staff skills or interests, available facilities, and limitations of budget. In systems-designed programs, however, activities should be carefully selected according to their ability to contribute to the achievement of objectives.

If the program is an instructional one, then the task is somewhat simplified. The activities must relate to the skills being taught. However, choices are more difficult when the objectives are oriented to treatment or behavioral change. For example, an objective dealing with increasing social skills or increasing concentration does not directly indicate that a particular activity should be chosen. The designer is thus free to select from a wide range of possibilities. A variety of factors must be considered, such as age, sex, carry-over value, feasibility, budget, facility constraints, and staffing concerns. The competent professional, however, will pick activities that have *inherent* characteristics that contribute to the objectives. Activity analysis is the procedure that enables and facilitates this selection process.

Activity analysis is a procedure for breaking down and examining an activity to find inherent characteristics that contribute to program objectives. It is a process that allows the therapeutic recreator to understand an activity and its potential contributions to behavioral outcomes. Activity analysis provides a more exact method of selecting activities in that activity components are analyzed before utilization for their behavioral and interactional requirements. In activity analysis, different activities and their therapeutic or instructional value can be compared so that better programming decisions can be made.

Breaking down activities into their component parts allows the therapeutic recreation specialist to become aware of what participatory skills and abilities are needed by the client in order to engage in the activity. The specialist can then determine if the activity is appropriate, or if modifications are needed.

Activity analysis occurs independent of clients. The specialist can take an activity and analyze it for its basic requirements and demands in terms of actual participation factors. Of basic concern are the physical, cognitive, affective (emotional), and social components of the activity as it is traditionally engaged in. Such an analysis considers just the activity itself. The goal is simply to understand the activity and its inherent characteristics. The process, however, has many applications in therapeutic recreation programming. If the program is instructional in nature, the process of activity analysis, combined with the functional assessment of a person with a disability, allows the instructor to know exactly what modifications of the activity are needed to accommodate that person. For example, an analysis of the physical requirements of the front crawl in swimming compared to the functional ability of an individual with cerebral palsy would indicate the exact areas needing adaptation; that is, the kick, or the coordination of arms and breathing.

On the other hand, if the program is rehabilitation- or treatment-oriented, an analysis of a selected activity, compared with the stated treatment goal, would allow the specialist to ascertain whether that activity would contribute to the desired behavioral or functional improvement objective. Bingo, for example, has no inherent social interaction requirements. The players merely listen for numbers, search their cards for those numbers, and cover them with tokens. Through analysis, an activity that is commonly billed as a social activity is discovered to possess none of the essential components of human interaction. Therefore, it is not an appropriate selection for a treatment goal dealing with social skills. It would, however, be a good activity for increasing concentration.

Admittedly, analysis is much more difficult for some activities than for others. Structured activities, such as games and sports, can, because of their exact rules and procedures, be more easily and more accurately analyzed and understood than unstructured activities, such as crafts, camping, or free play. Unstructured activities vary in their analysis outcomes, based on the context and situation surrounding the participation experiences. Nonetheless, the attempt at systematic analysis of activity components is beneficial for comprehending participation requirements and possible outcome behaviors, regardless of the limitations imposed by the nature or structure of the activities.

Activities also vary considerably in their participation requirements and demands. A casual evaluation of an activity can often be misleading. The complexity of many activities is frequently hidden because of an assumed familiarity. Thus, an activity like checkers is considered simple because it is so well known, whereas, in fact, the game requires advanced cognitive skills, including evaluation and decision-making (strategy) as well as the recall of countless rules governing the play. It is this type of information that is gleaned from employing a systematic and comprehensive activity analysis.

A variety of methods exists for analyzing activities. All of them have in common the desire to assist in the understanding of the nature and dynamics of activity. Peterson defines the general process as follows:

> Activity analysis is a process which involves the systematic application of selected sets of constructs and variables to break down and examine a given activity to determine the behavioral requirements inherent for successful participation.[1]

Activity analysis leads to a deeper understanding of activity components and participation requirements. Activity analysis provides—

1. a better comprehension of the expected outcomes of participation;
2. a greater understanding of the complexity of activity components, which can then be compared to the functional level of an individual or group to determine the appropriateness of the activity;
3. information about whether the activity will contribute to the desired behavioral outcome when specific behavioral goals or objectives are being used;
4. direction for the modification or adaptation of an activity for individuals with limitations;
5. useful information for selecting an intervention, instructional, or leadership technique; and
6. a rationale or explanation for the therapeutic benefits of activity involvement.

OVERVIEW OF ACTIVITY ANALYSIS

When an individual engages in an activity, action is required in *three behavioral areas: physical* (psychomotor), *cognitive,* and *affective* behaviors are all involved, regardless of the type of activity. For example, when playing Ping-Pong, the *physical* actions are obvious. The player must be able to grasp and hold a paddle, and have sufficient elbow, shoulder, and wrist movement to hit the ball, enough mobility to move quickly, and hand-eye coordination. *Cognitive* skills are also required. There are rules to remember, there is continuous scoring, and there are strategies to plan. These cognitive or mental requirements add to the totality of the involvement. *Affective* requirements for controlling or expressing emotions are also part of the action. An activity analysis of Ping-Pong, or any activity for that matter, examines each behavioral area.

[1]Carol Ann Peterson, "State of the Art: Activity Analysis," in *Leisure Activity Participation and Handicapped Populations: Assessment of Research Needs* (Arlington, Va.: National Recreation and Park Association and Bureau of Education for the Handicapped, United States Office of Education, April 1976), p. 82.

A game, such as checkers, that is normally considered a mental game also makes demands in all three behavioral areas. Cognitive requirements include knowledge of rules and strategy and concentration. Physically, the game requires sight, as well as the ability to grasp and move pieces. Affectively, checkers demands control of emotions when pieces are jumped and removed.

Besides the behavioral areas of involvement, we should also look at the social or *interactional* skills needed. Far too often, clients have problems with an activity (or refuse to play) because the interactional skills required are too demanding or just not part of their current functional ability. For example, a client may know the activity skills necessary to play volleyball but avoids the game because he or she cannot handle the verbal interactions needed to be a team member. The analysis of interactional requirements is, thus, critical for total comprehension of participation demands.

The therapeutic recreator must understand the demands in all four areas, realizing that they are complex and interrelated. Failure to be concerned with any one area could easily result in inappropriate program content. An example of this is selecting an activity for a group of mentally retarded teenagers and only looking at the physical demands of the activity. While conducting the activity, the leader becomes embarrassingly aware that the mental requirements or social demands are beyond the group's current functional level. An analysis ahead of time might have saved the situation, either by allowing the leader to plan for modifications or by selecting a more suitable activity.

The following pages present some major considerations in each area of concern. The information is far from complete. Additional factors can be identified for specific populations. The attempt here is to provide general material that cuts across all groups. Therapeutic recreators are encouraged to design their own activity analysis checklist, including items that are of specific concern to their clientele. A general checklist is presented as one example; it appears at the end of this section.

PHYSICAL REQUIREMENTS

All recreational activity requires some physical action. Often it is difficult to distinguish what action is required to participate from what action may be associated with an activity. Some activities do not require specific actions. There are many ways to fly a kite, whereas other activities, such as square dancing, have definite ways of moving. The task is to identify the actual demands of the activity.

One can begin analyzing the physical requirements of an activity by noting the basic body position, then determining the body parts involved. Each involved body part must be identified separately, such as fingers, hand, wrist, and elbow, or by grouping parts into larger categories, such as arm or upper torso. The amount of detail needed usually relates to the population that is receiving the recreational services. For example, more detailed information may be required when analyzing activities for the physically disabled than when doing so for the mentally ill.

The types of movement must also be determined. Common body actions are bending, stretching, twisting, reaching, grasping, and rotating. These actions are usually part of a movement pattern that can be identified in broad terms such as catching, throwing, kicking, striking, or running. Pinpointing the fundamental movement patterns in an activity helps to determine the complexity of an activity and also what skills need to be taught. When more detail is needed, the therapeutic recreation specialist can isolate the exact motions involved for each body part. An excellent example of this is found in Avedon's *Therapeutic Recreation Service* (1974, pp. 178–182).[2] This illustration identifies each body part and its position and describes in detail the movements required for archery. Such specific analysis, however, is rarely needed in most therapeutic recreation program situations.

It is also important to know the number and nature of the movements involved. For example, softball is extremely complex; it requires running, throwing, catching, and striking (batting), all with a high degree of accuracy. Bowling, on the other hand, has just one basic movement pattern. This type of information is crucial when it comes to the selection of activities for certain populations.

Coordination of body parts is another major factor to consider. Many activities require a high degree of coordination. Golf is a good example. It is a simple game by one standard, in that the entire game consists of one basic movement pattern, a swing of a golf club. However, coordination is critical, to which any frustrated amateur duffer can attest. Activities that require using few body parts in coordination are easier to participate in—an insight that has obvious implications for special populations. Scheduling activities that continuously frustrate a client because too much coordination is needed certainly blocks the therapeutic intent or the enjoyment in participation. Many special populations, whether mentally retarded, mentally ill, emotionally disturbed, cerebral palsied, blind, deaf, or elderly, may (each for a different reason) have difficulty with activities requiring high levels of body part coordination.

Hand-eye coordination is another critical area. Unfortunately, many basic recreational activities require some form of hand-eye coordination, whether the activity is a sport, a craft, or a table game. Again the issue is determining how much coordination is required for successful participation. An awareness that the level and amount of hand-eye coordination is extremely high in a certain activity may result in the selection of another activity to comply with the limitation of a person or group.

A variety of other physical factors can be analyzed. Among these are strength, speed, endurance, energy, flexibility, and cardiovascular activity. Determining how much or how little of these elements are involved in a given activity is equally important when selecting and modifying program content.

The different senses should also be considered as part of the physical

[2]Elliott M. Avedon, *Therapeutic Recreation Service: An Applied Behavioral Science Approach* (Englewood Cliffs, N.J.: Prentice-Hall, Inc., 1974).

requirements of activity participation. Sight is vital to successful participation in many activities, as is hearing. Rarely do we stop to analyze an
activity for these two essential areas. The inability of a client to hear clearly
in and of itself could make participation in many activities extremely frustrating, if not impossible. Smell and taste are not as often required for most
activities, but touch is inherent in most sports, games, and expressive arts.

Understanding the various physical demands of an activity is complex.
Indeed, the variety of factors to consider and their diversity makes the task
tedious. However, the result of such a process enables appropriate selection
of activities for treatment, instructional, or recreation programs. Knowing
where and how to modify an activity is also a result of the process.

COGNITIVE REQUIREMENTS

Cognition may be the most important requirement of activity participation,
since the mind regulates body movement as well as other behavioral aspects
of participation. Several aspects of cognition are important considerations
in activity analysis.

The number and complexity of rules need to be determined. Chess
and bridge have many rules, whereas creative dramatics has no inherent
rules. The leader may impose some, but the activity itself is rule-free. Not
only must rules be remembered, but the players must also regulate their
behavior according to them. Many individuals with mental retardation,
emotional disturbances, stroke and age related disabilities may have much
difficulty in playing games that have complex rules.

Memory retention is another vital area of cognition. It pertains not
only to rules but also to new information that needs to be processed, stored,
and used continuously during the activity. Both the amount and nature of
long- and short-term memory retention need to be analyzed before recommending the use of a certain activity.

Concentration needs should also be noted. Some activities require
intense, continuous concentration. Ping-Pong is a good example. Bowling,
however, requires intermittent concentration. The specialist must be aware
of the level of concentration required to perform an activity, as well as its
frequency.

Does the activity require verbalization or a command of language?
The act of speaking is actually physical, but generally language usage is
considered to be a cognitive function. Activities have differing degrees of
selecting, organizing, and using words. Bingo requires little verbalization,
whereas planning and putting on a skit requires a lot.

Strategy is another cognitive skill inherent in many recreational activities. It requires an ability to analyze alternatives and make decisions.
There is a big difference between the amount of strategy required in Chinese
checkers and a game of Old Maid, just as there is between tennis and
horseshoes.

The requirements of intellectual skill versus chance can also be considered in activity analysis. Some activities involve some mental functioning,

but the outcomes are pretty much chance-related. For example, Parcheesi, poker, or blackjack depend more on the luck of the deal or the roll of the dice than they do on intellectual skill.

The academic skills of reading, writing, and math should be analyzed in relation to most activities. For example, countless activities require the ability to keep score, which is a mathematical calculation. Frequently we take this ability for granted or overlook its complexity because an activity is primarily physical in nature.

Other cognitive concerns are basic factors, such as understanding directionality; spatial awareness; and object, person, part, and symbol identification and discrimination. Activities differ immensely in their utilization of these concepts. Typically, individuals acquire these abilities early in life, however, many adults (an acute psychotic, for example) temporarily may be unable to function in one or more of these areas.

The analysis of activities for an understanding of their cognitive demands is essential. More often than not, some cognitive inability makes a client's participation difficult, frustrating, or impossible. Cognitive requirements are as equally complex as physical requirements but by nature are more difficult to detect and are thus more likely to be overlooked by the therapeutic recreator.

INTERACTION AND SOCIAL REQUIREMENTS

Activities have different physical and cognitive requirements; they also demand varying degrees of interactional skills. In many activities, it is necessary to relate to others. The nature of the interaction may be cooperative or competitive, and there may be any number of people involved. An analysis of these inherent interaction patterns within activities is significant in selecting activities appropriately and helping clients to develop social skills.

Interaction Patterns Inherent in Recreational Activities

Elliott Avedon has developed a classification system of interaction patterns found in activities. It enables the therapeutic recreation specialist to understand quickly some of the dynamics of participation. Once an activity has been analyzed to determine which of the eight interaction patterns are inherent, the specialist can make a variety of judgments about the complexity, demands, or appropriateness of that activity for a specific individual or group. In addition, interaction analysis facilitates the selection and sequencing of activities for building social and interactional skills. Since many therapeutic recreation programs focus on social factors, it is advantageous to comprehend as much as possible about an activity's contribution in this area. The eight interaction patterns follow.[3]

[3]Ibid., pp. 162–170. Adapted by permission of Prentice-Hall, Inc.

Intraindividual. "Action taking place within the mind of a person or action involving the mind and a part of the body, but requiring no contact with another person or external object."[4]

Activities in this category are few and are seldom used in therapeutic recreation programming. Twiddling thumbs or daydreaming fall into this category. Intraindividual actions are, however, frequently engaged in by individuals, although they are rarely discussed in the professional literature or presented in programs.

Daydreaming and fantasizing are forms of leisure activity, although they have not traditionally been recognized as such. Needless to say, it is not a type of activity that can be programmed, but it is one that should be given permission to exist and be enjoyed.

Extraindividual. "Action directed by a person toward an object in the environment, requiring no contact with another person."[5]

Countless activities fall into this category. Anything done alone that involves an object fits the requirements. Watching television, engaging in a craft project, working in a garden, playing solitaire, and reading—all can be considered extraindividual activities.

Everyone engages in extraindividual activities. However, this category of activities is seldom directly addressed in therapeutic recreation programs. The reasons are usually time and resources. Because we are faced with providing programs for numbers of people, we tend to rely on group activities. Ironically, however, in the process of helping people prepare for independent leisure participation, we frequently overlook the fact that many ill and disabled individuals spend a large amount of time alone and thus need leisure skills that can be engaged in while alone. Extraindividual activities are therefore a must for program consideration. The ability to enjoy oneself while alone should be a basic concern of the therapeutic recreator who realistically confronts the needs of ill or disabled individuals.

[4]Ibid., p. 163.
[5]Ibid., p. 164.

Extraindividual activities can also serve another major function: they can be used as the first phase of a carefully sequenced plan for developing social interaction abilities. It is often easier for a client to engage in a social experience when an activity is the focus, as opposed to an emphasis on interacting with others. Assisting clients to engage in individual activity is therefore an important step in acquiring interactional skills. When a person is comfortable engaging in an activity alone and is receiving some degree of satisfaction from that involvement, it may then be possible for him or her to begin to interact comfortably with others.

Aggregate. "Action directed by a person toward an object in the environment while in the company of other persons who are also directing action toward objects in the environment. Action is not directed toward one another, and no interaction between participants is required or necessary."[6]

Many activities that can be done alone (extraindividual) can also be done in group settings. In therapeutic recreation, this is indeed common. Crafts programs, entertainment, and hobby groups are all examples of aggregate activities, as is the "infamous" game of Bingo. Aggregate activities require no interaction between participants. This quality, however, has several inherent therapeutic characteristics and applications.

Physical proximity to others is one characteristic. When individuals are together, all engaging in their own projects or activity, they have the opportunity to warm up to one another without feeling any pressure to interact. Each individual focuses on his or her own activity, but spontaneous interaction stimulated by the action often results. Borrowing a piece of equipment, sharing a success, or asking a question are all social responses that are natural and easy to make. In a program designed to develop social and verbal interactional skills, aggregate activities are ideal in the early stages when nonthreatening interactions are essential. Aggregate activities are frequently used within a sequenced program of social interaction development.

Aggregate activities, as well as extraindividual activities, can be either competitive or cooperative. Solitaire, a crossword puzzle, or a pinball game are competitive. The individual can learn competitive action without the reality or threat of another person as the opponent. Testing one's abilities against the game or task has a variety of therapeutic benefits. The ability

[6]Ibid., p. 165.

to compete in many areas of life appears to be an essential ingredient of survival in our culture. Competitive aggregate activities provide a simulated experience for acquiring this skill in a safe or supervised situation.

Cooperative extraindividual and aggregate activities, such as crafts, woodworking, writing, reading, and gardening, allow the clients to gain internal motivation and stimulation without competitive demands. Increasing one's ability to enjoy an activity without feeling the pressure of competition can be an important experience. When actions are initiated by the individuals themselves, and conducted without external expectations or demands, a feeling of self-sufficiency and independence may result.

Aggregate activities provide opportunities for those involved to master activities independent of others. Since many ill or handicapped people spend time alone, they should have a repertoire of activities in which they can engage without others. The aggregate pattern enables the therapeutic recreation specialist to facilitate the acquisition of such skills while still working in a group situation.

Inter-individual. "Action of a competitive nature directed by one person toward another."[7]

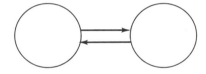

This interaction pattern is basic for many mental and physical activities. Chess, checkers, honeymoon bridge, singles tennis, badminton, and racquetball are examples. The pattern requires the ability to interact continuously with one's opponents and to apply the necessary skills with the intention of winning or at least enjoying the attempt. This competition simulates many interpersonal encounters in daily living in which individuals need to stand up for themselves in an interaction with another person.

Inter-individual activities vary in the amount and degree of necessary interaction. A game of checkers requires very little, if any, verbal exchange; other games require calling out scores, requesting information, or responding verbally in other ways. Inter-individual activities can be selected and sequenced to produce a progression of verbalization and other social responses.

Another therapeutic application of this pattern relates to the frequency of the interaction. A game like Ping-Pong requires continuous attention and response as the ball quickly moves from one side of the table to the other. In games like chess, however, there is no pressure to act immediately. Changes in frequency allow the specialist to provide a sequence of more and more challenging interactional activities.

[7]Ibid., p. 166.

Since the pattern is always competitive, it has the therapeutic quality of assisting people to deal with stress, pressure, and concepts of winning and losing. The therapeutic recreation specialist must focus on this aspect in order for it to be beneficial. Continuous losing can be destructive, as can be the overwhelming need always to win. Because inter-individual activities are competitive, they always have rules. A characteristic of these activities is playing by the rules and regulating one's behavior according to the rules in order to participate successfully. The players agree to interact and behave in certain ways, to their mutual benefit. The value of such agreement extends beyond the game into many life situations. In inter-individual activities, clients can experience appropriate role modeling for many other life interactions.

Unilateral. "Action of a competitive nature among three or more persons, one of whom is an antagonist or it."[8]

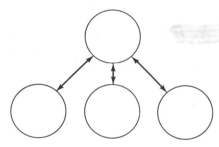

Many children's games have a unilateral pattern. Tag games, hide-and-seek games, and chase games are in this category. Fewer adult games fit it. Nonetheless, some characteristics of the unilateral pattern apply to the acquisition of interaction skills. Unilateral activities provide opportunities for role differentiation. In these kinds of games, all players except one have the same roles. It is the beginning stage of the recognition that different players have different functions, a concept that is further developed in the complex roles found in games such as basketball or softball. When just one person is "it," the concept of different roles is quickly learned and understood.

Several other benefits occur from unilateral activities. When working with mentally retarded individuals, it is often easier to teach beginning concepts of competition with unilateral activities. With other populations, unilateral activities put one person in the limelight. The competitive pressure also shifts from one player to another, thus removing the continuous, competitive pressure in other types of activities.

Multilateral. "Action of a competitive nature among three or more persons, with no one person as an antagonist."[9]

[8]Ibid., p. 167.
[9]Ibid., p. 168.

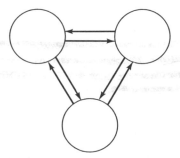

In multilateral activities, every player is against every other player. Games such as Scrabble, poker, and Monopoly are examples of activities that have this pattern. (Some social activities, such as cocktail parties, often appear to have this pattern also!) Multilateral activities have several characteristics that can be used for therapeutic outcomes.

Multilateral activities require each person to initiate competitive action with the others. For the individual who cannot tolerate sustained, competitive action with just one person, activities of this type allow for a diffusion of effort. In multilateral activities, the individual is often pressured to perform by a number of people simultaneously. This simulated experience has value for other real-life situations when the individual has to face pressures that come from a variety of people at the same time.

Multilateral activities place the responsibility for control directly on each individual, since each is an independent agent within the game. Decision making, strategy, and action are not shared by team members. The result can be a feeling of self-sufficiency for the individual who is ready for it. Obviously, many clients need to work up to this type of interaction pattern, since it places high demands on internal initiative and independence.

Intragroup. "Action of a cooperative nature by two or more persons intent upon reaching a mutual goal. Action requires positive verbal and non-verbal interaction."[10]

Examples of activities requiring this pattern include such things as musical groups (bands and choirs), dramatic plays, service projects, and square or ballroom dancing. Learning how to cooperate and function successfully as a group member is a difficult task, but one that most clients need. Unfortunately, without the motivation of competition, it is often hard to build the concepts of cooperation. Recreational activities of the intra-

[10]Ibid., p. 169.

group type do not inherently create cooperative action. Sensitive and astute leadership is needed to maximize the benefits of intragroup activities. Activities in this category are essential in helping to establish social skills, since so many interactions in life require compromise and cooperation. Family life, most social situations, and work are everyday examples that require intragroup interactional abilities. Programming activities in this category is overwhelmingly important if we wish to assist clients in the development of positive and cooperative interactional skills.

Many professionals feel that competitive activities are overemphasized in therapeutic recreation programs. The concept that fun has to involve doing someone else in or beating the other guy is indeed narrow. Enjoyment should be fostered through cooperative action as well.

Finding or creating good activities that utilize the intragroup pattern is a challenge for the therapeutic recreator. It is often difficult to establish a mutual goal that is attractive enough to the participants to facilitate positive interactions. Nevertheless, the benefits resulting from successful participation in intragroup activities make the effort well worthwhile.

Inter-group. "Action of a competitive nature between two or more intra-groups."[11]

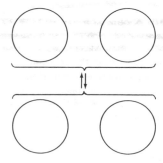

All team sports and games fall into this category. Softball, relays, doubles tennis, and bridge are examples. These activities are the most difficult to perform, since participants must cooperate with other team members as well as compete against their opponents. Far too often, clients are put into inter-group activities long before they are ready to handle the advanced interactional skills required. This often results in mass confusion, not to mention negative reactions. Therapeutic recreators should avoid introducing inter-group activities until they are sure the participants are functionally and developmentally able to handle the diverse interactions involved. Unfortunately, many traditional and familiar activities are of this type; we overlook their complexity because of their popularity.

Inter-group activities have many rather obvious therapeutic benefits. Learning to be a good team member is one. This interaction pattern represents many realistic life situations in which one group works against another group. The give and take needed to mount an effective attack can

[11]Ibid., p. 170.

be experienced through games, with carry-over to work, family, and other social situations.

An advantage of inter-group activities is that they often produce peer pressure among team members, which can effectively result in significant behavior changes in participants. This outcome, however, has both positive and negative implications. Good leadership is needed to influence the peer pressure desired. An understanding of group dynamics is needed to produce therapeutic peer pressure.

The fact that inter-group activities have the element of competition is another benefit, if handled wisely. The pressure to cooperate in order to win often brings a group together that otherwise could not or would not function as a unit. In this case, competition is a positive influence. Through the process, individuals frequently gain greater respect and liking for one another, which opens up other avenues of positive interaction.

Another therapeutic benefit of the inter-group pattern is the concept of a support system. To be a member of the team, to have a sense of belonging, and to experience unity within a group are all important and positive experiences. Many times, these experiences are missing in the lives of disabled individuals. Inter-group activities may facilitate the feeling of belonging and give individuals a base from which to develop other group ties.

Understanding the inherent interaction patterns found in activities contributes a great deal to our comprehension of the dynamics of involvement as well as to the therapeutic possibilities in the selection and sequencing process. Analyzing activities with the use of interaction patterns provides a valuable tool for the development of social interaction skills by enabling us to focus on the critical issues surrounding activity participation. Some therapeutic recreation specialists have developed assessment procedures for social skills utilizing these eight interaction categories as the basis for client analysis.

Other Social Factors

In addition to the interaction patterns inherent in activities, a variety of other social factors can be identified and used in the analysis process. Since the word "social" encompasses such broad categories of behavior in our culture, the list of factors could be extremely lengthy. Some of the more generic and useful items are presented below.

1. Does the activity provide opportunity for interaction with the opposite sex? No activity can be categorized as male or female, but traditionally, certain activities are participated in by one sex or the other in segregated programs. If meeting and enjoying members of the opposite sex is a client need, therapeutic recreation programs should present activities in which both sexes can engage mutually. Likewise, if sex-role identification is an issue, perhaps it is best to select activities that have the traditional male and female role orientation.

2. Does the activity facilitate social interaction by proximity? Often the goal is to increase social or verbal interaction; yet we erroneously select an activity like softball, where the players are spread out all over the field with little opportunity to communicate easily, thus eliminating any opportunity for either spontaneous or structured interaction.

3. How much physical contact does the activity require? Facilitating human contact may be a controversial subject, but there are times when assisting individuals to touch and be touched could be important. The issue is knowing whether an activity requires physical contact or whether it promotes spontaneous contact. Square dancing requires touch, whereas volleyball does not. The latter, however, may call for a pat on the back or a hug after winning or losing. Being able to cope with physical contact is a problem area for some psychiatric and emotionally disturbed patients. In such cases, it could be very inappropriate to select activities requiring too much contact before the individual is ready for it.

4. How much verbal communication is required in the activity? Although interaction is comprised of nonverbal as well as verbal communication, more often program goals deal with increasing or improving verbal-interaction skills. Analyzing activities for the amount and type of verbalization is therefore vital. Bingo requires no verbal interaction between clients, even though it is usually considered a social activity. Monopoly requires a lot of verbalization as the players buy and sell or share "Chance" and "Community Chest" cards.

5. How many participants does the activity require? Some activities have a set minimum and maximum number of participants. Checkers and Chess are two-person games. Other activities have a set number of players according to the official rules, but the number can be expanded or decreased. Volleyball is an example of such an activity. Other activities have no required number and thus can accommodate as many or as few participants as the resources, leadership, or facility can handle. Modern dance or creative dramatics fit this category. The activity selected must coincide with program goals and client needs. A two-person activity may be appropriate for encouraging a sense of being comfortable in a sustained interaction. A large-group activity may be appropriate for promoting self-initiated interactions among many people.

Other social or interactional items can be included in activity analysis, depending on the population served and their unique needs. Additional examples are included in Figure 8–1 on page 199.

EMOTIONAL (AFFECTIVE) FACTORS

Of all the behavioral areas of functioning, the affective domain causes the greatest difficulty in activity analysis. One problem is that of definition.

Affective behaviors are often difficult to deal with and, as a result, are often avoided. They are, however, a vital part of activity involvement and therefore cannot be excluded from examination. Therapeutic recreators are naturally concerned with how to recognize various emotional responses, since so much of therapeutic recreation programming focuses on developing, stimulating, and otherwise facilitating the appropriate expression of feelings.

Activities *do not* have set, inherent affective requirements that can be identified the way physical or cognitive requirements can be. Each client brings to an activity a lifetime of experience with a variety of ways of responding emotionally. An activity that causes excitement in one person fosters fear in someone else. Thus, there is no simple way to categorize the emotional responses or requirements of activities.

Basic Emotions

Six emotions are generally accepted as basic to the human experience. These six can therefore be generalized in relation to activity participation. The following descriptions are offered as guidelines for understanding possible emotional responses, but are in no way intended to be absolute. Individuals should be expected to vary in their responses. The therapeutic recreator can, however, be aware of possible outcomes and thus become a bit more prepared to cope with emotional reactions. Predominantly, we are concerned with what emotions are *likely* to be evoked or stimulated by the type of activity used.

Joy. We want people to feel good about themselves, to experience enjoyment, or at least to feel contentment. One thing that seems to produce this feeling in many cultures is winning. Any activity that involves competition, and in which the participants have a fairly equal amount of skill, should produce a sense of enjoyment for the winner. Unfortunately, the loser will probably sense a different emotional response. Very few people have really mastered the ability to feel good because of performing well even if they lose, or just feeling good for having participated. Our egos are too tied up with being the best, and that is quickly determined in any competitive activity.

Normally, enjoyment results from a pleasurable interaction with another person. Activities, therefore, that have a high possibility of creating social interactions are likely to produce some emotional feeling of joy and contentment.

Completing a task is another event that seems to bring good feelings to many people. Note the frustration level when individuals cannot complete a craft project because the time is up, or when tennis players have to get off the court in the middle of a set because the court was reserved by someone else. Contentment seems to be tied up with a sense of closure.

Guilt. Guilt is a very destructive emotion. It produces feelings of shame and inadequacy, and often results in counter-responses of resentment and hostility. Individuals feel guilty when they let someone else down.

This happens frequently in competitive, team situations. Players feel they are not good enough, or other team members convince a player that this is true. Being inadequate at something and then being forced to play and to have the outcomes affect others—this situation sets up a guilt response. People generally feel guilty when they hurt someone else. Any activity that has much combative contact has a high probability of producing guilt, whether the act of hurting was intentional or accidental.

Pain. Pain or hurt can be experienced through physical, mental, or emotional occurrences. We feel pain when we lose a game or when we have to acknowledge that we aren't as good as someone else. Competitive activities produce this response. There can only be one winner; someone always loses. We feel pain when we are rejected or eliminated. Activities that send an individual away to the sidelines or outside the circle can produce hurt. Musical chairs or a simple elimination dodgeball game selectively exclude more and more people as the activity continues.

Physical pain is easily understood. Lots of activities have a high risk of physical pain and should be carefully considered. Emotional or social pain is hard to predict, since it is more concerned with an individual's personality and previous experience.

Anger. Anger can be expected in a variety of situations. Any activity that requires physical restraint will normally produce anger in the person being held down or held back. King of the Mountain and wrestling are good examples of this.

Being struck by a person or object also produces anger (as well as the possibility of physical pain). Many activities require striking, directly or indirectly, and thus have a high potential for this emotional response. Obvious activities are boxing and fencing, but other activities, such as tag, volleyball, floor hockey, and dodgeball, have the potential of producing this response.

If someone needs to express anger, the activity can be analyzed similarly. It is often useful to select activities in which striking is a requirement of the action. However, the striking is best done through an object and toward an object. Softball, tennis, golf, and bowling allow for appropriate hitting within the rules and without danger to others.

Anger also needs to be understood as well in terms of symbolic attacks. Capturing the pieces on a Chess or Checkers board or sending a piece home in Parcheesi can produce the same response of anger as a direct physical blow.

Activities and situations that create a great deal of dependency on others can also result in anger and hostility. Although dependency is inherent in some activities, this condition is more often created by the therapeutic recreator.

An individual can become angry over a vast array of events or circumstances that the therapeutic recreator cannot know about and that are unrelated to an activity. Anger can result from defeat, frustration, or from not meeting one's own standards of performance. In these examples, the response is obviously not inherent in the nature of the activity, nor is it predictable unless the specialist is very familiar with the client.

Fear.   Fear is a strange emotion. In most cases, it is perceptual and usually unrealistic, but the felt response of the individual is real. Fear often results when individuals are insecure about their abilities to perform or when they are concerned about the judgments of others related to their abilities. People are afraid of failing or of not measuring up to expectations. These psychological fears often keep people from participating in order to protect themselves from perceived humiliation. Most often therapeutic recreators do not initially know what fears people have relative to activity involvement and thus cannot make many judgments about them ahead of time.

Some fears are easier to identify and understand, such as the fear of physical injury or the fear of social rejection. An activity can be analyzed to anticipate fear reactions to some of its characteristics.

Frustration.   This emotional response is a common one, and is frequently expressed during activity involvement. It is not inherent in activities, but is again a factor that the individual brings to a situation based on personality makeup and past experience. Frustration commonly occurs when one's abilities do not match the requirements of the task. A high-skill physical activity is likely to produce frustration because of the exact coordination of body parts required. Golf is a good example. Activities requiring a great deal of accuracy, such as archery and riflery, are likely to create frustration because the feedback is immediate. Other activities that do not have a well-defined outcome are less likely to be frustrating, such as crafts, or camping, or watching a television show.

Frustration is an expected response when two or more people are unequally matched in any competitive activity. It is also a common response when individuals are not performing at the level at which they know they are capable. Frustration is frequently seen when chance factors over which the individual has no control affect the outcome. It also occurs when individuals perceive that they are not meeting the expectations of others, particularly the leader.

Frustration levels vary a great deal. Some individuals are easygoing and are not easily frustrated. Others have high standards of performance and suffer a great deal of frustration in any activity. The therapeutic recreator has the task, regardless of individual personality factors, of selecting activities that can realistically be performed by clients.

Much more needs to be known about affective behaviors before activity analysis in this area can claim any real sophistication or accuracy. For the moment, awareness, observation, and common sense appear to be essential when considering this aspect of activity selection. The limited material presented here perhaps raises more questions than it gives answers. We hope that we are moving in the direction of being more concerned about affective stimuli and responses related to activity involvement. Predicting responses and being aware of possible outcomes appear to be important beginning points, as long as generalizations are not carried too far.

ACTIVITY ANALYSIS RATING FORM

The rating form (Figure 8–1) provides an example of a variety of items that has proven useful for analyzing a given activity. It also demonstrates different ways of rating activities, such as the absence or presence of characteristics, frequency ratings, simple checklists, and the use of Likert scales. It is not absolute; many other items could be added, and others presented could be deleted.

The reader is encouraged to select an activity and analyze it with the use of the form. Focus on the activity and its inherent requirements as it is traditionally engaged in. While doing this, try to keep your attention away from a specific disability or person. *Analyze just the activity itself.*

A therapeutic recreation specialist would not use a form such as this to analyze each activity under consideration for a program on a continuous basis. It serves as a learning tool. Most therapeutic recreators find that they can conduct an activity analysis in their heads after they have learned the procedures and have become familiar with the various items.

SELECTION FACTORS

The ability to analyze an activity thoroughly in all four behavioral areas enables the therapeutic recreator to more accurately select appropriate activities for predetermined therapeutic or instructional outcomes. Assessing client needs and specifying objectives have been previously discussed. Once objectives have been stated, the task of selecting the most appropriate activities for a program is undertaken. It is obviously valuable to use activities that have *inherent in their structure* the qualities that relate most directly to the objectives. *This information is only ascertained by activity analysis.* The process also allows several activities to be compared, so that the best ones can be selected and used.

Some professionals have found that the process of activity analysis has expanded their repertoire of assessment categories as well. For example, by realizing the many aspects of cognitive action involved in activity participation, practitioners have added these dimensions to their assessment of client needs, and, as a result, may end up with different or expanded objectives dealing with these areas.

The process of selecting activities for program content must also include a concern for a variety of other factors. These are briefly identified as follows:

1. Age. Although we cannot categorize activities specifically by age, certain activities are more appropriate at different stages of life. A common violation of this factor occurs when we program children's activities for adults. This situation is dehumanizing and humiliating. It occurs fre-

FIGURE 8–1 Activity Analysis Rating Form

ACTIVITY: _____

PHYSICAL ASPECTS

1. What is the primary body position required?
   prone   kneeling   sitting   standing   other

2. What parts of the body are required?
   arms _____   neck _____
   hands _____   head _____
   legs _____   upper torso _____
   feet _____   lower torso _____

3. What types of movement does the activity require?
   bending _____   catching _____
   stretching _____   throwing _____
   standing _____   hitting _____
   walking _____   skipping _____
   reaching _____   hopping _____
   grasping _____   running _____
   punching _____

4. Coordination between parts and movements:

	1	2	3	4	5	
Much						Little

5. What are the primary senses required for the activity?
   Rate: 0 = not at all: 1 = rarely; 2 = occasionally; 3 = often
   touch _____
   taste _____
   sight _____
   hearing _____
   smell _____

6. Hand-eye Coordination:

	1	2	3	4	5	
Much						Little

7. Strength:

	1	2	3	4	5	
Much						Little

8. Speed:

	1	2	3	4	5	
Much						None

9. Endurance:

	1	2	3	4	5	
Much						Little

FIGURE 8–1 (Continued)

10. Energy:

1	2	3	4	5

Much   Little

11. Flexibility:

1	2	3	4	5

Much   Little

12. Degree of cardiovascular activity involved:

1	2	3	4	5

Much   Little

SOCIAL ASPECTS

1. Interaction Pattern (check only one pattern)

_____ intra-individual: Action taking place within the mind or action involving the mind and a part of the body
—requires no contact with another person or external object

_____ extra-individual: Action directed by a person toward an object
—requires no contact with another person

_____ aggregate: Action directed by a person toward an object while in the company of other persons who are also directing action towards objects
—action is not directed toward each other
—no interaction between participants is required or necessary

_____ inter-individual: Action of a competitive nature directed by one person toward another

_____ unilateral: Action of a competitive nature among three or more persons, one of whom is an antagonist or "it"
—interaction is in simultaneous competitive relationship

_____ multilateral: Action of a competitive nature among three or more persons with no one person as an antagonist

_____ intra-group: Action of a cooperative nature by two or more persons intent upon reaching a mutual goal
—action requires positive verbal or nonverbal interaction

_____ inter-group: Action of a competitive nature between two or more intragroups

2. How many participants does the activity require?_____

FIGURE 8–1 (Continued)

3. How closely spaced are the participants?

	1	2	3	4	5	
Closely						Distant

4. Can everyone communicate with everyone else by nature of the activity?

Yes _____   No _____

5. Does the activity require cooperation or competition?

6. How much physical contact does the activity demand?

	1	2	3	4	5	
Much						Little

7. Does the activity promote sexual homogeneity or heterogeneity?
   Explain:

8. How structured is the activity?

	1	2	3	4	5	
Highly						Freely

9. Noise Level

	1	2	3	4	5	
High						Low

COGNITIVE ASPECTS

1. How many rules are there?

	1	2	3	4	5	
Many						Few

2. How complex are the rules that must be adhered to?

	1	2	3	4	5	
Complex						Simple

3. How much long-term memory is necessary?

	1	2	3	4	5	
Much						Little

4. How much immediate recall memory is necessary?

	1	2	3	4	5	
Much						Little

5. How much strategy does the activity require?

	1	2	3	4	5	
Much						Little

6. How much verbalization of thought process is required?

	1	2	3	4	5	
Much						Little

FIGURE 8–1 (Continued)

7. How much concentration is required?

	1	2	3	4	5	
Much						Little

8. How often are the following skills used?
   0 = never;   1 = rarely;   2 = occasionally;   3 = often

   Reading _____   Math _____
   Writing _____   Spelling _____

9. Intellectual skill required

	1	2	3	4	5	
Much						Little

10. Complexity of scoring

	1	2	3	4	5	
Very complex						Not complex

11. Rate the demands for the following identifications:

	Often				Never
Form and Shape	1	2	3	4	5
Colors	1	2	3	4	5
Size	1	2	3	4	5
Tactile	1	2	3	4	5
Objects	1	2	3	4	5
Classes	1	2	3	4	5
Numbers	1	2	3	4	5
Nonverbal Questions	1	2	3	4	5
Auditory Symbols	1	2	3	4	5
Visual Symbols	1	2	3	4	5
Concrete Thinking	1	2	3	4	5
Abstract Thinking	1	2	3	4	5
Body Parts	1	2	3	4	5

FIGURE 8–1 *(Continued)*

12. Check directionality required:
    Left/right _____
    Up/down _____
    Around _____
    Over/under _____
    Person/object _____
    Person/person _____
    Object/object _____

AFFECTIVE ASPECTS

1. Rate the opportunities for the expression of the following emotions during this activity

	Often				Never
Joy	1	2	3	4	5
Guilt	1	2	3	4	5
Pain	1	2	3	4	5
Anger	1	2	3	4	5
Fear	1	2	3	4	5
Frustration	1	2	3	4	5

ADMINISTRATIVE ASPECTS

1. Leadership: specific activity-skill expertise _____
                general activity-skill ability _____
                supervisory   _____
                none needed   _____

2. Equipment: none required   _____
                specific commercial product   _____
                can be made   _____

3. Facilities: none required   _____
                specific natural environment   _____
                specific man-made   _____
                  environment

4. Duration: set time   _____
                natural end   _____
                continuous   _____

5. Participants: any number   _____
                 fixed number or multiple   _____

quently, however, when working with mentally retarded adults and older people in extended-care facilities. Occasionally the opposite situation occurs. Children are asked to participate in activities that are above their physical, social, emotional, or mental development. For example, elementary-school–aged children may be pushed into team competition or learning social dance skills too soon. Successful programming considers the appropriateness of the activity to age and developmental factors.

2. Number of Clients. The sheer number of people to be served influences the selection process. Square dancing cannot successfully be done with fewer than eight people; likewise, individual leisure skills are difficult to schedule when the client population is large. Staff-client ratios, as well as budget considerations, enter into this critical area. However, program content should never be determined solely by expediency.

3. Facilities Available. A certain activity may be advantageous for an identified client need, but the absence of the required facility may render it impossible.

4. Equipment and Supplies. Many activities require specific equipment or many supplies; limited budgets often hinder buying them. In this situation, the therapeutic recreator must find a similar activity, one with the same characteristics and dynamics, but without the heavy emphasis on paraphernalia.

5. Staff Skills. Selecting an activity that the staff member does not have the skills to conduct is obviously inappropriate or even dangerous (for instance, an unqualified person taking clients swimming). However, program content does not need to be limited just to activities that the staff likes to do or can do. The staff should acquire skills through in-service training or professional development opportunities. In some situations, volunteers can supplement existing staff abilities. In either case, program content related to client needs should not be dictated by staff skills.

6. Carry-Over Value. Whenever possible, activities should have the greatest possible amount of carry-over value. Selection procedures can be based on knowledge of a client's future lifestyle and environment. The narrow focus on the immediate setting and its resources defeats the long-range goals of therapeutic recreation services.

The selection of activities for program inclusion requires attention to a vast number of variables. The nature of the program, and its goals and objectives are of primary concern. The nature and abilities of clients must also be considered. Constraints and characteristics of the agency and its resources are equally important. Consideration of these factors along with the information acquired through activity analysis should, however, enable the process of activity selection to be much more precise and appropriate.

ACTIVITY MODIFICATION

Activity analysis allows us to determine the appropriateness of selected activities for specific treatment, leisure education, or recreation participation objectives. It also serves a second basic function. It enables us to modify activities realistically and appropriately when needed.

Two major conditions require activity modification. The first occurs when working with disabled individuals in recreational participation, leisure activity skill development, or instructional programs. The analysis of the activity indicates the *actual participation requirements* for the physical, mental, and social areas. The individual is then assessed relative to these standard requirements. When certain functional abilities are absent or impaired, this indicates where a modification needs to occur. Sometimes the regulation of the activity is modified: for example, a rule is eliminated or simplified. Sometimes a procedure is changed; for instance, rolling a bowling ball from a stationary position. Sometimes a change is made in the equipment or the way it is used, as in adapting a pistol so that it can be triggered by mouth. Regardless of the type of modification, several factors should be considered:

1. Keep the activity and action as close to the original or traditional activity as possible. It's not much fun for a disabled individual to engage in an activity when the new version is so far removed from the traditional one.
2. Modify only the aspects of the activity that need adapting. A mentally retarded individual may need the rules of a game to be simplified but may be fully capable of performing the physical actions expected.
3. Individualize the modification. No two people with the same disability have exactly the same adaptation needs.

The second major condition that requires activity modification occurs most often in treatment or rehabilitation programs, where client needs have been assessed and treatment objectives written. An activity analysis determines the appropriateness or contribution of an activity to the treatment goal. The activity is analyzed, based on the variety of factors previously described, and it is judged appropriate to the attainment of the goal. A quick second analysis is made concerning the group members who will engage in the activity. This analysis reveals that some individuals may have difficulty with certain aspects of the activity. Minor modifications are then made for those individuals or for the group, so that the therapeutic benefits can be obtained.

Here is an example of this process. The treatment goal for a group of psychiatric patients is to increase contact with reality. The game of Parcheesi is selected and analyzed. It meets all of the physical, social, and mental requirements. It contributes to focusing attention and to staying in contact with reality. The individuals know how to play it and have the necessary control and skills. Therefore, Parcheesi is chosen as the activity.

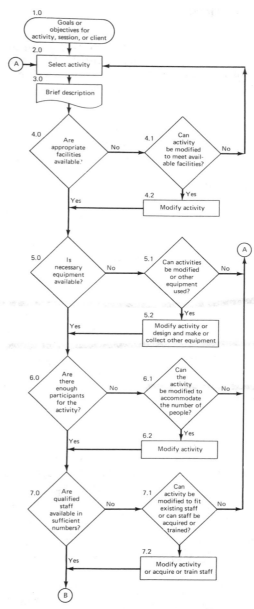

FIGURE 8–2 Selection of Activity and Modification Model

FIGURE 8–2 *(Continued)*

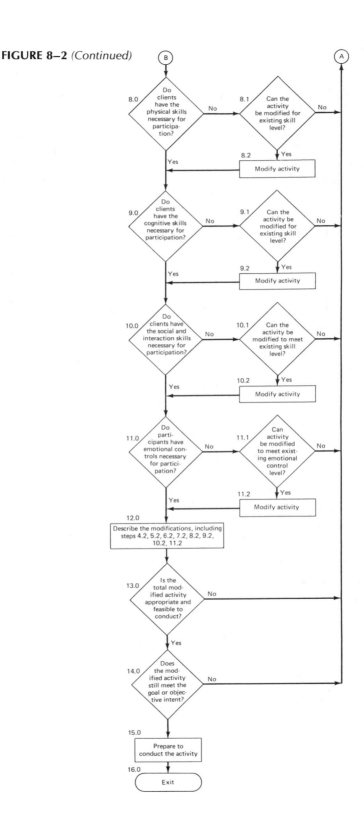

A quick analysis of the actual clients on the unit who would be involved in the program reveals that one client cannot grasp and move the pieces or roll the dice because he has attempted to cut his wrists, resulting in restrained movements of both arms due to the bandaging. The activity is modified for this person by assigning a partner to do the physical actions while the client makes all of the decisions. Because focusing attention and staying in touch with reality are the goals, the game is modified by decreasing the pieces from four to two and also decreasing the length of the game, and thus increasing the possibility of all clients being able to stay focused throughout the game. Over several sessions, the other pieces would be reinstated as the ability to focus attention increases.

In this case, the modifications were made to enable the therapeutic outcome of the activity; often, these minor modifications are necessary and

Goal or objective:

Selected activity: _____

Description:

Modifications from Step 4.2 (facilities)	Modifications from Step 8.2 (physical skills)

Modifications from Step 5.2 (equipment)	Modifications from Step 9.2 (cognitive skills)

Modifications from Step 6.2 (participants)	Modifications from Step 10.2 (social-interactional)

Modifications from Step 7.2 (staff)	Modifications from Step 11.2 (emotional control)

Description of complete modified activity

Decision based on feasibility and appropriateness of the modified activity to still meet the intent of the goal or objective:

_____ Accept   _____ Reject

FIGURE 8–3 Selection of Activity and Modification Worksheet

beneficial in the treatment context. Whether modifications are made to enable participation by a disabled person or for therapeutic purposes, activity analysis and functional assessment of the client are required. This process ensures that just the necessary adaptations are made.

The flow chart (Figure 8–2) serves as a helpful tool in learning activity modification procedures. It deals with administrative or operational concerns as well as with participation requirements. It can be used as a final check of an activity's appropriateness in the selection process or as a guide to where modification needs to occur. It summarizes the many aspects of activity analysis, and thus initially should be used in conjunction with an activity analysis rating form. A worksheet (Figure 8–3) provides the opportunity to examine the modified activity.

SUMMARY

Activity analysis is a practical and necessary tool of the therapeutic recreator in the program planning stage. In its purest form, activity analysis focuses on determining the inherent characteristics of activities. It enables a greater comprehension of participation requirements and gives insight into the dynamics of activity involvement. Practically applied, activity analysis makes it possible to select appropriate activities for therapeutic outcomes and facilitates sequencing and modification of instructional and recreation programs. Activity analysis gives more accuracy and accountability to program design efforts.

====== **Suggested References** ======

ADAMS, R. C., A. DANIEL, and L. RULLMAN, *Games, Sports, and Exercises for the Physically Handicapped* (4th ed.). Philadelphia: Lea and Febiger, 1982.

AVEDON, E. M., "The Structural Elements of Games," in *The Study of Games*, ed. E. M. Avedon and B. Sutton-Smith, pp. 419–426. New York: John Wiley and Sons, Inc., 1971.

———, *Therapeutic Recreation Service: An Applied Behavioral Science Approach*. Englewood Cliffs, N.J.: Prentice-Hall, Inc., 1974.

BERRYMAN, D., "Systems Utilization for Comprehensive Modular Planning of Therapeutic Recreation Services for Disabled Children and Youth." Final Progress Report, BEH Grant OEG-0-73-5171, New York University, May 1974.

BLOOM, B. S., ed., *Taxonomy of Educational Objectives, Handbook I: Cognitive Domain*. New York: David McKay Company, Inc., 1956.

CAILLOIS, R., *Man, Play, and Games*. London: Thames and Hudson, 1962.

———, "The Structure and Classification of Games," *Diogenes*, 12 (1955), 62–75.

CAMMERON, W., and P. PLEASANCE, *Education in Movement*. London: Basil Blackwell Company, 1965.

CRATTY, B. J., *Movement Behavior and Motor Learning*. Philadelphia: Lea and Febiger, 1967.

————, *Movement Perception and Thought.* Springfield, Il.: Charles C. Thomas, Publisher, 1969.

————, *Social Dimensions of Physical Activity.* Englewood Cliffs, N.J.: Prentice-Hall, Inc., 1967.

GARRISON, M., ed., *Cognitive Models and Development in Mental Retardation.* Monograph supplement to the *American Journal of Mental Deficiency,* 70, no. 4 (1966).

GODFREY, B. B., and N. C. KEPHART, *Movement Patterns and Motor Education.* New York: Appleton-Century-Crofts, 1969.

GUILFORD, J. P., *The Nature of Human Intelligence.* Toronto: McGraw-Hill Book Company, 1967.

————, and R. HOEPNER, *The Analysis of Intelligence.* Toronto: McGraw-Hill Book Company, 1971.

HARROW, A. J., *A Taxonomy of the Psychomotor Domain.* New York: David McKay Company, Inc., 1972.

HIRST, C. C., and E. MICHAELIS, *Developmental Activities for Children in Special Education.* Springfield, Il.: Charles C. Thomas, Publisher, 1972.

HUIZINGA, J., *Homo Ludens, A Study of the Play Element in Culture.* Boston: Beacon Press, 1950.

JOKL, E., and E. SIMON, eds., *International Research in Sport and Physical Education.* Springfield, Il.: Charles C. Thomas, 1964.

JONES, R. O., *A Theory of Thought Processes.* New York: Philosophical Library, Inc., 1969.

KRATHWAHL, D. R., B. S. BLOOM, and B. B. MARIA, *Taxonomy of Educational Objectives, Handbook II: Affective Domain.* New York: David McKay Company, Inc., 1956.

LOY, J. W., and G. S. KENYON, *Sport, Culture, and Society.* New York: Macmillan Publishing Company, 1969.

MCINTOSH, P. C., *Sport and Society.* London: C. A. Watts and Company, Ltd., 1963.

MEEKER, M. N., *The Structure of Intellect: Its Interpretation and Uses.* Columbus, Oh.: Charles E. Merrill Publishing Company, 1969.

MUNDY, J., *The Mundy Recreation Inventory for the Trainable Mentally Retarded.* Tallahassee, Fl.: Florida State University, 1966.

"Need Help with Activities? Ask a Computer," *Modern Nursing Home,* 27, no. 5 (1971), 39–41.

OVERS, R. P., E. O. O'CONNOR, and B. DEMARCO, *Avocational Activities for the Handicapped.* Springfield, Il.: Charles C. Thomas, 1974.

OVERS, R. P., and A. R. TROTTER, *Guide to Avocational Activities,* vols. 1, 2, & 3. Milwaukee, Wi.: Curative Workshop of Milwaukee, 1972.

PETERSON, C. A., "State of the Art: Activity Analysis," in *Leisure Activity Participation and Handicapped Populations: Assessment of Research Needs.* Arlington, Va.: National Recreation and Park Association and Bureau of Education for the Handicapped, United States Office of Education, April 1976.

————, "Therapeutic Applications of Activity Analysis," in *Expanding Horizons in Therapeutic Recreation IV,* ed. G. Hitzhusen, pp. 69–72. Columbia, Mo.: University of Missouri, Technical Education Services, 1977.

PETRIE, B. M., "Physical Activity, Games and Sport: A System of Classification and an Investigation of Social Influences Among Students of Michigan State University." Unpublished doctoral dissertation, Michigan State University, Department of Health, Physical Education, and Recreation, 1970.

PHILLIPS, J. L., Jr., *The Origins of Intellect: Piaget's Theory.* San Francisco: W. H. Freeman and Company, 1969.

PIERS, M. W., ed., *Play and Development.* New York: W. W. Norton & Co., Inc., 1972.

PINDERHUGHES, C. A., and J. P. Pederson, "The Psychodynamics of Recreation and Basis for Its Use as Therapy," *Recreation in Treatment Centers,* no. 4 (1965), 34–37.

SCOTT, M. G., *Analysis of Human Motion.* New York: Appleton-Century-Crofts, 1963.

SINGER, R. N., *Motor Learning and Human Performance.* New York: Association for Brain-Injured Children, 1968.

ULRICH, C., *The Social Matrix of Physical Education.* Englewood Cliffs, N.J.: Prentice-Hall, Inc., 1968.

WADSWORTH, B. J., *Piaget's Theory of Cognitive Development.* New York: David McKay Company, Inc., 1971.

WERTZ, D. J., J. R. HEALY, and R. P. OVERS, *Avocational Activities Inventory.* Milwaukee, Wi.: Milwaukee Median for Rehabilitation Research, Report 5, 1968.

WICKWIRE, G., "Activity Analysis for Rehabilitation," *The Archives of Physical Medicine and Rehabilitation,* 36, no. 9 (1955), 578–586.

9

Documentation
in Therapeutic Recreation
Nancy Navar[1]

PURPOSE: To present a rationale and overview of documentation and record-keeping in therapeutic recreation services. Descriptions and illustrations for various types of documentation are presented.

The importance of thorough and accurate record-keeping in therapeutic recreation cannot be overemphasized. In an effort to describe documentation as a crucial function of professional services, some administrators have coined the phrase, "If it's not in writing, it didn't happen." Such an exaggerated statement exemplifies the increasing importance that professional records are assuming in both clinical and community therapeutic recreation services.

RATIONALE FOR DOCUMENTATION

Although each agency may provide its own rationale for records and documentation, the following reasons are appropriate and apply to most agencies providing therapeutic recreation services.

Assurance of Quality Services

Recipients of therapeutic recreation services (participants, patients, clients, consumers, students) have a right to receive professional services that are of high quality. One way of assuring that programs are well planned

[1]This chapter was written by Dr. Navar and used with her permission. The authors acknowledge her expertise in the area of documentation and express appreciation for her contribution of this material.

and appropriate to client needs is to document the details of a particular program offering. The therapeutic recreation specialist, in essence, will be documenting what will happen in a particular program, what actually did happen, and how effective the program was.

The National Therapeutic Recreation Society has established *Standards of Practice for Therapeutic Recreation Service* that are applicable to both community and clinical therapeutic recreation services (see Appendix B). These standards provide minimal guidelines for the delivery of therapeutic recreation services and acknowledge the importance of thorough documentation.

Facilitation of Communication Among Staff

Accurate records about a program or a client can serve as a method of communication among staff members. Other staff members are not always available for an immediate verbal conversation. The written record of client or program progress can actually be considered a time-management technique that provides up-to-date information when personal contact is not feasible.

Residential settings provide twenty-four-hour services. This involves staffing for three different shifts. It is important that members of the staff on each shift have available up-to-date client information.

In both clinical and community settings, staff changes and turnover occur (due to attrition, promotion, leaves, illness, and so on). Continuity of program offerings and continuity of client care are ensured through accurate records that are available for new staff members.

Frequently, many disciplines are involved in providing services to the same clients (other allied health professionals, school personnel, and the like). To ensure consistency of intervention techniques, to avoid duplication of services, and to facilitate multidisciplinary or interdisciplinary team functioning, accurate program and client records and documentation must be available to staff members from all disciplines.

Professional Accountability

A professional can be expected to be held accountable for services provided. Accurate records are written evidence that services were provided or that plans for providing services are a reality.

Several years ago, providers of therapeutic recreation services were striving for professional recognition in both clinical and community settings. Now that therapeutic recreation specialists are recognized as professionals, they must accept the accompanying professional responsibilities. One major professional responsibility includes thorough and accurate documentation.

Another indicator of professionalism is the practitioner's desire and willingness to engage in self-regulation. Therapeutic recreation specialists can voluntarily facilitate the documentation process and, thus, assist in the self-regulation of their own therapeutic recreation department by following administrative guidelines established by their professional association. The

National Therapeutic Recreation Society has published *Guidelines for Administration of Therapeutic Recreation Service in Clinical and Residential Facilities.*[2] In addition to other administrative areas, these guidelines provide documentation suggestions for the following administrative concerns:

> Philosophy and Goals
> Administration
> Personnel Practices
> Staffing
> Areas and Facilities
> Equipment
> Evaluation and Research

In many instances, documentation provides a legal record that can be used to protect the client, the agency, or the professionals who provide services. Accurate, up-to-date records are critical to the concept of legal and professional accountability.

Compliance with Administrative Requirements

The content and methods of record keeping vary among settings. At times, both the content and format for record keeping will be determined by agency administration. In other instances, an administration may simply request particular types of data and the therapeutic recreation specialist will determine the method or format for collecting and recording the data. In still other situations, therapeutic recreation specialists will voluntarily initiate a particular type of record keeping because they feel it is important to collect and use the information, even if no one is requesting or requiring it.

All therapeutic recreation specialists should become familiar with their agency's documentation requirements. In addition, it is useful to investigate and discover the source of a particular requirement.

Some documentation procedures are unchangeable. Others are simply procedures that have been adopted in the past yet could be altered if they no longer are efficient and appropriate. By finding the source of a documentation procedure, the therapeutic recreation specialist will be able to determine which procedures are required and which procedures or record-keeping systems can be changed to better suit the needs of the therapeutic recreation department.

Several sources of documentation procedures are commonly found.

Agency Administration.   In some community recreation agencies, it is possible to identify the *individual* responsible for initiating or altering

---

[2]*Guidelines for Administration of Therapeutic Recreation Service in Clinical and Residential Facilities* is available for purchase from the National Therapeutic Recreation Society, National Recreation and Park Association, 3101 Park Center Drive, Alexandria, Va. 22302.

documentation procedures or record-keeping systems. This individual is typically the chief administrator or director. Changes in documentation procedures may often occur by obtaining approval of this individual.

In some clinical agencies, the approval of forms and records is the responsibility of the *medical records* committee, review board, or department. In this instance, alterations in documentation policies or procedures will entail a formal and thorough review of the proposed changes. In this situation, acceptance of new documentation procedures can be a very long and possibly tedious process.

Corporation and Multi-Facility Agencies.   Many long-term-care facilities, psychiatric hospitals, and other private agencies belong to a larger corporation, legal entity, or "chain." Some public agencies, such as Veterans Administration Hospitals, also are a part of a larger administrative structure. In these instances, a parent governing body provides standardized regulations or policies, which dictate record-keeping or documentation systems. The addition or alteration of record-keeping policies will often need the approval of corporate or administrative headquarters. Decisions are typically based on the applicability of documentation procedures for each member facility or agency.

Accreditation Agencies.   Many clinical and residential facilities must meet minimal standards determined by that agency's accreditation organization. An accreditation organization sets minimal standards for the purpose of providing quality services to consumers or clients. When an agency attempts to comply with accreditation standards, that agency may initiate corresponding documentation or record-keeping policies.

Accreditation standards may dictate the content of records but will seldom dictate the form that an agency must follow. Thus, the agency and, specifically, the therapeutic recreation department have much freedom in developing record-keeping policies and procedures that will comply with the intent of the accreditation standards.

Accreditation organizations that commonly affect agencies providing therapeutic recreation services include the following:

Joint Commission on Accreditation of Hospitals (JCAH)[3]
The five major accreditation programs operated by JCAH include:
Accreditation Program for Psychiatric Facilities (Consolidated Standards)[4]

[3]The Joint Commission on Accreditation of Hospitals provides a price list of its many publications. Publications Department, Joint Commission on Accreditation of Hospitals, 875 North Michigan Avenue, Chicago, Il. 60611.

[4]The Accreditation Program for Psychiatric Facilities (*Consolidated Standards*) of the Joint Commission on Accreditation of Hospitals (JCAH) provides standards for child, adolescent, and adult psychiatric, alcoholism, and drug abuse facilities. To date, this is the most comprehensive set of JCAH standards that affects therapeutic recreation services. Any therapeutic recreation specialist working in a facility accredited by JCAH's *Consolidated Standards* is responsible for complying with the standards *in each chapter* of the *entire Consolidated Standards* manual (approximate cost of 1983 edition: $30.00).

Accreditation Program for Hospitals
Accreditation Program for Long-Term-Care Facilities
Accreditation Program for Ambulatory-Care Facilities
Accreditation Program for Hospices

Commission on Accreditation for Rehabilitation Facilities (CARF)[5]

CARF provides different standards for the following types of rehabilitation programs:
Hospital-based rehabilitation
Outpatient medical rehabilitation
Infant and early-childhood developmental programs
Vocational evaluation
Work adjustment
Occupational-skill training
Work services
Activity services
Residential services
Independent-living programs
Psycho-social programs

Accreditation Council for Services for Mentally Retarded and Other Developmentally Disabled Persons (AC-MR/DD)[6]

AC-MR/DD provides standards for services that primarily serve developmentally disabled individuals. Guidelines for therapeutic recreation documentation are included in these standards.

American Camping Association (ACA)[7]

ACA provides an accreditation program for residential camps. Some hospitals and recreation agencies own or use camps to provide residential camping programs. Although accreditation of these camps is not required, most legitimate camping programs would desire accreditation by ACA.

Each accreditation agency will have standards that directly influence the type of documentation records that are maintained by the therapeutic recreation department. It is the professional responsibility of each therapeutic recreation specialist to become familiar with such standards and create or maintain the appropriate and meaningful corresponding documentation.

[5]A CARF standards manual may be purchased from the Commission on Accreditation of Rehabilitation Facilities, 2500 North Pantano Road, Tucson, Az. 85715.

[6]A copy of standards may be purchased from the Accreditation Council for Services for Mentally Retarded and Other Developmentally Disabled Persons, 5101 Wisconsin Avenue, N.W., Washington, D.C. 20016.

[7]American Camping Association standards may be obtained from the American Camping Association, Bradford Woods, 5040 State Road 67N, Martinsville, In. 46151.

Provision of Data for Program Evaluation and Improvement

One of the most important documents of every professional therapeutic recreation department is its therapeutic recreation *written plan of operation*.[8] (This document is explained in greater detail later in this chapter.) Unless the philosophy, purpose, goals, and objectives (all included in the written plan of operation) are documented, little meaningful program evaluation can occur.

In addition to departmental documentation, individual client treatment or program plans must be accurately documented when working in a clinical setting. Without complete records, it is almost impossible to judge whether the client's individualized program is meeting his or her needs. We cannot judge the success or failure of a client treatment plan or a program plan unless we can objectively review and evaluate that written plan.

Third, therapeutic recreation specialists must become more concerned about longitudinal program changes and effectiveness. A particular therapeutic recreation department may have an excellent program for the client it served in 1983. However, if the nature of the clients changed (because of a shorter stay, more multiple disabling conditions, and so on), the program would have to change. Documentation enables us to record these program changes over time and, consequently, better judge their effectiveness.

Longitudinal studies are becoming more common as means of program evaluation. In a longitudinal study, client functioning is investigated at various time intervals after discharge or termination from an agency's program.[9] The therapeutic recreation department needs accurate and complete records of the type of therapeutic recreation services clients received before discharge in order to participate fully in these longitudinal studies.

Summary of Rationale for Documentation

One of the simplest methods for keeping the issue of documentation in perspective is to follow this advice: "Do what you say and say what you do." In other words, the operation of the therapeutic recreation program

---

[8]In past years, many therapeutic recreation departments were able to function without having a written plan of operation. Now that therapeutic recreation specialists are considered to be professionals, corresponding professional responsibilities must be fulfilled. An important professional responsibility includes compiling a detailed and usable written plan of operation for each therapeutic recreation department. Both community and clinical therapeutic recreation departments should document their philosophy, purpose, goals, objectives, policies, and procedures. The reader is referred to the following article for a more detailed example of a written plan of operation for a clinical therapeutic recreation department:

Verdi, J., "Preparing a Policy and Procedure Manual for Therapeutic Recreation," in N. Navar and J. Dunn, eds., *Quality Assurance: Concerns for Therapeutic Recreation* (Champaign, II.: Department of Leisure Studies, University of Illinois, 1981).

[9]The Commission on Accreditation for Rehabilitation Facilities presently focuses its program evaluation concerns on a client's functioning after discharge. Detailed records are critical in this program evaluation process.

should correspond to its written statement of purpose and its written plan of operation; we should also keep accurate, detailed, and relevant records of each aspect of the therapeutic recreation program.

Although agencies will vary in their method of record-keeping, each therapeutic recreation department is concerned with accurate and complete documentation in order to (1) assure the delivery of quality services, (2) facilitate communication among staff, (3) provide for professional accountability, (4) comply with administrative requirements, and (5) provide data for program evaluation and improvement.

INDIVIDUAL CLIENT DOCUMENTATION

Client documentation is a major concern in clinical settings. In addition, some community therapeutic recreation specialists are concerned with individual client records such as the Individualized Educational Plan (I.E.P.) or client records required by a clinical-community referral system.[10] In most cases, however, individual client records are primarily a concern of therapeutic recreation specialists employed in clinical agencies. Although some community therapeutic recreation departments do choose to maintain individual client records, most do not. Therefore, the terminology and samples related to individual client documentation are clinically oriented.

Documentation related to the individual client is usually organized and stored in a main client record or chart. Since terminology varies among agencies, the terms "charting," "individual client documentation," and "client or patient records" are used interchangeably in this chapter.

Common Methods of Charting

There are two major methods for charting or client documentation: *source-oriented* record keeping and *problem-oriented* record keeping. In a source-oriented record-keeping system, each professional group or source keeps data separate from the other professional groups or sources. In the problem-oriented record-keeping system, there is a more coordinated documentation effort. The client record or chart is organized according to client problems rather than by each professional discipline. The mechanics, advantages, and disadvantages of both the problem-oriented and source-oriented record-keeping systems are discussed in the following sections.

---

[10]The Illinois Therapeutic Recreation Society of the Illinois Park and Recreation Association has developed guidelines for clinical-community client referrals. Although these guidelines are not yet in widespread use, they do provide excellent suggestions for developing a quality client-referral system between clinical and community therapeutic recreation services. Sample documentation forms are included in the following publication: *Therapeutic Recreation Discharge/Referral Process: Standards and Guidelines* (November 1981). It may be purchased from Illinois Therapeutic Recreation Section, Illinois Parks and Recreation Association, 250 East Wood Street, Palatine, Il. 60067.

Problem-oriented Record Keeping

Since 1958, Dr. Lawrence L. Weed has been attempting to improve the way that hospitals document patient care. Dr. Weed developed a documentation system called the *problem-oriented medical records* (POMR). The POMR system differs from the source-oriented system, since it focuses on the *problems* of the patient rather than the *source* of information. Ideally, the format of POMR will stay the same, no matter which clinical agency or professional group is using it.

Included in the POMR format are these five components:

1. data base, or initial assessment
2. problem list
3. initial plan
4. progress notes
5. discharge summary[11]

Each clinical agency or hospital that elects to use problem-oriented medical records may develop its own forms or specific methods for documenting each of these five components. The following pages provide examples and explanations of ways in which the overall agency and therapeutic recreation department may choose to address each POMR component.

Data Base. Any clinical agency will use a variety of data sources to gain information about a client. The specific data source used depends both upon the nature of the client problems and the quantity and qualifications of the professionals available to obtain the data.

Generally, a data base might include the patient's chief complaint or reason for admission to the hospital, personal and family history, medications and allergies, physical assessment, mental or emotional status, lifestyle information, employment status, leisure history, and so on. Some hospitals have the admission personnel or admitting physician obtain all or most of this information on a preliminary basis. For longer-term patients, more detailed assessment data are later obtained by each professional discipline. Therapeutic recreation is often one of the professional disciplines that contributes client assessment data.

In other hospitals or clinical agencies, more detailed client assessment data are obtained only when the preliminary assessment indicates that a referral is appropriate. In relation to therapeutic recreation services, more detailed data may need to be provided in any of the following areas:

Leisure profile: leisure participation patterns, leisure values and attitudes, leisure interests, and so on

[11]*Documenting Patient Care Responsibly,* Nursing 81 Books. (Horsham, Pa.: Intermed Communications Inc., 1981), p. 27.

Leisure skills: leisure or recreation skills and knowledge, prerequisite physical, mental, or emotional skills and knowledge

Social skills: behaviors, knowledge, listening or conversational skills

When the therapeutic recreation specialist contributes to the data base or initial client assessment, both formal assessment procedures and skilled clinical observations are useful data sources.

Problem List. A *problem* is any condition or situation that a patient cannot readily handle alone—one that requires intervention by one or more members of the health-care team.[12] Each clinical agency will provide guidelines for documenting a client's active, past, or potential problems.

In many agencies, all health-team professionals contribute to the development of the patient's problem list. In other agencies, the problem list may be developed by the physician or primary therapist. In either instance, many members of the treatment team will be used to help alleviate the clients' problems. Although therapeutic recreation specialists are certainly *not* qualified to diagnose the primary pathology, illness, or disability of a patient, they are often active contributing team members in the identification and treatment of a client's problems.

Not each of the patient's problems will be addressed by every member of the treatment team. A specific physical problem may be treated by the physician, nurse, and physical therapist, while the therapeutic recreation specialist need only be aware of the problem and take appropriate precautionary measures. A specific social problem may be simultaneously treated by a psychiatrist, a social worker, and a therapeutic recreation specialist. Yet a nurse or physical therapist may still enter a progress note based on observations related to the identified social problem.

Each agency will have a predetermined method for identifying patient problems. The therapeutic recreation specialist should become familiar with that method and determine an appropriate way of providing input to the patient's treatment plan.

Each client is an individual and has individualized problems. However, there are general categories of client problems that can be addressed by the therapeutic recreation specialist. The type of problems that the therapeutic recreation specialist will address depend both on the type of clients being served (children, adults, physically disabled, substance abusers, and so forth) and the role of the therapeutic recreation specialist on the treatment team. Sample problem areas that might be addressed by the therapeutic recreation specialist include:

Sample Rehabilitation / Treatment Problem Areas
Physical Fitness
   is easily fatigued
   complains of sore muscles

[12]Ibid.

Gross Motor Development
   locomotor skill deficiencies (running, jumping, and so on)
   lacks coordination
Cognitive Development
   short attention span
   difficulty with decision making
Social Skills
   atypical behaviors or mannerisms
   under- or overdeveloped cooperative or competitive actions
   difficulty listening or conversing
Emotional
   insufficient or inappropriate expression of feelings
   difficult adjustment to illness or disability
Independent Functioning
   inadequate decision-making skills
   undeveloped problem-solving ability
   difficulty with initiation of actions, choices

Sample Leisure Education Problem Areas
Leisure Attitudes
   lacks awareness of leisure
   lacks understanding of importance or role of leisure
   unable to relate leisure to own lifestyle
   unable to make informed leisure decisions
Leisure Activity Skills
   lacks variety of skills
   lacks desired expertise in skill area
   lacks knowledge of rules, procedures, etiquette
   lacks knowledge of solitary activities
Leisure Resources
   unaware of home or personal leisure resources
   lacks knowledge of community leisure resources
   unable to use leisure resources
   lacks money, transportation
Social Skills
   does not self-direct or initiate social involvement
   lacks conversational skills
   displays inappropriate social etiquette
   difficulty sustaining social conversations

Sample Recreation Participation Problem Areas
Independent functioning
Participation patterns
Self-expression
Use of opportunities and resources

Through client self-report or through the clinical observation of a client while in recreation participation situations, the therapeutic recreation specialist may identify treatment or leisure education problems of the client. The recreation participation component of the therapeutic recreation program is often used to identify client problems that will then be addressed through the leisure education or treatment (rehabilitation) components of the therapeutic recreation department's program offerings.

Each agency will have a predetermined method for giving priority to clients' problems. When using the POMR, each problem is numbered and the patient's chart is organized according to these numbered problems. After the patient's problems are identified, the health-care team can begin an initial plan.

The Initial Plan. Depending on the setting, the initial plan may be called the treatment plan, an individualized education plan (I.E.P.), a resident care plan, or an individualized client-program plan. When using POMR, the usual terminology is *treatment plan*.

The POMR treatment plan includes the following information:

the problem (with its corresponding number)
the goal and/or objective
plans for additional data collection (if necessary)
treatment plans
patient education plans

Client problems are listed in order of priority, and each problem is individually converted into a goal statement and behavioral objectives. The individualized client program plan contains a step-by-step outline of procedures to be followed in assisting the client to achieve the stated behavioral objectives.

Individual client program plans vary in complexity and specificity. Generally, the client program plan includes the following:

specific programs in which the client will participate
staff and client responsibilities
facilitation styles and approaches to be used by staff
frequency and duration of client involvement in programs
schedule for reevaluation of-the plan

Individual program plans or treatment plans should be written with enough detail so that all staff members understand the approach and can maintain consistency. The plan must be reevaluated, updated, and adjusted to address appropriately the changing needs and status of each client.

Whether a clinical agency chooses POMR or another form of record keeping, some form of individualized client program plan is required in clinical settings. Later in this chapter, individual client program planning related to therapeutic recreation is discussed in greater detail.

Progress Notes. Progress notes are the clinical method of documenting current information about a client into the client's main chart.

This information can indicate *progression, regression, or no change* in the client's condition relating to the specific problem or goal.

Some agencies may refer to *client status reports* or *anecdotal records*. For our purposes, these terms are synonymous with the phrase *progress note*.

The POMR progress notes have a specific format called SOAP notes. Each client problem requires its own SOAP data.

Basically, when a POMR progress note is written, the following format is followed:

Problem number and description

S—Subjective Data (what the client states about the problem; what the client says he or she feels)

O—Objective Data (what behaviors, signs, or factual data the staff observes or inspects)

A—Assessment (the conclusion the staff comes to, based on subjective and objective data, about the patient's problem)

P—Plan (what the treatment team plans to do about the problem now or in the future)

S for Subjective Data. As mentioned, subjective data include what the client says he or she feels or what the client states about the problem. Sample subjective data are presented in the following excerpt from a client's chart.

DATE	TIME	PROBLEM NO.	PROBLEM	PROGRESS NOTE
7/5/83	4:00 P.M.	2	Does not initiate social interaction	S: "I want to stay in my room." To TRS, "Leave me alone."

Since the progress note begins by listing the letter *S*, many agencies prefer that preliminary phrases such as "the patient states . . ." be omitted. Other agencies prefer that the subjective data be placed in context, as written in the following excerpt.

DATE	TIME	PROBLEM NO.	PROBLEM	PROGRESS NOTE
7/5/83	4:00 P.M.	2	Does not initiate social interaction	S: When TRS invited pt. to participate in group activity, pt. responded, "I want to stay in my room. Leave me alone."

If the patient is unable to provide subjective data, it is appropriate to request this information from the patient's family or significant others. In this case, document the source of the subjective information. A subjective entry may look like this: "Pt.'s mother states, 'Sue is lonely and could benefit from some social contact.' "

If no subjective information is available (if the patient was sleeping or refused to speak with you), just write the letter *S* and list the reason why subjective information could not be obtained. When other professionals read your note, they will know that you haven't just ignored the *S* category.

O for Objective Data.   The Objective section of the progress note contains factual information that you've obtained through observation. This information must be stated in specific behavioral terms that can be understood by everyone reading the chart. Personal opinions, conclusions, or generalized statements are not to be included in this section of the progress note.

DATE	TIME	PROBLEM NO.	PROBLEM	PROGRESS NOTE

O: Pt. refused TRS's request to attend evening social. While remaining in her room, client smiled and laughed while engaging in a 10-minute conversation with another 16-yr.-old pt. Pt. responded to questions from visiting pt. and initiated conversation related to favorite TV shows.

When writing objective entries into the progress note, record only significant findings. For example, if the patient's problem is anger or boredom, it can be significant that she engaged in a ten-minute conversation with another patient. It is not necessary to provide the content details of that conversation. In the preceding example, the patient's problem included the inability to socialize or sustain meaningful conversation. For that patient, it may be important to record sample content of the ten-minute conversation.

A for Assessment. As mentioned earlier, the assessment entry of the progress note records professional conclusions based on the subjective and objective data. (The term *assessment* should not be confused with the other meaning of client assessment as discussed in Chapter 10 or with collection of initial information in step 1—Data Base—of POMR.)

DATE	TIME	PROBLEM NO.	PROBLEM	PROGRESS NOTE
				A: Pt. has adequate conversational abilities for a 16-yr.old yet refuses to participate in a large-group social situation. In a 1:1 situation, with a peer, pt. interacted appropriately.

Assessment information can indicate progression, regression, or no change in the patient's condition relating to the specific problem. When documenting the Assessment section of a SOAP progress note, be sure to base your conclusions on the documented information from the subjective and objective sections of the progress note.

During the 1970s, it was common and appropriate to record in vague terms, such as "patient seems to be," "appears to," and so on. During the 1980s, many agency records policies will not permit such vagueness to be documented. The therapeutic recreation specialist should become informed concerning a particular agency's policy regarding progress notes and acceptable phrasing for documentation.

P for Plan. This section of the progress note includes what you plan to do about your patient's problem, now or in the future. This plan is based on your most recent assessment—the *A* data in that particular progress note. The plan can also be based on the following guidelines:

1. What additional information must be collected?
2. Have any other progress notes provided you with further directions?
3. Have any referrals been made for therapeutic recreation?
4. In what specific programs will the client participate?
5. What are the various staff and client responsibilities?

6. What intervention techniques will be used?
7. What is the planned frequency and duration of participation?
8. When will you reevaluate the plan?

The therapeutic recreation specialist must be careful to *relate the plan directly to the problem* under consideration. General or vague plans such as "enroll pt. in TR group" or "get pt. involved in activities" are not acceptable. Thoroughness and specificity are essential when writing the plan.

Excerpt from Patient's Progress Note:

DATE	TIME	PROBLEM NO.	PROBLEM	PROGRESS NOTE
				P: 1. TRS schedules two 30-minute sessions with pt. to reassess conversational skills and attitudes about group activities.
				2. Enroll pt. in leisure-planning class 5x/wk., starting 7/10/83, to increase opportunity for peer social contact.
				3. Focus on pt.'s social assets. Gradually talk about the importance of initiating conversations in friendships.
				4. Expose pt. to 3 new recreation activities of his/her choice.
				5. Reevaluate 8/10/83.

Progress notes and other types of documentation require a signature and date. Be sure to sign your progress note according to agency policy, using the appropriate professional abbreviation after your name.

FIGURE 9–1 Sample SOAP Note in POMR

PATIENT: Sue Smith			STAFF: Rhoda Williams, TRS	
			Signature	

DATE	TIME	PROBLEM NO.	PROBLEM	PROGRESS NOTE
7/5/83	4:00 P.M.	2	Does not initiate social interaction	S: "I want to stay in my room." To TRS, "Leave me alone." O: Pt. refused TRS's request to attend evening social. While remaining in her room, client smiled and laughed while engaging in a 10-minute conversation with another 16-year-old pt. Pt. responded to questions from visiting pt. and initiated conversation related to favorite TV shows. A: Pt. has adequate conversation abilities for a 16-year-old yet refuses to participate in a large-group social situation. In a 1:1 conversation with a peer, pt. interacted appropriately. P: 1. TRS schedules two 30-minute sessions with pt. to reassess conversational skills and attitudes about group activities. 2. Enroll pt. in leisure-planning class 5x/wk., starting 7/10/83 to increase opportunity for peer social contact.

The preceding SOAP progress note in its entirety would be documented as illustrated in Figure 9–1.

FIGURE 9–1 (Continued)

DATE	TIME	PROBLEM NO.	PROBLEM	PROGRESS NOTE
				3. Focus on pt.'s social assets. Gradually talk about the importance of initiating conversations in friendships.
				4. Expose pt. to 3 new recreation activities of her choice.
				5. Reevaluate 8/10/83.

Discharge Summary. The discharge summary is the final component included in the formal POMR method of charting or record keeping. Each agency will provide its own guidelines for both the content and format of the discharge summary.

Some agencies will use the SOAP format for the discharge summary. Other agencies will prefer a narrative summary or a standardized form combined with a narrative.

Typically, the therapeutic recreation specialist will have input into the discharge summary. Also, the therapeutic recreation specialist may be requested to write a summary of the client's involvement and progress in therapeutic recreation services. As therapeutic recreation services and other human services become more concerned with client functioning *after* discharge, greater importance will be placed upon discharge summaries.

A common slogan in many clinical agencies is, "Begin making plans for discharge the day the client is admitted." Unfortunately, few agency services truly abide by this guideline. Therapeutic recreation services actually could abide by this guideline if the focus of the therapeutic recreation programs was on the postdischarge leisure functioning of clients. Program goals, client goals, and corresponding client documentation could each be related to this end.

Given the diversity among agencies with regard to the discharge summary, there is no standard format or content appropriate to all therapeutic recreation specialists. The following ideas are presented as sample information that the therapeutic recreation specialist might include in a client's discharge summary:

1. *Major Client Problems or Goals.* This list or narrative will typically address either client problems or goals that the client achieved while receiving agency services. Therapeutic recreation's input includes problems and goals directly or indirectly related to present or future leisure functioning of the client.

2. Services Received by the Client. A summary would include the *type* of therapeutic recreation services that the client received. Many discharge summaries will also include the *frequency* and *duration* of the client's involvement in such services.

3. Client Responses to Treatment, Leisure Education, and Recreation Participation Services. Client responses to various services might include a summary of sequential client assessment information and a summary of highlights from client progress notes. Although some agencies do permit the addition of new information in a discharge summary, many agencies permit only a summary of previously documented client progress or status.

4. Remaining Problems or Concerns. The rehabilitation/treatment and leisure educational processes are seldom complete at client discharge time. Many clients will have remaining problems or potential problem areas after discharge. Many discharge summaries will enumerate and briefly explain problems and concerns related to the client's postdischarge leisure functioning.

5. Plan for Postdischarge Leisure Involvement. Too often clients are discharged from an agency without a clearly identifiable or clearly understood plan of action. Ideally, clients should be involved in the development of their postdischarge plan. When this is not feasible, because of the client's functional level, a written plan may still be quite useful.

The content of the discharge plan will certainly depend on the individual client's needs and abilities. Yet the client's future residence should also influence the content of the discharge plan. A client who is discharged from a hospital and referred to an extended-care facility will have a very different social and leisure environment than a client who will be discharged to live at home with family members. The discharge plan frequently accompanies the client when agency referrals are made. The discharge plan could also accompany the client who returns to a home environment. In each instance, client responsibilities and agency responsibilities should be clearly delineated.

Frequently, the client will be expected to complete a progress report, to be returned to the agency several weeks or months after discharge. Both the content and method of such a progress report or follow-up procedure should be included in the discharge plan.

At times, the agency will request that the TR specialist be included in the development of the discharge plan. In other instances, the TR specialist may initiate such involvement. The development of the discharge plan is one more method that can facilitate the future leisure ability of our clients.

Source-oriented Record Keeping

When an agency elects to chart according to the source-oriented record-keeping method, each professional group (including therapeutic recreation) keeps data on a client, separate from the other professional groups or sources. Each professional group does record in the client's main chart (client treatment record or individualized educational plan); yet, separate sections or pages of that chart are provided for each professional discipline.

If therapeutic recreation specialists wanted to read all of the current information concerning an individual client, they would need to read the nursing notes, the social worker's notes, and notes provided by each professional source. Proponents of the source-oriented record-keeping system claim that it is easier for a particular professional discipline to record all of its client information in one section of the client chart. Opponents of the source-oriented system claim that this method is cumbersome, since up-to-date client information is recorded in a variety of locations in the client chart.

The source-oriented system does not isolate and single out one client problem on which treatment is focused. Any professional making an entry or *progress note* in the chart may include observations about several identified problems; for instance, attention span, leisure skills, time management, conversational skills.

Although it is convenient for a staff member to enter all client observations in the same progress note, it is inconvenient in other respects. When a staff member reviews a client's chart, it is time-consuming to read each professional source's entries in order to sort out (1) the client's problems, (2) the interventions or professional disciplines addressing those problems, and (3) the client's responses to various services, programs, and interventions.

Figure 9–2 contains three source-oriented progress notes about the same client. Note the arbitrary format when the SOAP format is not used. Content may be included in any order. Each progress note may be documented on a different page of the client's chart.

The progress notes in Figure 9–2 all contain useful information for the nurse, the social worker, and the therapeutic recreation specialist. The source-oriented record-keeping method of charting does allow much information to be documented. However, from these three progress notes, it is not clear what Sue's problem really is, nor is it clear what action or staff intervention should occur next. In addition, each staff member must read all of the progress notes in order to obtain all the needed information about Sue. The source-oriented method of record keeping often results in overlapping, contradictory, or incomplete information about a particular client.

Summary of Individual Client Documentation

The two major methods for charting or client documentation are *source-oriented* record keeping and *problem-oriented* record keeping (POMR). In a source-oriented system, each professional group keeps data on a client separate from the other professional groups or sources. In the problem-oriented record-keeping system, all disciplines chart according to identified patient problems. Many agencies have developed their own format for charting, frequently combining aspects from both the source-oriented and POMR methods.

FIGURE 9–2 Sample Progress Notes: Source Oriented

Name: <u>Sue Stevens</u>

Age: <u>11</u>

Nurse's Notes

DATE	TIME	PROGRESS NOTES
7/5/83	10:00 A.M.	Pt. c/o being tired and states she misses her parents. Color pale. Pt. told she is no longer on medication. R. Smith, RN

Social Worker's Notes

DATE	TIME	PROGRESS NOTES
7/5/83	1:30 P.M.	Pt. states she doesn't like the children here and wants to go back to her regular school. Pt. c/o pain and asked to be excused from school and the activities today. Permission was granted to stay in room until evening activities. M. Jones, MSW

Therapeutic Recreation Specialist's Notes

DATE	TIME	PROGRESS NOTES
7/5/83	4:00 P.M.	Pt. states that she is bored after 3 weeks at the center and that she misses her parents and friends. When asked if she would like to visit some children in the activity room, pt. smiled and expressed a willingness to attend. When pt. arrived in activity room, she introduced herself to another girl. They sustained a social conversation for 20 minutes, smiling, laughing, and sharing school and family stories. Before returning to her room for supper at 5:00, pt. was overheard telling her new friend how she planned to be "sick" during school time tomorrow. N. Williams, TRS

TREATMENT PLANS

Treatment plans were discussed earlier in this chapter, in the section on problem-oriented medical records. Also, Chapter 2 introduced several issues related to the concept of treatment in therapeutic recreation services. The next section attempts to overview some of the remaining issues related to therapeutic recreation treatment plans. Sample client descriptions are presented for further discussion and development.

General Treatment Plans

Agency policy will determine both the format and process for the development of a client's treatment plan. In some agencies, one individual (physician, psychiatrist, primary therapist) will have the major responsibility for the development of a client's treatment plan. In these instances, the therapeutic recreation specialist has several options. One option includes the provision of therapeutic recreation services as supplemental to the primary treatment plan. Typically, this is not desirable, since the function and philosophy of therapeutic recreation coincides well with a treatment or rehabilitation philosophy. When auxiliary services are provided to clients yet not indicated in the client's primary care plan or treatment plan, the continuity and quality of client services is lacking.

Another option for the therapeutic recreation specialist involves a brief indication (documentation) in the treatment plan that therapeutic recreation services will be provided. In this instance, the therapeutic recreation specialist then develops a separate therapeutic recreation treatment plan, which will complement and expand the client's primary treatment plan. This method is frequently used by therapeutic recreation services as well as other disciplines. An important factor when using this documentation method is to design written and verbal communication methods to ensure timely feedback related to client progress.

A third option is to reeducate the person responsible for the development of the client's treatment plan. Many times, this individual may be unaware of the function of therapeutic recreation services in relation to client treatment. Ultimately, a desired goal for all therapeutic recreation services includes the education of co-workers concerning the role and function of therapeutic recreation in the treatment process. In the interim, therapeutic recreation specialists may still continue to provide and document quality treatment and program plans.

Team Treatment Plans

In some agencies, an identified team of professionals from many disciplines has the major responsibility for the development of a client's treatment plan. In these instances, the role of the therapeutic recreation specialist will still vary among settings.

At times, therapeutic recreation specialists will function in an interdisciplinary manner, providing team input throughout the development and implementation of the entire treatment plan. They will be involved in client assessment, problem identification, choosing goals, and the determination of services for a client.

Other agencies will expect each treatment team member to develop a specific aspect of the treatment plan. In these situations, the therapeutic recreation specialist will again need to develop a very detailed therapeutic recreation treatment plan. The next section of this chapter specifically addresses concerns related to the development of a therapeutic recreation treatment plan.

Writing the Therapeutic Recreation Treatment Plan

Because of the great variation in agency treatment plans, specific treatment plan formats are difficult to discuss. For the sake of the text, sample content and format for therapeutic recreation treatment plans are presented, as opposed to an overall treatment plan with therapeutic recreation integrated into it.

The treatment plan or individual client program plan is a step-by-step outline of procedures to be followed in assisting the client to achieve individual goals. Treatment plans should be written with enough detail so that all staff members understand the procedures and can maintain consistency. As the client progresses, the plan must be updated and changed.

Several guidelines for writing treatment plans were presented in the section on problem-oriented record keeping. Whether or not an agency uses the POMR format, these guidelines still have merit.

Information to Be Considered. Much information may be obtained from the client's chart. An up-to-date chart will contain client assessments from several disciplines, including therapeutic recreation. There is no need to duplicate efforts by reassessing what another discipline has already assessed. Therefore, the therapeutic recreation specialist should utilize all available relevant information before developing one's own assessments. The existing information and the TR assessment should be considered prior to the development of the client's treatment plan.

At times, the treatment plan must be written before all the necessary client information is gathered. In this instance, the treatment plan should specify what type of additional information is needed, who is responsible for obtaining this information, and a time schedule for documentation of the information.

Referrals: To and From Therapeutic Recreation Services. At times, specific referrals to therapeutic recreation will provide direction for the development of the treatment plan. The referral from a physician may indicate a specific physical condition or problem that needs to be addressed in the therapeutic recreation treatment plan. A referral from the psychologist or social worker may indicate a specific social, family, or behavioral concern that must be considered.

Many times, the therapeutic recreation specialist will discover a client problem or condition that warrants a referral to another discipline. When it is in accord with agency policy, the therapeutic recreation specialist may include a referral suggestion in the client's treatment plan. Since agency policies vary, the therapeutic recreation specialist must first identify the approved process for referrals in the particular agency.

Specification of Goals. Treatment plans will usually include individual client goals. Each client goal should be measurable. Although the format for documenting measurable client goals does vary among agencies, most agencies are now requiring that all professional staff record only *measurable* goals.

Sample Vague Goals (inappropriate)
To improve self-concept
To improve socialization
To increase responsible use of leisure

Sample Measurable Goals (appropriate)
To give and receive constructive criticism
To give and receive compliments
To maintain eye contact
To admit personal responsibility for own actions
To initiate/sustain a conversation
To demonstrate ability to make a leisure decision
To demonstrate knowledge of leisure resources

The preceding goals can be measured, although they are not yet written in measurable terms. In some treatment or clinical settings, the general (yet potentially measurable) goal is separated from the behavioral objective. The behavioral objective is usually very specific and contains the *conditions* and *criterion* needed to transform the goal into a measurable behavioral objective. The following sample documentation format (Figure 9–3) illustrates the separation of the client goals and behavioral objectives.

Other agencies will require that the therapeutic recreation specialist distinguish between *long-range* (long-term) and *short-range* (short-term) goals. There are no universal definitions for these terms. Long-range goals in one agency may imply four months, while another agency may consider long-range goals to imply one year.

In general, professionals have placed too much focus on long-range goals, to the neglect of short-range goals. When we see little or no progress in our clients, we may have set too difficult a goal. Several short-range goals will enable client and staff to recognize (and then document) progress.

Specific Programs. A major focus of any treatment plan is the specification of programs in which the client will be involved. Assume that the therapeutic recreation department has already conceptualized its programs

FIGURE 9–3 Sample Format: Client Goals and Objectives

NAME: Joe Ravan	NEEDS AREA: Social interaction skills
TREATMENT GOALS	BEHAVIORAL OBJECTIVES
1. To maintain eye contact	1. After 2 wks. of daily involvement in the TR social skills program, client will demonstrate the ability to engage in a 5-minute dyad conversation, maintaining appropriate eye contact throughout the conversation, as judged appropriate by the TRS.
2. To initiate and sustain social conversations	2. After 3 wks. of daily involvement in the TR social skills program, client will demonstrate the ability to a) initiate a conversation with a peer and b) appropriately sustain this conversation for 5 minutes, as judged appropriate by the TRS.

into categorizations that include treatment/rehabilitation, leisure education, and recreation participation. Each of these program areas may be further categorized into specific programs, such as resocialization (treatment focus), activity skill acquisition (leisure education focus), and so on. When this type of conceptualization has occurred, it is a relatively simple task to indicate (document) these programs in the client's treatment plan.

The most difficult situation arises when the therapeutic recreation department has neither comprehensively conceptualized nor documented a detailed description of the therapeutic recreation programs. Although not impossible, it is at best difficult, in this instance, to indicate stable, ongoing program involvement in the client's treatment plan.

In some instances, individual clients may have special needs that cannot be adequately addressed within an ongoing therapeutic recreation program. In these cases, the treatment plan should specify other mechanisms for dealing with individual clients. Frequently, one-to-one staff/client sessions, the utilization of nontherapeutic recreation staff, and volunteers are used to help meet the special or unique needs of individual clients.

Frequency and Duration of Participation. The treatment plan should indicate both the frequency and duration of the client's proposed involvement in various specific programs. Without such specification, it is difficult to tell whether the treatment plan is being implemented as originally designed.

Many staff members, while including the starting date of a client's involvement in programs, fail to indicate a tentative termination date. When it is not possible to estimate a realistic termination date, this date can coincide with the projected treatment plan review date. The accuracy and possible credibility of the treatment plan are dependent on the specificity of the plan.

Staff and Client Responsibilities. It is important to delineate and document both staff and client responsibilities. Each agency will have its own policy concerning the documentation of staff names in a client's chart. When last names are not permitted, professional titles (i.e., TRS) are usually included.

Whenever possible, the client should play an active role in his or her own treatment. For this reason, it is advisable to delineate and document specific responsibilities of the client. It is also advisable to document a plan for monitoring the implementation of these responsibilities.

Facilitation Styles and Approaches. To ensure consistent staff/client communication and interaction, it is important to suggest recommended facilitation styles or approaches for the staff to utilize. Such "hints for dealing with the client" will facilitate the treatment milieu or environment.

At times, the recommended interaction techniques are guidelines for those on the therapeutic recreation staff who are conducting the specific programs. In other instances, suggestions for interacting with clients during nonprogrammed times are useful. Consistency in staff/client interactions, both within a specific program and external to a specific therapeutic recreation program, can facilitate the treatment process.

Schedule for Reevaluation. Too often, staff members fail to indicate when the treatment plan will be reevaluated. The unfortunate result is that treatment plan reviews become a haphazard occurrence and not in the client's best interest. If a plan is not working, it should be changed. If the client has achieved all, or most, of the treatment plan goals, the plan should be updated and made relevant.

Signatures and Dates. Most agencies require that the designer of the treatment plan sign and date the completed plan. Other agencies require that each staff member involved in the client's treatment indicate this involvement in writing.

In some agencies, such a routine loses its meaning and becomes a meaningless ritual. However, the rationale behind such a procedure is sound. Signatures imply a personal awareness of professional responsibilities in relation to the client's treatment plan. They also can serve as a quality assurance mechanism, documenting professional accountability and timely communication.

Many agencies will include the client's signature on the treatment plan. This procedure documents the client's involvement and input into their own treatment process.

Figures 9–4 and 9–5 present sample client descriptions, which can be used for further discussion in relation to client treatment plans. We will first look at Figure 9–4.

Treatment plan design is a complex process. In the example of Figure 9–4, the therapeutic recreation specialist made several professional decisions.

FIGURE 9–4 Client Description, Example 1

NAME: Gary   EDUCATION: GED
AGE: 20   HOMETOWN: Podunk City
I.Q.: 100   (population: 9,000)
      OCCUPATION: unemployed

Excerpt from Social Worker's Notes

Gary has held several part-time jobs since he dropped out of high school at age 16. At age 17, he received a small inheritance, completed his H.S. equivalency courses, and bought a car. For the past 2 years, Gary has been unemployed, living with a distant relative.

Excerpts from Psychologist's Notes

Depressed mood (sad, irritable, feeling hopeless, feelings of worthlessness)
Sleeps 12 hours/day
Low energy level
Low self-esteem
Difficulty concentrating or thinking
Lacks social interaction
Not involved in recreation or pleasurable activities

Excerpts from Therapeutic Recreation Specialist's Notes

Present leisure involvement: sleeping, listening to music, pool, video games
Past leisure involvement: team sports in high school, going to the bar, cruising in his car
Client stated that he "never thought much about leisure, since that was for rich people."
Client stated that there was "nothing fun to do" in Podunk City, so he just stayed at home most of the time.

NOTE: Although the preceding excerpts are incomplete, much preliminary information is available for the development of a temporary treatment plan.

SAMPLE THERAPEUTIC RECREATION TREATMENT PLAN

DATE: 8/14/83   NAME: Gary

Data Sources

Assessments:	Psychiatry	NO	Social Work	YES
	Psychology	YES	Nursing	NO
	Therapeutic Recreation	NO		
Interviews:	Psychiatry	NO	Social Work	NO
	Psychology	NO	Nursing	NO
	Therapeutic Recreation	YES		

FIGURE 9–4 (*Continued*)

Problem Areas

  1. Expressed dissatisfaction with present leisure lifestyle

  2. Lack of knowledge of leisure and leisure resources

  3. Lacks variety in age-appropriate leisure activity skills

Goals

  1. To develop an awareness of leisure and one's personal responsibility for leisure utilization

  2. To develop knowledge of leisure resources

  3. To develop awareness of leisure activity and social opportunities

  4. To develop leisure-planning and decision-making skills

Plan

  1. TRS will conduct formal TR assessment by 8/25/83.

  2. Enroll pt. in "Singles Survival" classes (leisure education focus) MWF 3:00–4:00 P.M., 8/15/83–8/25/83. Focus on:
    a. planning for social opportunities
    b. awareness of community leisure resources

  3. Involve pt. in "Activity Exploration" process (recreation participation focus).
    a. TRS will explain activity opportunities to pt. by 8/15/83
    b. Pt. will initiate attendance at 4 activity sessions/week and record attendance in daily log (provided by the psychologist).

  4. Enroll pt. in "Values Clarification" sessions (leisure education focus) TTh 3:00–4:00 P.M., 8/15/83–8/21/83. Focus on:
    a. leisure awareness
    b. personal responsibility for leisure
    c. planning and decision-making skills

  5. Compliment pt. when social interaction or activity involvement are self-initiated.

  6. Redirect conversation when pt. complains of boredom or blames others for his actions.

  7. Reevaluate 8/25/83.

P. Alexander, TRS
Signature

FIGURE 9–5 Client Description, Example 2

FACILITY: Residential School for Emotionally Impaired Youth

NAME: Sue   EDUCATION: 5th grade

SEX: Female   HOMETOWN: Kalamazoo

AGE: 10

I.Q.: 120

Background Information

Client has been in residence at this special school since September 1, 1983. When previously enrolled in public school, client was unable to sit still in class for more than 10 minutes. She would walk around the classroom disturbing other students. Sue seldom completed in-class or homework assignments. She had few friends and lacked social skills appropriate for her age. She was regularly involved in quarrels and fistfights at school and at home with her brother (age 12).

Excerpts from public school referral

> lacks gross-motor coordination
> lacks cooperation skills with peers
> reads at 4th-grade level
> math abilities include: multiplication, long division, understanding of decimals; has difficulty with word problems
> disruptive classroom and playground behavior

Grades: Math—A   Reading—D   Science—D
            Spelling—A   Social Studies—E   Phys. Ed.—D

Plan

1. Client will participate in the following therapeutic recreation programs, 9/15–10/15/83.

MWF	2:00–3:00	Movement Exploration Group (treatment focus)
TTh	2:00–3:00	Cooperative Play Group (treatment focus)
MWF	6:00–7:30	Home Activities Group (leisure education focus)
TTh	6:00–7:30	Outdoor Adventure Group (leisure education focus)
Sat.	1:00–3:00	Community Trips (recreation participation focus)
Sun.	1:00–3:00	Family Activities (recreation participation focus)

2. Compliment client when the following behaviors occur:
   a. cooperates with peers
   b. attends to task longer than 10 minutes
   c. establishes and maintains eye contact and proper social distancing longer than 1 minute
   d. listens to and follows directions having more than 1 component

FIGURE 9–5 *(Continued)*

3. Gently yet directly remind client to engage in the preceding behaviors when she fails to do so. If necessary, role-model appropriate behavior and have client imitate this behavior.

4. TRS will contact physical education instructor by 9/20 to coordinate client's physical activities program.

5. TRS will request that cottage parents record client's evening free time activities and cooperative behaviors in daily log, beginning 9/15. TRS will evaluate this log on 9/25.

6. Goals for Movement Exploration Group (treatment focus)
   a. To increase attention span and concentration ability
   b. To develop the ability to follow directions involving sequential steps
   c. To improve body awareness and control, spatial awareness, and proper social distancing

7. Goals for Cooperative Play Group (treatment focus)
   a. To develop the ability to successfully engage in aggregate play for 30 minutes
   b. To develop the ability to successfully engage in dyad cooperative play for 20 minutes

8. Goals for Home Activities Group (leisure education focus)
   a. To develop skills in 3 solitary recreation activities that can be performed at home
   b. To develop skills in 2 family recreation activities

9. Goals for Outdoor Adventure Group (leisure education focus)
   a. To develop knowledge of 2 small-group outdoor play activities
   b. To develop leisure-planning skills useful in neighborhood outdoor activities

10. Goals for Community Trips (recreation focus)
    [These are program goals rather than client goals.]
    a. To monitor client's ability to follow directions
    b. To monitor client's ability to cooperate with peers

11. Goals for Family Activities (recreation focus)
    [These are program goals rather than client goals.]
    a. To monitor client's ability to cooperate with family members
    b. To monitor client's attention span

12. Reevaluate 10/15/83.

S. Murphy	9/15/83
Signature	Date

Sample professional decisions include:

What data sources are available? What information do I have? (Not all assessments or interviews are complete.)
What are the patient's major problems?
Which problems are priorities?
Which problems are within the domain (scope) of therapeutic recreation?
How can the problems be converted into goals?
Which goals are within the domain of therapeutic recreation services?
Are the goals (potentially) measurable?
What specific programs will help the client achieve these goals?
What facilitation styles or interaction techniques will be useful?
Does the patient have any unique needs (goals) that cannot be addressed in ongoing programs?

When writing the treatment plan, care should be taken that the client's original problems and goals will be addressed through implementation of the plan. Continuity and consistency throughout the treatment plan are essential.

Figure 9–5 presents a different type of patient, a different format for a treatment plan, and a different set of professional decisions. In addition to the professional decisions that were presented for the therapeutic recreation specialist dealing with Gary, in Figure 9–4, new professional decisions were made by the therapeutic recreation specialist dealing with Sue (Figure 9–5).

What other (non-TR) staff needs to be contacted?
What will these staff members be requested to do?
What specific client behaviors will be addressed in each program area?

It is very possible that each client will present a challenge to the therapeutic recreation specialist, who may have to make new professional decisions for each client. Yet there are specific stable guidelines that the therapeutic recreation specialist can use when formulating client treatment plans. Such stability relies greatly on the existence of a well-conceptualized, comprehensive therapeutic recreation program.

One stable assumption that will facilitate treatment plan design is the belief that every client has a right to be involved in the recreation participation component of the therapeutic recreation continuum of services. The second guideline involves a brief analysis of the client in relation to the remaining scope of therapeutic recreation services. Which of the following areas includes the client's greatest needs? problems? potential goals?

Treatment Component of TR Services
Are there predominant physical, mental, emotional, or social behavioral areas that will greatly inhibit the client's leisure involvement and lifestyle?

Leisure Education Component of TR Services
Does the client have an adequate awareness of the role of leisure and the ability to solve problems and make responsible leisure decisions?

Does the client have adequate social skills to initiate and participate in leisure pursuits?

Does the client have knowledge of the existence of, and the ability to use, available leisure resources?

Does the client have an appropriate repertoire of leisure activity skills?

"Meeting individual needs" does not necessarily imply a totally different treatment plan for each client. A well-conceptualized and well-implemented comprehensive therapeutic recreation program should help meet the major needs of the majority of clients served. The uniqueness of each client's treatment plan occurs when each client is assessed and professionally guided into the specific programs that will address individually determined needs. Uniqueness, or individualized client planning, will also occur through the type of staff/client interaction that occurs within each specific program area. Thus, while the content of treatment plans may be very similar for several clients, the treatment process will still be individually determined.

As stated earlier, each facility will provide its own *format* for treatment plans. In the instances where the therapeutic recreation department develops its own treatment plan, a usable, practical format should be chosen.

The *length* of the therapeutic recreation treatment plan will also vary among agencies. The plan must contain a sufficient amount of detail to be useful yet not be so lengthy that it becomes unfeasible to document on a regular basis.

Many therapeutic recreation departments have discovered that the treatment plan documentation time may be lessened by having a thorough written plan of operation that contains detailed program goals and objectives. Such a document is especially useful when *behavioral objectives* are required in the treatment plan.

The treatment plans described in Figures 9–4 and 9–5 contain no behavioral objectives. (The reader is referred to Chapter 5 for instructions related to the mechanics of writing behavioral objectives.) If the agency required the inclusion of behavioral objectives in the client's treatment plans, they usually would be listed after each client goal or after each program area.

Example 1. Client: Gary (Figure 9–4)

Goal 4.   To develop leisure planning and decision-making skills

Objective.   After one week of participation in the Values Clarification Group, client will demonstrate the ability to develop leisure-planning and decision-making skills by verbally—
1. identifying one leisure decision to be made postdischarge;
2. identifying possible alternatives;
3. evaluating the pros and cons of each alternative;
4. making a decision;
5. explaining how the decision will be implemented, as judged appropriate by the TRS.

Example 2. Client: Sue (Figure 9–5)

Movement Exploration Group

Goal. To develop the ability to follow directions involving sequential steps.

Objective. Upon request of the TRS, the student will demonstrate the ability to follow directions involving sequential steps by accurately responding to one out of the following two statements:
1. "Run when the music plays; stop when the music stops; begin skipping when the music begins again."
2. "Choose a color square on the floor as your home base. When the music begins, gallop in a clockwise circle around the room. When the music stops, return to home base and sit down," as judged appropriate by the TRS.

The reader will notice that to include such detail in the treatment plan would be very time-consuming. When such goals and behavioral objectives are detailed in the specific therapeutic recreation program plans, the treatment plan need only refer to the specific program to be included in the individual's plan. Thus, the documentation of the treatment plan is less time-consuming. Figure 9–6 illustrates how a thoroughly designed specific program can assist in the documentation of the client's plan.

In this section, we have attempted to provide examples and detailed information about treatment plans. It is acknowledged that each agency

FIGURE 9–6 Segment of a Shortened Therapeutic Recreation Treatment Plan

CLIENT: Sue

1. Client will participate in the following therapeutic recreation programs, 9/15–10/15/83.

MWF   2:00–3:30   Movement Exploration Group

Goals	Objectives
1. Attention span	1. 10 minutes
	2. 15 minutes
	3. 30 minutes
2. Sequential directions	1. 3 requests
	2. 5 requests
3. Spatial awareness	1. with objects
	2. with one person
	3. with four people

TTh   2:00–3:00   Cooperative Play Group

(Continue referring to selected goals and behavioral objectives as indicated in the therapeutic recreation program plan.)

S. Murphy	9/15/83
Signature	Date

will have its own policies and procedures related to the development and specification of treatment plans. Thus, the examples and information provided here must be read for their contributions to general concepts and principles. The major issue remains: therapeutic recreation can be included in treatment plans. This inclusion, however, is dependent on the therapeutic recreation specialist's knowing how to develop treatment plans appropriately. In addition, there is great value in having a thoroughly developed, comprehensive therapeutic recreation program with highly developed specific programs that can be immediately and directly included in the individual's treatment plan.

PROGRESS NOTES

The *formats* for progress notes were discussed earlier in this chapter, in the section concerning problem-oriented medical records. This discussion will consider some general issues related to the *content* and *procedures* in documentation progress. The issues addressed in this section have applicability for both POMR and source-oriented record keeping as well as other types of record-keeping systems.

Content of Progress Notes

Frequently, beginning professionals are unsure what to include in progress notes. What really is significant information? Although not exhaustive, the following list of guidelines can be used to determine the relevance of content to be included in progress notes:

> progress toward attainment of client goal
> regression from attainment of client goal
> new patterns of behavior
> consistency of behavior
> verbal information provided by the client
> successful or unsuccessful attempts at a task
> appropriate or inappropriate interactions with staff, peers, visitors
> client responses to questions, instructions, requests
> initiative with actions, ideas, problem-solving, decision making
> follow-through or lack of follow-through with commitments

Even with such guidelines, many practitioners are unsure of the significance of some client behaviors. General behavior and participation patterns, specific behavioral cues, and environmental cues are all potentially significant information to be included in progress notes.

Is Attendance Significant? The significance of a behavior will vary greatly among clients. While it may be significant that Mrs. Smith did not choose to attend the evening social, it may also be significant that Mrs.

Jones attended yet did not participate. Such observations become useful when they are documented and, thus, become available to all staff.

One frequent error made by many professionals is mistakenly documenting a client's *attendance* as evidence of participation. While it is often important to indicate that an individual client attended a particular activity, the documentation of attendance is insufficient content for a "progress note" and certainly insufficient information in general.

The following questions will help the therapeutic recreation specialist decide whether or not a client's attendance at a specific activity is truly a significant behavior:

> Did the client attend voluntarily?
> Did the client respond to staff or peer requests?
> Did the client merely *observe* the activity?
> Was the client *actively participating* in the session?
> Did the client assume a *leadership* role?

Notice the difference in explanatory information and resulting clarity or lack of clarity in the following two sample progress notes:

Incomplete Progress Note:

3/28   Pt. attended a pizza party Friday night.

R. Thomas, TRS

Signature

More complete Progress Note:

3/28   Pt. voluntarily participated in Friday's pizza party. He offered three appropriate suggestions to help organize the pts. assigned to cooking, willingly volunteered to help with cleanup, and courteously thanked the participants at the end of the two-hour social.

R. Thomas, TRS

Signature

Physical Cues. In addition to general behavior and participation patterns such as those previously mentioned, there are specific behavioral cues that often need to be documented. Again, the significance of these cues depends on the client, the setting, and the purpose for documenting.

The following sample *physical cues* are often observable and can help to accurately describe a client's behavior:

> *Dress:* sloppy, neat, formal, clashing colors and so on.
> *Posture:* slouched, erect, arms crossed and so on.
> *Movement:* jerky, fast, slow, tapping foot, wringing hands, shuffling feet and so on.
> *Social distancing:* touching, moving away from, ignoring, moving close to and so on.

Face: lips quivering, jaws clenched, eyes red, maintaining eye contact, cheeks flushed and so on.

Environmental Cues. The following *environmental cues* are often significant, since they help to place a client's behavior in a realistic context:

weather conditions
temperature
surrounding objects (cluttered room, open space)
social patterns (quiet small-group discussions versus loud, active, competitive game)
positioning (front of room, alone, behind table)
setting (indoors, outdoors, familiar area)

General behavior patterns, the circumstances surrounding attendance, physical cues, and environmental cues are all potentially significant information. The documentation of such information will help the therapeutic recreation specialist keep objective and accurate client records.

The following sample progress notes provide examples related to the use of physical and environmental cues:

Incomplete Progress Note:

5/30   Pt. voluntarily participated in the holiday outing.

J. Johnson, TRS

Signature

More Complete Progress Note:

5/30   Pt. voluntarily participated in the holiday outing. Although the weather was cold and rainy, pt. arrived in his cut-offs and dirty T-shirt.

J. Johnson, TRS

Signature

Assume that the previous client was working on grooming skills and appropriate dress. The second progress note, although brief, still provides more relevant information. The inclusion of physical and environmental cues can help place the client's behavior into a meaningful context.

How to Document Progress Notes

When recording observations of clients, it is crucial to document in an accurate, complete, and timely fashion. Although the frequency and timeliness of client documentation varies greatly among settings, the accuracy of recording client progress is an important consideration, regardless of the setting.

Behavioral Language. We have already discussed the importance of selecting only significant, or potentially significant, client behaviors for documentation. Once a behavior has been observed and deemed important, it is necessary to write about this behavior using *behavioral language.*

The mechanics involved in constructing a behavioral objective were discussed at length in Chapter 5. Although the recording of client progress need not be in the form of an objective, similar guidelines are useful. That is, the behavior, the conditions, and the criteria are clues to the content of an accurate progress note.

Appropriate Progress Note:

12/12/83   While pt. was attending the evening social in the day room, in the presence of 15 other people, she suddenly ran to the corner of the room and began crying loudly. This crying lasted approximately 1 minute, until I escorted her into the hallway. O'Brien, R.N., then talked with the pt. and escorted her to her room.

K. O'Malley, TRS
Signature

Inappropriate Progress Note:

12/12/83   Pt. seemed sad at the evening social.

K. O'Malley, TRS
Signature

Consistency in Information.   Consistency in charting and other forms of documentation is very important. Very often, a client's behavior during a therapeutic recreation session differs from that same client's behavior in other situations. Recording this behavior variance requires attention to detail and surrounding circumstances. It is important that the therapeutic recreation specialist not provide contradictory information about a client. In other words, *do not contradict what another professional charted unless you explain what you mean.*

Sample Contradictions:

Nursing note: 5/20   Pt. insists on using his w/c rather than crutches.

S. Smith, RN
Signature

TR note: 5/20   Pt. walked with crutches today.

S. Murphy, TRS
Signature

More Complete Note:

TR Note: 5/20   Pt. voluntarily walked to afternoon TR session on crutches. Smith (RN) indicated that pt. refused to use his crutches earlier same day.

S. Murphy, TRS
Signature

In addition to maintaining consistency among disciplines, the therapeutic recreation specialist must *be careful to maintain consistency in documen-*

tations over time. It is advisable to check back to what you have charted previously. For example, on January 23, the TRS documented that pt. Alexander was actively participating in two out-trips each week. On February 23, the TRS charted that pt. Alexander's social skills were improving because she was attending two out-trips each week.

The content of the preceding documentation simply indicates a carelessness on the part of the therapeutic recreation specialist. Had the TRS reread January's progress note, the TRS would have realized that pt. Alexander's participation in out-trips had remained constant. It was then inconsistent to imply that pt. Alexander's social skills were improving because of an increased number of out-trips.

The conscientious professional will maintain consistency in documentation. Such consistency is one indication of an organized and well-implemented approach or program plan.

Meaningful Phrases. The therapeutic recreation specialist should document only meaningful information. Vague phrases, such as "seems to be" and "appears to" have little meaning when recorded.

The trend in the 1970s was to use these phrases to help protect the staff from documentation errors. In reality, these phrases have been greatly overused and have made many professionals look uncertain. Rather than writing, "Pt. seems to be enjoying herself," use descriptive, behavioral language, as in the following example: "Pt. smiled and laughed while conversing with peers. When asked if she was having a good time, pt. responded, 'You bet! This is a great activity!' "

Documenting Incidents. Each agency will have a special form for documenting accidents, incidents, or unusual occurrences (that is, client injury, broken equipment, runaway client, and so on). When a client is involved in an incident or unusual occurrence, this information should also be reported in the client's main chart. An entry in the client's chart after an incident should include the following information:

When and where the incident occurred

Findings at the scene (facts; visual or material information)

Care of client pre- and postincident

Client's comments

Who was notified

What preventive steps are/were taken

Do *NOT* chart the fact that an incident report was filed, as legal counsel to most agencies will advise. However, the details surrounding the incident must be charted.

Writing Mechanics. Although some agencies are beginning to document progress notes with computer terminals, most progress notes are still hand-written. It is essential that each entry be legible and written in ink. Only standard medical and agency-approved abbreviations may be used.

If a documentation error is made, there will be a specific agency policy indicating how to correct it. A common method of correcting writing errors includes the following three procedures:

1. Draw a single line through the error.
   This avoids corrections, which create the appearance of tampering.
2. Write the correction above the crossed-out portion.
3. Initial and date the correction.
   This procedure helps to authenticate the correction.

               arrived NN 3/17
Sample Correction:

      Pt. ~~invited~~ . . .

When to Document Progress Notes

How often should a progress note be written? Three factors relate to this question: agency regulations and requirements, TR staff-time usage, and delivery of quality services.

Agency Regulations. Each agency will specify the required frequency of progress notes. For example, some general hospitals require daily charting, a psychiatric facility may require weekly progress notes, and an extended-care facility may require monthly or quarterly progress notes. The therapeutic recreation specialist should inquire about the agency's charting requirements and follow the same documentation schedule required of other team professionals.

TR Staff-Time Usage. A common complaint among therapeutic recreation specialists, as well as other allied health professionals, is the lack of time for documentation. Time for documentation and charting should be regularly scheduled into the therapeutic recreation specialists' daily, weekly, or monthly schedules. Thus, there is no longer any valid excuse that alleviates the therapeutic recreation specialist from the professional responsibility of performing accurate and timely client documentation.

Although historically, therapeutic recreation specialists chose to spend most of their work day in direct client contact, this approach is no longer feasible or desirable. Many therapeutic recreation departments have paralleled their documentation time allotments with other professional disciplines in their facility. Although there is no national standard, some therapeutic recreation departments allocate 30 to 50 percent of staff time for administrative issues (documentation, charting, planning, conferences, committee work, in-service training, program evaluation, continuing education, and so on).

Delivery of Quality Services. The third, and most important, rationale for timely documentation is the delivery of quality services. As discussed in the first part of this chapter, timely documentation helps to facilitate communication among staff members, thus enabling improved professional services. The therapeutic recreation specialist may choose to write in a client's chart more frequently than is required if more frequent documentation provides important information about an individual client.

Progress notes are a critical aspect of individual client record keeping. The professional therapeutic recreation specialist will be expected to provide client documentation and progress notes regularly and accurately.

RECORDING CLIENT OBSERVATIONS

There are several observational and recording methods available to assist the therapeutic recreation specialist in accurately documenting observations made of clients. The appropriateness of the method depends upon the type of observation being made, the purpose for making the observation, and the feasibility of the recording method.

The next several pages address the recording of client observations in general. The information obtained from such preliminary documentation can be useful in more formal records, such as treatment plans, progress notes, program records, and referral information. Specific documentation formats are presented for illustrative purposes only. Many other formats for documenting observations of clients are possible.

Many times, our observations of clients and corresponding documentation records need to be very specific and accurate. In these instances, there are formal recording methods that enable the therapeutic recreation specialist to obtain objective data about a client's behavior. The four methods presented here include the *interval* recording method, the *tally* method of recording, the *duration* method, and the *instantaneous time sampling* method.

Interval Recording

The interval recording method is typically used when we want a running account of the occurrence or nonoccurrence of a behavior (or group of behaviors). Here are some sample behaviors appropriate for the interval recording method.

Sample Behavior	Possible Interval
engaging in isolated play	15 seconds
biting one's lip	1 minute
staring into space	1 minute
crying (fairly frequently)	15 seconds
engaging in cooperative play	1 minute
inappropriate rocking	1 minute
interrupting a conversation	15 seconds

FIGURE 9–7 Sample Interval Recording

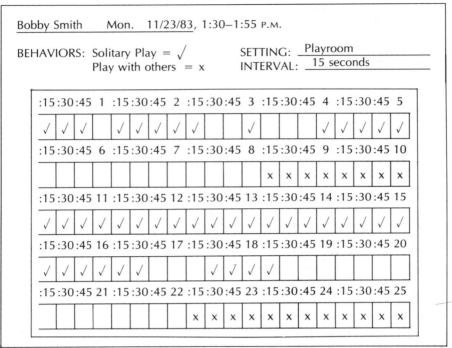

Bobby Smith   Mon.   11/23/83, 1:30–1:55 P.M.

BEHAVIORS: Solitary Play = √   SETTING: Playroom
                 Play with others = x   INTERVAL: 15 seconds

It is important to determine the size of the intervals on the basis of how often the behavior occurs. Choose an interval size that is large enough to allow you to observe the behavior but small enough to show separate occurrences of the behavior.

If the behavior occurs at least once during an interval, the observer records a mark on the data sheet; if an interval passes without a behavior's occurring, no mark is recorded. A mark is recorded whenever the behavior occurs during an interval, even if the person started the behavior during a previous interval. Figure 9–7 is an example of interval recording.

Several conclusions can be drawn from a visual analysis of this documented observation. For example, during a twenty-five-minute playroom session, the client (1) engaged in five minutes' of play with other children, (2) engaged in eleven minutes' of solitary play, and (3) was observed not playing for nine minutes.

If these behaviors (solitary play, play with others, and nonplay) were recorded by the interval method over several sessions, it would be possible to determine if there was a pattern to Bobby's behaviors. Once the patterns were discovered, possible intervention techniques and environmental influences could be altered to help Bobby change his use of the playroom.

The interval recording method provides a means of recording behaviors that would be very difficult to observe reliably in any other way. Although this method is time-consuming and usually requires an independent person to observe and record behaviors, it is useful when—

you want to do a rough estimate of both the frequency and duration of the behavior;

the rate of behavior is low enough to count;

it is not easy to tell exactly when a behavior starts and stops.

Tally Method

The tally method of recording is often used when you are interested in knowing the *frequency* or the number of times that a person engages in a specific behavior. The procedure simply involves scoring a tally mark each time the subject engages in the behavior during the observation period. A wide variety of behaviors can be recorded using the tally method.

Sample Behaviors: Treatment/Rehabilitation	Tally Record
number of times client responds assertively	///
number of times client follows directions	##+
number of times client independently walks to activities	##+ ///
number of times physical aggression is shown	//
number of times client seeks attention by shouting	///
number of times client whines	//

Sample Behaviors: Leisure Education	Tally Record
number of leisure resources identified	///
number of craft projects completed	//
number of answers volunteered	##+ ##+
number of times client initiates conversation	##+ //
number of sit-ups performed	##+ ##+ ##+
number of questions asked	//
number of leisure decisions made	##+

Sample Behaviors: Recreation Participation	Tally Record
number of activities chosen	##+
number of times client attends music group	///
number of leisure resources used	##+ /
number of people attending an activity	##+ ##+

The next example (Figure 9–8) uses the tally method to record a client's frequency of engaging in four different social behaviors. The client's behaviors are documented during four different therapeutic recreation groups.

FIGURE 9–8 Sample Tally Recording for One Client

Marcia Jones   Week of 11/25

Behaviors	Exercise Group	Music Group	Social Hour	Leisure Education Group
Asks questions of leaders	ⅲ	ⅲ //	ⅲ ⅲ	ⅲ ///
Asks questions of peers			//	
Volunteers answers	ⅲ	ⅲ ⅲ		ⅲ ⅲ
Initiates conversation			///	

Figure 9–8 records the frequency of one client's behaviors in four social/conversational areas during a week's time. The tally method can also be used to record behaviors of several individuals, as illustrated in the following document (Figure 9–9).

Through a visual analysis of this tally documentation of behavior frequency, one can report an increase or decrease in participation in the assertiveness group. Since we recorded two types of behaviors (contribution to the discussion and initiation of discussion topics), facts may be concluded in two behavioral areas.

The tally method is useful to the staff when the behavior can be defined very clearly and when you are interested in knowing the number of times the behavior occurs. The tally method is also commonly presented to clients as a method of keeping track of their own behaviors. Sample behaviors appropriate for client self-reporting might include

> number of times I exercised during a week
> number of TV shows watched
> number of times anger was expressed assertively
> number of times I overcame a temptation to get off my diet
> number of social contacts initiated
> number of community resources used

The *frequency* of a behavior may be converted into *percentages* (for example, percent of shooting accuracy) or into *rate,* which is a frequency

FIGURE 9–9 Sample Tally Recording for a Group of Clients

ASSERTIVENESS GROUP   A = Contributes to discussion
B = Initiates topic for discussion

CLIENTS	11/26		11/28		11/30		12/2		12/4		12/6		1/4		1/6	
	A	B	A	B	A	B	A	B	A	B	A	B	A	B	A	B
Steve	///	/	////	//	////	//	₮HT	//	HHT	//	HHT	//	HHT	/	HHT	//
Mary	//		//		///	/	///	//	////	///	HHT	///	HHT	//	HHT	//
Barb	HHT	/	///	/	///	/	HHT	/	////	/	///	/	////	/	///	/
Joe	//				//		//		//		//		//	/	///	/
Skip	///	/	//	/	//	//										
Tom	//		//		//		//		//		//		//		//	
Selah	HHT /	HHT	HHT	HHT /	////	///	///	/	///	/	///	//	///	/	///	/

per unit of time (for instance, client gets out of seat two times per minute). The therapeutic recreation specialist will find the tally method of documenting behavior quite simple and useful in many situations.

Duration Method

The duration method is often used when you are interested in knowing how much time is spent in a specific behavior. If someone can observe constantly for the entire observation period, and if you are observing the behaviors of only one person, the duration method may be the most accurate method of recording. A variety of behaviors can be recorded using the duration method.

Sample Behaviors: Treatment/Rehabilitation
engages in/sustains conversation with staff
attends to task at hand
plays video game (attention span)
walks without tiring

Sample Behaviors: Leisure Education
engages in/sustains conversation with peers
engages in calisthenics
follows rules and procedures of card game
stays attentive/involved in group planning exercise

Sample Behaviors: Recreation Participation
watches TV

hoes garden plot (maintains interest)

A sweep second hand on a clock or a stopwatch is a useful aid when recording duration. Begin timing the behavior at its onset, and cease timing when the behavior ceases. Record the duration of the behavior. The duration record or data sheet might look like this:

11/26   ACTIVITY ROOM COFFEE HOUR   CLIENT: Nancy Brown
                                      OBSERVER: Pat Stevens, TRS

BEHAVIOR: Engages in conversation with peers
TOTAL LENGTH OF SESSION: 30 minutes
TIME STARTED: 6:00 P.M.
TIME ENDED: 6:30 P.M.
TOTAL DURATION (read from stopwatch): 15 minutes

In the preceding example, Nancy was observed for thirty minutes by the therapeutic recreation specialist. The TRS maintained an unobstructed (and unobtrusive!) view of Nancy for the entire thirty minutes. Whenever Nancy conversed with another client, the TRS started a stopwatch concealed in her hand. When Nancy ceased interacting, the watch was stopped until the next interaction began. Nancy engaged in conversation with peers for fifteen minutes, or 50 percent of duration of the coffee hour.

The duration method of recording observations is somewhat time-consuming, since accurate observations do demand a great deal of attention on the part of the observer. The therapeutic recreation specialist should choose the duration method of recording behavior only when the behavior is readily and easily observed by this method.

Instantaneous Time Sampling

Many times, it is not possible to obtain a trained observer who can spend the time recording behaviors using the previously mentioned recording methods. In this instance, the instantaneous time-sampling method can be useful. It involves the observer's watching the subject or group of subjects for an instant at the end of predetermined time intervals and deciding whether or not the subject(s) engaged in the behavior. Sample behaviors appropriate for instantaneous time sampling include the following:

Sample Behaviors: Treatment/Rehabilitation
following directions to do *x*, *y*, or *z*

sitting alone

staying in own room

responding appropriately to reality-oriented questions

Sample Behaviors: Leisure Education
engaging in social conversation
playing a new table game
reading community resource pamphlets or bulletin board
utilizing facility's leisure resources
correctly identifying leisure opportunities or choices

Sample Behaviors: Recreation Participation
number of clients watching TV
number of clients interacting with peers
working in the garden
listening/attending to music
playing cards

To use this method of observation, divide the observation period into small intervals (usually fifteen seconds to fifteen minutes), depending upon how frequently the behavior occurs. At the end of each time interval, look at the subject and record whether or not the behavior is occurring. This type of "spot checking" is frequently used in therapeutic recreation services.

This method can be useful when observing a group or several clients. Simply scan the group (in the same direction each time) and count the number of subjects engaged in the behavior and total number of clients in the room. At the end of the session, determine the percent of subjects engaging in the behavior by adding up the number recorded as engaging in the behavior in all observations and dividing this by the sum of all those present in all observations.

For example, the therapeutic recreation specialist wants to determine how successful the new "free play" period is for a group of 8-year-olds. The following observations were recorded:

Mon.   10/21/83   FREE PLAY GROUP, 2:00–3:00 P.M.

	2:00–2:15	2:15–2:30	2:30–2:45	2:45–3:00	TOTAL
Total children in room	15	15	15	15	60
Children playing	15	7	5	3	30

The children were observed playing thirty times during the one-hour period. Divide thirty by sixty (total children across each observation) to show that only 50 percent of the children were playing appropriately during the entire free-play hour. From this percentage, the therapeutic recreation specialist might initially conclude that—

the free play period is too long;

the children may need to learn specific play skills before they will take advantage of a free play period;

the play period needs to be more structured.

Any number of preliminary conclusions can be further investigated.

In another instance, the instantaneous time-sampling method may be used to evaluate the amount of interaction that the recreation aides have with a group of patients during a nonprogrammed time after supper. In this example, the therapeutic recreation specialist suspects that the aides may need an in-service training that helps them interact more frequently with the patients. Before the TRS concludes than an in-service training period is needed, the TRS decides to find out exactly how much interaction occurs between the aides and the patients. The following data sheet or observation record would be useful in this situation.

12/10   ACTIVITY LOUNGE, 6:00–8:00 P.M.   OBSERVER: Ray Thomas, TRS

	NO. OF STAFF INTERACTING	NO. OF STAFF PRESENT		NO. OF STAFF INTERACTING	NO. OF STAFF PRESENT
6:05			7:05		
6:15			7:15		
6:25			7:25		
6:35			7:35		
6:45			7:45		
6:55			7:50		

In this example, the observer enters the activity lounge every ten minutes between 6:00 and 8:00 P.M. The observer counts the number of staff persons interacting with clients, counts the number of staff persons in the room, and records these numbers in the appropriate columns of the data sheet. When counting, the observer always scans the room from left to right, deciding immediately whether or not each staff person is interacting with a patient.

The instantaneous time-sampling method of observing and recording behaviors is useful when an observer cannot devote an entire session solely to other methods of observation. It is also useful for determining the involvement of a large group of people at once.

Summary of Observation Recording

These formal methods of observing and recording client behavior (interval, tally, duration, instantaneous time sampling) are not always feasible. Yet they are considered to be reliable methods of obtaining client data and can be selectively used in a variety of therapeutic recreation situations.

If a therapeutic recreation specialist is familiar with both the purposes and techniques of each *formal* observation method, it is very probable that one's *informal* observational skills will improve. Less formal does not imply less accurate or less important. Through the selective use of formal observation techniques and through consistent improvement in less formal observational procedures, the therapeutic recreation specialist should develop observational skills that will enable accurate and detailed recording of client behaviors.

OTHER DOCUMENTATION ISSUES

A major portion of this chapter has focused on documentation related to individual clients or groups of clients. The final section includes other types of documentation concerns and records that are of concern to therapeutic recreation specialists.

Policy and Procedure Manual

Most therapeutic recreation departments in either community or clinical settings already have a *policy and procedure manual.* Included in such a manual are agency policies and departmental procedures that are of concern to employees. Examples include the following:

Personnel Policies
position descriptions
position qualifications and selection procedures
vacation, sick leave, and overtime policies
insurance and benefit information
salary information
employee rights and responsibilities
volunteers (policies, training, evaluation)
personnel evaluation procedures
continuing education policies

Facility/Equipment/Supplies
vehicle use
use of buildings, rooms, and so on
purchasing procedures
repair and maintenance procedures
safety and sanitation procedures
off-grounds or overnight policies
housekeeping services

Administration/Supervision
organizational structure
supervision methods and procedures

communication mechanisms (within and external to department and/or agency)
fiscal management
procedures related to in-service training, continuing education
contractual services and in-kind services procedures

Such a general policy and procedure manual is important to the administrative operation and efficiency of both the overall agency and the therapeutic recreation department. Administrative efficiency is improved when policies and procedures are regularly reviewed and updated.

Written Plan of Operation

In community settings, the written plan of operation may be the same document as the policy and procedure manual. In many clinical settings, additional information (beyond that included in a policy and procedural manual) is required.

In clinical settings, a comprehensive written plan of operation is, or soon will be, imperative for each therapeutic recreation department. In relation to this written plan, two issues should concern the therapeutic recreation specialist: therapeutic recreation's involvement in the overall agency's written plan of operation and the specific therapeutic recreation department's written plan of operation.

Agency Plan. Therapeutic recreation services should be included in the overall agency's written plan of operation. Each agency is required "to formulate and specify in a written plan for professional services its goals, objectives, policies, and programs so that its performance can be measured."[13] This plan describes the services offered by the agency and describes how the various services interact and interrelate.

Many therapeutic recreation practitioners who are making efforts to be involved in the agency's accreditation process are disappointed if an accreditation surveyor fails to review the therapeutic recreation department. Frequently, accreditation surveyors will review or evaluate only those professional services that are reflected in the documentation of the overall agency's philosophy, goals, or major professional services. If therapeutic recreation is not adequately documented or described in the agency's written plan of operation, it may not be viewed as a major professional service. In these instances, the accreditation surveyor may choose not to review the therapeutic recreation department.

The therapeutic recreation administrator has a responsibility to attempt to integrate therapeutic recreation into the agency's overall written plan of operation. Without such a documented integration, therapeutic recreation will be seen as less important than those professional disciplines that are documented in the agency's written plan of operation.

Very often, therapeutic recreation specialists in clinical settings *are*

---

[13]This standard (4.1) is taken from the 1981 JCAH *Consolidated Standards.* Although specific standards may change, this statement adequately reflects the intent of a written plan of operation.

directly involved with *patient management* concerns (that is, client assessment, treatment plans, progress notes, treatment plan reviews, and discharge summaries). To qualify for inclusion in the agency's written plan of operation, an agency may also expect involvement in *program management* concerns. Several program management concerns are briefly described below. Although terminology may vary among agencies, involvemer:t in the following program management functions is typical when a service (such as therapeutic recreation) is viewed as a major professional service.

1. Quality Assurance Process. In general, quality assurance may be broadly interpreted to mean the provision of continuously improved patient care. Quality assurance implies that there are formal, documented mechanisms that will ensure accountability in the provision of quality patient services. These formal administrative procedures typically involve the review and evaluation of an agency's functioning. Quality assurance is often an umbrella term that includes more specific administrative functions, such as patient care monitoring, utilization reviews, and program evaluation.

If an agency is accredited by the Joint Commission on Accreditation of Hospitals (JCAH), quality assurance may be very specifically described as a "well-defined, organized program designed to enhance patient care and the correction of identified problems."[14] In addition, specific accreditation programs within JCAH have provided standards that specify essential components of the quality assurance program.[15]

Accreditation standards are reviewed and revised on a regular basis. All accreditation standards can, in a general sense, be considered as a quality assurance mechanism. The therapeutic recreation specialist should be familiar with the entire accreditation manual that concerns his or her particular agency. Regardless of the specific accreditation organization of concern, each accreditation manual will provide specific guidelines for documentation that will be useful in quality assurance programs.

2. Utilization Reviews. A utilization review program in a clinical agency

---

[14]This standard (9.1) is taken from the 1981 JCAH *Consolidated Standards.* The term *quality assurance* has several meanings. In the *Consolidated Standards,* therapeutic recreation specialists are responsible for complying with 1) quality assurance standards directly related to activity services, 2) quality assurance standards listed in the chapter on quality assurance, and 3) standards throughout the entire accreditation manual.

[15]The 1981 JCAH *Consolidated Standards Manual* states that the quality assurance program includes five essential components:
1. problem identification
2. problem assessment
3. problem correction
4. problem correction monitoring
5. program monitoring

For more detailed information concerning the JCAH quality assurance process, the reader is referred to:

Joint Commission on Accreditation of Hospitals, *Quality Assurance Guide for Psychiatric and Substance Abuse Facilities* (Chicago: Author, 1981).

Navar, N. and J. Dunn, eds., *Quality Assurance: Concerns for Therapeutic Recreation* (Champaign, Il.: Department of Leisure Studies, University of Illinois, 1981).

attempts to demonstrate (document) how effective the agency is at appropriately allocating its resources. Typically, the utilization review program will address underutilization, overutilization, and inefficient scheduling of the agency's resources. A therapeutic recreation department that is well integrated in the overall agency's functioning will frequently be involved in the utilization review program.

3. Patient Care Monitoring.   Patient care monitoring procedures will typically be specified in the agency's written plan of operation. These procedures help assure that the treatment planned and provided for patients is evaluated and updated according to the needs of the patients.[16] When therapeutic recreation services are an integral function in a patient's treatment plan, they will be included in the facility's patient care monitoring program.

Quality assurance, utilization reviews, and patient care monitoring are three of many possible program management functions that will concern therapeutic recreation specialists in clinical facilities. For too long, there has been hesitancy on the part of therapeutic recreation specialists to initiate involvement in such administrative functions. Therapeutic recreation administrators should become both knowledgeable and skilled in selective program management functions in their agency. Such involvement typically requires that the therapeutic recreation administrator investigate and initiate the necessary corresponding documentation mechanisms.

Therapeutic Recreation Written Plan.   Regardless of the extent that therapeutic recreation is included in the agency's written plan of operation, each clinical therapeutic recreation department should also have its own written plan of operation. It is almost futile to expect that any clinical therapeutic recreation department could attempt to continue functioning in an "age of accountability" without such documentation.

There exists no universal format for a therapeutic recreation department's written plan of operation. The intent of such a plan should guide the therapeutic recreation specialists to design a format that is both comprehensive and useful. The major purpose of designing a therapeutic recreation written plan of operation is to assure high-quality client care. The assumption here is that the delivery of high-quality client care is greatly facilitated when administrative goals and procedures assist specialists in implementing high-quality client services. A written plan of operation documents these concerns.

What should be included in a therapeutic recreation plan of operation? The following suggestions are presented as guidelines. Each therapeutic recreation department will ultimately include those items that are relevant to its particular therapeutic recreation service program.

---

[16]This standard (11.1) is taken from the 1981 JCAH *Consolidated Standards.* Although terminology varies among agencies, the concept of patient care monitoring is typically included in clinical settings.

1. What is the philosophy of therapeutic recreation in *your agency?*
2. What are the goals of the comprehensive therapeutic recreation program?
3. What are the components of the comprehensive therapeutic recreation program (treatment/rehabilitation, leisure education, recreation participation)?
4. How are clients involved in each program component (by referral, requirement, voluntary participation, or based on client goals, and so on)?
5. What are the goals of each program component?
6. What specific programs are provided?
7. How are specific programs and the comprehensive TR program evaluated? How often?
8. What type of client assessment process is used? How is it used? When is it used? Who is qualified to perform client assessments? How are his or her qualifications reviewed?
9. What policies and procedures are used by therapeutic recreation personnel? (The policy and procedure manual is usually included as part of the written plan of operation.)
10. How does the therapeutic recreation department or therapeutic recreation services interact with other professional services?
11. What is the role of therapeutic recreation in relation to *patient management* functions (intake, assessment, treatment plans, progress notes, treatment plan reviews, discharge summaries, aftercare)?
12. What is the role of therapeutic recreation in relation to *program management* functions (professional staff organization, quality assurance, utilization reviews, patient care monitoring, staff growth and development, research, patient rights, and so on)?

It is obvious that the documentation of a thorough written plan of operation is a lengthy process. Some therapeutic recreation departments will simply need to revise or improve on a policy and procedure manual, which can be expanded into a more comprehensive written plan of operation. Other therapeutic recreation departments, especially those that are just beginning to document their services, will have a lengthy, tedious task to undertake. Very few therapeutic recreation programs or departments will be expected to design or document a comprehensive, usable written plan of operation overnight. The wise therapeutic recreation administrator will first comprehensively conceptualize both the content and format of the therapeutic recreation written plan of operation. This "master plan" can then be included in the beginning written plan of operation. As long as a realistic tentative time line for the completion of the comprehensive plan is included, those on the therapeutic recreation staff will have the confidence that they are on their way to completing an appropriate written plan of operation.

Professional Style for Documentation

The effectiveness and usefulness of any form of documentation is greatly dependent on the quality of the documented information. One guideline that will facilitate any documentation effort is: *know your audience.*

Who will be reading this information? Documentation styles will vary, depending on the recipients of the information.

A second guideline is: *provide sufficient background information.* Certain documentation procedures inherently include this information (for instance, treatment plans typically include client demographics, assessments, and so on). Reports, program evaluations, news releases, interagency communications, and other records should include sufficient background information to provide the reader with an adequate perspective on the information.

The third and final guideline regarding documentation style is: *write with clarity.* Professionally written documents should ensure that the reader receives the information that the writer intended. Frequently, we use a different vocabulary for documentation than we would for conversation. The following lists provide examples of commonly misused words and phrases:

Inappropriate in Professional Documentation	Possible Alternatives
kids	children
a lot (a lot of toys)	many, several, approximately ten toys
good	appropriate, feasible
bad	inappropriate
sort of, kind of	(omit these phrases!)
in order to	to
in regards to	in regard to, or concerning
to have fun	provide enjoyable leisure/recreation experiences or activities
incompetent	does not have the skill

Many times, the use of an absolute lessens the credibility of the written statement. Since there usually is an exception to each idea, the therapeutic recreation specialist would increase the clarity and credibility of the written word by using absolutes infrequently.

Commonly Misused Absolute	Possible Alternatives
must/should (Tom should swim)	could
all the time	frequently
all (all the clients)	most, many
everyone	most
never	seldom
will (Exercise will help)	may

Redundant words can greatly interfere with the clarity of written documents. Care should be taken to K.I.S.S. (Keep it sweet and simple).

Commonly Used Redundant Phrases	Possible Alternatives
necessary requirements	requirements
cooperate together	cooperate
ask the question	ask
for a period of two weeks	for two weeks
all of	all
check up on	check
later on	later
during the time	while
come in contact with	meet
evaluate the value	evaluate
final outcome	outcome
as a general rule	as a rule

Too often, an accurate or important issue is overlooked or discounted if the documentation is not professionally written. It is the responsibility of each therapeutic recreation specialist to communicate effectively through written documents that adhere to a professional style.

Computer Use in Therapeutic Recreation

So far, we have assumed that all documentation efforts will occur through traditional methods, such as writing, typing, and printing. Although discussion here concerning the use of computers in therapeutic recreation will be cursory, the progressive therapeutic recreation specialist is already aware that computers will be a major method of documentation and communication in the near future.

Many clinical agencies and community recreation agencies are already using computers to facilitate administrative functions. Some of these functions include

> budget, payroll
> statistics related to clients and consumers (attendance, demographic information)
> evaluation of programs
> aftercare reports and information
> clerical functions (word processing)

Some hospitals have already begun to chart client progress notes and treatment plans through the use of computer terminals. As computers continue to be used to perform administrative functions, computer advocates and computer critics will continue to surface.

The therapeutic recreation specialist is encouraged to recognize that the age of computers is just beginning. Each therapeutic recreation specialist has the opportunity to be receptive to discovering how computers may be of assistance in therapeutic recreation services. Beyond documentation and administrative efficiency, there are several areas where therapeutic recreation services could be enhanced by the use of computers. Some of these potential uses are briefly described next.

1. Some studies have begun that utilize video games in the treatment of brain injuries and other types of specific disabilities.
2. The development of computer software for individual instruction is already realized in education. In which content areas would individualized instruction be useful for the recipient of therapeutic recreation services?
3. The medical professions have used computers to increase the availability of diagnostic services. What are the implications of computer use for select areas of client assessment?
4. Education has used computer "tutor" programs to assess cognitive functioning, to identify student needs, and to prescribe programs for remediation. Are these functions also applicable in therapeutic recreation services?
5. Special services, focusing on specific disabilities, have already been operationalized in progressive settings throughout the country. For example, some physically disabled individuals have found success in communicating via the computer through the use of synthetic speech devices, mouth sticks, or head pointers. Computer use with mentally retarded individuals has provided detailed task analysis, opportunities for drill and practice, and well-defined reinforcement schedules. Are there any implications here for therapeutic recreation?
6. There is no denying that use of the computer is a fast-growing leisure activity. Will therapeutic recreation specialists be influential in this area, or will they "let the computer experts" design the leisure content of tomorrow?

Therapeutic recreation specialists have the opportunity to initiate, direct, and develop the utilization of computers for therapeutic recreation services. There is great opportunity to begin the development of appropriate software that has applications to treatment and leisure education programs. There exists a timely challenge to study the use of computers in recreation participation programs. In addition, there are many assistive functions, such as assessment and charting, that can utilize the current computer technology in the provision of therapeutic recreation services.

SUMMARY

Documentation in therapeutic recreation services is of major importance. Both community and clinical therapeutic recreation specialists will be involved in a variety of documentation efforts. While documentation may not be as enjoyable or as rewarding as direct client service, it must be realized that high-quality documentation is one aspect of professional responsibility. Knowledge of and skills in documentation ultimately aid in giving high-quality service to clients. Thus, they are vital tools of the therapeutic recreation specialist.

================================== **Suggested References** ==================================

Accreditation Council for Services for Mentally Retarded and Other Developmentally Disabled Persons, *Standards for Services for Developmentally Disabled Individuals*. Washington, D.C., 1981.

BERGER, M. M., *Working with People Called Patients*. New York: Brunner/Mazel Publishers, 1977.

BJORKQUIST, D. C., *Supervision in Vocational Education: Management of Human Resources*. Boston: Allyn and Bacon, Inc., 1982.

CALHOUN, M. L., and M. HAWISHER, *Teaching and Learning Strategies for Physically Handicapped Students*. Baltimore: University Park Press, 1979.

COHEN, D. H., and V. STERN, *Observing and Recording the Behavior of Young Children*. New York: Teachers College Press, 1975.

Commission on Accreditation of Rehabilitation Facilities, *Standards Manual of the Commission on Accreditation of Rehabilitation Facilities*. Tucson, 1982.

Illinois Therapeutic Recreation Section, *Therapeutic Recreation Discharge/Referral Process: Standards and Guidelines*. Palatine, Il.: Illinois Parks and Recreation Association, 1982.

IRVIN, D. M., and M. M. BUSHNELL, *Observational Strategies for Child Study*. New York: Holt, Rinehart and Winston, 1980.

JACKSON, D. A., G. M. DELLA-PIANA, and H. N. SLOANE, JR., *How to Establish a Behavioral Observation System*. Englewood Cliffs, N.J.: Educational Technology Publications, 1975.

Joint Commission on Accreditation of Hospitals, *Consolidated Standards Manual for Child, Adolescent, and Adult Psychiatric, Alcoholism, and Drug Abuse Facilities*. Chicago, 1981.

————, *Quality Assurance Guide for Psychiatric and Substance Abuse Facilities*. Chicago, 1981.

LEVY, R., *The New Language of Psychiatry*. Boston: Little, Brown and Company, 1982.

National Therapeutic Recreation Society, *Guidelines for Administration of Therapeutic Recreation Service in Clinical and Residential Facilities*. Alexandria, Va.: National Recreation and Park Association, 1982.

NAVAR, N., and J. DUNN, eds., *Quality Assurance: Concerns for Therapeutic Recreation*. Champaign, Il.: Department of Leisure Studies, University of Illinois, 1981.

Nursing 81 Books, *Documenting Patient Care Responsibly*. Horsham, Pa.: Intermed Communications, Inc., 1981.

SPITZER, R. L., A. E. SKODOL, M. GIBBON, and J. B. W. WILLIAMS, *DSM III Case Book: A Learning Companion to the Diagnostic and Statistical Manual of Mental Disorders* (3rd ed.). Washington, D.C.: American Psychiatric Association, 1981.

TURNBULL, A. P., B. B. STRICKLAND, and J. C. BRANTLEY, *Developing and Implementing Individualized Education Programs*. Columbus, Oh.: Charles E. Merrill Publishing Company, 1978.

10

Assessment
Julia Kennon Dunn[1]

PURPOSE: Assessment is a vital aspect of therapeutic recreation programming. This chapter is designed to provide a comprehensive overview of client assessment. Definitions, procedures, and common uses of assessment are presented. The current status of therapeutic recreation assessment procedures is explored, and various existing procedures are reviewed. Desired qualities for appropriate assessment instruments are delineated. The role of assessment in relationship to program planning is explored and described. Information on the selection of assessment procedures is provided in detail.

DEFINING ASSESSMENT

Gathering information about an individual is the basic focus of assessment. Individuals have been tested, evaluated, and measured in such areas as physical functioning, overall health, mental status, personality, social development, educational achievement, intellectual abilities, and vocational potential. Aspects of interests, beliefs, attitudes, preferences, and motivation have been measured and classified according to a number of variables. Representative standards of performance (norms) have been generated for groups characterized by age, sex, level of education, social status, vocation, and diagnostic category. For various professionals in medicine, health, education, and the social sciences, a need exists to describe individuals in terms of their similarities and differences compared to other individuals and groups. The process of gathering information to formulate these descriptions is referred to as assessment. Definitions of assessment in other

---

[1]This chapter was written by Julia Kennon Dunn and used with her permission. The authors acknowledge her expertise in the area of assessment and express appreciation for her contribution of this material.

professions serve to provide an understanding of the scope and functions encompassed in the concept of assessment. In special education, assessment is defined as an "evaluation of the way in which individuals perform a variety of tasks in a variety of settings or contexts and the meaning of those performances in terms of the individual's total functioning."[2] Sundberg defines personality testing as "the set of processes used by a person or persons for developing impressions and images, making decisions and checking hypotheses about another person's pattern of characteristics which determine his or her behavior in interaction with the environment."[3] The function of decision making is seen as important in both psychology and education by Thorndike and Hagen, who state that "the role of measurement procedures is to provide the information that will permit these decisions to be informed and appropriate."[4] Though Sundberg used the term *testing* and Thorndike and Hagen used *measurement*, both of these terms can be seen as part of the assessment process. Measurement is the quantification or assigning of numbers to variables or properties of individuals in a systematic way. The use of measurement is based on measurement theory, a branch of applied statistics that provides underlying rules and operations for measurement. Testing is the use of tests in order systematically to gather information about an individual.

In general, assessment is commonly understood to be a process of gathering and interpreting information about an individual for some purpose. By examining these various definitions and relating them to the practice of therapeutic recreation, a more specific definition of assessment can be formulated. *For therapeutic recreation, assessment can be defined as a systematic procedure for gathering select information about an individual for the purpose of making decisions regarding that individual's program or treatment plan.*

The definition of therapeutic recreation assessment identifies individualized program planning as its purpose. In making programmatic decisions, appropriate information is needed to enable those decisions to be useful. Practicality in the gathering of such information is an essential requirement of assessment. In order to efficiently achieve the purpose of assessment, the type of information needed must be determined. The kind of decisions to be made will indicate the nature of information that is needed. A variety of factors will influence the determination of what decisions are to be made: agency characteristics, existing programs, the purpose of the assessment, and the characteristics of the client group. For example, many agencies provide only short-term treatment. Assessment, in this situation, would need to be efficient and focus on areas of functioning that could be dealt with during the specified time period. A lengthy, time-consuming assessment would leave little time for actual program

[2]J. Salvia and J. E. Ysseldyke, *Instructor's Manual: Assessment in Special and Remedial Education,* 2nd ed. (Boston: Houghton-Mifflin Company, 1981), p. 1.

[3]N. D. Sundberg, *Assessment of Persons* (Englewood Cliffs, N.J.: Prentice-Hall, Inc., 1977), pp. 21–22.

[4]Robert L. Thorndike and E. P. Hagen, *Measurement and Evaluation in Psychology and Education,* 4th ed. (New York: John Wiley and Sons, 1977), p. 1.

involvement. Therefore, duration of intervention is an important factor in deciding what and how much information can, and should, be gathered.

Another focus of the assessment definition is the issue of a systematic procedure. It is essential that information gathered for decision making be acquired in an organized, systematic manner. A systematic procedure will allow itself to be repeated in similar circumstances and will enable individuals to be compared to themselves at an earlier time or to other individuals in terms of a specified group of characteristics or performance. When a systematic procedure is utilized, it is more likely that the information will be accurate and valid.

Systematic methodologies of assessment are implied in such terms as test, measurement, evaluation, questionnaire, interview, observation, survey, inventory, data summary, scale, chart, profile, and checklist. These descriptors give an indication of the format in which the information is gathered, recorded, and analyzed.

The remainder of this chapter will utilize the basic definition of therapeutic recreation assessment provided in this section. The concept of a systematic procedure to gather select information about the individual for the purpose of making program decisions for that individual appears to be generally accepted by therapeutic recreation professionals. A current problem in the practice of therapeutic recreation seems to be in the selection and utilization of assessment procedures.

BATTERIES AND MULTI-METHOD PROCEDURES

In many cases, assessment procedures have been designed to gather information regarding one specific type of behavior, knowledge, or belief. In cases where more information is needed than can be gathered from one procedure, several procedures are frequently combined to form a *battery*. Batteries are formed when more information is needed within a related conceptual framework than is available on a single assessment instrument. Such a situation commonly exists in therapeutic recreation. For example, if a comprehensive knowledge of an individual's functional abilities related to leisure were needed, a battery of assessment instruments would be created, including (1) social functioning, (2) cognitive functioning, (3) physical functioning, and (4) emotional functioning. Batteries do create some problems in administering, scoring, and interpretation, since different instruments use different procedures or methodologies. This inhibits the combining of scores into a "battery score." When procedures are significantly different, it is recommended that their scores be reported separately.

In some situations, *multiple procedures* are needed to assess a *single behavior, belief, or type of knowledge*. This *multi-method approach* yields a more accurate and in-depth understanding of a single assessment focus. For example, in assessing an individual's social behavior, two methods could be used. A social behavior observation checklist type of assessment could be used by the staff. Secondly, the individual's subjective perspective on his or her own behavior could be assessed using a self-report questionnaire. This situation illustrates the use of a multi-method approach to gain a more in-depth understanding of a single component of an individual's behavior.

These concepts of batteries and multi-method approaches to assessment indicate some of the complexities involved in assessment of selected information. The range of behaviors demonstrated in leisure, recreation, and play make the assessment process both complicated and challenging.

THERAPEUTIC RECREATION ASSESSMENT: STATE OF THE ART

Assessment has received a great deal of attention in recent years. This attention has largely been prompted by the issue of accountability. Services provided in health care and public settings are no longer simply assumed to be beneficial. Proof is expected. The decisions that are made regarding programs must be demonstrated to be appropriate for the client and to contribute to the client's goals and treatment plan. In therapeutic recreation, assessment is the process that has the potential to individualize a program to the unique characteristics or needs of a single client. If individualized programs are going to be a component of therapeutic recreation delivery systems, reliable and valid assessment procedures must be utilized.

The development of assessment procedures for therapeutic recreation programming is in an early stage. As a result, several problems have inhibited the availability and effective use of assessment in program planning. These difficulties can be grouped into four areas: general lack of assessment procedures, developmental inadequacies, utilization problems, and staff qualifications.

Lack of Assessment Procedures

At the current time, very few adequate and appropriate assessment procedures have been developed for use in therapeutic recreation. Because of the need for assessment procedures and the general lack of them, professionals have been forced into taking one of two paths. Often, procedures have been borrowed from other professions for use in therapeutic recreation programming. These borrowed procedures frequently do not relate to leisure, and, therefore, their results are not generalizable to the conceptual framework of leisure behavior. The second option has been to develop an assessment at the agency level. This development has frequently suffered because of insufficient knowledge of assessment techniques and design. The absence of appropriately designed and validated procedures has left the practitioner with limited options in the selection and use of assessment in program planning.

Developmental Inadequacies

Appropriate procedures for the development of assessments do exist. Unfortunately, in many of the locally constructed assessments, these procedures have not been followed. Many of the existing locally developed procedures that have been evaluated have been found unrefined[5] and to have little reliability and validity.[6] Many procedures have been developed for a particular agency or program and are so agency-specific that they do not represent a generalizable understanding of leisure behavior.[7] What appears to be the case in many locally developed procedures is that the initial methods of assessment development are followed, but because of the immediate need for the assessment, complete testing and validation procedures are not carried out. Development must go beyond the item-writing stage to item analysis, establishment of reliability and validity, and the development of the manual, if a fully developed appropriate assessment procedure is to result.

By far the most fundamental problem in assessment development in therapeutic recreation is the lack of a sound conceptual framework for the assessment.[8,9] A conceptual framework of leisure behavior, based upon research and theoretical constructs, is essential to the development of any assessment procedure. Without such a foundation, little faith can be placed in the interpretation of assessment results.

Problems in Utilization

Apart from the conceptual framework issue in assessment development, other difficulties exist in utilization of assessment procedures. Assessments should be developed for a particular purpose. They then should be utilized for that purpose. In many instances, agencies have taken an assessment procedure developed for research in leisure behavior and employed it as the initial phase of individual program planning. Though the procedure may be reliable and valid in the research process, it doesn't mean that it will be of value when employed for another purpose. Little confidence can be placed in the results of a procedure that is not employed for its intended purpose.

Some assessments exist that measure *one* aspect of leisure functioning. Though these procedures may have the essential features of a quality assessment, they are frequently used to represent the entire scope of leisure functioning. As an illustration, this is similar to utilizing eyesight to indicate overall physical health. Though the two are related, a physician cannot presume that if an individual's eyesight is 20/20, one is in excellent physical health.

---

[5]W. B. Kinney, "Clinical Assessment in Mental Health Settings," *Therapeutic Recreation Journal*, 14, no. 4 (1980), pp. 39–45.

[6]William A. Touchstone, "The Status of Client Evaluation in Psychiatric Settings," *Therapeutic Recreation Journal*, 9, no. 4 (1975), pp. 166–172.

[7]Peter A. Witt, Peg Connolly, and David Compton, "Assessment: A Plea for Sophistication," *Therapeutic Recreation Journal*, 14, no. 4 (1980), pp. 5–8.

[8]Nancy Navar, "A Rationale for Leisure Skill Assessment with Handicapped Adults," *Therapeutic Recreation Journal*, 14, no. 4 (1980), pp. 21–28.

[9]Witt, Connolly, and Compton, "Assessment."

Staff Qualifications

The role of the therapeutic recreation professional has changed over the years. Today, more professional expertise is being expected and required. Therapeutic recreation programs have become more sophisticated, and so must the professional who plans, implements, and evaluates those programs. Until recent years, professional preparation did not include the topic of client assessment. Only recently has this topic been included in undergraduate therapeutic recreation curricula and continuing education efforts at conferences, symposia, and workshops. However, even now, the time allocated to the topic is minimal and the content is introductory. Education in the development of assessment procedures is, for the most part, only available in graduate curricula through courses in education or psychology. Thus, it is safe to say that few therapeutic recreation professionals have had the opportunity to learn the strategies needed for the development or use of assessment procedures. Despite this lack of opportunity, some professionals have developed usable procedures. However, these procedures have rarely gone past the initial development stage, to be evaluated in their own right.

Needs for the Future

Therapeutic recreation as a profession needs to be more conscious of the criteria for quality in assessment procedures. Individual professionals need to adequately examine their alternatives and qualifications before embarking on the development of client assessment procedures. Appropriate methodologies must be employed in the development and use of assessments. Only when using appropriately developed and selected assessments can professionals have confidence in the results, thus allowing their programmatic decisions to be informed and appropriate for their clients.

USING ASSESSMENTS IN THERAPEUTIC RECREATION

General Phases of Assessment

As has already been stated, the ultimate use of assessment results is in making decisions for individual program planning. Cone and Hawkins have explained assessment by dividing it into five phases.[10] Each phase provides information for a different level of decision making. Decisions, according to this model, can be made in relation to screening and general disposition, defining a problem, pinpointing a problem and designing intervention, monitoring progress, and follow-up. The first three phases relate to decisions to be made at the initial stage of treatment planning, and the last two phases relate more to evaluation decisions made during or after intervention.

[10]J. D. Cone and R. P. Hawkins, eds., *Behavioral Assessment, New Directions in Clinical Psychology* (New York: Brunner/Mazel Inc., 1977).

Screening and general disposition serve to determine the general type and areas of difficulty of a problem. The decisions made at this level are to identify the problems that need further definition.

Definition of the problem includes the classification of the problem and formulation of conclusions about the client's personal resources, environment, and probable cause of the problem. A decision is made during this phase as to the general type of intervention needed by the client.

Pinpointing and designing the intervention serves to narrow the focus on the client and environment. Decisions identifying the behaviors that will be targeted for change and recommending the method of intervention are made. Information gathered in this phase of assessment serves as baseline data or results to which later findings can be compared to measure change.

Monitoring progress provides feedback on a client's progress in relation to the identified treatment goals and objectives. Decisions made while the intervention is taking place allow the program to be flexible regarding the changing needs and rate of progress of the client.

Follow-up is the assessment process that takes place after the completion of an intervention or program or a client's discharge. This assessment enables measurement of long-term effects of the intervention and its generalizability to other environments or situations. Decisions made at this level are those related to program evaluation and would serve as data to support decisions related to program change.

Phases of Therapeutic Recreation Assessment

Therapeutic recreation utilizes assessment in three phases similar to Cone and Hawkins's model. Three general types of decisions can be made related to the individual's therapeutic recreation program plan: screening or placement, pinpointing an area in need of improvement, and monitoring progress.

Screening or program placement provides initial information for decisions regarding placement into existing program components (that is, treatment, leisure education, and/or recreation participation). A client who generally lacks basic functional abilities, as indicated from the results of assessment, would be placed in treatment-related programs, whereas a client with adequate functional abilities but generally inadequate leisure abilities would be placed in leisure education programs. It is quite possible that a given client could have assessed needs in both categories and, thus, be placed in these two different program categories simultaneously.

Pinpointing an area in need of improvement is the second level of therapeutic recreation assessment. A general screening decision can be made to give an indication of the program component or components (treatment, leisure education, or recreation participation) where a client should be placed. However, a client's abilities may vary within the content areas of these three program components. It is, therefore, necessary to assess a client's abilities in more depth. Though a client may generally lack functional abilities socially and cognitively, he or she may have adequate emotional and physical skills. The deficit areas would then be examined more specifically to determine the target behaviors for particular program intervention. Further, this client may be able to participate in other levels of programming in leisure education or recreation participation to expand needed leisure abilities. This phase of assessment would yield information that may indicate a combination of specific programs to address the broad area of leisure functioning as well as a specific focus on one central area, such as social functioning. Results from assessments would also give an indication as to the most appropriate facilitation technique or environmental situation. Details of the clients' strengths, weaknesses, and areas of adequate functioning are evident from this phase of assessment. From these results, the decisions are made regarding the specific program plan.

Monitoring the client's progress in the various programs allows for evaluation decisions to be made while the client is participating and involved. Such decisions might include: to continue involvement in the program, continue on the present time schedule, alter the program, terminate the program, or refer to another program.

At this stage in therapeutic recreation assessment development, no provision has been made for follow-up. Rarely do therapeutic recreation professionals have the opportunity to see clients after discharge, as do counselors or other allied health professionals. However, as referral procedures are advanced and the importance of carry-over value and generalizability realized, follow-up procedures may be possible. Now follow-up assessment procedures are possible for therapeutic recreation only for research purposes in which personnel and financial resources are allocated.

Functions of Therapeutic Recreation Assessment

As described previously, therapeutic recreation assessment can be thought of as the first step, and contributing to the evaluation stage, in individualized program planning. In the three phases of assessment, the decisions made have two basic functions, *descriptive* and *evaluative*. Information gathered prior to program implementation serves to describe a client, so that goals and objectives can be established. This *description* will determine placement decisions and help to pinpoint strengths and weaknesses of the client for individualized program planning. Describing the client will help the therapeutic recreation specialist determine if the client can be placed in the ongoing programs of the agency or will need adaptations for program involvement.

The second function of assessment is that of *evaluation*. Evaluating the progress of a client serves the monitoring function of assessment. As previously discussed, this information is evaluative in nature and occurs during program implementation. Another function of evaluating a client's progress, beyond individualized program decisions, is the contribution to overall program evaluation. The client's success in the program, in addition to other factors, provides information to the program developer concerning the worth or value of each specific program (see Chapter 7: Program Evaluation).

Assessment in Individual Program Planning

In the individualized program planning process, assessment is the first step and a part of the evaluation stage. It is imperative that all phases of individualized program planning be compatible with the assessment findings, for it is from the descriptive function of the assessment that goals and objectives for the program are developed. The placement into specific programs, selection of activities, and designation of facilitation techniques are determined based on those goals and objectives. The plan is then implemented based on decisions made in previous stages. Finally, it is evaluated using the client's monitored progress based on a comparison with initial-phase assessment results.

ASSESSMENT PROCESS

Before direct client assessments can be utilized effectively, it is necessary for therapeutic recreation professionals *to understand and be able to implement the entire assessment process effectively.* The assessment process can be conceptualized as a series of steps between the selection or development of an assessment procedure and the development of an individualized program plan. To begin the process, it is assumed that an assessment procedure has been selected or developed according to specified criteria. The assessment process then follows with understanding the assessment procedure, collecting needed resources, administering the procedure to clients, determining results, interpreting results, and making the decisions related to the individual's program plan. Figure 10–1 provides a model of the total process.

Understanding the Assessment Procedure

It is essential that every professional staff member who will be assessing the client or making programmatic decisions have a thorough understanding of the designated assessment procedure. This understanding includes how the results are to be used in the individual's program planning process; the procedure's background and development; the reliability and validity of the obtained results; instructions for administering, scoring, and interpreting results; time and resources needed for administration; and the role of the person administering the assessment.

Before conducting an assessment, a careful review of the accompanying manual as well as practice in the administration of the instrument prepares the therapeutic recreation staff member to conduct and score the assessment. Professional knowledge of leisure behavior and therapeutic recreation contribute to the judgments involved in interpretation of results and programmatic decision making. Following this educational preparation for assessment, it is necessary to prepare the actual assessment environment.

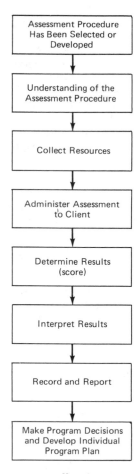

FIGURE 10–1
Assessment Process

Collecting Resources

Many assessments require "test kits" or supplies for administration. These requirements may be as simple as a test form and a pencil. Other procedures call for the organization of slides and a projector, play equipment, or objects for the client to manipulate or identify. Some assessments specify different space and situational needs, ranging from a small quiet room with a table and chair to a large play area with equipment and other participants. In certain observational assessments, situations may need to be contrived or stimuli provided to elicit specific behaviors. All resources, materials, environments, and situations need to be organized, checked for usability, and scheduled in advance of the actual administration.

Administering the Assessment to Clients

Prior to seeing the client for assessment purposes, the therapeutic recreation specialist has become familiar with the selected procedure and has gathered all necessary resources. When meeting with a client for the purpose of assessment, several personal factors need consideration. The establishment of rapport with the client can alleviate test anxiety by facilitating a relaxed atmosphere. Discussing the purpose of assessment and explaining its significance in the planning process may encourage the client's cooperation and motivation to complete the process. With children, special consideration should be given to their age and social development. A warm and relaxed approach is, in most cases, effective with young children. With children or adults, if there is an intent to compare assessment results to those of other individuals, particular attention should be paid to utilizing similar strategies for establishing rapport with all clients. Therapeutic recreation specialists, for example, might begin by introducing themselves and explaining the intent of the assessment; for instance, "From your answers, we can better understand your awareness of leisure, so that together we can better plan a program for you while you're here." There are some situations in which establishing rapport is not a necessary part of the administration. These assessments call for the therapeutic recreation specialist to assume an unobtrusive role. An observation in which the client's knowledge of being observed would inhibit the reliability and validity of the results is an example of the unobtrusive role of the administrator. In this situation, the observation is done in such a way that the client is not directly aware of being assessed. Not all observations are unobtrusive; some require the obvious presence of the observer, who is actively recording data. These observers should be explained and their purpose recognized. If the presence of observers affects the client's behavior patterns, several days of data collection, to allow the client to accept and eventually ignore the observer's presence, may be needed to acquire appropriate and useful information.

Other personal factors can affect the administering of an assessment. The client's current abilities and limitations may influence that client's performance on an assessment procedure directed at other behaviors. A client with visual impairments may not be able to read the leisure attitude survey, or a client with a bad cold may not perform at his or her level of capability on a fitness test. The administrator's inadvertent provision of cues or hints or conveying expectations will affect the client's responses. It is important for the administrator to conform to standardized instructions and be consistent in methods for establishing rapport. Any deviation from these directions or unique personal characteristics of the client should be recorded for consideration in the interpretation of results.

In addition to personal influences, the environment can also affect a client's performance or response to an assessment. The physical environment includes all stimuli that can be physically perceived by the client, such as distracting noises or sights, room temperature, and lighting. Any of these environmental influences that might invalidate the results because of their effect on the administration of the assessment should also be recorded for consideration in the interpretation of the assessment results.

In administering an assessment procedure, both personal and environmental factors need examination. When possible, steps should be taken to eliminate distracting and inappropriate influences in the assessment situation. If these unusual circumstances do occur, they should be documented for consideration during interpretation and decision making. In the case that such situations are extreme, the assessment can be terminated and repeated at another time, when personal situations have changed or environmental variables are better controlled.

Determining Results

Every reputable assessment procedure has an established method for scoring or determining results. Assessments involving open-ended questions or demographic data usually require the organization of that information into logical documentation. In this sense, the results are the individual responses. Such demographic results, in general, only lend themselves to a comparison with results of other individuals or criteria of performance in terms of placing an individual in a norm group. The interpretation of such results is either concrete, as in factual information requiring little or no interpretation; or abstract and unstructured, as is an interview, which requires a great deal of subjective, judgmental interpretation. In the case of the latter, without documented support for such interpretation, the assumptions made become suspect and debatable. Such assessment methods tend not to provide usable information for therapeutic recreation program planning, though they are used to assess such areas as mental status and psychological adjustment by appropriately qualified psychologists, psychiatrists, and mental health professionals.

In the majority of assessments, results are determined by scoring. Scoring implies that numbers have been utilized to represent the degree of performance, strength of belief or attitude, and amount of knowledge or frequency of behavioral occurrence, among other characteristics. The assigning of numbers for the purpose of measurement is not a casual decision, but is founded in mathematic and statistical theory. Assessments using scoring procedures to determine results have specified techniques for scoring and interpreting those scores. Professionals assessing clients with scored assessments need to follow the established scoring procedure to determine results.

Results determined by scoring methods are objective and nonjudgmental. Judgment is utilized in interpretation. Scores are only numbers assigned to represent measurement. Their significance is determined by interpretation. On a test, for example, a client circling 4s (representing level of agreement on a 5-point scale where 1 = strong disagreement and 5 = strong agreement) on five items of an attitude scale, resulting in a score of 20, is an example of a score. In an observation, a rater would record a 2, indicating a previously described level of performance displayed by the client. These numbers do not imply the reason for the behavior or attitude or the relationship of the behavior or attitude to any criterion or group of individuals. It is in the next phase of the assessment process, interpretation, that meaning is assigned to scores.

Scoring is usually a relatively simple task, which is accomplished by following the directions in the manual that accompanies the assessment.

Scores may be computed on the assessment form or on a separate score sheet. Depending on the method of determining scores, time may become a factor. Some procedures simply take more time to score than others. If time is a major factor in the selection of an assessment procedure, the amount of time needed to determine scores should be considered.

Interpreting Results

Once results or scores have been determined, judgment is made regarding the meaning of the results. More than any other, the interpretation phase of the assessment process calls upon the therapeutic recreation specialist's expertise. It is here that results are put into a context so that they can be used for decision making.

In interpreting results, both instrumental and situational (personal and environmental) influences need consideration. Instrumental variables are those qualities or limitations of the particular assessment. Like scoring, interpretation guidelines are usually provided in the accompanying manual. These guidelines for interpretation describe the meaning of scores. Interpretation is influenced by the reliability and validity of the results, the norm group used for comparison, the conceptual framework on which the assessment is based, and the process used in validation. *Reliability is a measure of relationship that indicates the consistency or accuracy of scores.* It is represented by a number from 0 to 1, with 1 indicating perfect reliability. The closer to 1 a reliability coefficient is, the more accurate are the results. *Validity is the determination of the degree to which an assessment measures what it intends to measure.* It indicates how well the assessment fulfills its purpose. Validity is determined in a variety of ways, depending upon the purpose of the assessment procedure. If a procedure's results are judged to be valid, more confidence can be placed on them in making interpretations.

Some assessments provide specific guidelines for interpretation. These usually include relating the results acquired from one individual to those established for a norm group or criterion variable. Norm groups are samples of people with similar characteristics. Norm groups might be described by age (10-year-olds), education (college graduates), occupation (accountants), and situation (income, housing, geographical location), among others. By comparing individual scores to those of a norm group, the interpretation would include the determination of the degree of similarity or difference between the individual and group results.

Often, scores of the individual are interpreted in terms of the conceptual framework or other criterion. The conceptual framework that allows the classification of activities according to various characteristics also permits the interpretation to relate assessment scores of an activity participation to groups of activities. For example, if an individual indicates regular participation in tennis, softball, bowling, and racquetball, an interpretation can be made that this person participates in sports (category of activities that is supported in the conceptual framework).

Other criteria that might be used for interpretation might be the relationship of scores to the highest possible score. In an assessment measuring an individual's ability to identify local leisure resources, the actual number of local resources might be the criterion used in interpretation. For example, scores might be interpreted to say the individual has an understanding of the resources because he or she correctly identified 65 percent of those presented.

In addition to instrumental factors, situational influences also need to be considered in interpretation of assessment results. Regardless of the quality of the assessment procedure, conditions of administration can cause invalid and unreliable results to occur. Such factors are those mentioned earlier related to the current state of the client, the ability of the professional conducting the assessment, and the environment. Assessments should be administered under the conditions specified in the manual. Any variance from these conditions must be noted and considered in the interpretation process. As more conditions in the assessment process vary, less confidence can be placed in the reliability and validity of the results. If too many extraneous variables are believed to have influenced the assessment results, a reassessment of the client should be considered.

One of the most influential elements in interpretation is the judgment of the therapeutic recreation specialist. This factor alone is enough to restrict the use of therapeutic recreation assessments to therapeutic recreation specialists. Their educational and experiential background provides the foundation for understanding leisure and leisure behavior. This understanding is essential in the interpretation of results and translating those results into programmatic decisions. For those assessment procedures with less specific interpretation guidelines, professional judgment becomes more important. It is this informed judgment that is used in the interpretation. The more specific the interpretation guidelines, the less judgment is needed in the interpretation phase. However, this does not negate the importance of expert judgment. Program decisions must be made utilizing the interpretation, and it is imperative that these decisions be both informed and appropriate.

It is crucial that professionals have confidence in the results obtained through the assessment procedure they are utilizing. Without this confidence, results become meaningless and useless. Careful consideration of all influencing elements in the assessment process will enable more appropriate interpretations and, thus, better decisions.

Recording and Reporting

Prior to making decisions, the results and interpretations need to be recorded and reported. The method of documentation of assessment is usually determined by the specific agency. Most agencies provide areas within patient charts for such information. This information, written in summary form, with support for interpretation, is usually documented as part of the treatment plan. Results from assessments used in evaluating or monitoring a client during program involvement may appear as an entry in a client's progress notes. Other situations call for departmental record keeping. In such circumstances, the therapeutic recreation department determines how and what is to be reported in its files. In the reporting of assessment results, thought must be given to the potential audiences who might review the results. In preserving a client's confidentiality, careful consideration should be given to deciding who has access to such information.

Documenting assessment is essential to accountability efforts. This documentation contains more than just the individual client's results. It contains information that states that clients were assessed, that the assessment results are reflected in program decisions, and that the assessment's effectiveness was evaluated in terms of its use in the program planning process.

Making Decisions

The final stage of the assessment process is making decisions regarding a client's individualized program plan. These decisions yield the goals and objectives of the individual program plan and are based on the purpose of the assessment. Compatibility of decisions to the purpose is essential. If the assessment was designed to be used for screening or placement into programs, then the decisions should reflect the fact that each client was appropriately placed in programs. Likewise, if the assessment is designed for monitoring a client's progress within the program, it should yield evaluation-based decisions.

Concluding Comments

The assessment process includes administrative preparation tasks as well as the direct administration to the client. It is important for the therapeutic recreation specialist to understand the entire assessment process and the factors that influence it. Each phase is important and contributes to the overall process. The entire process needs to be compatible with established purposes and guidelines for assessment utilization. The successful understanding and implementation of the process will influence both the information available and the appropriateness of decisions made in programming.

INTEGRATING ASSESSMENT INTO COMPREHENSIVE PROGRAMS

Since assessment is a relatively new aspect of the comprehensive program planning process, many programs are being implemented without the use of assessment information. Ideally, for assessment to have its greatest impact, comprehensive therapeutic recreation programs and the assessment procedures would be developed together. When this is not the case, assessment procedures are usually selected or developed to be implemented within the existing program approach. Whether the assessment is part of a new program or is being integrated into an existing program, it is important to understand the designed or existing comprehensive program, determine what needs to be assessed, describe the client population, project the intended utilization of the results, and identify factors that may affect the assessment situation.

Understanding the Comprehensive Program

A thorough understanding of the designed or existing comprehensive program will provide insights into the nature of assessment that is needed. Information should be gathered concerning the comprehensive program itself and its specific program offerings, the planning process, the clients, the agency, and the staff. A variety of forms can be used to assist in gathering and describing this information. General comprehensive program information should be listed, such as the title, purpose, goals, and referral procedures. Figure 10–2 provides a form that can be used for this general overall program description.

Many comprehensive therapeutic recreation programs are developed utilizing the concept of specific programs. Specific programs may be classified by the continuum service components of treatment, leisure education, and recreation participation.

When specific programs are developed and used, a brief but very accurate description can be given by providing information about their purpose, objectives, and classification within the therapeutic recreation continuum. Figure 10–3 provides a form that can be used to display this information easily and quickly.

Further, the existence of individual program planning as a part of overall programming must be examined. Figure 10–4 provides a form that lists some questions to consider in describing the individual program planning process.

Clients are the primary focus of all program planning. It is, therefore, important to generally describe the client population served by the therapeutic recreation comprehensive program. This description is general, and examines the clients as a group. Such characteristics as age ranges, sex ratios, environmental situation, primary and secondary disabling conditions, severity of disability, and average length of stay serve to generally describe the client population. Figure 10–5 provides a form to describe the basic nature of clients.

Agencies vary in the type of services provided and the role of the therapeutic recreation department and specialist within the department. A description of these elements will enhance the understanding of the role of the comprehensive therapeutic recreation program within the overall agency program. Further, it will indicate the role of the therapeutic recreation staff members and their involvement in the planning of agency services delivered to the client. Figure 10–6 provides a form for the description of this agency information.

The therapeutic recreation staff's education and experience in therapeutic recreation and assessment will greatly affect assessment utilization in program planning. Time available to implement the entire

FIGURE 10–2 Comprehensive Program Description

This form is designed to consolidate information about a comprehensive therapeutic recreation program and factors influencing that program, in order to make decisions regarding the use of client assessment.

Comprehensive program title _____

Purpose of the comprehensive program _____

_____

_____

_____

Comprehensive program goals _____

_____

_____

_____

On what basis are clients referred to and accepted into your program? _____

_____

On what basis are clients placed into specific programs or activities? _____

_____

FIGURE 10–3 Description of Specific Programs

SPECIFIC PROGRAM	PROGRAM PURPOSE	TERMINAL PROGRAM OBJECTIVES	CLASSIFICATION*

*Treatment, Leisure Education, or Recreation Participation.

FIGURE 10–4 Description of the Procedure for Individualized Treatment or Program Planning

PROGRAM

Are individual program plans completed for each client?   YES   NO

If yes, on what are the clients' goals/objectives based?	How are these factors determined?	When are the factors identified?

How are clients' programs changed? _____

_____

How are clients terminated from your program? _____

_____

FIGURE 10-5 Client Description

CLIENTS

What is the primary disabling condition of the clients served? _____

What is the severity of the disabling conditions? _____

What are any secondary disabling conditions? _____

What is the average stay of a client in the agency? _____

What are the age ranges of clients? _____

In general, from what background or environmental situation are the clients? _____

What is the sex ratio? Describe _____

FIGURE 10–6 Agency Description

AGENCY

Type of agency ————————————————

General focus of agency

———— treatment of disabling conditions

———— adjustment to new or existing life situations

———— provision of community services requested by the public

———— other (specify)

Describe the relationship of therapeutic recreation to the agency. ————

————————————————————————————————

————————————————————————————————

————————————————————————————————

If a treatment team directs client programs, describe the relationship of therapeutic recreation staff to the treatment team. ————

————————————————————————————————

————————————————————————————————

————————————————————————————————

FIGURE 10–7 Staff Description

STAFF

What are the academic and experiential qualifications of your staff?

		THERAPEUTIC RECREATION	ASSESSMENT
STAFF	TIME AVAILABLE	ACADEMIC EXPERIENCE	ACADEMIC EXPERIENCE

In the blank to the left of "Staff," indicate which of these staff members are/would be responsible for client assessment.

Indicate the amount of time allocated per week for each member of the staff for assessment, including administering, scoring, interpreting, and making recommendations from the results.

assessment process is also necessary for integrating assessment into program planning. By utilizing a form, such as the one found in Figure 10–7, decisions can be made regarding continuing education and time scheduling for the staff implementing the assessment process.

Through understanding the designed or existing comprehensive program, decisions can be made to adjust procedures or conditions to allow for assessment use. Also influencing this integration process is the determination of the purpose of assessment and how it will be used in program planning.

Focus of Assessment

In addition to describing the program and purpose of assessment within the program, the specific target of the assessment should be determined. What is to be assessed? For example, in a clinical setting, functional abilities and leisure abilities might both be the target of assessment. Specifically, assessment would focus on gathering information about a client's physical, social, cognitive, and emotional functioning. In addition, assessment would also focus on leisure and self-awareness, knowledge of resources, leisure skills, and social interaction. The specific content areas may be influenced by agency requirements and clients' characteristics. Agencies accredited by such external bodies, such as the Joint Commission on Accreditation of Hospitals, will need to meet their specified standards for activities and leisure assessments. Necessary components of assessment identified by JCAH include interests, current skills, aptitudes, talents, needs, life experiences, capacities, and deficiencies.[11] Client characteristics may influence an exaggerated focus on one or more areas. For example, in planning programs for physically disabled children, a more in-depth assessment may be needed to gather information on their physical and mobility skills. Clients' characteristics will affect not only the assessment purpose but also its methodology. The nature and severity of the disabling condition is a central factor in determining what assessment methodologies can be used. Observation, for example, may be the only way in which information can be gathered on someone who is nonverbal.

Utilizing Results

Though the purpose of the assessment probably indicates the ultimate use of the assessment as making decisions for program planning, the specific strategies for utilization should be planned. This might include policies and procedures concerning when and how often a client will be assessed, the types of decisions to be made (that is, screening or evaluation), and by whom the results will be used. Assessment results will obviously be used by the therapeutic recreation staff, but will they also be used by the treatment team? the client's physician? the client? appropriate designated others?

---

[11]Joint Commission on Accreditation of Hospitals, *Consolidated Standards Manual for Child, Adolescent, and Adult Psychiatric, Alcoholism, and Drug Abuse Programs* (Chicago: 1981).

Factors Affecting the Assessment Process

Planning for client assessments also requires an ability to foresee environmental or personnel elements that may potentially affect the assessment process. Among these factors may be such things as space available for assessment, staff time designated for the assessment process, and qualifications of the staff to use assessment procedures. Decisions may need to be made to adjust these elements to allow for the successful integration of assessment into the existing program operation. Space and needed equipment and materials will have to be allocated and scheduled for use. The therapeutic recreation staff needs to be prepared through continuing education, in-service training, and study of the selected assessment procedure. Staff time needs to be scheduled to allow for the appropriate utilization of the assessment procedure.

Integration of assessment into the current program operation requires a thorough understanding of the program, clients, staff, and agency. Plans need to be made for utilization of assessment results as well as correcting environmental and personnel factors that could potentially invalidate assessment results through these influences.

ESSENTIAL CHARACTERISTICS OF ASSESSMENT

Assessment procedures will not provide the information needed unless they are valid, reliable, and usable. These three elements are essential to any assessment procedure. Basically, validity refers to the ability of a procedure to measure what it was designed to measure. Reliability is a measure of the consistency or accuracy of the results, and usability refers to the practicality of the procedure, given the situation. Each of these areas will be described in greater detail, since all are so important within assessment.

Validity

Validity is an estimate of the degree to which assessment results fulfill their intended purpose. Three general types of validity are utilized to evaluate assessment results based on the intended purpose of the assessment procedure. These three types of validity are content validity, criterion-related validity, and construct validity.

Content Validity. *Content validity is a judgment concerned with the ability of the assessment to measure the content or subject matter of the procedure and the behavioral changes sought in the clients.* Therefore, content validity is asking two questions. First, how well does the assessment measure the subject or content? Subject or content relates to knowledge and understanding of certain concepts. For example, in leisure education, several areas of knowledge based on content have been established (such as, knowledge of resources and activity skills). The content validity would demonstrate that each of these areas was appropriately represented in the items of the assessment. Secondly, if the focus of the assessment is a measure of behavioral change, content validity then is concerned with the representativeness of the behavioral items to the total behavioral concept being measured.

Content validity is strongly related to the representative sampling of the conceptual framework. It can be established by comparing the assessment content (items) to the universe of content and/or behaviors being assessed.

Criterion-Related Validity. *Criterion-related validity assumes a comparison of assessment results to another criteria measure of the same content or behavior.* This comparison can be with a future criterion, which yields a predictive validity, or with another valued measure, which yields a concurrent validity. In estimating criterion-related validity, multi-methods can be used. Predictive validity, then, is the attempt to predict future behavior by the measure of present behavior. As an example of a multi-method approach, a client may be assessed using a test of leisure ability at discharge, in the hopes that it will predict future community adjustment. At a later date, after discharge, a multi-method procedure is utilized to assess community adjustment. The results of these two assessments are then compared. The better the relationship between the two, the better the prediction of the leisure ability assessment. (This does assume a conceptual relationship of leisure ability to community adjustment.)

In concurrent validity, more than one procedure is used to assess similar content. By administering two assessments at one time or in close succession and comparing the results, estimates of the validity of the results of the assessment in question are established. This would be useful in the development of a new procedure or in the consideration of replacing a time-consuming procedure with one that is more time-efficient.

Criterion-related validity is represented statistically. Scores are compared from one procedure to the criterion measure, and that relationship is numerically indicated by a positive or negative number between 1 and 0. As the relationship approaches 1 or -1, the predictability of the assessment in question is increased. A relationship of $r = .73$ is a better predictor than one of $r = .52$. The positive number indicates a positive relationship. In other words, a client who scores high on the assessment will score high on the criterion. Conversely, a negative number ($r = -.82$) indicates that a client who scores low on the assessment will score high on the criterion or vice versa. Thus, as validity coefficients or relationships are reported in assessment procedures, the type of validity reported is usually criterion-related.

Construct Validity. Construct validity is concerned with the interpretation of the assessment. It assumes the existence of an underlying construct (such as, leisure ability), which influences the results. This allows scores to be interpreted as a reflection of that construct. A construct is viewed as a psychological trait or quality that is assumed to explain an aspect of behavior. *Construct validity, therefore, is concerned with the degree to which assessment results can be interpreted in terms of such constructs.*

Verifying construct validity involves empirically researching hypotheses that would demonstrate relationships, described by the existence of the construct. Construct validity is not demonstrated in a single research project or statistical calculation. Rather, its evidence is determined by combined procedures which validate the conceptual framework or theory and the assessment simultaneously. Both content and criterion-related validity contribute to construct validity. Therefore, the procedures used in their establishment also serve as part of the variety of methods used in demonstrating construct validity.

Validity is absolutely essential in any assessment procedure. Depending on the assessment's purpose, either content or criterion-related validity may be demonstrated. Research concerning the conceptual framework on which the assessment is based contributes to the construct validity.

Reliability

Reliability refers to accuracy or consistency of a measurement. Reliability is reported in terms of a statistical relationship or coefficient (labeled *r;* for example, $r = .62$) computed from the results (scores) gathered from one or more administrations of the assessment to a sample for which the procedure was designed. As previously mentioned, the reliability coefficient (*r*) is represented by a number between 0 and 1, with 1 indicating a perfect relationship or reliability. The closer to 1 the reliability coefficient is, the more accurate or consistent are the results of the procedure.

These statistical procedures conducted on test results yield four types of reliability: stability over time, equivalence of forms, internal consistency, and an inter-rater reliability. The intended use of the results of an assessment will dictate which type of reliability is important for the situation. In evaluating reliability of an assessment, two criteria are necessary: the specific purpose of the assessment and the degree to which the procedure's results are reliable for that purpose.

Estimating Stability. The test-retest method of determining reliability indicates how stable the results of an assessment are over time. Test-retest is conducted by administering a procedure at two different times to the same sample of individuals and comparing the results between the two. This type of reliability is important in measuring educational and psychological constructs that remain the same over time.

Measure of Equivalence. The use of equivalent or alternate forms provides two equal forms to measure the same content. In this case, the reliability is the relationship between the results of the equivalent forms.

Internal Consistency. Two methods are available to estimate the internal consistency of an assessment procedure. They both require one administration of the test. The *split-half* method divides the test in half, and each half functions as an equivalent form. A statistical formula (Spearman-Brown) is employed to estimate the reliability of the whole test. The *Kuder-Richardson* method also estimates reliability from the scores obtained from one administration. Internal consistency here is also measured using a statistical formula. Unlike split-half, the Kuder-Richardson formulas do not require dividing the test. Each of these reliability estimates has advantages and disadvantages that should be carefully weighed when evaluating assessment procedures.

Inter-Rater Reliability. In observation methodologies, the observer, or rater, is considered part of the assessment instrument. Reliability, as previously discussed, is a comparison of procedures or parts of procedures. In inter-rater reliability, then, the results of one rater are compared with those of another rater who observed the same event or situation. High reliability indicates that with the instructions on forms or training of observers, the observers agree about the description of what they see.

Reliability and Validity. Reliability does not guarantee that an assessment measures what it says it will. The relationship between reliability and validity can be illustrated simply by a series of items on a test. If these items were answered in the same way on repeated testings, the test results would have a high reliability, but those results do not mean that the test measures leisure ability. Thus, high reliability does not indicate validity. Validity, however, is affected by reliability. The accuracy of results contributes to the validity of those results. When examining reliability and validity, it is important to consider the interaction between the two elements.

Usability

The usability of an assessment refers to its practical use. Considerations of usability include time, cost, staff qualifications, ease of administration and scoring, and ease of interpretation and application. Usability as it relates to an agency and department deserves consideration.

SELECTION OF AN ASSESSMENT PROCEDURE

Whenever possible, an assessment procedure should be selected. Unfortunately, in therapeutic recreation, few procedures are available; therefore, choices are few. Because of the time and expertise needed to develop an assessment, selection should be the primary consideration in planning for assessment integration in program planning. Figure 10–8 illustrates the process of assessment selection.

Specifying the Purpose

The first step in selecting an assessment procedure is to identify the purpose of the assessment. Purposes of assessment within the program planning process are based on the type of decisions that will be made using the assessment results.

Each assessment also has a specified purpose. This purpose is usually related to the content and interpretation of the assessment. Both purposes need to be identified at this stage. A criticism of current assessment utilization in therapeutic recreation is that procedures that were intended for

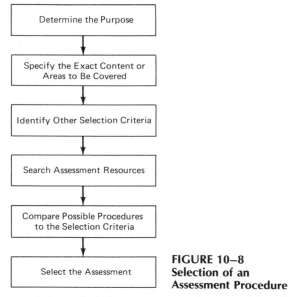

FIGURE 10–8
Selection of an
Assessment Procedure

purposes other than program planning (usually research) are actually being used in the planning process. Selecting and using an assessment for a purpose it was not intended to fulfill will diminish the value of the results determined during utilization.

Specify the Content

Secondly, the specific content or areas to be covered by the assessment should be determined. For example, if the purpose is to provide information for placing a child in a play group, according to his or her level of social play skills, then the assessment should examine solitary, parallel, associative, and cooperative play behaviors.

Identify Selection Criteria

After the identification of purpose and content focus, other criteria expected of the procedure need to be specified. The reliability, validity, and usability are essential criteria by which to evaluate any assessment. Based on common problems in achieving these criteria identified by Thorndike and Hagen[12] and Gronlund,[13] six desired qualities should be expected of therapeutic recreation assessments. They should (1) fulfill their intended purpose, (2) have the ability to gather specified information, (3) gather that information accurately, (4) utilize an appropriate method, (5) be appropriate for clients, and (6) be appropriate for the agency and situation.[14]

[12]Thorndike and Hagen, *Measurement and Evaluation.*

[13]N. E. Gronlund, *Measurement and Evaluation in Teaching,* 3rd ed. (New York: Macmillan Inc., 1976).

[14]Julia K. Dunn, "Improving Client Assessment Procedures in Therapeutic Recreation Programming," in *Expanding Horizons in Therapeutic Recreation X,* ed. G. L. Hitzhusen (Columbia, Mo.: University of Missouri, 1983), pp. 61–84.

Ability to Fulfill the Purpose. As previously mentioned, the ultimate purpose of assessment in therapeutic recreation is to provide information to assist in making decisions for individual program plans. A more specific use of a particular assessment may be affected by the type of decisions that need to be made. Once the purpose(s) has been described, the standard for evaluation of a particular assessment becomes the extent to which it fulfills that purpose. The degree to which the assessment achieves these criteria can be addressed by the following questions.

Does the assessment selection consider the existing or potential program? Since assessment functions as part of program planning, it is essential that it be selected based on the needs of the existing or potential program.

Are the nature of the program and the assessment parallel? The parallel nature indicates a similarity of content and purpose. Regardless of how programs are broken down into component areas, the assessment used in programs should share the focus of the program and gather information related to program content. For example, to be parallel, an assessment used in a leisure education program should focus on an individual's level of leisure ability and the content areas in the leisure education program (leisure and self-awareness, leisure skills, social interaction, decision making, and leisure resources).

Is the program designed to utilize the assessment results? As the attempt has been made to match the assessment to the program, the program must also be able to accept the assessment results. For assessments to be effective, their results must be utilized as they were intended. For example, if a screening assessment was selected to provide information in order to make the decision about whether to place clients in leisure education or treatment programs and there was no difference between the treatment or leisure education program in actual operation, then the results of assessment would not be useful for program decision making.

How do the results of combined assessments affect overall program planning? In this chapter, "program planning" has primarily referred to individual program planning. However, it is also important to relate the assessment of individual clients to the overall therapeutic recreation program planning process. As the results from a variety of clients are reviewed, general trends may appear. Thus, by monitoring clients' assessment results, therapeutic recreation programming can be reviewed and altered to better meet general client needs.

Ability to Gather Specified Information. This criterion directly relates to the procedure's validity. The validity of existing assessments should be evaluated in terms of the validation process and the conceptual framework.

Accuracy in Gathering Information. Assessments are expected to yield reliable or accurate results. As previously stated, reliability is reported as a statistical relationship. The level of the reported reliability should be evaluated according to the appropriateness of the type and the sample on which the reliability was computed.

Method is Appropriate for the Purpose. Another quality desired of assessment procedures is that the method of assessment be appropriate for the purpose and content. The decision has been made as to what is to be assessed. The next step is to determine the most appropriate method. In therapeutic recreation, three general methods are utilized: tests, observations, and interviews.

Tests can be thought of as systematic methods of gathering data that are quantified for analysis. Observations are methods, both structured and unstructured, in which an observer watches and records an individual's behavior.

Interviews are verbally presented questions, and are usually less organized than either tests or observations. Interviews are not considered here as the verbal presentation of a test. Rather, they are seen as an unstructured verbal exchange. Specific questions may be part of the interview, but flexibility is inherent. For, with the use of a variety of communication techniques, more in-depth information can be gathered. An advantage of the interview technique is that it allows for the acquisition of unanticipated, yet valuable, information. Other procedures are restricted in the amount and degree to which they measure behavior or characteristics. However, because of its unstructured format, validity can be threatened. The interview is, perhaps, the most misused technique in therapeutic recreation. It requires advanced communication skills, insight in determining results, and experienced levels of judgment for interpretation. Interpretation of interview results by unqualified individuals is highly suspect because of its demand on judgment rather than measurement.

In terms of measuring change and addressing the issue of accountability, the use of tests and observation is preferred to unstructured interviews. It is for this reason that this chapter's focus is in the area of tests and observation with measurement-related results.

In selecting an assessment procedure, it is important to evaluate the method according to the content it is designed to measure. The strategy that has the best probability of gathering the needed information would be the method of choice.

Appropriateness to Clients. In evaluating assessments for selection, it is essential that they be examined in terms of their appropriateness to clients. Clients should be described according to characteristics such as age, literacy, cultural background, ability to communicate, life situation, length of attention span, and general behavioral patterns. With this knowledge, review of the assessment instrument can be conducted according to the following criteria: clarity of directions, general readability and understandability of items, length of the entire process, and fairness to the client.

Practical for the Situation. Agencies differ, and that difference can affect the assessment process. The agency can influence assessment content, staff qualifications, availability of time and space, and the client population served. A careful examination of the agency and situations that could potentially influence any phase of the assessment process should be undertaken.

Reading the Manual. Criteria related to a variety of different concerns are important in evaluating assessment procedures. Since assessment is in the early stages of development in therapeutic recreation, it is extremely important to monitor the quality of the procedures that are being considered for use.

The quality of any procedure should be evident through the information presented in its manual. Therefore, it is essential in evaluating an assessment to examine the specified criteria as reported in its manual. According to the American Psychological Association's *Standards for Educational and Psychological Tests,* a manual should include: (1) the purpose of the assessment, (2) an introduction and the background of the assessment's development and the conceptual framework, (3) qualifications needed by staff members who are to utilize the assessment, (4) directions for administration, (5) equipment and supplies needed, (6) directions for scoring, (7) directions or guidelines for the interpretation of results, (8) report of reliability, (9) report of validity, and (10) any norms computed.[15]

Search Assessment Resources

Once criteria have been identified, the search for possible assessment procedures can begin. After thorough development, assessments are usually published by established companies and organizations. These published tests are described and reviewed in several comprehensive bibliographical sources. The most important of these sources is the most recent edition of the *Mental Measurements Yearbook,* edited by Buros.[16] These yearbooks cover almost all commercially available assessments. Other valuable sources are *Tests in Print,*[17] the *Journal of Educational Measurement,* and the *Journal of Counseling Psychology.* The majority of assessment procedures reviewed in these sources are educational or psychological in nature. Few assessments related directly to leisure or recreation are listed in these sources; however, they should be consulted, depending upon the purpose of, and content desired from, the procedure. In therapeutic recreation, assessments are available from the developers or have been published in related literature, specifically *Therapeutic Recreation Journal;* the *Journal of Leisure Research; Leisure Sciences; Testing for Impaired, Disabled, and Handicapped Individuals,*[18] and *Expanding Horizons in Therapeutic Recreation.*[19] Information is also available through a variety of continuing education programs and universities.

[15]American Psychological Association, *Standards for Educational and Psychological Tests* (Washington, D.C.: 1974).

[16]O. K. Buros, *The Eighth Mental Measurements Yearbook* (Highland Park, N.J.: Gryphon Press, 1978).

[17]O. K. Buros, *Tests in Print* (Highland Park, N.J.: Gryphon Press, 1965).
O. K. Buros, *Tests in Print II* (Highland Park, N.J.: Gryphon Press, 1974).

[18]American Association of Health, Physical Education, and Recreation, *Testing for Impaired, Disabled, and Handicapped Individuals* (Washington, D.C.: 1974).

[19]*Expanding Horizons in Therapeutic Recreation, Volumes I - X* (Columbia, Mo.: University of Missouri, 1974–1983).

As several potential procedures are located, each should be evaluated according to the specified criteria. For published procedures, other opinions on the value of the procedure are noted in reviews. Reviews of therapeutic recreation assessments do appear in the literature and should be sought out for their contribution to evaluation.

Compare Possible Procedures to Criteria

As several procedures are discovered, they should then be compared to the purpose, content identified, and the program in which they will be used. A useful procedure for this comparison has been provided in Figure 10–9. A comparison of the purpose of the assessment and its intended use within the program in addition to other factors related to the clients agency, and staff will indicate the degree of compatibility of a particular procedure to the program. By asking a series of questions concerning both the program and several assessments, the professional staff can determine the most compatible procedure for a particular program. Some evaluation criteria may be more important than others. As assessments are evaluated, the higher priority criteria should be considered first.

Select the Assessment

When selecting a procedure, the "best match" using the criteria questions and priority concerns would help in determining the preferred assessment. The ultimate goal is to choose the assessment that is most compatible with the existing or potential program. It is unlikely that any one procedure will be the "perfect match" unless the program and assessment were developed concurrently. Possible alternatives might be to alter the program, to combine assessments into a battery, or to evaluate other procedures. The assessment that best fulfills the evaluative criteria would, thus, be the procedure of choice. The decision is then made and the assessment is ordered and integrated into the program planning process.

ASSESSMENTS IN THERAPEUTIC RECREATION

Several appropriate assessments have been developed and are in use within the field of therapeutic recreation. The following selected procedures represent different methods of assessment and are designed for different client groups. They are presented and reviewed to highlight their major characteristics and differences.

Therapeutic Recreation Assessment— Fairview Hospital

General Description. Through a self-report questionnaire and behavioral observation, the Therapeutic Recreation Assessment attempts to gather information related to psychiatric clients' leisure needs and abilities and to identify general problems in functioning. The self-report question-

FIGURE 10–9 Criteria for Assessment Selection: Program Compatibility

ASSESSMENTS

PROGRAM DESCRIPTION		PROCEDURE DESCRIPTION				
Program: What decisions will be made based on assessment results?		What kinds of decisions can be made from assessment results?				
What is the program focus?		What is the assessment focus?				
In general, what is to be assessed?		In general, what does the procedure assess?				
What are subcategories of what is to be assessed?		What factors or subcategories are identified?				
What is the preferred method of assessment?		What is the method?				
Client: What is the target population?		What is the target population?				
Are there any unique characteristics?		Is there provision for unique client characteristics?				
Agency: Are there any agency criteria for assessment?		What special characteristics would meet agency criteria?				
Staff: What are the staff qualifications?		What qualifications are needed to use assessment?				
How much time is available for assessment process?		How long does the assessment take to administer, score, interpret?				

299

naire is largely an interest survey, with items that address leisure awareness, activity preferences, and participation patterns. The observation is loosely structured, including social interaction, emotional expression, and cognitive and physical performance. Results in these categories are determined in two to five observations within therapeutic recreation programs. In addition to the observation and self-report questionnaire, background data are also gathered, including information from admission notes, client history, test records, progress notes, and team discussions.

The structure of this assessment is based on the criteria identified by the standards of the Joint Commission on Accreditation of Hospitals and the therapeutic recreation continuum model (Leisure Ability philosophy). The Therapeutic Recreation Assessment is seen as a component of the planning process and serves the administrative function of documenting the initiation and progress of intervention efforts.

Validity and Reliability. Content validity is addressed in terms of the JCAH standards and the continuum model. Further, since this is a locally developed assessment, it has been written in conjunction with the Fairview Hospital program and, thus, demonstrates content validity in that relationship. No reliability is reported.

Manual and Forms. The Therapeutic Recreation Assessment has no manual, but, like some other locally constructed procedures, has been published in the therapeutic recreation literature. The background of the procedure is discussed as well as the forms. Two forms are presented: the Therapeutic Recreation Interest Survey and the Therapeutic Recreation Assessment. The Interest Survey is the self-report questionnaire. The Assessment is a combination of observation data (Figure 10–10) and treatment planning (Figure 10–11). This form is considered part of the patient's chart, and serves as documentation of the individual program plan.

Usability. The Therapeutic Recreation Assessment is limited in availability. It is published as a chapter in *Quality Assurance: Concerns for Therapeutic Recreation.*[20] Since it was developed for one specific program, its generalizability to other programs has not been established. The function of the assessment form as a tool for documentation seems time-efficient.

Comments. The Therapeutic Recreation Assessment is highly representative of many assessment procedures currently existing in therapeutic recreation. It is an example of the necessity to report a summary of assessment results and to document the treatment plan. Caution should be taken when developing or utilizing such procedures. This type of procedure requires a greater amount of staff judgment than other, more structured

[20]Mary Ellen Erlandson, "The Therapeutic Recreation Assessment Process: Meeting JCAH Standards," in *Quality Assurance: Concerns for Therapeutic Recreation,* ed. N. Navar and J. Dunn (Champaign, Il.: Department of Leisure Studies, University of Illinois, 1981), pp. 68–89.

**FIGURE 10–10
Items from
Therapeutic Recreation Assessment—
Fairview Hospital***

Fairview Hospital
Achievement through excellence

2321 South Sixth Street, Minneapolis, Minn. 55454

_____ Admission note

_____ History and Physical

_____ Psychosocial history

_____ All testing, outside records

_____ POMR charting

_____ Dr's progress notes

_____ Observed in 2-5 TR sessions

_____ Discussed with team

_____ Relative Interview

_____ Family Health History

_____ Intake Evaluation

SOCIAL INTERACTION: Peer interaction _____

Assertiveness _____

Self-Presentation _____

Role with peers _____

Response to authority _____

Response to conflict _____

Need for structure _____

Other: _____

*Material used with permission of Mary Ellen Erlandson.

procedures. As such, the reliability and validity of its results are variable, depending upon the reliability of the staff's judgment.

State Technical Institute's Leisure Assessment Process (STILAP)

General Description.   STILAP is an assessment designed to measure the general scope of leisure activity skills in order to provide a basis for program decision making regarding a more balanced and increased leisure skill repertoire. It was designed as a program planning tool for the State Technical Institute and Rehabilitation Center (STIRC). The Center's clients included adults aged seventeen to sixty, with physical, mental, emotional, and/or social handicapping conditions, who were enrolled in the Institute's program for vocational rehabilitation and trade education.

STILAP is a self-report activity checklist that measures participation and interest in 123 leisure activities, representing fourteen categories of leisure participation. The fourteen categories include physical skills done alone; physical skills done with others regardless of skill level; physical skills requiring others; activity skills that depend on the outdoor environment; physical skills that are not seasonal; physical skills with carry-over to later years; physical skill—cardiovascular; mental skills done alone; mental skills requiring others; appreciation skills—mental or emotional stimulation; creative construction or self-expression; enjoyment or improvement of home;

**FIGURE 10–11 Therapeutic Recreation Assessment Treatment Plan—
Fairview Hospital***

Assessed Areas of Concern	Strengths
Treatment Goals	Treatment plan/approach

Date _____ Therapist _____

Frequency: In accordance with program _____; 5 days/week _____.

    6 days/week (adult) _____; other (specify) _____

    Swimming (off-unit activities) as code permits _____

Duration: Duration of hospitalization _____ other (specify) _____

Date _____ Referring physician _____

*Material used with permission of Mary Ellen Erlandson.

social skills; and leadership or community service.

STILAP is administered to the client as an independent self-report with a follow-up interview. It requires knowledge of a variety of communication techniques in addition to a professional background in therapeutic recreation.

Validity and Reliability. Content validity is addressed through the compatibility of STILAP with the therapeutic recreation program at STIRC. No other validity or reliability data are reported.

Manual and Forms. The entire STILAP procedure has been presented in a chapter of *Expanding Horizons in Therapeutic Recreation VI*.[21] Included are the basic assumptions that are the basis of the conceptual foundation, purpose, administration and scoring procedures, and guidelines for use in program planning.

The activity checklist, or MSI form, is completed by the client or staff with client (see Figure 10–12). Directions are included on the form, as well as the listing of the 123 activities.

[21]Nancy Navar, "Leisure Skill Assessment Process in Leisure Counseling," in *Expanding Horizons in Therapeutic Recreation VI*, ed. D. J. Szymanski and G. L. Hitzhusen (Columbia, Mo.: Technical Education Services, University of Missouri, 1979), pp. 68–94.

FIGURE 10–12 Directions and Sample Items from STILAP*

```
STATE TECHNICAL INSTITUTE AND REHABILITATION CENTER - - - - - LEISURE ASSESSMENT - - - - - -
                              STILAP ACTIVITY CHECKLIST

NAME: _____   TRADE AREA: _____   DATE: _____   INTERVIEW DATE: _____   STAFF: _____

DIRECTIONS:  Following is a list of various leisure activities.

    1. Circle "M" (much) for those activities you participate in regularly (daily, every other day, when in season, etc.).
    2. Circle "S" (sometimes) for those activities you have experienced but not on a regular basis.
    3. Circle "I" (interested in) for those activities you would like to learn (you may or may not have done these before, but you
       are still interested in learning more about the activity).

       M S I—1.  Pool/billiards/snooker      M S I—17.  Horseback riding
       M S I—2.  Dieting/nutrition           M S I—18.  Miniature golf
       M S I—3.  Bowling                     M S I—19.  Golf
       M S I—4.  Roller skating              M S I—20.  Hunting
```

*Material used with permission of designer, Nancy Navar.

FIGURE 10–13 Partial Profile Worksheet from STILAP*

STILAP PROFILE WORKSHEET

NAME: _____ DATE: _____ STAFF: _____

	YES	NO	M's	S'	Interest Areas	Prescription Choice
1. Physical skill that can be done alone (1–7; 9–36; 121)						
2. Physical skill that she/he can participate with others regardless of skill level (3–7; 9–36; 121)						
3. Physical skill that requires the participation of one or more others (38–51)						
12. Skill which enables enjoyment/improvement of the home environment (82–83; 94–109)						
13. Physical or mental skill which enables participation in a predominantly social situation (3–4; 18–19; 66; 87–89; 93; 116–120)						
14. Leadership and or interpersonal skill which enables community service (112–120)						

*Material used with permission of designer, Nancy Navar.

The activity checklist requests clients to indicate their level of participation as "much" or "some," and their interest in each of the listed activities. These activities have been analyzed according to their ability to meet the fourteen competency areas, so a client's response on each activity can then be transferred to the appropriate category on the profile sheet. Figure 10–13 illustrates the profile sheet where scores are recorded and areas of program focus are identified. The form has been revised from the 1979 version and is partially presented here in its revised state.

Usability. STILAP is available from one of the developers and has been published in *Expanding Horizons in Therapeutic Recreation VI.*[22] Its reported use is in the program of the State Technical Institute and Rehabilitation Center of Plainwell, Michigan.

Comments. STILAP is limited to measurement of participation and interest in leisure activity skills, one component of leisure education. Therefore, careful consideration should be given to its ability to represent the total construct of leisure ability.

The Comprehensive Evaluation in Recreational Therapy (CERT) Scale

General Description. The CERT Scale is a systematic behavioral observation designed for monitoring three categories of behaviors. CERT was designed for short-term psychiatric settings serving adolescents and adults; however, it is usable in other psychiatric settings. The behaviors measured include the following:

General: attendance, appearance, attitude toward recreation therapy, coordination of gait, and posture.

Individual Performance: response to therapist's structure, one-to-one, decision-making ability, judgment ability, ability to form individual relationships, expression of hostility, performance in organized activities, performance in free activities, attention span, frustration tolerance level, strength/endurance.

Group Performance: memory for group activities, response to group structure, leadership ability in groups, group conversation, display of sexual role in the group, style of group interaction, handles conflicts in group when indirectly involved, handles conflict in group when directly involved, competition in group, attitude toward group decisions.

Validity and Reliability. Content validity has been addressed in the identification of behaviors included in the procedure. Other behavioral scales were reviewed for content, and practicing recreation therapists were used as an expert panel for behavior identification. At the time of publication, methods to describe the predictive validity of results were being

[22]Ibid.

undertaken. Inter-rater reliability was computed using the specified scaling system (0–4) between five therapists rating thirty-eight patients at one mental health facility and reported at .51, with a range of .25 to 1.00. When the range of the scale was reduced to three rather than five degrees (0–1, 2–3, 3–4), the same reliability check ranged from .67 to 1.00, with the average being .91.

Manual and Forms. The CERT Scale is published as a journal article and does not have a specific manual. The article does include the background and development of the procedure, reports reliability and validity, and describes the scoring procedures and use of results.

The scale form lists each behavior and five descriptors of the degree of that behavior, ranging from 0, "normal," to 4, indicating a severe problem. Figure 10–14 is a representation of several items on the CERT Scale. Its designation as a monitoring tool is addressed on the form, with space available (columns) to record repeated observations.

Usability. The CERT Scale is not available as a published form with an accompanying manual, but was published in the *Therapeutic Recreation Journal.*[23]

Comments. The CERT Scale is designed to monitor twenty-five behaviors commonly displayed in recreation activities. However, the procedure does not guarantee that these behaviors will occur. Therefore, observation of several different activities may be needed to observe all of the behaviors listed. Some items (behaviors) seem loosely defined and would merit further item analysis. In adapting a scale like the CERT, it is important to establish reliability and content validity of the results for the program in which it will be used.

The Mundy Recreation Inventory for the Trainable Mentally Retarded[24]

General Description. The Mundy Inventory is designed as the preliminary stage of the "Habilitation Recreation Program Planning Process." Its purpose is to "assess a client's performance and abilities to determine the selection of recreation activities for that client's program." The general focus is cognitive and physical functioning as they relate to recreation participation. It is frequently combined with components of the *Purdue Perceptual-Motor Survey* into the Florida State University Diagnostic Battery of Recreative Function for the Trainable Mentally Retarded. This combination expands the functional assessment to include perceptual-motor abilities.

[23]Robert A. Parker, C. H. Ellison, T. F. Kirby, and M. J. Short, "The Comprehensive Evaluation in Recreation Therapy Scale: A Tool for Patient Evaluation," *Therapeutic Recreation Journal,* 9, no. 4 (1975), pp. 143–152.

[24]Jean Mundy, "The Mundy Recreation Inventory for the Trainable Mentally Retarded" (unpublished manuscript, 1966).

FIGURE 10–14 Sample Items from CERT Scale‡

F. PERFORMANCE IN ORGANIZED ACTIVITIES

(0) Grasps situation	
(1) Needs minimal instructions	
(2) Needs frequent instructions	
(3) Needs constant instructions to participate	
(4) Unable to participate	

G. PERFORMANCE IN FREE ACTIVITIES†

(0) Acts on own initiative	
(1) Participates after activity has started	
(2) Participates after encouragement	
(3) Starts & stops; have to encourage often	
(4) No interest and/or refuses	

H. ATTENTION SPAN

(0) Attends to activity	
(1) Occasionally does not attend (preoccupied)	
(2) Frequently does not attend (distracted)	
(3) Rarely attends to activity	
(4) Does not attend (detached)	

•Evaluate after three days.
†Evaluate from evening and weekend activities.
‡Material used with permission of Robert Parker.

FIGURE 10–14 *(Continued)*

I. FRUSTRATION TOLERANCE LEVEL																		
(0) Participates without appearing frustrated																		
(1) Occasionally becomes frustrated																		
(2) Often becomes frustrated																		
(3) Appears frustrated most of the time																		
(4) So frustrated unable to participate																		

Categories addressed by the Mundy Inventory include object identification; action concepts; color concepts; amount, position, direction, place, and space; following directions; rhythm; manipulation skills; and motor skills. Items in each of these categories are assessed through the administrator's visual observation and judgment of the client's performance on a given set of tasks. Because of the level of experience and judgment required in determining the degree of success of each task and in utilization of the final results, a professional is needed to administer, score, and interpret results. Responses are recorded while the assessment is administered. This often necessitates two professionals for every administration, one to present the directions or task and one to record responses.

Validity and Reliability. Criterion-related (concurrent) validity and reliability have been addressed in a study by Cannon, Moffett, and Moffett.[25] They validated the Florida State University Battery from the results of scores obtained from fifty-eight randomly selected residents of a training center for the mentally retarded. Scores were determined by judges' ratings, total battery scores, and scores from the Mundy Inventory and the *Purdue Perceptual-Motor Survey,* prior to program intervention and after intervention. Criterion-validity of the judges' ratings and the Mundy Inventory were $r = .66$ at pre-test and $r = .63$ at post-test. Between the Mundy Inventory and the Purdue, $r = .67$ at pre-test and $r = .74$ at post-test; between the Mundy Inventory and the FSU Battery, $r = .51$, pre-test, and $r = .58$, post-test. In this validation, all correlations were found to be significant at the .05 level. Test-retest reliability on the Mundy Inventory was computed, and showed little change in scores from the first to the second administration (one- and two-week time periods).

[25]F. C. Cannon, H. W. Moffett, and L. O. Moffett, "Diagnostically-designed Recreation Program for Trainable Mentally Retarded Children," *Journal of Leisure Research,* 2, no. 2 (1970), pp. 93–103.

Manual and Forms. The Mundy Inventory's manual includes the conceptual framework of program planning without background on the procedure's development. Directions are provided for administration, scoring (see Figures 10–15 and 10–16), and interpretation. A profile or summary form is included, in which results are organized for decision making.

Usability. The Mundy Inventory has not been published, and, therefore, has limited access. It is available from the author, Jean Mundy.[26] This procedure is somewhat time-consuming but provides a variety of results in the areas of cognitive and physical functioning. Financial demand is placed on the agency, because it must acquire the equipment needed for administration.

Comment. It should be noted that the Mundy Inventory is a component of a specific programming process demanding a variety of professional skills in planning, implementing, and evaluating. As such, when evaluating the Inventory's potential use, consideration should also be addressed to the Habilitative Programming Plan. In relation to basic functioning, the Mundy Inventory assesses only cognitive and physical areas. For a comprehensive view of "recreative functioning," components would need to be added to address social and affective areas.

Leisure Diagnostic Battery (LDB)

General Description. The Leisure Diagnostic Battery is one of the most comprehensive measures in therapeutic recreation. It has four major purposes:

1. To enable the assessment of individuals' current level of leisure functioning
2. To determine areas where improvement of current leisure functioning is needed
3. To determine via post assessment the impact of offered services on leisure functioning
4. To facilitate research on the structure of leisure to enable a better understanding of the value, purpose, and outcomes of leisure experiences[27]

To achieve these purposes, eight component assessments were devised. Each of these addresses a factor thought to affect leisure functioning.

Component: Leisure Preferences Inventory
Purpose: To determine relative strength of preference in six domains of leisure activities and to assess preferred modes of involvement.

Component: Playfulness/Spontaneity Scale
Purpose: To determine an individual's degree of playfulness/spontaneity.

---

[26]Jean Mundy, Leisures Services and Studies Program, 215 Stone Building, Florida State University, Tallahassee, Fla. 32306.

[27]Peter A. Witt, G. Ellis, *The Leisure Diagnostic Battery User's Guide* (Denton, Tx.: Division of Recreation and Leisure Studies, North Texas State University, 1982), p. 6.

FIGURE 10–15 Sample Items and Directions: Motor Skills—Catching Section. Mundy Recreation Inventory for the Trainable Mentally Retarded*

VI. MOTOR SKILLS

Equipment needed: 16" softball and a 7" rubber playground ball.

This section is to inventory some of the basic motor skills involved in many recreation activities. Since the subjects have usually been taught not to throw or kick a ball inside, an example of their behavior and functioning can best be gained in the out-of-doors or in a gymnasium.

The examiner is to stand approximately 10 feet in front of the subject. Three attempts are allowed for each task with the score for any task recorded as the average of the three attempts.

The examiner should explain that he will throw the ball and the subject is to catch it and then throw it back to him. In this way, an assessment can be made of the throwing and catching at the same time.

Item 84: Throw the ball underhanded to the subject, just above the waist. The ball should be thrown directly in front of the subject and slightly above his waist in a trajectory no higher than the subject's head. If it is a bad throw, the examiner is to repeat the throw. A bad throw on the part of the examiner is not counted as one of the three attempts given the subject.

Item 85: Throw the ball directly in front of the subject and slightly below his waist. If it is a bad throw, repeat.

Item 86: Throw the ball slightly to the right of the subject, at about waist height.

Item 87: Throw the ball slightly to the left of the subject, at about waist height.

Item 88: Throw the ball directly in front of the subject, slightly over his head, where he will have to take at least one and not more than two steps backwards in order to make the catch.

Item 89: Throw the ball directly in front of the subject, slightly below his waist but not quite to him, so he will have to take at least one and not more than two steps forward to make the catch.

Item 90: Throw the ball far enough to the right of the subject (a little past his arm's reach) that he will have to move to make the catch.

Item 91: Throw the ball far enough to the left of the subject (a little past his arm's reach) that he will have to move to make the catch.

Items 92, 93: These can be checked when the subject throws the ball back to the examiner after each catch, by asking that some of the throws be underhanded and some of the throws be overhanded.

Items 94–96: The examiner should explain he will roll the ball to the subject, who is to kick it back to him. The examiner is to roll the ball to the subject and directly in front of the subject. (Item 94 is designed to find out the subject's dominant or preferred foot. The remaining two items are to check performance with both the right and left foot, regardless of the dominant or preferred foot.)

*Material used with permission of Jean Mundy.

FIGURE 10–16 Sample Items and Scoring: Motor Skills—Catching Section. Mundy Recreation Inventory for the Trainable Mentally Retarded*

VI. MOTOR SKILLS

Circle the appropriate answer. The throwing and catching may be administered together but should be scored separately.

Catching
84. Above the waist
   3. completes catch
   2. raises hands, grasps, but misses
   1. grasps but does not raise hands
   0. no attempt
85. Below the waist
   3. completes catch
   2. lowers hands, grasps, but misses
   1. grasps but doesn't move the hands down
   0. no attempt
86. Right quadrant
   3. completes catch
   2. moves hands to the right, grasps, but misses
   1. grasps but does not move hands to the right
   0. no attempt
87. Left quadrant
   3. completes catch
   2. moves hands to the left, grasps, but misses
   1. grasps but does not move hands to the left
   0. no attempt
88. Moves backwards
   3. completes catch
   2. moves backwards after ball, grasps, but misses
   1. grasps but does not move backwards
   0. no attempt
89. Moves forward
   3. completes catch
   2. moves forward, grasps, but misses
   1. grasps but does not move forward
   0. no attempt
90. Moves right
   3. completes catch
   2. moves right, grasps, but misses
   1. grasps but does not move right
   0. no attempt
91. Moves left
   3. completes catch
   2. moves left, grasps, but misses
   1. grasps but does not move left
   0. no attempt

*Material used with permission of Jean Mundy.

Component: Knowledge of Leisure Opportunities Test
Purpose: To determine an individual's knowledge of leisure opportunities.

Component: Leisure Barriers Inventory
Purpose: To determine problems that an individual encounters when trying
to participate in activities during free time.

Component: Leisure Needs Scale
Purpose: To determine the degree of ability of an individual to meet certain
needs via leisure experience.

Component: Intrinsic Motivation Scale
Purpose: To determine the degree to which individuals are internally motivated to undertake leisure activities and experiences or are influenced by
extrinsic reward or sanction.

Component: Perceived Competence Scale
Purpose: To determine the degree of competence or ability individuals perceive themselves as possessing.

Component: Locus of Control Test
Purpose: To determine whether individuals believe events in their lives to be
under their own control (internal locus of control) or are a result of fate,
luck, or powerful others (external locus of control).[28]

The LDB is focused on assessing the leisure functioning of handicapped children and youth. Version A is designed for nine- to fourteen-
year-old normal, orthopedically impaired, and higher-functioning,
educable mentally retarded individuals. Version B is focused for use with
lower-functioning, educable mentally retarded individuals. For these client
groups, five LDB (diagnostic) scales are used to assess leisure functioning:
(1) Perceived Leisure Competence Scale, (2) Perceived Leisure Control
Scale, (3) Leisure Needs Scale, (4) Depth of Involvement in Leisure Scale,
and (5) Playfulness Scale. Each of these scales contributes to an overall
measure of feelings of freedom, the underlying foundation of leisure functioning.

Three additional scales are available to assess specific problems that
may inhibit feelings of freedom. These include Leisure Barriers Inventory,
Knowledge of Leisure Opportunities Test, and the Leisure Preferences
Inventory.

Validity and Reliability. Reliability was determined on each of the
diagnostic scales and the total battery for stability of scores (test-retest) and
for internal consistency (Chronbach's alpha). Scores from a pilot testing of
over 1300 children were used in various validation studies. For Version A,
the test-retest of the LDB was .89, with the five scales individually ranging
from .82 to .62. Chronbach's alpha reliability range on individual scales
was .86 to .96. For Version B, test-retest reliability ranged from .79 to .46
on the different scales, while alpha ranged between .71 and .82, with the
Perceived Freedom Scale being .90 to .92.

[28]Ibid., pp. 4–5.

FIGURE 10–17 Item Response Format—Leisure Diagnostic Battery*

	SOUNDS LIKE ME	SOUNDS A LITTLE LIKE ME	DOESN'T SOUND LIKE ME
13. When I'm doing recreation activities, I can keep bad things from happening.	A	B	C
14. I can do things that will make other people better players.	A	B	C
15. I can do things during recreation activities that will make other people like me more.	A	B	C

*Material used with permission of Peter Witt and Gary Ellis. Leisure Diagnostic Battery. Denton, Texas: Division of Recreation and Leisure Studies, North Texas State University, 1982.

Construct validation was addressed through an extensive literature review to identify the factors of the construct of leisure functioning and factor analysis to confirm the relationship of each of those factors to the construct. Comparison with other established scales yielded a measure of predictive validity. During some of the validation studies, the LDB scale scores were compared with the Piers-Harris Self-Concept Scale, the Crandall Social Desirability Scale, and the Coopersmith Self-Esteem Scale.

Version A scales are judged to have a high degree of construct validity. One scale, the Knowledge Test, seems lower than is desired in terms of stability. The low reliability estimates in Version B reduce its validity, resulting in somewhat questionable results.

Manual and Forms. A variety of materials is available beyond the instrumentation of the LDB. They include the *LDB User's Guide, LDB Remediation Guide,* and *LDB Background, Conceptualization, and Structure.*[29] Through these, all necessary information is available to understand and effectively utilize the LDB.

The instrumentation includes separate scales for each of the component areas. In Version A, the Perceived Leisure Competence, the Perceived Leisure Control, the Leisure Needs, the Depth of Involvement in Leisure Experiences, the Playfulness, and the Barriers to Leisure Experience scales contain approximately twenty items each. Items are structured to generate a response of "sounds like me," "sounds a little like me," or "doesn't sound like me" (see Figure 10–17). The Leisure Preferences Scale is a sixty-item procedure with a forced-choice response type. The Knowledge of Leisure Opportunities Scale includes twenty-eight multiple choice items (Figures 10–18 and 10–19). Forms are designed to be completed by the clients and administered on an individual or a group level. Summary

[29]*The Leisure Diagnostic Battery Users Guide, The LDB Remediation Guide,* and *The LDB Background, Conceptualization, and Structure* are all available through the Division of Recreation and Leisure Studies, North Texas State University, Denton, Tx.

FIGURE 10–18 Item Response Format, Forced Choice—Leisure Diagnostic Battery*

11. I would rather:	A	Talk on the telephone	(M)
	B	Play with a puppet	(C)
12. I would rather:	A	Play a game of pool	(S)
	B	Paint a doghouse	(C)
13. I would rather:	A	Dress in a funny costume	(D)
	B	Read the comics	(M)
14. I would rather:	A	Paint like an artist	(C)
	B	Go skating	(S)
15. I would rather:	A	Play badminton	(S)
	B	Sing for people	(D)

*Material used with permission of Peter Witt and Gary Ellis. Leisure Diagnostic Battery. Denton, Texas: Division of Recreation and Leisure Studies, North Texas State University, 1982.

forms are provided for the Barriers to Leisure, Leisure Preferences, and Knowledge of Leisure Opportunities Scales.

Version B provides the same scale structure, with a different representation of items. Rather than children circling a letter to represent the "like me" sequence, they point to one of three faces; for instance, "like me" is equivalent to ☺ . In items requiring forced or multiple choice, the choices are presented by pictures. Scoring is done by the professional administering the assessment.

Usability. The LDB is available from the developers. It is a new procedure, which can be used in a variety of settings, including schools. This procedure provides a unique "community-based" approach to leisure assessment. The time needed to administer it (forty-five minutes to one hour) may seem prohibitive. However, it provides a variety of information easily integrated into the decisions needed for individual program planning.

Comments. The LDB provides extensive materials, which have been well-developed. The conceptual foundation has been well-established and provides a basis for construct validity, absent in most other assessment procedures utilized in therapeutic recreation programming.

Recreation Behavior Inventory (RBI)

General Description. The Recreation Behavior Inventory is an indirect observation procedure designed to "assess the client's level of performance in a selected sample of cognitive, sensory, and perceptual-motor skills and behaviors which are either important developmental milestones or frequently required for successful participation in a variety of play and recreation activities."[30] Eighty-seven behaviors have been identified and are

[30]Doris L. Berryman and Claudette B. Lefebvre, *Recreation Behavior Inventory* (Denton, Tx.: Leisure Learning Systems, 1981).

FIGURE 10–19 Item Response, Multiple Choice—Leisure Diagnostic Battery*

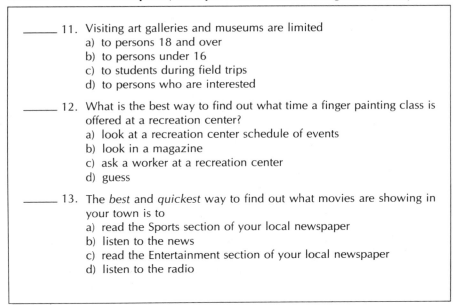

> _____ 11. Visiting art galleries and museums are limited
>   a) to persons 18 and over
>   b) to persons under 16
>   c) to students during field trips
>   d) to persons who are interested
>
> _____ 12. What is the best way to find out what time a finger painting class is offered at a recreation center?
>   a) look at a recreation center schedule of events
>   b) look in a magazine
>   c) ask a worker at a recreation center
>   d) guess
>
> _____ 13. The *best* and *quickest* way to find out what movies are showing in your town is to
>   a) read the Sports section of your local newspaper
>   b) listen to the news
>   c) read the Entertainment section of your local newspaper
>   d) listen to the radio

*Material used with permission of Peter Witt and Gary Ellis. Leisure Diagnostic Battery. Denton, Texas: Division of Recreation and Leisure Studies, North Texas State University, 1982.

assessed by observation in twenty different recreational activities. Each activity is designed to elicit specific behaviors, which can then be rated on a three-point scale. The behaviors have been grouped into approximately thirty behavioral categories, representing the domains of sensory, cognitive, and perceptual-motor behavior.

The assessment is designed to provide specific performance levels, which are then used as the basis for program design for individuals in treatment or classroom settings. The primary client focus of the RBI is children, though reportedly it has been used with adult psychiatric patients and nursing home residents.

Validity and Reliability. Content validity was established in three ways. First, relevant literature and research were reviewed to establish the representativeness of behavioral tasks to the stages of human growth and development. Secondly, analysis of a cross-section of play and recreational activities was undertaken to determine the behaviors commonly found in them. Finally, the appropriateness of the behaviors and tasks previously identified was validated by review by a panel of experts.

Reliability was calculated through the use of inter-class correlation, incorporating both variance of persons and variance for error. Three raters, observing 55 clients over all 87 behaviors, yielded a mean correlation coefficient of .94, with the range being .62 to 1.00.

FIGURE 10–20 Activity Example—Recreation Behavior Inventory*

ACTIVITY: WHAT AM I DOING?	BEHAVIOR(S):
MATERIALS NEEDED: None	*Visual Recall* 72 Remember actions *Symbol Identification* 114 Identify actions

DESCRIPTION:	(SUGGESTED ORGANIZATION)
114 Leader pantomimes a behavior and asks the participants to identify the action. This will acquaint them with the activity. Leader pantomimes a new and different behavior or action	PPPPPPPp L Participants (P): up to 8

for each participant individually to identify. Sample actions are: rock a baby, drive a car, play a piano, cutting paper (using index and second finger as shears), brush teeth, deal cards, tie shoes, comb or brush hair. Each participant is given two trials at random to identify the action. Each participant is given only one chance on each trial. No sounds may accompany the action. No coaching is allowed by leader or other participants. Leader and observer should review all actions beforehand so that the observer will recognize correct response, in addition to making certain all pantomimes are clearly understandable.

72   Leader asks each participant individually if he or she can remember one of the performed actions; e.g., "How did I rock the baby?" Participant must *perform* that same action. To perform the action is a way to illustrate that one remembers the action. Leader should intervene to inform observer what actions are acceptable. Each participant is given two trials at random to recall the action. Each participant is given one chance on each trial to recall the action. All participants are given two trials. No coaching is allowed by leader or other participants.

SUGGESTED ACTIONS:

1. Drinking	10. Eating
2. Sleeping	11. Combing or brushing hair
3. Finger to lips for silence	12. Brushing teeth
4. Waving hello or goodbye	13. Driving a car
5. Swinging a bat	14. Playing a piano
6. Throwing	15. Cutting paper
7. Putting on a pair of pants	16. Dealing cards
8. Jumping a rope	17. Tying shoes
9. Running	

*Material used with permission of Doris L. Berryman and Claudette B. Lefebvre.

FIGURE 10–21 Activity Score Sheet—Recreation Behavior Inventory*

Observer: _____

Date: _____ Center: _____

NAMES

ACTIVITY: WHAT AM I DOING?

Scoring: The Activity leader will inform you what behavior you are observing and when you should assign your score for each participant. Each participant will be given two trials (though not successively), so you should indicate a successful performance by placing hash marks (I, II) in the appropriate column. When that behavior is completed, you may refer to your hash marks to assign a score for each participant depending on the stated criteria.

If for some reason the participant is not assessed, score a one (1) and comment in the appropriate space.

COMMENTS

BEHAVIOR: 114 *Symbol Identification of Actions (Two trials)*
1. Could not identify actions on either trial
2. Identified action on only one trial
3. Identified actions on both trials

BEHAVIOR: 72 *Visual Recall of Actions* (Two trials)
1. Could not recall actions on either trial
2. Recalled action on only one trial
3. Recalled actions on both trials

*Material used with permission of Doris L. Berryman and Claudette B. Lefebvre.

Manual and Forms.   The RBI is packaged in a loose-leaf binder and available through Leisure Learning Systems. The manual includes extensive directions for administration and scoring as well as background data, reliability, and validity. Each of the activities (Figure 10–20) is described, and scoring sheets for group evaluation are presented (see Figure 10–21).

Usability.   The RBI is available for a cost. It takes a significant amount of time to administer; however, the actual activities used for observation could be considered programmatic, and, thus, serve a dual purpose.

Comments.   The RBI seems to be a well-conceptualized measure of cognitive, sensory, and perceptual-motor skills and behavior. If a comprehensive assessment of leisure functioning is needed, the RBI will need to be supplemented with other assessments that target additional functional abilities such as social skills.

The various assessment procedures described, illustrate those currently available for use in therapeutic recreation. This is not a comprehensive list. Rather, assessment procedures were selected to represent diversity of method, content, and population.

SUMMARY

Client assessment has been identified as a critical issue in therapeutic recreation. Client assessment procedures are the major tool used to individualize program planning, thus contributing to accountability. Because therapeutic recreation is in the early stage of assessment use, few procedures exist. Many of the existing assessment procedures are problematic due to inappropriate development and utilization. This chapter has served to introduce the concept of client assessment as a component of the program planning process. Concepts of assessment have been presented and related to utilization. The processes involved in the selection of assessment have been outlined. In order to utilize client assessments effectively in program planning, professionals must be familiar with their use, their relation to program planning, and criteria for their evaluation.

========================= **Suggested References** =========================

ALLEN, M. J., and W. M. YEN, *Introduction to Measurement Theory.* Monterey, Ca.: Brooks/Cole Publishing Co., 1979.

American Association of Health, Physical Education, and Recreation, *Testing for Impaired, Disabled, and Handicapped Individuals.* Washington, D.C.: 1975.

American Psychological Association, *Standards for Educational and Psychological Tests.* Washington, D.C.: 1974.

ANASTASI, A., *Psychological Testing* (4th edition). New York: Macmillan Inc., 1976.

BARLOW, D. H., ed., *Behavioral Assessment of Adult Disorders.* New York: Guilford Press, 1981.

BERRYMAN, D. L., and C. B. LEFEBVRE, *Recreation Behavior Inventory*. Denton, Tx.: Leisure Learning Systems, 1981.

BRADBURN, N. M., and S. SUDMAN, *Improving Interview Method and Questionnaire Design*. San Francisco: Jossey-Bass Inc., Publishers, 1980.

BUROS, O. K., *The Eighth Mental Measurements Yearbook*. Highland Park, N.J.: Gryphon Press, 1978.

CONE, J. D., and R. P. HAWKINS, eds., *Behavioral Assessment, New Directions in Clinical Psychology*. New York: Brunner/Mazel Inc., 1977.

CORMIER, W. H., and L. S. CORMIER, *Interviewing Strategies for Helpers: A Guide to Assessment, Treatment, and Evaluation*. Monterey, Ca.: Brooks/Cole Publishing Co., 1979.

DUNN, J. K., "Improving Client Assessment Procedures in Therapeutic Recreation Programming," in *Expanding Horizons in Therapeutic Recreation X*, ed. G. L. Hitzhusen, pp. 61–84. Columbia, Mo.: University of Missouri, 1983.

ELLIS, G. D., P. A. WITT, and S. NILES, *The Leisure Diagnostic Battery Remediation Guide*. Denton, Tx.: Division of Recreation and Leisure Studies, North Texas State University, 1982.

ERLANDSON, M. E., "The Therapeutic Recreation Assessment Process: Meeting JCAH Standards," in *Quality Assurance: Concerns for Therapeutic Recreation*, ed. N. Navar and J. Dunn, pp. 68–69. Champaign, Il.: Department of Leisure Studies, University of Illinois, 1981.

GILBERT, J., *Interpreting Psychological Test Data*. 2 vols. New York: Van Nostrand Reinhold, 1978, 1980.

GRONLUND, N. E., *Measurement and Evaluation in Teaching* (3rd ed.). New York: Macmillan Inc., 1976.

HALPERN, A. S., J. P. LEHMANN, L. K. IRVIN, and T. J. HEIRY, *Contemporary Assessment for Mentally Retarded Adolescents and Adults*. Baltimore: University Park Press, 1982.

HARROW, A. J., *A Taxonomy of the Psychomotor Domain*. New York: Longman Inc., 1972.

HUTT, S. J., and C. HUTT, *Direct Observation and Measurement of Behavior*. Springfield, Il.: Charles C. Thomas, Publisher, 1974.

KINNEY, W. B., "Clinical Assessment in Mental Health Settings," *Therapeutic Recreation Journal*, 14, no. 4 (1980), pp. 39–45.

KRUG, J. L., "A Review of Perceptual-Motor/Sensory Integrative Measurement Tools," *Therapeutic Recreation Journal*, 13, no. 2 (1979), pp. 41–43.

LIDZ, C. S., *Improving Assessment of School Children*. San Francisco: Jossey-Bass Inc., Publishers, 1981.

LYERLY, S. B., *Handbook of Psychiatric Rating Scales*. Rockville, Md.: National Institute of Mental Health, 1973.

MASH, E. J., and L. G. TERDAL, *Behavioral Assessment of Childhood Disorders*. New York: Guilford Press, 1981.

McKECHNIE, G. E., *Manual for Leisure Activities Blank*. Palo Alto: Consulting Psychology Press, 1975.

MUNDY, J., "The Mundy Recreation Inventory for the Trainable Mentally Retarded." Unpublished manuscript, 1966.

MUNDY, J. and L. ODUM, *Leisure Education: Theory and Practice*. New York: John Wiley and Sons, 1979.

NAVAR, N. "Leisure Skill Assessment Process in Leisure Counseling," in *Expanding Horizons in Therapeutic Recreation VI*, ed. D. J. Szymanski and G. L. Hitzhusen, pp. 68–94. Columbia, Mo.: Technical Education Services, University of Missouri, 1979.

———— "A Rationale for Leisure Skill Assessment with Handicapped Adults," *Therapeutic Recreation Journal*, 14, no. 4, 1980, pp. 21–28.

NIE, N. H., C. H. HULL, J. G. JENKINS, K. STEINBRENNER, and D. H. BENT, *Statistical Package for the Social Sciences* (2nd ed.). New York: McGraw-Hill Book Co., 1975.

PARKER, R. A., C. H. ELLISON, T. F. KIRBY, and M. J. SHORT, "The Comprehensive Evaluation in Recreation Therapy Scale: A Tool for Patient Evaluation," *Therapeutic Recreation Journal*, 9, no. 4 (1975), pp. 143–152.

SALVIA, J., and J. E. YSSELDYKE, *Assessment in Special and Remedial Education* (2nd ed.). Boston: Houghton-Mifflin Co., 1981.

————, *Instructor's Manual: Assessment in Special and Remedial Education* (2nd ed.). Boston: Houghton-Mifflin Co., 1981.

SULZER-AZAROFF, B., and G. R. MAYER, *Applying Behavior-Analysis Procedures with Children and Youth*. New York: Holt, Rinehart and Winston, 1977.

SUNDBERG, N. D. *Assessment of Persons*. Englewood Cliffs, N.J.: Prentice-Hall, Inc., 1977.

THORNDIKE, R. L., and E. P. HAGEN, *Measurement and Evaluation in Psychology and Education* (4th ed.). New York: John Wiley and Sons, 1977.

WEHMAN, P., and S. J. SCHLEIEN, "Relevant Assessment in Leisure Skill Training Program," *Therapeutic Recreation Journal*, 14, no. 4 (1980), pp. 9–20.

WILSON, S. J., *Recording: Guidelines for Social Workers*. New York: The Free Press, 1976.

WITT, P. A., *The Leisure Diagnostic Battery User's Guide*. Denton, Tx.: Division of Recreation and Leisure Studies, North Texas State University, 1982.

WITT, P. A., P. CONNOLLY, and D. COMPTON, "Assessment: A Plea for Sophistication," *Therapeutic Recreation Journal*, 14, no. 4 (1980), pp. 5–8.

WITT, P. A., and R. GROOM, "Dangers and Problems Associated with Current Approaches to Developing Leisure Interest Finders," *Therapeutic Recreation Journal*, 13, no. 1 (1979), pp. 19–31.

WOODY, R. H., ed., *Encyclopedia of Clinical Assessment*. 2 vols. San Francisco: Jossey-Bass Inc., Publishers, 1980.

APPENDIX A

Philosophical Position Statement of the National Therapeutic Recreation Society[1]

Leisure, including recreation and play, is an inherent aspect of the human experience. The importance of appropriate leisure involvement has been documented throughout history. More recently, research has addressed the value of leisure involvement in human development, in social and family relationships, and, in general, as an important aspect of the quality of life. Some human beings have disabilities, illnesses or social conditions which limit their full participation in the normative social structure of society. These individuals with limitations have the same human rights to, and needs for, leisure involvement.

The purpose of therapeutic recreation is to facilitate the development, maintenance, and expression of an appropriate leisure lifestyle for individuals with physical, mental, emotional or social limitations. Accordingly, this purpose is accomplished through the provision of professional programs and services which assist the client in eliminating barriers to leisure, developing leisure skills and attitudes, and optimizing leisure involvement. Therapeutic recreation professionals use these principles to enhance clients' leisure ability in recognition of the importance and value of leisure in the human experience.

Three specific areas of professional services are employed to provide this comprehensive leisure ability approach toward enabling appropriate leisure lifestyles: *therapy, leisure education,* and *recreation participation.* While these three areas of service have unique purposes in relation to client need, they each employ similar delivery processes, using assessment or identification of client need, development of a related program strategy, and monitoring and evaluating client outcomes. The decision as to where and when each of the three service areas would be provided is based on the assessment of client needs and the service mandate of the sponsoring agency. The selection of appropriate service areas is contingent on a recognition that different clients have differing needs related to leisure involvement in view of their personal life situation.

[1]Approved by the Board of Directors of the National Therapeutic Recreation Society (a branch of the National Recreation and Parks Association), May 1982.

The purpose of the *therapy* service area within therapeutic recreation is to improve functional behaviors. Some clients may require treatment or remediation of a functional behavior as a necessary prerequisite to enable their involvement in meaningful leisure experiences. *Therapy*, therefore, is viewed as most appropriate when clients have functional limitations that relate to, or inhibit, their potential leisure involvement. This distinction enables the therapeutic recreator to decide when *therapy* service is appropriate, as well as to identify the types of behaviors that are most appropriate to address within the therapeutic recreation domain of expertise and authority. In settings where a comprehensive treatment approach is used, *therapy* focuses on team-identified treatment goals, as well as addressing unique aspects of leisure-related functional behaviors. This approach places therapeutic recreation as an integral and cooperative member of the comprehensive treatment team, while linking its primary focus to eventual leisure ability.

The purpose of the *leisure education* service area is to provide opportunities for the acquisition of skills, knowledge and attitudes related to leisure involvement. For some clients, acquiring leisure skills, knowledge and attitudes are priority needs. It appears that the majority of clients in residential, treatment and community settings need *leisure education* services in order to initiate and engage in leisure experiences. It is the absence of leisure learning opportunities and socialization into leisure that blocks or inhibits these individuals from participation in leisure experiences. Here, *leisure education* services would be employed to provide the client with leisure skills, enhance the client's attitudes concerning the value and importance of leisure, as well as learning about opportunities and resources for leisure involvement. Thus, *leisure education* programs provide the opportunity for the development of leisure behaviors and skills.

The purpose of the *recreation participation* area of therapeutic recreation services is to provide opportunities which allow voluntary client involvement in recreation interests and activities. Human beings, despite disability, illness or other limiting conditions, and regardless of place of residence, are entitled to recreation opportunities. The justification for specialized *recreation participation* programs is based on the clients' need for assistance and/or adapted recreation equipment, limitations imposed by restrictive treatment or residential environments, or the absence of appropriate community recreation opportunities. In therapeutic recreation services, the need for *recreation participation* is acknowledged and given appropriate emphasis in recognition of the intent of the leisure ability concept.

These three service areas of therapeutic recreation represent a continuum of care, including *therapy, leisure education,* and the provision of special *recreation participation* opportunities. This comprehensive leisure ability approach uses the need of the client to give direction to program service selection. In some situations, the client may need programs from all three service areas. In other situations, the client may require only one or two of the service areas.

Equally important is the concern of generalizing therapeutic recreation services across diverse service delivery settings. The leisure ability approach of therapeutic recreation provides appropriate program direction regardless of type of setting or type of client served. A professional working in a treatment setting can see the extension of the leisure ability approach toward client needs within the community environment. Likewise, those within the community can view therapeutic recreation services within a perspective of previous services received or possible future needs.

All human beings, including those individuals with disabilities, illnesses or limiting conditions, have a right to, and a need for, leisure involvement as a necessary aspect of the human experience. The purpose of therapeutic recreation services is to facilitate the development, maintenance, and expression of an appropriate leisure lifestyle for individuals with limitations through the provision of *therapy, leisure education,* and *recreation participation* services. The National Therapeutic Recreation Society is the acknowledged professional organization representing the field of therapeutic recreation. The National Therapeutic Recreation Society exists to foster the development and advancement of this field in order to ensure quality professional services and to protect the rights of consumers of therapeutic recreation services. In order to provide consistent and identifiable services throughout the field, the National Therapeutic Recreation Society endorses the leisure ability philosophy described herein as the official position statement regarding therapeutic recreation.

APPENDIX B

National Therapeutic Recreation Society Standards of Practice for Therapeutic Recreation Service[1]

STANDARD I. SCOPE OF SERVICE

Comprehensive therapeutic recreation program services are available to all clients in the agency/facility.

CRITERIA

A. Treatment services are available which are goal oriented and directed toward (re)habilitation, amelioration and/or modification of specific physical, emotional, mental, and/or social behaviors.

 1. When interdisciplinary teams are utilized, the therapeutic recreation staff functions as part of that team.

 2. The therapeutic recreation staff determines appropriate goals relative to therapeutic recreation and interventions to achieve the goals.

 3. There is a written plan for implementing the therapeutic recreation goals.

 4. There is periodic evaluation of the therapeutic recreation treatment program plan in accordance with standards of regulatory agencies.

 5. The treatment goals and plan are modified according to the results of the evaluation and needs of the client.

B. Leisure education services are available.

 1. Program Development and Implementation
   a. There is an established method for assessing leisure function.
   b. When appropriate, leisure counseling is available for clients and/or families.
   c. There is an established method for referral and follow-up when needed to assist clients make successful adjustment in the use of community leisure resources.

[1]Approved by the Board of Directors of the National Therapeutic Recreation Society (a branch of the National Recreation and Parks Association), October 1980.

2. Program Content
   a. Opportunities are provided to explore and develop new activity skills that have carry-over value at home and in the community.
   b. Identification and instruction are provided in the use of appropriate leisure resources available in the client's community.
   c. Opportunities are provided for exploration of leisure concepts, attitudes, and values.

C. There are general recreation services which provide a wide range of activities designed to meet the needs, competencies, capabilities and interests of clients during leisure time.
   1. Orientation
      a. Clients are assisted in orienting themselves to the physical surroundings and are helped to achieve maximum mobility and independence.
      b. Clients receive orientation to the available leisure programs, facilities, and resources with initial entrance into the program.
   2. Program Development and Implementation
      a. Participant committees, when appropriate, are used in planning and implementing the general recreation program.
      b. There is an established method for assessing the needs, interests, competencies, and capabilities of all clients.
      c. Activities take into consideration the cultural, economic, social and educational backgrounds of clients.
      d. The therapeutic recreation program is carefully and consistently integrated with other programs to achieve maximum use of agency/facility resources.
      e. Provision is made for each client to participate at his/her optimal level of functioning and to progress at his/her own speed.
      f. Provision is made for clients to use their own initiative in selecting and participating in recreational activities.
      g. Provision is made for clients to assume leadership responsibilities.
      h. Activities are modified and special aids or adaptive equipment are utilized to assure success experiences and sequential development for each client.
      i. Provision is made for bedside/home-bound activities when and where appropriate.
   3. Program Content
      a. Opportunities are provided for clients to participate in activities which utilize physical behaviors (sensory-motor domain), mental behaviors (cognitive domain), and emotional behaviors (affective domain).
      b. In day and residential facilities, opportunities are provided for clients to participate in daily periods of activity.
      c. Opportunities are provided for individual, small, and large group participation.
      d. The program provides both regularly scheduled activities and special events.
      e. The program provides for the utilization of a wide variety of public and private community resources and services.
      f. The program provides for various levels of integration of the client population with the general population.

STANDARD II. OBJECTIVES

Specific objectives are stated for each type of therapeutic recreation service based upon the philosophy and goals of the therapeutic recreation unit/agency/department and translated into operational terms.

CRITERIA

A. The statement of objectives is in writing.

B. The statement is prepared by the therapeutic recreation staff in consultation with appropriate professional staff of the agency/facility (e.g., medical, educational, recreational, and/or designated representative of the administration).

C. The statement is used as a program planning and evaluation tool.

STANDARD III. INDIVIDUAL TREATMENT/PROGRAM PLAN

The therapeutic recreation staff develops an individualized treatment/program plan for each client referred to the unit/agency/department.

CRITERIA

A. The plan is based on complete and relevant diagnostic/assessment data.
   1. The plan reflects the client's physical, social, mental, and emotional aptitudes and skills and current level of leisure functioning.
   2. The plan indicates precautions, restrictions, or limitations related to an individual's participation as determined by the diagnosis/assessment.

B. The plan is stated in behavioral terms that permit the progress of the individual to be assessed.

C. The plan is periodically reviewed, evaluated and modified as necessary to meet the changing needs of the client.

D. The plan differentiates among short-term, long-term, and discharge/transition goals.

E. The plan is documented in the personal record of the client.

F. The plan reflects an integrated approach.
   1. The plan is consistent with interdisciplinary treatment goals for the client.
   2. When feasible, the client and/or his/her family assist in developing and implementing the therapeutic recreation treatment plan.
   3. The plan reflects the client's goals and expectation of benefits to be derived from the therapeutic recreation program.

STANDARD IV. DOCUMENTATION

Therapeutic recreation personnel record specific information on assigned clients for the client/participant's record on a regular basis in accordance with the policies and procedures of the agency.

CRITERIA

A. The individualized therapeutic recreation treatment/program plan is recorded in the client/participant's record. It should include:

1. The referral document or reason for referral.
2. Assessment data.
3. Identification of client's problem and needs.
4. Treatment objectives.
5. Methods and plans for implementation of the therapeutic recreation program.
6. Methods and plans for evaluation of the objectives.

B. Progress of the individual and his/her reactions to the therapeutic recreation program are systematically recorded in the client/participant's record and reported to all appropriate parties (e.g., interdisciplinary team, parents, etc.)

1. Subjective interpretation of client progress is supported with concise behavioral observations.
2. Documentation of progress is directly related to the treatment goals.

C. A discharge/transition plan is included in the personal record and should include:

1. A summary of the treatment/program implemented and the client's progress.
2. An assessment of the client's current level of leisure function.
3. Recommendations for post-discharge/transition planning.
4. Information regarding appropriate community recreation resources and referral information as indicated.

D. Client records are reviewed regularly by therapeutic recreation staff in accordance with standards of regulatory agencies and documentation of such review is entered in the personal record.

STANDARD V. SCHEDULING OF SERVICES

Specific times are allocated for therapeutic recreation programs.

CRITERIA

A. The master schedule is established in cooperation with other programs and services provided for the client.

B. Each client receives a schedule of the comprehensive therapeutic recreation program or has easy access to posted schedules and schedule changes.

STANDARD VI. ETHICAL PRACTICES

Therapeutic recreation service delivery is designed to respect the personal rights of the individual clients and their families.

CRITERIA

A. It conforms with the local, state and federal guidelines such as the "Patients Bill of Rights" and Mental Health/Mental Retardation Act.

B. It conforms with the National Recreation and Park Association/National Therapeutic Recreation Society Code of Ethics.

Relaxation: A Program System

Carolyn Lemsky, TRS[1]

INTRODUCTION

The following pages contain a complete systems-designed program, utilizing the technology and methods presented in chapters 3–6. Frequent reference is made in those chapters to this appendix for illustration and application of the information. In addition, this appendix provides the only example of a complete program system, including all parts in appropriate format and sequence.

---

[1]Materials used with the permission of the designer, Carolyn Lemsky.

PROGRAM: Relaxation

Purpose: To present basic concepts related to stress and relaxation, and to teach relaxation techniques for self-control of tension.

Program Objectives

TPO 1. To demonstrate knowledge of the concept of relaxation
    EO 1. To demonstrate knowledge of the potential benefits of using relaxation techniques
    EO 2. To demonstrate an awareness of stress and its sources
    EO 3. To demonstrate the ability to identify physical manifestations of stress

TPO 2. To demonstrate the ability to perform relaxation techniques
    EO 1. To demonstrate relaxed diaphragmatic breathing
    EO 2. To demonstrate basic physical warm-ups and relaxation activities
    EO 3. To demonstrate progressive relaxation
    EO 4. To demonstrate the centering technique

IMPLEMENTATION DESCRIPTION

Population

This program is designed for a group of 5 to 10 individuals with emotional or psychiatric problems. It can be used with adolescents or adults. It is desirable to group participants by similar ages, so that discussions can be more relevant. Clients must have receptive and expressive language and be able to make verbal contributions to the group that are authentic and relevant in nature. Each participant must be able to concentrate for 20 minutes at a time on a task that is mainly cognitive. Individuals with physical limitations can be incorporated into the program with minor modifications based on their individual needs.

Program Length and Duration

This program is designed with 8 sessions, each lasting 50 minutes. The sessions are optimally scheduled twice a week for a period of 4 weeks. A period of less than 4 weeks does not allow adequate time for learning and practicing the techniques. A period lasting longer than 4 weeks may not provide enough contact with the group to motivate them or enable appropriate practice between sessions.

The program does require work outside the scheduled session times.

Program Context

This program can be implemented in any agency serving the described population. Thus, the program could be used with inpatient, outpatient, or partial-hospitalization clients. It could be utilized within clinical or community-based settings.

Staff

One professional staff member is needed for every 5 clients. The staff member must have a knowledge of and ability to teach relaxation techniques, the ability to lead group discussions, knowledge of the psychiatric and emotional conditions of the participating clients, and the ability to utilize intervention and behavioral-management techniques.

Facility

A quiet room, free of distractions, where lights may be dimmed is essential to conduct this program. This room should have enough floor space for participants to lie down.

Equipment

A mat or blanket for each participant
Tapes or records of semiclassical music (suggestions for appropriate selections are found in the reference section)
Record player or tape recorder
Paper and pencils
Handouts (described in text of system materials and presented in the appendix)

ADDITIONAL IMPLEMENTATION INFORMATION

Session Content and Sequence

Information on the sequence of content to be presented is found on the *Sequence Sheet* within the text of the materials. The *Sequence Sheet* provides direction for the sequence within each session as well as the sequence of the total program.

Program Content and Process

The objectives, and the exact content and process related to each objective, are described in the *Content and Process Sheets* found within the text of the materials.

A Note on the Discussions

Much of the learning in this program is based on discussion. A leader must, therefore, be capable of guiding discussions according to the needs and experiences of the group members. Stimulating discussion may require that the leaders contribute information and personal experiences; however, they should not dominate the session. Instead, they should build as much as possible on the responses of clients.

Evaluation of the Performance Measures

Evaluation of client performance should be conducted on an ongoing basis. Participants will be meeting most of the criteria stated in the performance measures during discussions. It is therefore necessary that leaders record progress made during or directly after conducting a session. Notes made during the session should be taken in as unobtrusive a way as possible. Before each session, it is advisable for leaders to review the performance measures relevant to the content being covered.

A Note on the Use of Music

Tapes of semiclassical music and dimming the lights during warm-ups and relaxation exercises is advised. Participants should optimally be provided with information on, or assistance in, obtaining music for home practice.

A Note on Instructions

Instructions on the Content and Process Sheets are presented in a narrative style. This is to facilitate an understanding of how the material may be presented. Leaders are to note this style, but should not memorize or read the instructions while conducting group sessions. Instead, an attempt should be made to reproduce the relaxed, conversational tone when giving instructions to the group.

ORDER OF THE MATERIALS WITHIN THIS PROGRAM SYSTEM PACKAGE

Terminal Program Objectives Sheets

These sheets contain the Terminal Program Objectives (TPOs), the Enabling Objectives (EOs), and Performance Measures (PMs) that accompany each Enabling Objective.

Content and Process Sheets

These pages specify the exact content and process that will be presented within the program to address each Enabling Objective.

The Sequence Sheet

This is a session-by-session breakdown of content sequencing, with time estimates for material and activities within each session.

The Performance Sheet

This is a form that enables the monitoring of the accomplishment of objectives for each participant.

References

Appendices

Objectives and Performance Measures

PROGRAM: Relaxation

TERMINAL PROGRAM OBJECTIVE: 1. To demonstrate knowledge of the concept of relaxation

ENABLING OBJECTIVE	PERFORMANCE MEASURE

1. To demonstrate knowledge of the potential benefits of using relaxation techniques.	1. Upon request, the client will demonstrate knowledge of the potential benefits of using relaxation techniques by stating (either verbally or in writing) one of the following concepts related to the benefits of relaxation:
	
	  a. increase in a sense of control over behavior when tense,
	  b. decrease in physical tension, or alleviation of some symptom related to physical tension,
	  c. decrease in feelings of anxiety or some symptom of anxiety,
	
	as judged appropriate by the therapeutic recreation specialist.

2. To demonstrate an awareness of stress and its sources.	2. Upon request, the client will demonstrate an awareness of stress and its sources by stating one personal source and one symptom of stress that he or she has experienced, as judged appropriate by the therapeutic recreation specialist.

3. To demonstrate the ability to identify physical manifestations of stress.	3. Upon request, the client will demonstrate the ability to identify physical manifestations of stress by:
	
	  a. locating a symptom of tension using another client or leader as a model, and
	  b. verbally identifying muscle tension in his or her own body,
	
	as judged appropriate by the therapeutic recreation specialist.

Objectives and Performance Measures

PROGRAM: Relaxation

TERMINAL PROGRAM OBJECTIVE: 2. To demonstrate the ability to perform relaxation techniques.

ENABLING OBJECTIVE	PERFORMANCE MEASURE
1. To demonstrate relaxed diaphragmatic breathing.	1. Upon request, the client will demonstrate the ability to perform diaphragmatic breathing as characterized by: a. the abdomen (not the chest) rising with each breath, b. breathing at a relaxed and natural pace (approximately 12–15 cycles/minute) for two minutes, as judged appropriate by the therapeutic recreation specialist.
2. To demonstrate basic physical warm-ups and relaxation activities.	2. When given the names of 2 of the 9 regularly used physical warm-up and relaxation activities introduced in the program and upon request, the client will demonstrate the identified activities as characterized by the following: a. proper body positioning and movements as described on the C & P sheets, and b. proper breathing for 5 repetitions of the activity or 1 minute (depending on the activity), as judged appropriate by the therapeutic recreation specialist.

3. To demonstrate progressive relaxation.

3. Upon request, the client will demonstrate the progressive relaxation technique as characterized by:

   a. tensing and relaxing muscles as described in the progressive relaxation process,

   b. achieving an average score of 3 for at least 2 out of 3 sessions of progressive relaxation as recorded on Form I, Relaxation Data Sheet,

  as judged appropriate by the therapeutic recreation specialist.

4. To demonstrate the centering technique.

4. Upon request, the client will demonstrate the centering technique as characterized by:

   a. maintaining proper body position

   b. appropriate breathing

  throughout one complete presentation of the techique, as judged appropriate by the therapeutic recreation specialist.

Content and Process Description

TPO No.: __1__ EQUIPMENT: _____

EO No.: __1__ To demonstrate knowledge of the potential benefits of using relaxation techniques

CONTENT	PROCESS
1. The importance of practice	Review the content at the left for participants as an introduction to practice discussions.
a. In order for the techniques we will learn during our group sessions to be effective, they must be practiced. The relaxation response must become natural for it to work for you in times of stress.	It is important that these attitudes be reinforced throughout the course. Suggestions for doing so are found in the rationale and in the introductions of many of the activities.
b. Keep track of your independent practice using some kind of record sheet or diary.	
c. To start with, practice before you go to sleep at night or at a time when activity in the area where you will be relaxing is at a minimum.	
It is suggested that you do not try to practice after meals because this may interfere with and slow up the digestive process.	
2. Personal applications of relaxation techniques	Five minutes per session are set aside for discussion of practice as it is recorded by the participants.
	The leader gives a summary of the techniques learned in the group and asks participants to discuss their experiences with

them both inside and outside of class. The leader should also practice techniques outside of class and be prepared to give personal input to stimulate discussions.

Suggestions for discussion are offered within the instructional process.

The leader should think of the discussion questions provided as guidelines. The most appropriate way to present the material for discussion is dependent on the leader and participants. Sections labeled *Discuss* are intended only as a point of departure for leaders.

It is therefore advisable that the leader prepare for each session by reviewing the content and thinking about discussion questions and other methods of presentation which she/he feels would be appropriate for the group.

Review the content at the left for participants as an introduction to relaxation techniques.

It is important that this content be reinforced throughout the course. Suggestions for this are found with the instructional processes. The leader should also remember to include this content where appropriate in practice discussions.

3. Applications of individual techniques

4. Potential benefits of relaxation

   a. Increased sense of control over behavior when tense
   b. Decrease in physical tension, or alleviation of some symptom related to physical tension
   c. Decrease in feelings of anxiety or some related symptom.

Content and Process Description

TPO No.: 1

EO No.: 2   To demonstrate an awareness of stress and its sources

EQUIPMENT: Blackboard & chalk or poster and marker

CONTENT	PROCESS
1. Stress defined	Present the content at the left very briefly.
Any aspect of the environment which requires the individual to make an adaptive change in behavior may be considered stress.	The leader should invite questions from the group, and adapt the presentation to the participants.
Animals faced with an attacking predator must either run away or fight. The fear of death or injury experienced by the animal motivates this survival-oriented reaction.	
Predators, because they must eat, feel some stress which motivates them to hunt. That stress may be identified as hunger. Stress motivates adaptive reactions.	
Stress is not always negative. Some stress is necessary to keep us active.	
Everyone has the ability to adapt to stress. However, when the amount of stress in the environment is too great, the individual may not react appropriately.	
2. Identifying stressful situations	The leader asks the group to list some common sources of stress on the blackboard or poster. Some examples of common sources of stress may be found at the left. As each source of stress is recorded, the group is asked to identify what appropriate adaptive behaviors are required.
a. Identifying sources of stress	
External stress	
Fear generated because of something in the environment—real physical danger.	Once the group has recorded 5 to 10 sources of stress, the leader gives a brief explanation of the content at the left regarding internal and external sources of stress. The group should be able
Internal stress	
Anxiety which is self-generated and has no apparent cause in the environment.	

Some common sources of stress people experience
  Death of a relative or friend
  Marital problems
  Social obligations
  Disagreements with family or friends
  Financial problems
  Employment difficulties
b. Identifying the behaviors associated with stressful situations
c. Identifying feelings associated with stressful situations
The source of stress depends partially on how a situation is experienced. External stress is determined by the extent to which the state of mind of the individual controls how the situation is experienced.
3. Physiological reactions related to stress
Fear and anxiety cause some physical responses, which are the body's way of getting ready to handle danger. These physiological events are called the fight or flight response.
This response occurs in three stages identified by Dr. Hans Selye.
a. Alarm: Danger is recognized in the environment, and a message is sent to a part of the brain called the hypothalamus, which is involved in producing feelings of fear and anger. The hypothalamus releases a hormone called adrenaline A which sets off the following reactions:
Lungs puff as in chest breathing, to increase the body's oxygen supply.
Skin becomes pale as blood moves to organs and muscles where it will be needed.
Perspiration begins to flush out wastes and cool body.

to differentiate between fear and anxiety at the end of the explanation. The leader then asks the group to go through the list of stressors which has been formulated and identify which are external stressors, which result in fear, and which are internal stressors, which are anxieties.

During the above process, the leader should not encourage participants to discuss at length their individual difficulties. If the conversation is kept general, the attention of the participants may be maintained and the length of the discussion kept brief. The leader may want to emphasize issues relevant to the entire group.

The information at the left is reviewed by the leader.
The following are some questions intended to help the leader summarize the content at the left:
"What is fear?"
"What is anxiety?"
"At a time when you remember feeling stressed, do you remember experiencing any of these physical reactions?"
"When would these physical reactions be helpful?" (Focus: when there is a physical danger which must be avoided.)
"When would these reactions be harmful?" (Focus: when there is no physical danger to be avoided, and these reactions contribute to the individual's feelings of stress.)
"How can chest breathing contribute to feelings of anxiety?" (Focus: by triggering the fight or flight response, or by the individual unconsciously associating feelings of anxiety with chest breathing.)

Content and Process Description

TPO No.: __1__

EO No.: __2__   To demonstrate an awareness of stress and its sources (*continued*)

EQUIPMENT: Blackboard & chalk or
<u>poster and marker</u>

CONTENT	PROCESS
All functions not necessary for fight or flight shut down, and blood leaves the digestive tract, causing the sensation of the stomach dropping. Bowels and bladder relax. b. Resistance: The individual responds to the danger with some action. c. Exhaustion: Messages are sent to glands from the hypothalamus to stop the secretion of adrenaline A. The individual feels weary and out of breath. These reactions occur when we sense something which makes us afraid or anxious. These reactions occur unconsciously, whether they are necessary or not. Some things we do unconsciously may cause a feeling of stress. Tense muscles and chest breathing, which are parts of the fight or flight response, may cause the individual to feel anxiety, which in turn may set off the fight or flight response. Going through the stages of the fight or flight response is very taxing, both physically and emotionally. Prolonged or frequent periods of stress may lead to heart disease, ulcers, and other physical illnesses. It may also lead the individual to feel helpless or cause him or her to feel unable to handle stress.	"What are some of the possible consequences of prolonged periods of stress?" (Focus: physical damage, as in the case of heart disease and ulcers; emotional damage, which may cause the individual to feel he or she is incapable of handling stress effectively.) Note: The leader should prepare for the presentation of this material by referring to sources as listed in the reference section. An understanding of this information on a more detailed level will facilitate the leader's ability to answer questions and lead discussions effectively. Recommended reading: Tanner, *Stress*, pp. 15–29; Benson, *Relaxation Response*, pp. 39–53 (see Suggested References).

Content and Process Description

TPO No.: ___1___

EO No.: ___3___   To demonstrate the ability to identify physical manifestations of stress

EQUIPMENT: Copies of Form II CTASS Appendix C–1 or blackboard/poster, pencils, large box or suitcase with heavy removable objects inside

CONTENT	PROCESS
1. Identification of physical manifestations of stress. (See Appendix C–1 for CTASS forms.)	Before clients arrive, leader places box at center of room.
	Have the participants sit in a formation conducive to informal communication (e.g., a circle with participants seated cross-legged).
	The leader should use the following as an example of how this session might run. The leader should be prepared to communicate the content to participants on the basis of the group's responses and questions.
	Discuss: Ask, "What do you think relaxation is?" (Focus: to get participants to express their ideas about what relaxation is)
	Ask, "What do you do to relax?" (Focus: some activities feel relaxing, rest is relaxing, etc. The intent of asking this question is to get participants to recognize that there are things we do specifically to relax.)
	Ask, "Has there ever been a time when you wanted to relax but couldn't? A time when you felt nervous or tense?" The leader might want to give examples to get the group going (e.g., going to the dentist, taking an exam).

Content and Process Description

TPO No.: __1__

EO No.: __3__   To demonstrate the ability to identify physical manifestations of stress
(continued)

EQUIPMENT: Copies of Form II CTASS
Appendix C–1 or
blackboard/poster,
pencils, large box or
suitcase with heavy
removable objects inside

CONTENT

PROCESS

Pick a situation which most of the participants indicate is familiar. Ask, "How did you feel?" What physical sensations can you remember?" (Focus: any physical manifestations of stress; e.g., , "butterflies in the stomach," feeling "tight," etc.)

The leader may want to begin with an example; e.g., the leader sits facing the group and says, "I am going to show you what I look like waiting in a dentist's office." The leader then tenses legs, arms, and perhaps taps foot or bites nails.

Ask, "How do you think I was feeling?" (Focus: nervous, anxious, stressed)

Ask, "How could you tell I was feeling that way?" (Physical manifestations of stress)

The leader gives a few more examples of how stress is manifested. These should include the obvious (e.g., nail-biting, foot-tapping) as well as the subtle (e.g., muscle tension) stress behaviors. Group members should be given the opportunity to act out their contributions themselves. Questions from the group should be answered by group members when possible.

Pass out CTASS (Form II in Appendix C–1).

2. Physical tension is the result of an unconscious reaction to stress.

Explanation: The participant's muscles were ready for the heavier load. She/he didn't have to think about it. It just happened, as a result of his or her expectations.

Excess muscle tension, or other physical reactions, results from similar processes. These processes are set into motion by our expectations of the environment.

We can feel more relaxed by controlling physical tension. The relaxation techniques we will learn are to be used in controlling tension.

Introduce the form by telling participants that it is a list of the things we have been talking about. The participants may keep it as a summary of the session. The leader may want to have pencils available so that she/he can read through the form aloud, answering questions to help participants fill it out.

An alternative to using this form is listing stress behaviors participants come up with on a blackboard or poster. However, the CTASS handout has an advantage, since it can be kept by the participants.

Discuss: Ask, "We've been talking about some of the things we do when we're nervous. Can you think of any reasons why we do them?" (Focus: fright, anxiety, etc.)

The leader begins the next exercise by telling a participant to move the heavy box to the center of the room. The leader then gives a false reason for asking that participant to leave the room (e.g., getting something from another room). While the participant is gone, the leader removes the heavy object from the box and places it out of sight. The leader asks the other participants not to tell the one who has left what she/he has done, and to watch while the participant picks up the box again. Upon reentering the room, the participant is asked again to pick up the box.

Discuss: Ask, "Why do you think she/he reacted this way?" (Focus: because she/he expected the box to be heavier.)

Ask, "Do you think she/he would have reacted differently if we had told him or her that the box is now light?" (Focus: our expectations of a situation can determine how we react to it.)

The leader presents closure in the form of an explanation.

The leader asks if the participants have any questions or concerns regarding the material covered.

Content and Process Description

TPO No.: 2
EO No.: 1   To demonstrate relaxed diaphragmatic breathing

EQUIPMENT: Mats or blankets

CONTENT	PROCESS
1. Breathing from the diaphragm means taking deep breaths, which cause the abdomen (as opposed to the chest) to rise.	Ask participants to lie on the floor in a complete prone position. Have them place their right hand on their stomach over the navel.
Even though this is the most natural way to breathe (infants and most people breathe this way while they are sleeping), some of us get into the habit of chest breathing.	Ask participants if their hand is rising when they breathe in. Leaders should watch to see that participants are in the correct position and whether or not their hands are rising. Because participants may begin to alter their natural breathing patterns when trying to concentrate, remind them to breathe slowly and naturally. Counting aloud to the group, as in the following example, may aid participants in breathing naturally.
Getting deep, full breaths increases the flow of oxygen to vital organs and, in this way, aids in relaxation.	"Take a nice easy breath. Now, I–N–H–A–L–E and E–X–H–A–L–E." The words *inhale* and *exhale* should be stretched to sound for the duration of an average breathing cycle. The best way to time this is to stay with your own relaxed breathing pattern and watch those of participants. This is only necessary if participants are having trouble.
	Assure the participants that diaphragmatic breathing may not come naturally, and with practice it will become easier.
	Review the content while allowing participants to continue to practice for a few minutes.
2. Diaphragmatic breathing allows the body to function in an integrated way.	*Discuss:* Ask, "Do you feel relaxed after doing this kind of breathing? When do you breathe with quick shallow breaths (chest breathing)? How do you feel when you are breathing this way?" (Focus: chest breathing usually occurs with arousal of some kind and is not conducive to relaxation.)
Quick, shallow breathing causes a generalized feeling of stress or arousal, which may not be warranted by the activity or the environment being experienced.	

Content and Process Description

TPO No.: __2__

EO No.: __2__ To demonstrate basic physical warm-ups and relaxation activities

EQUIPMENT: Mats or blankets

CONTENT	PROCESS
1. The purpose of warming up	Have participants stand in a circle at arm's length from one another.
a. The warm-up serves as a transition into a session of relaxation activities.	Introduce the warm-ups by reviewing the purposes of warming up. Tell participants that the beginning of each session will be spent doing warm-ups and that you will be starting with some simple movements or stretches.
b. The warm-up functions as a physical preparation by— helping to prevent injuries by easing muscles into physical activity;	Explain that most of the warm-ups include breathing with the movements. Tell them it is important in getting full benefit from the warm-up to pay careful attention to the breathing instructions.
helping to identify points of physical tension and initiating the process of releasing it; encouraging body awareness.	
c. The warm-up aids in mental preparation for a session of relaxation by providing an activity which is relatively easy to concentrate on and is therefore useful in clearing the mind of daily stress.	
2. The processes of warm-up activities.	
Total Body Stretch—Warm-up Activity A	Introduce the total body stretch by asking the participants to stretch as if they had just awakened from a night's sleep. The leader may want to demonstrate if the group is slow in getting started.
a. Make your body as long as possible, stretching your hands over your head.	*Discuss:* Ask, "Why do you think we want to stretch in the morning?" (Focus: it helps to get blood back in to muscles that haven't been working all night. That is how we get started in the morning, so it is a logical place to begin with warming up.)
b. Stretch the right side, making it as long as possible, leaving the left side relaxed.	Take participants through steps verbally and with demonstrations.
c. Repeat above for left side, leaving right side relaxed.	
d. Make your body as wide as possible, stretching your arms out to the side, and standing in a straddle.	
(Repeat 2 or 3 times.)	

Content and Process Description

TPO No.: __2__

EO No.: __2__   To demonstrate basic physical warm-ups and relaxation activities (*continued*)

EQUIPMENT: __Mats or blankets__

CONTENT	PROCESS
Rotating Joints—Warm-up Activity B	Take participants through steps verbally and with demonstrations.
a. Move all of your fingers as if you were trying to get sticky crumbs off of them.	Keep the movements of participants gentle and easy. If participants are moving too fast, help them out with an image—for example, trying to imagine that they are underwater, weightless, or in a pool filled with jello.
b. Rotate your wrists as if you were stirring thick batter with a spoon in each hand.	
c. Rotate your elbows as if you were drawing large circles with your hands.	
d. Rotate your shoulders as if your arms were the blades of a windmill moving slowly.	
e. Rotate your neck by first trying to touch your right ear to your shoulder, then touching your chin to your chest—trying not to let your shoulders move.	
f. Rotate your neck in the other direction, starting with your left ear to your left shoulder.	
(Each step should be repeated 4–5 times.)	
Siren—Warm-up Activity C	Tell the participants that this activity is intended to help integrate breathing with body movement.
a. Begin by bending over as if to touch your toes, allowing your knees to bend.	Take participants through the steps verbally and with demonstrations.
b. Take a deep diaphragmatic breath. (It is nearly impossible to breathe from the chest in this position.)	
c. Start as soft and low pitched a tone that you can make, saying "Ah. . . ."	

348

d. As you straighten up slowly, gradually make the sound louder and higher in pitch until you are standing up straight with your hands over your head, and the tone is as high and loud as you can make it.

e. Gradually reverse the process so that you end up in the bent-over position.

f. Repeat the siren 4–5 times, getting smoother and faster until you can feel your voice and body working together.

Take participants through steps verbally and with demonstrations. Participants should be reminded to pay close attention to the breathing associated with the movements.

Seated Stretch—Warm-up Activity D*

a. Sit comfortably with both of your legs stretched out in front of you, your arms over your head, until your palms come together.

b. Look up at your hands, and as you begin to breathe out, bend slowly forward from the hips, keeping your legs flat. Stretch your arms out as far as they will go, and as you exhale all your air, reach forward and grasp your ankles or your feet, whichever you can reach.

c. Pull gently, stretching your spine as far as it can go.

d. Release your grip and come up slowly, breathing in deeply, bringing your hands back up over your head until the palms touch. (Repeat 2 or 3 times.)

Bridge—Warm-up Activity E†

a. Lie on your back and relax until you are as flat on the floor as you can be.

b. Draw your knees up until your feet are close to your buttocks. Relax arms at sides, palms down on floor.

Take participants through steps verbally and with demonstrations.

*From *The Centering Book* by Gay Hendricks and Russell Wills, p. 122. Copyright © 1975 by Prentice-Hall, Inc., Published by Prentice-Hall, Inc., Englewood Cliffs, N.J. 07632.
†Ibid., p. 123.

Content and Process Description

TPO No.: __2__

EO No.: __2__   To demonstrate basic physical warm-ups and relaxation activities *(continued)*

EQUIPMENT: <u>Mats or blankets</u>

CONTENT	PROCESS
c. As you inhale, raise your body gently off the floor by pressing down your feet. Keep your neck and shoulders relaxed as you arch your back into a bridge. d. Exhale and lower yourself to the original position. Relax and let your body sink deeply into the floor. (Repeat 3 or 4 times.) *Shoulder Stand*—Warm-up Activity F* a. Sit on the floor with your legs drawn up to your buttocks and your hands next to your buttocks. b. Roll back, bringing your knees over your forehead and sliding your hands under your lower back to support you. Relax in this position, making sure that your back and neck are relaxed. c. Begin to raise your legs gently until they are straight above you. Do not strain, but find a position that is straight but not uncomfortable. d. Relax in this position and breathe deeply, letting all of the unnecessary tension leave your body. e. When you're ready to come down, lower your knees slowly to your forehead, then roll your back down to the floor slowly and gently. When you are all the way down	Take the participants through steps verbally and with demonstrations. It may be necessary to demonstrate the complete process before asking participants to perform the shoulder stand. Have the participants hold this position for 10 seconds at first. This may be increased to a minute in later sessions.

350

to the floor, relax your body completely, feeling yourself totally supported by the floor.

Cobra—Warm-up Activity G†

a. Lie on your stomach, stretching your feet out behind you and placing your palms down next to your armpits.

b. Rest your forehead gently on the floor.

c. Begin to breathe in smoothly, and as you do, begin raising your head, then your neck.

d. As you breathe in more, continue to raise your neck and your spine, without lifting your hips and pelvis, until your chest is off the floor as far as it will go comfortably.

e. When you get to the top, relax in that position, then exhale slowly and roll yourself back down until your forehead again touches the floor.

f. Relax your shoulders, your neck, and your back . . . letting yourself sink into the floor.

(Repeat 2 or 3 times.)

Corpse—Warm-up Activity H‡

a. Lie on your back on the floor, and let your body sink down until it is completely supported by the floor.

b. Close your eyes and sink back in total relaxation, letting your mind and your body recharge with pure, fresh energy.

Take participants through steps verbally and with demonstrations. The Cobra should always be done after the shoulder stand, to stretch the spine in the opposite direction. This should be pointed out to participants.

Tell participants that the Corpse is used between and after exercises like the foregoing.

Discuss: Ask, "Can you tell me why the Corpse might be useful in between exercises?" (Focus: to get ready for the deep relaxation necessary to do the warm-ups described previously.)

Ask, "When else might we want to use the Corpse?" (Focus: any time we want to relax fully and have an appropriate place to lie down.)

*From *The Centering Book* by Gay Hendricks and Russell Wills, p. 125. Copyright © 1975 by Prentice-Hall, Inc. Published by Prentice-Hall, Inc., Englewood Cliffs, NJ 07632.
†Ibid., p. 126.
‡Ibid., p. 128.

Content and Process Description

TPO No.: __2__

EO No.: __2__   To demonstrate basic physical warm-ups and relaxation activities (*continued*)

EQUIPMENT: Mats or blankets

CONTENT	PROCESS
Salute to the Sun—Warm-up Activity I*	Demonstrate the complete process of Salute to the Sun, doing the correct breathing and not speaking. One leader may demonstrate while the other points out the inhale-exhale breathing pattern which goes with the movements. Explain that the breathing is as important as the movements. The hardest thing about the exercise is coordinating the breathing and the movements, and eventually this will become natural, but it will take practice.
a. Stand up comfortably straight. You should feel light and relaxed. Take a few deep breaths, feeling lighter and more relaxed with each one.	
b. Inhale, bending back gently with your arms over your head and your back slightly arched.	Have one leader demonstrate while the other gives the directions and points out the breathing process.
c. As you exhale, bend over forward as if to touch your toes. Do this gently; don't strain.	Have the participants practice a few times at their own speed. Tell them to let their natural breathing determine the speed of the movements.
d. Place your palms on the floor, letting your knees bend, and as you do, begin to inhale.	If any of the participants feel light-headed, tell them to watch until they feel better, and then try the salute again, paying careful attention to their natural pace of breathing.
e. As you complete this inhalation, stretch your right foot out behind you, letting your left knee bend.	
f. As you exhale, shift your weight to your palms, and bring your left foot behind you. This should leave you in a "push up" position.	

352

g. As you begin to inhale, let your knees and legs drop gently to the floor. You are now in the position which begins the Cobra.

h. Sway your buttocks back toward your heels, and continuing to inhale, run your chin, then chest, then stomach against the floor and end in the arched position of the cobra.

i. Curl your toes under, getting ready to bear weight. As you exhale, swing your buttocks up until you are in a V position.

j. As you inhale, bring your right knee toward your hands.

k. As you exhale, bring your left knee in until you are in a squat with your palms on the floor.

l. As you inhale, straighten your knees until you are in a bent-over position with your knees straight and your arms hanging down.

m. Continue to inhale, straightening your back vertebra by vertebra, slowly and smoothly, ending with your arms over your head and your back slightly arched.

n. As you exhale, bring your hands back to your sides and end in the comfortable position that you started in.

Discuss: Ask, "How did that feel? Did you have trouble getting your breathing and the movements to work together? Was this exercise relaxing?" (Focus: this is a Yoga exercise used first thing in the morning. It aids in stretching out the body, and is good for gaining energy upon waking or before doing an unpleasant task. The effect of getting body and breathing together is somewhat like centering. After doing this exercise, many people feel energized and relaxed. This may take practice.)

Ask, "When do you think we could use Salute to the Sun?" (Focus: any time we feel the need to become more in touch with our bodies and breathing—for example, before a session in relaxation, or any time we feel nervous and there is the time and a quiet, appropriate place to do it.)

*Adapted from *The Complete Yoga Book*, and used by permission of Schocken Books Inc. Copyright 1977 by James Hewitt, pp. 259–263.

Content and Process Description

TPO No.: __2__

EO No.: __3__ To demonstrate progressive relaxation

EQUIPMENT: Mats or blankets, copies of Form I, Data Relaxation Sheet, Appendix C–2

CONTENT	PROCESS

1. Rationale for progressive relaxation*
 Introduction
 a. The procedures are called progressive relaxation training.
 b. Progressive relaxation training consists of learning to tense and release various muscle groups throughout the body.
 c. An essential part of learning how to relax involves learning to pay close attention to the feelings of tension and relaxation in your body.
 d. Learning relaxation skills is like learning other motor skills.
 e. We employ tension in order to ultimately produce relaxation.
   1. Strong tension is noticeable, and you will learn to attend to these feelings.
   2. The initial production of tension gives us some "momentum," so that as we release the tension; deep relaxation is the result.
	Present the rationale to the group.
	 Ask if anyone has any questions.
	 Note: In order to prepare for the session, leaders should read through Appendix C–2. Leaders should take themselves through progressive relaxation if they have not had this experience.
	 The leader may want to use additional images in the progressive relaxation process. For example, participants can be asked to imagine they are squeezing a ball or an orange.
	 If clients claim that, even after a relaxation session, they still feel tense, it is helpful to have them imagine relaxing scenes such as lying on a beach in the warm sun.

2. See Appendix C–2 for Form I. As the participants go through the relaxation process, they will be scored using Form I. The self-report section is to be filled in after the progressive relaxation process is completed. This section is intended to measure the overall sensation the client is having after participating in progressive relaxation.	Present Form I to clients. Review the purpose of the form and the scoring process. If the participants have difficulty understanding the form, the leader may use demonstrations. For example, the leader may tense a muscle group, and not relax it, then have the participants score the performance.

354

Honesty in completing this portion of the form should be stressed. Progressive relaxation may not produce complete relaxation during the first few sessions. For some people, the process does not work at all. Form I is only intended to provide a record of what has happened during the progressive relaxation sessions.

3. Progressive Relaxation Process†

"This is an activity that can help us learn to relax our bodies and minds by tensing and releasing muscles. We cannot be tense and relaxed at the same time, so if we learn to relax, we avoid wasting energy through muscle tension. If you ever feel tense, while asking a question or taking a test or any time, you can use the feeling of relaxation to feel better."

"Let's begin by lying on your backs on the floor and not touching anyone else. Wiggle around a little until you find a way of lying down that is completely comfortable. Now close your eyes and think of your hands. Feel the bones inside them, feel the muscles that move the bones, feel the weight of them on the floor. Now make a fist with your hands and clench tightly. Hold your hands tightly (10 seconds). Now relax and feel the soothing, tingling feeling of relaxation come into your hands." (Pause 10 seconds or so between instructions.)

"Now draw up your arms and tighten your biceps—making muscles like a strongman. Hold them tightly (10 seconds). Now relax and feel the tension drain out of your arms." (Pause)

*From Bernstein and Borkovec, Progressive Relaxation Training, p. 162.
†From The Centering Book by Gay Hendricks and Russell Wills; pp. 41–45. Copyright © 1975 by Prentice-Hall, Inc. Published by Prentice-Hall, Inc., Englewood Cliffs, NJ 07632.

Content and Process Description

TPO No.: __2__

EO No.: __3__ To demonstrate progressive relaxation (*continued*)

PROCESS

CONTENT

"Shrug your shoulders now, pushing them as if to push them through your ears. Hold them tightly there (10 seconds). Now let them go and feel all the tension drain out of your body." (Pause)

"Continuing to keep your eyes closed, open your mouth as far as it will go, stretching the muscles at the corners of your mouth. Hold it tightly (10 seconds). Relax and enjoy the tingling feeling as the tension dissolves in your mouth." (Pause)

"Now press your tongue against the roof of your mouth and tighten your jaw muscles. Press tightly and hold it (10 seconds). Now let go and relax. Let the peaceful feeling of relaxation flow through your body." (Pause)

"Now tighten the muscles of your chest, stomach, and abdomen. Draw all of the muscles in tightly and hold them tense (10 seconds). Now let them go, feeling the soothing feeling of relaxation pour in." (Pause)

"Now tense the backs of your legs by straightening your feet. Hold your legs tensely (10 seconds). Now relax them and let all of the tension go." (Pause)

"Now tense your feet by curling the toes. Keep them curled tightly (10 seconds). Now relax your toes and feel the delicious feeling of relaxation come into your feet." (Pause)

"Your whole body is feeling loose and relaxed now. Feel yourself completely supported by the floor, and breathe deeply, and as you breathe in, let each breath fill your body with deeper and deeper feelings of relaxation." (Pause)

"Let the soothing feeling of relaxation fill your body. Each breath takes you deeper and deeper into relaxation." (Pause 30 seconds to 1 minute.)

"Now you will be coming out of relaxation in a moment, and you will feel rested and alert. I will count backward from ten to one, and as I do, feel your body becoming alert at your own rate."

"Ten, nine, eight, feel the alertness returning to your body. Seven, six, five, feel your toes and fingers begin to move. Four, three, move your arms and legs. Two, eyes. One, get up slowly, feeling completely rested and alert."

4. Instant Relaxation—Whole Body*

This relaxation exercise can be done sitting, standing, or lying down. It gives an individual a skill to counter tension in all kinds of situations.

"Let's close our eyes."

"Now tense every muscle in your body at the same time. Legs, arms, jaws, fists, face, shoulders, stomach. Hold them . . . tightly. Now relax and feel the tension pour out of your body. Let all of the tension flow out of your body and your mind . . . replacing the tension with calm, peaceful energy . . . letting each breath you take bring calmness and relaxation into your body." (Pause)

Instructions: leader provides narrative directions as written under Content.

*Ibid., pp. 46—47

Content and Process Description

TPO No.: __2__

EO No.: __3__   To demonstrate progressive relaxation (*continued*)

EQUIPMENT: Mats or blankets, copies of Form I, Data Relaxation Sheet, Appendix C–2

CONTENT	PROCESS
"Now tense your body again and hold it for a few seconds. Then let go, relaxing and feeling all of the tension flow out of your body." (Pause)	
"And now tense every muscle in your body and at the same time, take a deep breath for a few seconds. Then say 'Relax' to yourself, and when you do, let your breath go and relax." (Pause)	
"Take a deep breath and hold it about ten seconds. Then say 'Relax' to yourself and let yourself go." (Pause)	
"When you feel like relaxing, just take a deep breath, hold it a few seconds, say 'Relax' to yourself, and let it all go. You can do this wherever you are, because nobody can hear you or see you. Practice this again by yourself two or three times." (Pause)	
"Now let's open our eyes slowly, feeling calm and alert."	
5. Instant Relaxation—Specific Parts*	*Instructions:* leader provides narrative directions as written under Content.
"Now we are going to go through various parts of the body, telling each part to relax; as you tell each part to relax, you will be able to feel a soothing feeling of relaxation enter that part of your body. Now let your attention go to your feet." (Pause) "Tell your feet to relax."	*Discuss:* "This is another instant exercise. How well did it work for you? Do you think you could use this technique successfully now, or do you feel you need more practice?" (Focus: personal reactions to the exercise)
This process is repeated for selected parts of the body.	

*Ibid., pp. 48–51.

Content and Process Description

TPO No.: __2__

EO No.: __4__   To demonstrate the centering technique

EQUIPMENT: Mats or blankets

CONTENT	PROCESS
1. An introduction to centering. a. There is powerful energy in our bodies. This energy may be focused by concentration. We can learn to use this energy to our advantage through centering.	*An Experiment in Centering* Have participants find partners near to their own body build. (The leader may want to pair participants.) The leader introduces this activity by telling participants that just by thinking about it they can make themselves heavier or lighter. Tell one member of each pair to stand tall and light. Suggest to them to send all of their thoughts upward. Next have their partners take them around the waist and try to lift them. Caution participants to get a firm hold and lift slowly and gently. Now have those participants who were thinking light, think heavy. Tell them to imagine themselves nailed to the floor. Now have the participants' partners try to lift them again. It should be harder. The participants should feel heavier than before. The best way to insure this effect is to give strong images for light and heavy, and allowing plenty of time to let participants concentrate. Have participants reverse roles and try the exercise again. *Discuss:* "What do you think made your weight seem to change?" (Focus: our conscious will, energy, or body tension can be focused.) *Explain:* In the next session, we will learn something called centering. With centering, we focus our energy on our centers and that helps us to feel good about ourselves and gives us a sense of strength.

Content and Process Description

TPO No.: 2

EO No.: 4   To demonstrate the centering technique (continued)

EQUIPMENT: Mats or blankets

CONTENT	PROCESS
2. Centering is a way to gain a feeling of solidness by concentrating on the center of the body.	Present the concept of centering to the group.
3. Activities in centering.	Take participants through the centering exercises.
Feeling the Center—Centering Activity A*	Have participants lie on the floor.
Instructions:	Note: The beginning portion of this exercise combines centering with diaphragmatic breathing. It is therefore suggested that it be used in its entirety for the first session. A shortened version, which may be used in subsequent sessions, is indicated by the bracket.
"Most of the time we use only a small part of our lungs when we breathe. If we can learn to fill our bodies with breath by breathing more deeply and smoothly, we can increase the energy that flows through our bodies. Let's begin by letting our bodies relax . . . becoming very comfortable and closing our eyes."	
"And now, becoming aware of your feet and moving them around a little to become aware of how they feel, send them a message to relax. Let all of the tension go out of them and feel them rest comfortably on the floor."	
"Now relax your legs. Let go of them and let them sink into the floor, feeling relaxed and heavy."	
"Let the feeling of relaxation enter your chest and stomach. Feel the middle of your body become soothed and relaxed. Breathe deeply and smoothly, letting all of the tension go out of your body."	

"Now let your neck and face relax. Feel the tension draining out of your face as you feel the soothing feeling of relaxation enter your face and your neck."

"Relax your arms and your hands, feeling them resting comfortably, completely supported. Breathe deeply, sending the feeling of relaxation to your arms and hands." (Pause 30 seconds.)

"The center of your body is where it balances. For many people, the balance point is just below the navel. As you breathe in, imagine that your breath is pouring into your body through the center of your body. Let yourself feel the energy rushing into your body through the center, just below the navel. Feel your breath flow into your body, up through your chest, filling your head. Hold the breath inside you for a moment, then let it flow out, carrying with it any tension you feel. Breathe through your center, filling your body with energy, then let the breath flow out of you, relaxing your body completely." (Pause 10 breaths)

"Let yourself feel the center of your body, so that you can come back to it when you want to relax and feel balanced. Anytime you have something in your head that you don't like, breathe it out and then replace it with pure, clean energy when you breathe in."

"Now feel the alertness coming back into your body. Feel your feet and hands begin to stir. Feel your muscles begin to move. Open your eyes, feeling rested and full of energy."

This section comprises the essential images of centering. If used alone, a few moments of breathing before and after should be provided for participants to relax and breathe at their own pace.

*From *The Centering Book* by Gay Hendricks and Russell Wills, p. 123. Copyright © 1975 by Prentice-Hall, Inc. Published by Prentice-Hall, Inc., Englewood Cliffs, NJ 07632.

Content and Process Description

TPO No.: __2__

EO No.: __4__ To demonstrate the centering technique *(continued)*

EQUIPMENT: __Mats or blankets__

CONTENT	PROCESS
Quick Centering Breath—Centering Activity B* Instructions: "Focus all of your attention on your center. Send all of your thoughts and feelings down to that point below your navel." (Pause) "Now begin sending each breath all the way down to your center." (Pause) "Each time you breathe, send the breath to your center." (Pause) "Now that you know how to get in touch with your center, you can focus on that point when you feel nervous or angry, or whenever you want to feel better . . . it's always there when you need it." *Instant Centering*—Centering Activity C† Instructions: "Have the students put all their thoughts in an elevator up in their heads. Then have them punch the button and send the elevator down to their centers." "Have the students imagine an hourglass inside them, the top in their heads, the bottom in their centers. Have them let the sand slowly fill up the bottom." "Have the students imagine a light shining out from their centers, and have them vary the intensity of the light."	This activity may be done in any position. The leader should take the group through this activity verbally. Pauses should be about 10 seconds in duration. The leader should present these images to the group as tools to use when centering. *Discuss:* Ask, "Can you think of any other images which might help you in centering?" (Focus: the best images to use in centering are the ones which work best for the individual.) Participants may present their ideas to the group. The leader may ask the group to try and think of an image to present to the group at the next session.

*Ibid., pp. 24–25.
†Ibid., pp. 25–26.

			SESSION	TIME
		Sequence Sheet*		
TPO	EO	DESCRIPTION	NO.	(MIN)
		Introduction to course General overview of what the course will cover Format of sessions: Sessions will be 50 minutes long. There will be a warm-up, introduction or review of a technique, discussion of practice, a final relaxation activity before leaving. Participants may be asked to prepare for the next class by observing something to report to the class, doing a reading, home practice, etc.	1	10
2	2	A. Purpose of warming up; warming up activities A and B		10
2	4	B. An experiment in centering		10
1	4	C. Identification of physical manifestations of stress		15
1	2	D. Give assignment: Tell participants to look out for a situation when they feel tense for next session's discussion. Take a few minutes to listen quietly to music.		5
2	2	A. Warm-up activities A and B (review) Warm-up activities C, D, and E introduced.	2	10
2	1	B. Diaphragmatic breathing		10
1	2	C. Discussion of Parts 1 and 2: "Identifying sources of stress"		20
2	4	D. Concept of centering Centering activity A		10
2	4	Evaluation of Centering		
2	2	A. Warm-up activities A, C, and D (review) Warm-up activities E, F, and G	3	5 10
1	2	B. Discussion Part 3		20
2	1	C. Review diaphragmatic breathing		3
2	4	D. Quick Centering Breath		5
1	1	E. Discussion of practice Observe half of participants for evaluation of breathing and centering		7

			SESSION	TIME
TPO	EO	DESCRIPTION	NO.	(MIN)

Sequence Sheet* *(Continued)*

TPO	EO	DESCRIPTION	SESSION NO.	TIME (MIN)
2	1	A. Warm-up activities E, F, and G (review)	4	5
		Warm-up activity I introduced		10
2	3	B. Progressive Relaxation, parts 1 (rationale) and 2 (basic process)		20
1	1	C. Discussion of practice		10
2	4	D. Clients choose a centering activity		5
		Observe second half breathing and centering.		
2	2	A. Warm-up activities E, F, and I (review); repeat 15 times	5	15
2	3	B. Progressive Relaxation, part 2		20
1	1	C. Discussion of practice		10
2	4	D. Choose Centering Activity		5
		Evaluate Centering if necessary		
2	2	A. Warm-up activities E, F, G, and I repeat 15 times	6	20
2	3	B. Progressive Relaxation, part 3		20
		Instant Relaxation		
1	1	C. Discussion of practice		10
2	2	A. Warm-up activities E, F, G, and I repeat 15 times	7	20
2	3	B. Progressive Relaxation, part 3		15
		Instant Relaxation		
1	1	C. Discussion of practice		15
		Check evaluations for TPO 1		
2	2	A. Warm-up activities E, F, G, and I	8	15
2	4	B. Progressive Relaxation, part 4		15
		Talking to your body		
1	1	C. Discussion of practice		15
		D. Present closure		5

*Evaluation should take place on an ongoing basis. Performance Measures should be reviewed prior to each session, and clients' progress should be recorded during or directly after groups.

Performance Sheet

PROGRAM: _____   Relaxation

STAFF: _____
DATE: _____

ENABLING OBJECTIVES

NAMES	TPO 1, EO 1. Knowledge of benefits	EO 2. Stress and its sources	EO 3. physical manifestations	TPO 2, EO 1. Diaphragmatic breathing	EO 2. Knowledge of warm-ups	EO 3. Progressive relaxation	EO 4. Centering techniques										
1.																	
2.																	
3.																	
4.																	
5.																	
6.																	
7.																	
8.																	
9.																	
10.																	
11.																	
12.																	
13.																	
14.																	
15.																	

====================== **Suggested References** ======================

BENSON, HERBERT, *The Relaxation Response.* New York: William Morrow & Co., Inc., 1975.

BERNSTEIN, DOUGLAS A., and THOMAS D. BORKOVEC, *Progressive Relaxation Training.* Champaign, Ill.: Research Press, 1973.

HENDRICK, GAY, and RUSSELL WILLS, *The Centering Book.* Englewood Cliffs, N.J.: Prentice-Hall, Inc., 1975.

HEWITT, JAMES, *The Complete Yoga Book.* New York: Schocken Books, Inc., 1978.

STEIN, MARK L., *Good and Bad Feelings.* New York: Morrow Junior Books, 1976.

TANNER, OGDEN, *Stress.* Alexandria, Va.: Time-Life Books, 1978.

APPENDIX C-1

Form II: Cues for Tension and Anxiety Survey Schedule (CTASS)[1]

Individuals have different ways that indicate to them that they are tense or anxious. Check below the ways that apply to you. (This form is for you to keep. You don't have to share it with anyone if you don't want to.)

1. You feel tense in:
   a. your forehead (   )
   b. back of your neck (   )
   c. chest (   )
   d. shoulders (   )
   e. stomach (   )
   f. face (   )
   g. other parts _____

2. You sweat (   )

3. Your heart beats fast (   )

4. You can feel your heart pounding (   )

5. You can hear your heart pounding (   )

6. Your face feels flush or warm (   )

7. Your skin feels cool and damp (   )

[1]Reprinted with permission from J. R. Cautela and D. Upper, "The Behavior Inventory Battery: The Use of Self-report Measures in Behavioral Analysis in Therapy, in *Behavior Assessment: A Practical Handbook,* ed. M. Hersen and A. S. Bellak (Elmsford, N.Y.: Pergamon Press, 1976).

8. You tremble or shake in your:
   a. hands ( )
   b. legs ( )
   c. other _____

9. Your stomach feels like you are just stopping in an elevator ( )

10. Your stomach feels nauseous ( )

11. You feel yourself holding something tight (like a steering wheel or the arm of a chair) ( )

12. You scratch a certain part of your body ( ): Part you scratch: _____

13. When your legs are crossed, you move the top one up and down ( )

14. You bite your nails ( )

15. You grind your teeth ( )

16. You have trouble with your speech ( )

APPENDIX C-2

Relaxation Data Sheet[1]
Form I

[1]Adapted from a handout provided by Mark Anderson and Glenn Riske in "Clinical Applications of Relaxation Techniques," National Parks and Recreation Congress 1981, Minneapolis, Minn.

NAME: _____

0 = no response to instructions
1 = tenses, no relaxation
2 = relaxation, no tension
3 = tenses and relaxes

	Session I	Session II	Session III	Session IV	Session V
Is the face relaxed and smooth?					
Is the jaw slack?					
Are the shoulders down and at rest?					
Is the small of the back off the floor?					
Are the legs relaxed and at rest?					
Are the feet tilted out and at rest?					
Is the body motionless (not restless)?					
Average Score					
Self-Report n/r = no relaxation R = relaxation (+, −) T = tense					

Score at least three sessions for each participant.

Comments:

APPENDIX D

Abbreviations Used in Charting[1]

Abbreviation	Meaning
$\bar{a}$	before
$\overline{aa}$	of each
ac	before meals
ad lib	as patient can tolerate
AMA	against medical advice
B & B	bowel and bladder
bid	twice a day
BJM	bones, joints, muscles
BM	bowel movement
BMR	basal metabolic rate
BP	blood pressure
BRP	bathroom privileges
$\bar{c}$	with
C–5	cervical lesion at the fifth vertebra
Ca	cancer
cap	capsule
cath	catheterize
CN	cranial nerves
CNS	central nervous system
CP	cerebral palsy
CVA	cerebral vascular accident—stroke
CVR	cardiovascular respiration

[1]Scout Lee Gunn, *Basic Terminology in Therapeutic Recreation and Other Action Therapies* (Champaign, Ill.: Stipes Publishing Co., 1975), pp. 73–77.

Abbreviation	Meaning
d	day
D & C	dilatation and curettage
D & V	diarrhea and vomiting
DD	developmental disability
DOA	dead on arrival
DTR	deep tendon reflexes
DTs	delirium tremens
ECG/EKG	electrocardiogram
ECT	electroconvulsive therapy
EEG	electroencephalogram
EMR/EMH	educable mentally retarded or handicapped
EST	electroshock therapy
FUO	fever of unknown origin
FWB	fully weight-bearing
fx	fracture
GI	gastrointestinal
GU	genitourinary
Hb	hemoglobin
hs	hour of sleep
HT	hypertension
IM	intramuscular (into the muscle)
IQ	intelligence quotient
IUD	intrauterine device
IV	intravenous (into the vein)
L–5	lumbar lesion at the fifth vertebra
LD	learning disability
LKS	liver, kidney, spleen
LPN	licensed practical nurse
MA	mental age
MD	muscular dystrophy
ML	midline
MS	multiple sclerosis
n	normal
noc	night
NP	neuropsychiatric
NPO	nothing by mouth
NSR	normal sinus rhythm
NWB	no weight-bearing (as in crutch walking)
ō	other
OBS	organic brain syndrome
OD	overdose
OR	operating room
OT	occupational therapy

Abbreviation	**Meaning**
OTR	registered occupational therapist
p̄	after
pc	after meals
PND	postnasal drip
post op	after surgery
pre op	before surgery; also means pre op medication
prep	prepare for surgery
PRN/prn	given as needed
pt	patient
PT	physical therapy
PWB	partially weight-bearing
q̄	every
qid	four times a day
qod	every other day
RN	registered nurse
ROM	range of motion
RT	recreation therapist
Rx	prescription/treatment
s̄	without
sig	instructions (when to take drugs)
SOB	shortness of breath
stat	immediately
T–5	thoracic lesion at the fifth vertebra
tab	tablet
tach	tachycardia
T & A	tonsils and adenoids
TB	tuberculin/tuberculosis
tid	three times a day
TMR/TMH	trainable mentally retarded or handicapped
TRS	therapeutic recreation specialist
TR	therapeutic recreation
up ad lib	allow patient to move around as much as patient feels is possible
VD	venereal disease
VDG	gonorrhea
w/c	wheelchair
x̄c	except
♀	female
♂	male

Index